DARK
VOYAGE

H	K	HK	Course	Wind	Weather	Daily Remarks on Board the Marlborough

Journal of A Voyage in the Good Ship Marlborough

George Wm. Babcock Commander Bound On A

Five Months Cruize Against the Enemies Of

The United States of America from Rhode Island

Kept by John Linscom. Bss. Capts. Clerk.

1777 Octr. 23d. We Set Sail from Swanzey and Came to Anchor att fall River
and after wind being thick a fog John

Wednesday 24th we weighed anchor and went through Seconnett passage got a ground & Lay 3 hours we got

25 we came to Anchor off Tarpaulin Cove in Martha Vineyard Sound

26 we weighed Anchor and went to holms hole to get Some more hands

27 the Captain and Some more of the Officers ashore engaging hands

28 Officers Still on Shore

29 weighed Anchor and went to Old Town

30 Officers Ashore to Collect men

31st the Barge men went Ashore to fill water

1778 1: the pilot got the Ship Under way the Capt. came off and Brought 30 men & stay came to anchor again

2 We Set Sail from Old Town in Martha Vineyard Bound to Sea

With a Fair Wind and Prosperous Gale & 96 Men & Boys on Board

H	K	HK	Course	Winds	Weather	Remarks for Sunday Janry. 4th. 1778
2			E.B.S.½S.	W.NW	Clear	Cape Poage on Martha Vineyard Bore S.W.S.
4						Distant 3 Leagues
6			E.			
8	6	1	E.S.E.	NW½W	Do.	Sancutty head of Nantuckett Bore S.S.W. distant
10	5	1				3 Leagues in Latt. 41.15 N & Long. 68.48 W.
12	6					from whence I take my Departure
2	5	1				handed the Mizn. T.S. T.G.S. Flyg S.& Sett 2 refs in M.T.S. T.Sail
4	5	1				
6	6	1	E.S.E.	Do.	Do.	Set the Mizn. T.S. & Sprit Sail Set a one ref out of each T. Sail
8	6	1				handed the Sprit S. & unbent the Cables Coild them down the hold
10	5					
12	5					

Course	Distance	S. Lat.	Departure	Latt. by D.R.	Latt. by Obser.	M. Distance	S. Long.	Long. in
25.19	166	N	S	E W			E W	
		96	45			39..46	45	60	67..52¼

DARK VOYAGE

* * * * * *AN* * * * * *

American Privateer's War

* * * * * *ON* * * * * *

Britain's African Slave Trade

CHRISTIAN McBURNEY

WESTHOLME
Yardley

Facing title page: Cover page to the ship's log for the *Marlborough* kept by John Linscom Boss on the ship's voyage to Africa and back. (*Morristown National Historical Park*)

©2022 Christian McBurney
Maps by Tracy Dungan

Westholme Publishing, LLC
904 Edgewood Road
Yardley, Pennsylvania 19067
Visit our Web site at www.westholmepublishing.com

ISBN: 978-1-59416-382-1
Also available as an eBook.

Printed in the United States of America.

To my father, who inspired my interest in history

Contents

Maps

A gallery of illustrations follows page 114.

Preface

The contrast is glaring in the extreme. On the one hand, the American Revolutionary War, from 1775 to 1783, was a glorious struggle for the causes of freedom, equality, liberty, and the dignity of the individual. Thomas Jefferson's rousing words in the Declaration of Independence— "that all men are created equal, that they are endowed by their Creator with certain unalienable rights, that among these are life, liberty, and the pursuit of happiness"—have inspired millions across the globe for almost 250 years. The word "men" originally was intended to apply only to adult white males, but over time its meaning has been extended to women and people of all races, colors, and creeds. Democracy (the rule of the many and not just the few), representative and balanced government, the rule of law—these and more are the gifts that the new United States bestowed on the world as a result of the American Revolution. The Revolutionary War that secured American independence also set an example as the first time a colony earned its independence from a European power.

At the same time the American Revolutionary War was about to commence, one of the worst tragedies in world history was continuing unabated: the Atlantic slave trade. European and American mercantile firms sent ships across the ocean to purchase African captives and bring them to the Caribbean islands, Brazil, and the North American mainland. At the time, Great Britain dominated the Atlantic slave trade, but other European countries and what would become the United States also participated in it. Between 1771 and 1775 alone, on average, each year more than ninety thousand African captives were carried across the Atlantic Ocean to the New World. There the Africans were forced into a lifetime of unpaid work and permanent bondage, with their children consigned to the same unimaginably miserable fates. Each year thousands died during the voyage across the Atlantic, called the Middle Passage, and thousands more died in the seasoning time, the initial period of enslavement. It was a horrible, abominable trade, and it is mind boggling to believe it ever existed, especially by today's moral standards.

The years before the commencement of the American Revolution saw an emerging recognition, particularly in the North, that the African slave trade was a wrong and should be banned on moral grounds or at least restricted. This became another source of tension with Britain, whose government officials sought to avoid any interference with the slave trade.

Some American Patriots, also called Whigs, were not blind to the inconsistency of proclaiming their rights to freedom and liberty from British oppression while themselves denying those very rights to enslaved people. This development was a significant step in world history in the movement toward the abolition of the slave trade and slavery itself, but there was still a long way to go. There was an even longer path toward treating Black people as the social and political equal of whites.

What follows brings the glory of the American Revolutionary War and horror of the African slave trade together in one tale. The tale is told through the extraordinary voyage of the American privateer *Marlborough* to West Africa and the men who sailed on it with the bold goal of attacking British slave trading interests.

The conduct of the officers and sailors of the *Marlborough* and its owners presented glaring inconsistencies. On the one hand, as with other American privateersmen, they risked their freedom and very lives to attack British maritime shipping. American privateers helped the cause of American independence by harming British maritime trade and seizing goods that the American military desperately needed. At the same time, they shared in the booty they captured, enriching themselves. It was a form of self-interested capitalism that had beneficial effects for the American war effort.

On the other hand, the men of the *Marlborough* and other American privateersmen desperately wanted to seize British slave ships filled with enslaved Africans for their own selfish and awful interests. When they did capture British slave ships, they in effect became slave traders, hoping to sell their captives for as high a price as possible. They did not show compassion for the hundreds of captives crammed aboard the British slave ships they captured or worry about the trauma the enslaved Africans had already suffered. Instead, the Americans sought to treat the captives the same as any nonhuman cargo seized on board an enemy ship. While such a motive at the time was not seen as offensive by many Americans, by today's standards it is repugnant.

Not only did the officers and men of the *Marlborough* capture several British slave ships during their voyage to Africa, they went further than other American privateersmen. They substantially damaged a major British slave post on the West African coast. Captain George Waite Babcock and his crew on the *Marlborough* inflicted more damage to the British slave trade than any other American privateer during the Revolutionary War.

The actions of the officers and sailors of the *Marlborough*, as well as those of other American privateersmen who intercepted British slave ships at sea, had a stunning unintended consequence. The British slave trade by 1778 had not only been disrupted, it had virtually collapsed. American privateersmen interfered with the conduct of the British slave trade to such an extent that British slave merchants substantially reduced their investments in African slave voyages. As a result, during the early years of the Revolutionary War, the number of enslaved Africans shipped across the Atlantic Ocean declined dramatically, perhaps as much as sixty thousand and possibly more.

All wars in the eighteenth century tended to cause a temporary decline in African slaving voyages. Slave merchants were more hesitant to make the substantial investments needed for long slave voyages if they feared their ships and human cargo would be captured or destroyed. But the Revolutionary War caused a much greater decline in the African slave trade than any war prior to it. And in the period from August 1776 until the active role of the French navy on the American side in August 1778, American privateers inflicted almost all of the damage on British slave trade interests. The new United States had only a fledgling Continental navy that was no match for the Royal Navy. But hundreds of pesky American privateers sailing from dozens of ports along the Atlantic Coast wreaked immense financial losses on the British merchant economy, including on Britain's lucrative slave trade. This is the first book to detail and emphasize the role of American privateers in disrupting that slave trade.

The officers and sailors on the *Marlborough* and other American privateersmen who intercepted British slave ships wanted to harm British economic interests and profit from their endeavors. They were not motivated to help Africans avoid being sold in the slave trade. Far from it. Still, their actions did substantially reduce the African slave trade and prevent tens of thousands of Africans from becoming enslaved in the New World. This was a positive impact, even if the reduction was both unintended and temporary. The privateersmen can be viewed as heroes or villains—or both.

The pages that follow are a microhistory of a voyage of the Rhode Island privateer *Marlborough* to Africa and back in early 1778. While it is a microhistory, the *Marlborough*'s story also provides the opportunity to learn about American privateering, the British slave trade, the Rhode Island slave trade, and the stunning impact American privateers had on the British slave trade during the Revolutionary War. For example, in Africa the officers and crew of the *Marlborough* came across a fascinating array of African leaders and European and American slave traders who were willing to assist them in attacking the British.

The *Marlborough*'s remarkable voyage to Africa is a tale that has never been told. The idea and funds for the voyage came from John Brown, one of the most prominent merchants in Providence, Rhode Island—and an investor in two prior slave trading voyages. The commander of Brown's ship was virtually unknown at the time. But George Waite Babcock of Exeter, Rhode Island, would prove himself to be an able and courageous commander. The ship Brown built and Babcock captained—the sleek, twenty-gun, double-decker brig *Marlborough*—carried a crew of Rhode Island and Massachusetts sailors across the Atlantic to the heart of the British slave trading empire in West Africa. This is their story, demonstrating courage, patriotism, glaring moral inconsistencies, and more.

* * * *CHAPTER ONE* * * *

John Brown, Great Britain, and the African Slave Trade

George Waite Babcock, the commander of a newly built, trim, and graceful two-masted brig, the twenty-gun privateer *Marlborough*, appeared on the outside calm and undaunted, but inside he must have been tense with anticipation. The strain on his emotions increased by the second as his brig, under full sail on a dark and windy Christmas Eve in 1777, approached the enemy warship's usual station. Babcock knew that the Royal Navy sloop *Kingsfisher* would be expecting Babcock's vessel and preparing to attack it. Minutes earlier, Royal Artillery cannon had fired at the *Marlborough*, missing but alerting the *Kingsfisher*'s commander, Captain Alexander Graeme, that a "rebel" vessel was heading his way.

It was Graeme's task, Babcock knew, to stop any American privateer or merchant ship from attempting to run the Royal Navy's blockade of the Sakonnet Channel, on the east side of Aquidneck Island in Narragansett Bay, Rhode Island. British forces had seized Newport, one of the top five ports in the colonies, as well as the rest of Aquidneck Island on which Newport stood, in December 1776. Since then, the Royal Navy had imposed its blockade on the three main entries into and out of Narragansett Bay, including the smallest and shallowest one, the Sakonnet Channel.

Finally, Babcock spotted the *Kingsfisher*—far to his rear. Babcock must have breathed a sigh of relief, knowing that his *Marlborough* could easily outrun the older and slower *Kingsfisher*.[1] Still, Babcock heard the report of a bow gun fired by the *Kingsfisher*. Babcock ordered his gunners to fire three cannon shots from the stern in retaliation. None of the shots hit its mark. Meanwhile, the *Marlborough* sped beyond the range of the British sloop's guns. Realizing a chase was hopeless against such a fast sailor, Captain Graeme gave up and returned his ship to its prior station.[2]

An exhilarated Babcock and his crew raced down the remainder of the channel and entered the open water of Rhode Island Sound. Babcock sailed his vessel into Massachusetts waters to Bedford (now New Bedford) and spent the night there. The next day, Babcock tried to enlist more sailors. The *Marlborough* then sailed to Tarpaulin Cove off Naushon Island, one of the Elizabeth Islands in Vineyard Sound. After spending Christmas there, the *Marlborough* sailed to Martha's Vineyard, where Babcock rounded out his crew. Finally, on January 2, 1778, Babcock ordered the *Marlborough*'s crew to sail the brig to the northeast in the open sea. They were starting their voyage to a destination some 3,800 miles away—the west coast of Africa.

Africa! Why would Babcock sail to that distant and foreign land? Africa was where slave traders historically sailed to purchase captives to carry to the Caribbean or North America. But the *Marlborough* was no slaver, it was a privateer—a private, armed ship with government authority to attack and capture enemy shipping. It is likely that none of the *Marlborough*'s officers or crew had ever made a voyage to Africa.

After capturing an enemy vessel, a privateer's officers and crew, as well as its investors, would share in the profits gained from selling the vessel and its cargo. Most American privateers headed to the Caribbean, to capture British merchant ships laden with goods to supply the sugar-cane plantations on the British-held islands. Other privateers sought to intercept British supply ships for the British army in North America, especially off Nova Scotia or Newfoundland in Canada. An occasional adventurous privateer even operated off the coast of Great Britain itself.

But Africa? No American privateer was known to have ventured there. It seemed an odd decision. And one fraught with danger, since it required a long voyage to a coast known to be unhealthy for ship crews and could be infested with Royal Navy warships.

The man most responsible for sending the *Marlborough* to West Africa was its primary owner, John Brown of Providence. He was one of Rhode

Island's most prominent and enterprising merchants. He and his brothers were the dominant merchants in Providence. By closely examining John Brown's background, his experiences, and the Atlantic world he lived in, it will become apparent that sending the *Marlborough* to Africa was not so odd a decision after all. Indeed, from the perspective of an investor in privateers, it was a brilliant one. Brown's privateer would play a key role in disrupting an important industry in Britain, the African slave trade, and thus help weaken America's opponent in its war for independence.

To conceive of and pull off a privateer voyage to Africa, several factors in Brown's life converged. He was a firm Patriot and was naturally bold; he was experienced in investing in merchant vessels and privateers that sailed throughout the Atlantic world; he generated from his various businesses excess cash needed to finance the construction of a new, twenty-gun brig and supply it for a long voyage; and he had knowledge of, and experience with, slave trading in Africa.

A number of New England maritime investors possessed the first three qualities. But few Patriot merchants active in investing in privateers had Brown's knowledge of the African slave trade. That made him well situated to think of, plan for, and implement his idea to send his new privateer to Africa.

Brown was not a substantial slave merchant, but he had financed two African slave voyages prior to the American Revolution, in 1764 and 1769. With this experience, he knew what it took to plan and execute a voyage to Africa and back, when other investors in privateers might shrink from such a daunting prospect.

Brown had another advantage compared to merchants from other colonies: he came from Rhode Island, the colony that held the dubious distinction of leading all North American colonies in slave trading. Thus, he had opportunities to converse regularly with slave merchants and slave ship captains, gaining even more information about African voyages, the peoples of Africa, and British slave trading posts on the coast of West Africa.

Brown was fully aware of the importance of the slave trade to Great Britain's economy. He knew that if his privateer had free rein on the coast of West Africa, it could cause substantial damage to Britain's slave trading operations there and at the same time enrich him and his investors, as well as the ship's crew.

In the first three quarters of the eighteenth century, Great Britain was the world's leading slave trading country. By 1775, British merchants from Liverpool, Bristol, London, and a few smaller ports annually sponsored around 150 to 200 slave ships that sailed to the coast of West Africa and purchased on average about thirty-five thousand to forty-five thousand en-slaved people.[3] The British vessels transported their captives across the At-lantic Ocean and landed them mostly in British colonial possessions in the Caribbean islands (then also called the West Indies), but also to other places in North America, including what would become the United States. These British merchants invested in ships that were specially outfitted for slave voyages and capable of carrying from two hundred to five hundred captives in a single voyage. From 1642 to 1807 (the year Great Britain finally out-lawed the slave trade), British slave ships carried more African captives than any other country, 3,247,000. This compares to, during the same pe-riod, Portugal and its colony of Brazil, 3,061,000; France, 1,188,000; Hol-land, 541,000; and what would become the United States, 292,000.[4]

In the quarter century prior to the American Revolution, Great Britain's domination of the Atlantic slave trade peaked. From 1751 to 1775, its ves-sels carried 832,000 enslaved people, compared to Portugal and Brazil, 529,000; France, 326,000; Holland, 132,000; and what would become the United States, 85,000.[5]

A British slaving voyage typically had three legs, thus giving rise to the name the triangular trade. Starting from Britain, the slave ship sailed to the African coast carrying goods mainly manufactured in Britain, such as muskets, gunpowder, pottery, and textiles, which were used to trade for African captives. Then the ship carried the captives across the Atlantic through the dreaded Middle Passage, a six-week-or-so voyage from Africa to the Americas, during which many enslaved Africans died. The ship's destination typically was to a Caribbean possession of Britain, where the surviving captives were ultimately sold to local plantation owners. Next, the ship's captain purchased sugar, rum, or molasses in the Caribbean to bring back to Britain to sell to British wholesalers.

Britain's slave trade was not close to being its most important industry, but it was a significant part of the British economy. Those who invested in or worked in the slave trade benefitted directly. British investors and mer-chants earned the profits from their investments. Slave ship crews were paid better wages than the crews on other mercantile voyages. British slave ship captains were highly compensated.

Many more British people indirectly benefitted from the trade. Owners and workers of manufacturing businesses who made goods for export to Africa thrived from the trade. British ship builders constructed vessels for the trade. British craftsmen were employed to fit out slave ships, including building decking to separate the captives and wooden barrels to hold water and provisions for the long voyages. London banks sometimes extended credit to the ship owners, and insurance firms earned hefty premiums insuring them. And the British government benefitted from ever-increasing port duties and customs receipts from sugar, molasses, and rum imported into Britain.[6]

Sugar was the key. Europe craved sugar, which was almost unknown to most Europeans before the seventeenth century. England became the major consumer. Because of increased production, the price of sugar dropped, making it affordable to most English households. Pastry-cook shops, filled with sweet jams, cakes, and gingerbread, appeared in city and town corners everywhere. The English added sugar to their tea and coffee in coffee-houses, where sweetened chocolate milk was also served.[7]

As early as 1660, only a few decades after Britain acquired its first sugar-producing Caribbean islands, sugar was England's most valuable import from its American colonies. The value of sugar imports, and related products, molasses and rum, far outstripped the value of imports of tobacco from the colonies of Virginia and Maryland, and rice from South Carolina. For a century and a half, until overtaken by cotton in 1820, sugar was Great Britain's largest import.[8]

Sugar plantations in the Caribbean created fabulous fortunes. Planters who survived mosquito-borne diseases and became rich frequently moved back to the mother country, buying impressive manorial estates, riding in splendid carriages accompanied by liveried servants, wearing satin and other finery, and holding banquets that rivaled those of King George III. The Earl of Shelburne, a British statesman, declared in 1778 on a trip to the English countryside, "there were scarcely ten miles together throughout the country where the house and estate of a rich West Indian was not to be seen."[9]

Slave labor was indispensable to the production of sugar. Plantation owners in the Caribbean islands used gangs of enslaved workers to cultivate, harvest, and process sugar cane into sugar. "All this great increase in our treasure," wrote Joshua Gee as early as 1729, "proceeds chiefly from the labor of negroes in the plantations."[10] A British writer in 1745 summed up the significance of the African slave trade and slave labor to Great Britain's prosperity:

> [I]s it not notorious to the whole world, that the business of *planting* in our *British colonies* . . . is carried on by the labor of *Negroes*, imported tither from Africa? Are we not indebted to those valuable people, *the Africans* for our *sugars, tobaccos, rice, rum,* and all other *plantation produce?* And the greater

the number of *Negroes* imported into our colonies, from Africa, will not the exportation of *British* manufactures among the *Africans* be in proportion, they being paid for in such commodities only? . . . May we not therefore say . . . Great Britain owes all its *increase* and *splendor* to the commerce of its *American* and *African colonies* . . . ?[11]

If slave labor was the key to developing and maintaining successful sugar plantations, the African slave trade was the key to the continuation of slave labor. This was because of the need of sugar plantation owners to replenish their slave stock annually by purchasing new captives.

An outstanding feature of British Caribbean plantation slavery in the mid-eighteenth century was that natural births of enslaved people failed to exceed natural and unnatural deaths. Most plantations experienced excess deaths over births. For example, at one Barbados plantation, from 1754 to 1775, there were 73 births and 117 deaths.[12]

There were a number of reasons why natural births of enslaved people in the British Caribbean failed to exceed natural and unnatural deaths. For one, in the effort to maximize profits quickly from the plantations, plantation owners preferred adult men to work in the fields and perform heavy lifting. Accordingly, women and girls constituted only about one-third of the imported African captives. In addition, due to primitive and unhealthy conditions in which the enslaved women lived and worked, deaths of children during or shortly after childbirth was shockingly high.[13] On one Jamaican plantation, just 159 of the 345 children whose births were recorded over the years survived childbirth and several weeks afterward.[14]

Furthermore, the death rate was high for all enslaved people in the British Caribbean. For a start, the environment on the islands was dangerous for any human beings, Black or white. Malaria and yellow fever were common as were other fatal diseases.

The death rate among enslaved people increased as a result of the grueling and harsh work required for cultivating and harvesting sugar cane. Enslaved laborers were often forced to work twelve to fifteen hours per day, much of it in oppressive heat and in the sun. Once harvested, sugar-cane stalks had to be brought to mills within hours. So as not to overload the mills, the crop was planted so it would be ready for harvest at staggered times, resulting in a period of intense harvesting that could last up to six months. The cruelly unhealthy working conditions left the enslaved even more vulnerable to deadly diseases.

The first three years or so of a newly imported enslaved individual's life, called the seasoning period, took a heavy toll. Arriving weak and vulnerable after the arduous Middle Passage voyage, the new arrivals had to adjust to new work, food, diseases, and rules; they died in droves.[15]

Crucially (and shockingly), Caribbean planters in the mid-eighteenth century intentionally provided their enslaved people with minimal food, shelter, and clothing. With the profits from their plantations, they could have done much more. They made the mind-boggling cruel calculus that so long as the slave trade persisted, it was cheaper to buy replacement workers from Africa from slave ships arriving at island ports than to spend money improving the working and living conditions of the enslaved laborers who had already been purchased. It is noteworthy that in the 1770s in the British Caribbean, a newly imported enslaved African adult male could be purchased for about £35 to £55, but he could cost his master £550 a year in feeding him food imported from Britain or North America.[16]

Discipline imposed on the enslaved in the Caribbean was brutal. Henry Dalrymple, the son of a West Indian planter, spent years in English schools. In 1773, he returned to his home island of Grenada to visit his family's 250-acre plantation. He quickly gained a new perspective on the brutality of the slave system. In the marketplace of Saint George, the largest town on the island, "Negroes were flogged every day by the particular orders of their masters. They were tied down upon the ground," Dalrymple later testified to Parliament, "and every stroke brought blood and very often took out a piece of the flesh." This intentional use of terror and disregard for human life and dignity were used to preserve the slave system. Dalrymple added that the "general opinion" among planters was that "it was more profitable to import slaves and work them out than to breed them."[17]

Captain James Samuel Smith of the Royal Navy visited several plantations in the Windward Islands in 1777. He wrote, "The ill treatment of slaves is too well known and universal to be denied. I do affirm I have seen the most cruel treatment made use of at several of the West India Islands, particularly at Antigua." Once Smith met with an old school chum from England who then managed a plantation on Antigua. Smith witnessed whippings of enslaved people, and it shocked him. "A poor Negro laid stretched flat on his face on the ground, at his peril to move an inch till the punishment is over." Smith described the whip that was used as having an end "the size of a man's thumb" and "tapering longer than a coachman's whip." He continued, "At every stroke a piece [of flesh] was taken out by the particular jerk of the whip, which the manager . . . takes care to direct. This I have often seen for not getting a sufficient quantity of grass for the manager [to feed his horses] . . . and many such trifling things."[18]

As a result of the high mortality rate among the enslaved and the low natural birth rate, British Caribbean planters had to import massive numbers of African captives just to maintain their enslaved populations. The British slave trade was thus vital to replenish the slave stock of the British Caribbean plantations. From 1751 to 1775, the British Caribbean islands imported approximately the following numbers of captives: Jamaica, 230,000; Barbados 110,000; St. Kitts (officially St. Christopher), Antigua, Grenada, and Dominica in total, 210,0000; and St. Vincent, Montserrat and Nevis, and Trinidad and Tobago in total 20,000.[19]

Perhaps the most devastating statistic is to compare the number of Africans carried to the British Caribbean to their populations when slavery was prohibited. Adam Hochschild writes, "When slavery ended in the United States [in 1865], less than half a million slaves imported over the centuries had grown to a population of nearly four million." By comparison, notes the same author, when slavery ended in the British Caribbean in 1834, "total slave imports of well over two million left a surviving slave population of only about 670,000." Enslaved people in what would become the United States, even if they were kept in control through a system of terror, were apparently better fed and housed than their counterparts in the Caribbean and typically did not work in as debilitating conditions as in the Caribbean. As a result, American enslaved families grew in numbers by natural birth, while those in the British Caribbean did not, and therefore British planters each year had to replace dead enslaved people with new captives from Africa.[20] After reviewing his statistics, Hochschild concludes, "The [British] Caribbean was a slaughterhouse."[21]

The British slave trade was also the key business that prevented the British Caribbean islands from becoming allies of the new United States during the American Revolution. The same astute British observer who in 1745 summed up the significance of the triangular trade and the role of slave labor to Great Britain's economy also pointed out that Britain's slave traders, who made it possible for British Caribbean planters to replenish between two and five percent of their slave stock annually, kept the British Caribbean colonies tied to Great Britain.[22] A modern historian of Jamaica, Trevor Burnard, writes that it was not fear of slave rebellions that kept Jamaica allied with Britain during the Revolutionary War but instead the continuation of Britain's transatlantic slave trade.[23]

The year 1774, the eve of the American Revolution, was a high point for Britain's slave trade to its Caribbean islands. In that year, British slave ships carried almost thirty-nine thousand African captives to British-controlled Caribbean islands. The year 1775 was also a strong one for British slave traders.[24]

In addition to his knowledge of the British slave trade, John Brown was familiar with the slave trading business in what would become the United States. While Brown knew it, some readers may be surprised to learn that merchants of what would become the United States overall played a comparatively small role in the African slave trade. While the slave trade lasted they carried a total of about 292,000 captive Africans across the Atlantic and outfitted only about 2.4 percent of all slaving voyages.[25] However, in the twenty-five years leading up to the American Revolution, from 1751 to 1775, North American ships carried a higher percentage than that, 4.4 percent. During this period, North American ships annually carried on average 3,380 enslaved Africans to the New World.[26]

Comparatively few of the enslaved people carried across the Atlantic disembarked in what would become the United States—less than 400,000 of the approximately 12.5 million forced across the ocean from 1501 to 1867, or about 3.2 percent of the total. The Caribbean and South America (mostly Brazil) accounted for ninety-five percent of the captives arriving across the Atlantic from Africa.[27] From 1751 to 1775, 116,000 African captives were imported into the thirteen mainland North American colonies.[28] Most of these African captives were carried on British slave ships.

While slavers in what would become the United States were small players overall in the Atlantic slave trade, John Brown lived in Rhode Island, the colony that dominated the slave trade among the thirteen mainland colonies. More than half of the North American slave trading voyages in colonial times emanated from Rhode Island, with the rest coming mostly from New York City, Boston, and other coastal New England ports.

Why tiny Rhode Island dominated the slave trade is not clear. With some of the best natural deep harbors in North America in Narragansett Bay, Rhode Islanders naturally took to the sea. But Boston merchants overshadowed them, and Rhode Island merchants lacked the large hinterland of farms to draw on for trade that Boston, New York, and Charleston merchants could.

Rhode Island merchants began to trade for molasses with the Caribbean islands and with it produced distilled rum in abundance. In a report sent to London in 1764, Governor Stephen Hopkins stated Rhode Island had more than thirty distilleries, "erected at a vast expense, constantly employed in making rum from molasses." That industry, Hopkins wrote, was "the main hinge upon which the trade of the colony turns, and many hundreds of persons depend immediately upon it for subsistence."[29]

Rhode Island merchants cast their eyes on the transatlantic slave trade as an outlet for their rum. While most of the distilled rum was not used in the slave trade, historian Jay Coughtry concludes, "the slave trade was simply the most profitable method of selling rum, Rhode Island's most important export."[30] Eventually, about twenty-two percent of the rum distilled in colonial Rhode Island was used as a commodity to exchange for African captives.[31]

Rhode Island rum was higher proof than other rums and most other spirits, and it became the preferred liquor for trading for captives on Africa's Gold Coast. African sellers of captives sometimes called Rhode Island slave ship captains Rum Men.[32]

Of the slave trading ports in colonial Rhode Island, Newport was dominant, with Providence, Bristol, and Warren coming in far behind. Many of Newport's top colonial merchants engaged in the African slave trade. Aaron Lopez and the Vernon brothers, Samuel and William, sent the most voyages to Africa from Rhode Island.[33] (William Vernon would play an important administrative role for the Continental navy during the Revolutionary War.)

Yet while the importance of the slave trade to Newport's economy was significant, its role has sometimes been exaggerated.[34] Some historians closely examining the matter have concluded that the trade was not an important part of Newport's economy.[35] The proportion of Newport vessels sailing for Africa compared to total voyages appears to support the conclusion. In 1763, according to the report Hopkins sent to London trade officials, Newport employed 352 vessels in the North American coastal trade and sent 184 more ships to foreign ports. Of the latter, 150 sailed to the Caribbean in the carrying trade—transporting mostly provisions, spermaceti candles, and lumber to the West Indies.[36] According to Hopkins, the entire colony of Rhode Island sent on average per year eighteen vessels to Africa.[37] Another observer in the same year stated that Newport merchants had a slave trading fleet of "20 sail of vessels." Newport custom house records show that between 1763 and 1774, from fifteen to twenty-two African voyages a year cleared Newport Harbor.[38] Recent scholarship supports these numbers, although finding that custom house records numbers slightly undercount the African voyages.[39]

Still, merely taking into account the relatively few African slave voyages commencing from Newport annually does not reflect the full significance of the slave trade to Newport's colonial economy. Slave voyages required a much greater investment than other voyages. Spending time on the African coast purchasing captives and completing the three legs of the triangular journey on average took Rhode Island slavers about a year, and frequently longer.[40] Meanwhile, at least two trips to the Caribbean could be taken more safely in the same time. Longer voyages meant increased costs feeding the crew and paying the crew's wages, since there were more days afloat. Slave ship captains received a higher wage than on other voyages (mostly by being able to claim several "privilege slaves" from the surviving captives they brought to market). Insurance rates were high. In 1774, Newport merchant Aaron Lopez was pleased to learn that his London agents had secured insurance at only seven percent.[41]

Moreover, to guard the captives and protect against the real risk of slave insurrections, additional costs were required. The crews were about one-third larger than needed on a carrying trade voyage.[42] Chains, additional weapons, and gunpowder were purchased mainly to prevent or suppress uprisings among the captives. John Brown, as principal owner of the slave ship *Sultan*, described the arsenal his ship carried when it departed Rhode Island in 1769. The sixteen-man crew had on board the 160-ton vessel "six swivel and two carriage guns, four blunderbusses, fourteen or fifteen small arms and a number of pistols with sufficiency of ammunition."[43]

Brown and other merchants willing to finance slave trading voyages recognized that African voyages entailed substantial risks that exceeded those of losing a ship from storms or other causes of shipwrecks that loomed over any sea voyage. As mentioned, there was the risk of insurrections among the enslaved captives. There was also the risk of deadly diseases for the white officers and crew of the slave vessel. For example, in 1774 alone, four captains of Rhode Island slavers and one from Boston died of illness on the African coast.[44] White crew members probably had a higher death rate on African slave ships than the African captives.[45] Slave merchants also had the market risk that by the time the vessel arrived at its far-away North American destination, the market for selling African captives might have turned. Given the high costs and risks of a slave voyage, slave merchants often spread the risk by syndicating partial ownership interests in the voyage to other merchants.

Financing a slave voyage was a high-risk, high-reward venture, similar to gambling, playing the lottery—or privateering. Slave merchants were willing to take such risks for a portion of their portfolio of voyages but not for the bulk of them. One author of a study of Newport slave trading concludes, "the slave trade simply provided an alternative set of markets and carried risks and opportunities similar to those of privateering. Potential losses outweighed potential gains for most merchants." As support for the last point, the author noted, "Only a quarter of Newport's leading merchants ever succumbed to the seduction" of the slave trade.[46]

No comprehensive study of the profits of Rhode Island slavers has been undertaken. Such a task would be extremely complex, and it is unlikely that sufficient contemporary records needed to make accurate calculations exist. A careful study of the profitability of the British slave trade from 1761 to 1807 led to the conclusion that average profits stood at 9.5 percent.[47] On 110 African slave trading voyages from 1757 to 1784 for which there is good documentation, Liverpool slave trader William Davenport was found to have a profit margin of 10.9 percent.[48] These profit margins are substantial but were not remarkable or excessive for British merchants.[49] It can be assumed that Rhode Island slavers on average earned similar profit margins, even if some experienced losses on some voyages and extraordinary profits on others.

While no comprehensive study has been done, the annual revenues and profits from Newport's carrying trade to the Caribbean and the coastal trade from Nova Scotia to Georgia likely each far outstripped the annual revenues and profits from the African slave trade. Common sense would indicate that this was the case in 1763, for example, when Stephen Hopkins reported that Newport sent out 352 vessels in the coastal trade with the other thirteen colonies and Canada, and 150 more to the Caribbean, while only about 18 ships departed for Africa.[50]

One way to gauge the importance of the slave trading business is to make weighted adjustments to the numbers of slave voyages compared to other clearances. Starting with Hopkins's 1763 numbers but assuming twenty African voyages were made from Newport rather than eighteen, I would increase the number of African slave voyages by a factor of four, based on the increased investment required for African slave voyages and their relatively high profits compared to North American coastal voyages. I would increase the number of Caribbean and other foreign destination voyages by a factor of two. This works out to clearances for Africa being the equivalent of about 10.5 percent of all of the clearances from Newport in 1763.[51] Using an entirely different approach, based on the value of Rhode Island exports to foreign destinations found in the British Customs office from 1768 to 1772, I arrive at the rough conclusion that African slave voyages generated about twelve percent of the annual revenues of Newport merchants.[52] Accordingly, it can be concluded that the African slave trade was a significant part of Newport's colonial economy, but not a major or dominant one.

One reason some Newport merchants likely occasionally resorted to slave trading was that the bills of exchange their ship captains received for selling African captives could be used to repay amounts the Newport merchants owed to London merchants. Bills of exchange issued by slave trading houses, whether in Jamaica or Charleston, were typically guaranteed by British banks, and thus they were like money. That was crucial at a time when cash was scarce in colonial America. Governor Hopkins estimated that remittances from trading in African captives paid for one-third of goods Rhode Island merchants purchased from British merchants.[53]

While Rhode Island was a small player in the worldwide slave trade prior to the American Revolution, carrying on average 2,400 African captives per year, as decades passed, the number became substantial. In all, over fifty-nine thousand Africans were involuntarily taken aboard Rhode Island ships in the colonial period.[54] The human suffering Rhode Island slavers caused African captives and their families left behind is impossible to measure.

It has already been discussed that the slave trade directly supported Rhode Island's most important industry, distilling and selling rum. The slave trade also supported other Rhode Island industries, including ship building, sail and rope making, barrel making for rum, water, and provisions, and blacksmithing for shackles. Local farmers sold provisions and livestock for the long voyages.

If each year Rhode Island merchants did not send out many slave ships to Africa, they did send out numerous ships to the Caribbean in the carrying trade. Because most British Caribbean islands raised little other than sugar cane, they had to import the bulk of their food. New England merchants, such as John Brown and his brothers, regularly sent ships to the Caribbean, bringing livestock, cheese, butter, dried fish, and other foodstuffs to feed the white colonials and their enslaved people, as well as spermaceti candles and lumber. Thus, the carrying trade supported the slave system in the Caribbean.

Brown knew most of Rhode Island's slave merchants and ship captains. In order to keep up with the latest developments—an important part of being a successful merchant—he talked with his fellow merchants and ship captains frequently. As a result, he gained valuable knowledge about Africa and its most unique—and horrible—commercial trade, such as where British slave traders preferred to trade and where Britain maintained forts and slave trading posts.

Brown may have first learned about the slave trade from his father, who dispatched the first slave ship to sail from Providence. Captain James

Brown sent the *Mary* to Africa in 1736, the year of John's birth. This vessel sold its human cargo in the Caribbean, with the exception of three enslaved people brought back to Providence.[55]

The Brown family did not return to the slave trade until 1759, when the firm of Obadiah Brown and Company, the successor to Captain Brown's business and controlled by Obadiah Brown, the uncle to John and his brothers, dispatched a rum-laden schooner, *Wheel of Fortune*, to Africa. John's older brothers, Nicholas and Joseph, invested in this venture. Twenty-three-year-old John did not. The Seven Years' War raging between Britain and France at the time made the voyage a risky venture. According to Obadiah's insurance book, the ship was "taken," probably by a French privateer. The capture occurred before any enslaved Africans were embarked on board. The loss was estimated as twenty thousand pounds.[56]

In 1764, the North American maritime economy was mired in recession. The Brown brothers (in order of age, Nicholas, Joseph, John, and Moses) then operated through the firm of Nicholas Brown & Company based in Providence. Eager to enter into a profitable venture during the economic downturn, they decided to invest in a slave voyage to Africa. Moses would later claim that John was the driving force behind the voyage.

On September 10, 1764, the Browns' vessel, the *Sally*, a one-hundred-ton brigantine (i.e., a small brig), embarked from Newport to the west coast of Africa on its slaving voyage. The ship's commander was one of the Brown brothers' favorites, Esek Hopkins, the future commander in chief of the Continental navy. After a two-month crossing, the *Sally* arrived on the West African coast.

The *Sally*'s voyage turned out to be one of the deadliest ever undertaken from Rhode Island. The mortality rate of African captives on board Rhode Island slave vessels in the Middle Passage was about twelve percent.[57] But Hopkins far exceeded that shocking average. Of the 196 Africans purchased by Hopkins, at least 109 perished. Eight were killed in a failed insurrection in the Middle Passage (two more later died of their wounds), and a few others committed suicide during the voyage. Most captives died of disease. The inexperienced Hopkins, on his first slaving voyage, spent too long on the African coast. Many Rhode Island slave captains preferred purchasing enslaved people from British-owned slave trading posts and forts where captives were held in holding pens for arriving slave ships.[58] While prices for captives were higher at slave trading posts and forts, purchasing captives in bulk meant spending less time in Africa. Hopkins instead traded for a few captives at a time with local African merchants and chiefs. Hopkins lacked connections to African sellers, so this process took a lot of time. Meanwhile, the captives he purchased were kept in hot, fetid, and cramped quarters, ideal conditions for breeding diseases of many varieties.

When Hopkins finally landed in Barbados in October 1765, he found the market for selling African captives poor. Sailing his vessel on to Antigua, he sold the surviving enslaved people, but for low prices, largely because of their bad physical conditions. The ultimate loss suffered by the Browns is not known because of incomplete records on the sales, but the Browns at one point estimated that "we shall lose at least £2,000 by the voyage."[59] In addition to the terrible loss of life among the African captives, three white crewmembers died on the trip. The slave trade was not for novices—merchants could lose a substantial part of their investment, and the captives on board could suffer horribly.

In the wake of the *Sally*'s disastrous voyage, three of the four Brown brothers—Nicholas, Joseph, and Moses—never again invested in the transatlantic slave trade. Brother John, however, did not have any qualms about investing in African slave trading voyages. He invested in another voyage to Africa in 1769, this time by the *Sultan* out of Newport.[60]

Almost ten years after the *Sally* left Rhode Island, Moses Brown repented his involvement in the slave trade. In 1773, he experienced a profound emotional crisis, brought about by the death of his wife, Anna. Moses emerged as a convert to the Society of Friends, whose followers were called Quakers. As did many other Quakers, Moses became an ardent opponent of slavery and the slave trade. In 1773, he gathered ten of his family and friends, and his ten enslaved people, and announced that he was freeing the latter. "I am clearly convinced that the buying and selling of men of what color [what]soever is contrary to the Divine Mind . . . and is contrary to that justice, mercy, and humanity enjoined as the duty of every Christian," he wrote in his articles of manumission, later filed in Providence probate court records.[61] Moses's biographer, Mack Thompson, observed that he "no doubt considered his act an atonement for his part in the slaving venture of the *Sally* eight years before."[62]

Moses Brown's antislavery views were not widespread prior to the American Revolution. The conviction that the slave trade and slavery itself were completely wrong and should be banned took time for most white Americans to realize. Given how horrible both institutions were, that fact today is difficult to comprehend. But most white Americans at this time believed in the inferiority of Blacks, and both the slave trade and slavery had been practiced in North America since the times of their forebears. Slavery was mentioned in the Bible, and the transatlantic slave trade had been started by Portugal in the fifteenth century with voyages to Brazil. The first country to ban the slave trade, Great Britain, did not do so until 1807.

The American Revolution was a crucial catalyst for the worldwide antislavery movement. It was, in fact, prior to the outbreak of the Civil War the most important event in America promoting the antislavery cause. When the rebellion against Crown rule began, there was little antislavery activity anywhere else in the world. (Britain's antislavery movement did not begin until 1787.)[63] As with any great worldwide movement, the antislavery campaign made slow progress, in fits and starts. The American Revolution proved to be a major leap forward for the cause of ending the African slave trade, as well as slavery itself.[64]

With American colonists declaring their beliefs in "liberty" and "natural rights" and denouncing a British plot to "enslave" them by imposing taxes without representation, it is not surprising that some were moved to question the plight of those whom the colonists themselves had actually enslaved. After all, at this time, around twenty percent of the population of the thirteen colonies consisted of Black people, most of whom were enslaved. Historian W. E. B. Du Bois put it more bluntly: "the new philosophy of 'freedom' and the 'rights of man,' which formed the cornerstone of the Revolution, made even the dullest realize that, at the very least, the slave-trade and a struggle for 'liberty' were not consistent."[65]

In North America, prior to the American Revolution, organized political opposition to slavery and the African slave trade began with the Quakers. They were, however, viewed as a fringe religious group, and larger and mainstream religious groups, such as Congregationalists and Baptists, were slow to follow. But as the rhetoric for freedom and liberty grew louder and colonial resistance to Crown rule increased, the first organized opposition to the slave trade in American history appeared.

While Massachusetts had a small enslaved population and only a few slave merchants, an effort to limit the importation of enslaved people into the colony arose. As early as 1763, the great Patriot orator James Otis of Massachusetts, in an influential pamphlet arguing that colonists ought not to be taxed without their consent, asserted that there were laws higher than acts of Parliament. While not necessary to do so to make his main point, he delved into race relations. He exclaimed, "The colonists are by the law of nature free born, as indeed are all men, white or black. . . . Does it follow that 'tis right to enslave a man because he is black?" Speaking of the African slave trade, he said, "Nothing better can be said in favor of a trade that is the most shocking violation of the law of nature, has a direct tendency to diminish the idea of the inestimable value of liberty, and makes every dealer in it a tyrant."[66]

A few Congregationalist ministers and a new generation of college graduates began to express their opposition to the slave trade and even to slavery itself. In 1766, the Boston town meeting instructed James Otis, Samuel Adams, and Thomas Cushing to push for "a law to prohibit the importation and purchasing of slaves" in Massachusetts. Over the next eight years, several bills to accomplish that goal were passed in the Massachusetts colonial legislature. But they never made it into law because the royal governor refused to sign the bills, as he had no authority from London to do so. The slave trade was too profitable for Britain to give up.

Rhode Island saw its own antislavery movement arise, even though the colony continued to dominate the North American slave trade and had the highest percentage of Blacks of any New England colony (about six percent). Rhode Island's dominant politician at the time was Stephen Hopkins of Providence. He served as governor of the colony four times and would sign the Declaration of Independence. Raised in rural Smithfield as a Quaker, he became widely read even though he received no formal schooling. In 1765, he demonstrated his learning by writing a respected pamphlet opposing Parliament's Sugar Act.

Hopkins had once owned an enslaved woman, whom he insisted he kept to care for his ailing mother and his children. His brother Esek had dabbled in the slave trade as captain of the doomed *Sally*. But Stephen Hopkins's views on slavery and the slave trade evolved. By the eve of the American Revolution, he, Moses Brown, and the Reverend Samuel Hopkins (no relation) of Newport became a powerful triumvirate in Rhode Island opposing the slave trade and slavery. They knew that because Rhode Island did not have a royal governor, its legislature, the General Assembly, could enact antislavery bills without the need of royal approval, and that because the colony was so small, royal officials in London might not bother to invalidate the laws.

On May 17, 1774, the town meeting of Providence recommended a stoppage of "all trade with Great Britain, Ireland, Africa and the West Indies." The ban would prohibit Rhode Islanders from carrying African captives to British-controlled Caribbean islands. The town meeting further instructed its representatives to the Rhode Island General Assembly to support an act banning the importation of enslaved people and another freeing all enslaved people born in the colony after they reached maturity.[67] With Stephen Hopkins and Moses Brown working behind the scenes, the General Assembly at least complied with one request, banishing the importation of African captives in June of that same year.[68]

The same sentiments were felt in pockets throughout the North prior to the American Revolution. In Philadelphia, a rising young physician, Benjamin Rush, wrote a pamphlet in 1773 demanding an end to the importation of enslaved people into Pennsylvania. Rush went even further, declaring that the "intellects of the Negroes" and their "capacities for virtue and happiness . . . show us that they are equal to the Europeans."[69] This was going too far for even most abolitionists of the day. The idea that Blacks and whites were equal in rights and talents and therefore deserved equal treatment was an idea rejected by most whites of the day. Progress in social thinking would take more than a century to mature. In reaction to Rush's pamphlet, some Philadelphians refused to use him, and his medical practice dropped by at least half.[70]

Even Virginia, with its extensive tobacco plantations worked by gangs of enslaved people, saw a strong movement to limit slave imports. The reasons were not primarily based on equality, humanitarian impulse, or an objection to slavery. Rather the planters realized that with their tobacco economy stalled, they had a surplus of enslaved workers, and limiting slave imports would maintain their values. In addition, some politicians wanted to attract settlers to Virginia's mountainous west, but whites hesitated to go there if they had to compete with slave labor.

From 1759 to 1772, Virginia's House of Burgesses attempted to increase tariffs on slave imports with the goal of reducing the imports to a trickle. But in London, under pressure from Bristol and Liverpool slave merchants, the Board of Trade quashed the effort.

In July 1774, as part of the overall rising tide against George III's colonial policies and efforts to adopt policies not to import British goods, a nascent popular movement arose in several Virginia counties opposing further slave importations. In Fairfax County, at a meeting chaired by George Washington, a series of influential resolves, known as the Fairfax Resolves and penned by George Mason, were adopted. The seventeenth resolve stated in part, "during our present difficulties and distress, no slaves ought to be imported into any of the British colonies on this Continent." The resolve made it clear that the request was at least in part based on moral grounds: "We take this opportunity of declaring our most earnest wishes to see the entire stop forever put to such a wicked, cruel and unnatural trade."[71] Washington and Mason were both substantial slaveholders. Nonetheless, Washington carried the resolves to Philadelphia to present to delegates at the First Continental Congress.[72]

London's refusal to limit the importation of African captives was yet another bone of contention Americans had with Britain's perceived overbearing rule. Because of the importance of the African slave trade to Britain's Caribbean colonies, British officials would not permit its North American colonies to even limit the importation of African captives. In 1788, looking back to the years leading up to the Declaration of Independence, George Mason wrote (with some exaggeration) that the desire of the colonies to prohibit the slave trade "was one the great causes of our separation from Great Britain."[73]

In Providence, John Brown was fully aware of these antislavery developments, but antislavery arguments made no impression on him. When the *Marlborough* sailed for Africa in January 1778, Brown owned several enslaved people. In a list of taxable tangible personal property he owned in Providence submitted to town officials, Brown recorded the following: "5 horses, 1 cow, two Negro men, 3 carriages, and 1/4 part of 3 other Negroes."[74] Brown did not bother to provide the names of any of the enslaved people he listed.

While Brown may have been willing to finance slave trading voyages in 1775, he was not allowed to do so. Astonishingly, the First Continental Congress had banned American participation in the slave trade.

That Congress was called in reaction to the harsh punishments Parliament inflicted on Boston for dumping a massive shipload of tea in Boston Harbor rather than allowing it to land and have tax paid on it. Parliament passed four acts, called the Coercive Acts, including one that closed the port of Boston. To the surprise of British government officials in London, Whig delegates from twelve of the thirteen American colonies (all except Georgia) met in Philadelphia to coordinate a response to the Coercive Acts.

Delegates decided to try peaceful economic pressure to persuade the British government to change its policies. On September 27, on a motion by Richard Henry Lee of Virginia, delegates unanimously resolved to import no goods from Great Britain after December 1, 1774.[75] The so-called Continental Association containing the various nonimportation pledges was signed by delegates of the twelve colonies on October 20.

Not surprisingly, delegates realized the importance of the slave trade to Britain's economy. The second article of the Continental Association began,

"We will neither import nor purchase, any slave imported after the first day of December next." Given that British merchants dominated the slave trade, including in sending captives to North America, this pledge was primarily designed to harm British economic interests. Henry Laurens, a prominent Patriot from Charleston, South Carolina, and once perhaps the leading slave importer in North America, succinctly summarized the economic argument for ending slave imports by British ships. "Men-of-war, forts, castles, governors, companies and committees are employed and authorized by . . . Parliament to protect, regulate, and extend the slave trade. . . . Bristol, Liverpool, Manchester, Birmingham, etc., live upon the slave trade," he wrote.[76]

Remarkably, the delegates to the First Continental Congress went much further. They pledged that after December 1, 1774, "we will wholly discontinue the slave trade, and will neither be concerned in it ourselves, nor will we hire our vessels, nor sell our commodities or manufactures to those who are concerned in it."[77] American merchants could not even finance their own slave voyages or engage in the slave trade with a country other than Great Britain.

How this happened is not certain. The heady ideas of the Fairfax Resolves brought by Washington, and reinforced by similar language from a young Thomas Jefferson, likely played a crucial role. The key committee determining what products would be subject to nonimportation included on them Lee of Virginia and Thomas Cushing of Massachusetts, both of whom opposed the slave trade. Notably, the committee did not have any delegates from South Carolina or Georgia, the two colonies with the strongest demand for slave imports.

In form, the Continental Association was an agreement to boycott trade with Britain and a boycott of the entire slave trade. The delegates did not vote on it as a binding resolution; instead, they all signed it as a pledge to abide by it.[78] All the colonies passed resolutions adopting the Continental Association, even eventually Georgia. With Whig local organizations ready to enforce the Continental Association, it became in effect a binding obligation. According to the Continental Association's own terms, any merchant who violated it would be ostracized—no one would be permitted to trade with him. With the Whigs in ascendancy in most of the thirteen colonies, few merchants, even with neutral or Tory leanings, dared to violate the Continental Association and risk business failure.

Henry Laurens advised a Charleston merchant on January 10, 1776, that the list of products that could not be imported into the colonies included "slaves from any place."[79] In Baltimore in 1775, the masters of vessels entering the port had to swear that they did not carry "any Slave or Slaves."[80]

One of Rhode Island's delegates to the First Continental Congress was the respected Samuel Ward of Westerly. In a December 1774 letter to fellow delegate John Dickinson of Pennsylvania, Ward exulted, "The people [in Rhode Island] are universally satisfied with the proceedings of Congress, and determined to adhere to the Association." Ward added, as if in disbelief, "Even the merchants who suffer the most by discontinuing the slave trade assure me they will most punctually conform to that Resolve and the country in general is vastly pleased with it."[81] Ward, a former three-time governor of Rhode Island whose support mostly came from Newport, was well positioned to know whether the colony's slave traders were willing to abide by the ban.

Whether Newport slavers would truly abide by the ban remained an open question. An initial indication that Newport merchants would comply with the ban was the scramble to send out ships to Africa before the prohibition took effect on December 1, 1774. In the first ten months of 1774, thirteen slave ships cleared out of Newport for Africa and two sailed from nearby Bristol. In the single month of November, after learning of the ban shortly to take effect, five ships sailed out of Newport and one out of Bristol, bound for Africa. Three of them departed with just two days to spare.[82] Several Newport slaving vessels that could not be made ready to sail by December 1 were reportedly kept in port.[83]

Newport's Samuel Hopkins, one of the key antislavery leaders in the thirteen colonies, observed that Congress's ban on the slave trade "falls heaviest on this town." He said that the ban was unpopular since it was considered to be detrimental to the interests of its residents.[84] Still, after December 1, all of Newport's and other Rhode Island merchants complied with the ban. Two prominent Newport slave merchants, Christopher and George Champlin, informed their English joint venturers that their younger brother, Robert Champlin, had sailed their sloop out of Newport bound for Africa nine days prior to the December 1 deadline. But they also warned, "By the resolves of the Continental Congress, all trade is stopped from this continent [mainland North America] to Africa [starting] 1st December last, since which no vessel has sailed for thence, nor will any till our troubles are settled."[85]

While American merchants generally abided by the ban, some American ship captains did not. They had more flexibility than did merchants, and they could sail from a variety of international ports and under different flags.

American ship captains who violated the slave trade ban did so by sailing not from North American ports but from Caribbean ports. For example, Captain Robert Champlin, brother of the Newport merchants, commanded two slave voyages between British-held Jamaica and Africa in 1775 and 1776.[86] Another Newport captain, Stanton Hazard, arrived at the French-controlled Caribbean Island of Guadeloupe in September 1775. A group of New England ship captains then in Guadeloupe saw Hazard's preparations and became concerned he was about to sail on a slave voyage to Africa in violation of Congress's ban. They met with Hazard and insisted that he not go through with it.[87] The threat of Hazard being ostracized hung in the air. Nonetheless, Hazard, who would become a committed Tory, ignored them and proceeded to the African coast, trading Rhode Island rum for African captives.[88]

On April 6, 1776, the Continental Congress stepped back from its total ban prohibiting Americans from participating in the slave trade. The main thrust of the resolution was a momentous one: to permit American merchants to export goods and merchandise to any foreign country, and to import goods and merchandise from any foreign country—except those "subject to the King of Great Britain."[89] The resolution added that "no slave be imported into any of the thirteen United Colonies." No mention was made of the ability of Americans to participate in the slave trade with other countries. Violation of the April 1776 resolutions could result in forfeiture of the goods and merchandise.

A fair reading of the two resolutions is that American merchants could not deal in enslaved people with Britain or any of its colonies, and they could not import enslaved people into the thirteen mainland colonies, but they could purchase captives in Africa from non-British interests and sell them to French, Spanish, or Portuguese slave buyers in the New World. However, it is not clear this was practical on a wide scale, as those countries had their own monopolies and rules limiting who could participate in their slave trading systems.

Importantly, the new prohibitions did not apply to goods and merchandise that were "made prize of" by an American privateer capturing a British ship on the high seas.[90] This provision would become relevant to John Brown in 1778.

Brown disagreed with his brother Moses's views that the slave trade was morally wrong. John had no compunction against trading in human flesh.

Yet he did abide by Congress's 1774 ban prohibiting participation in the slave trade and the 1776 ban prohibiting the importation of enslaved people. Still, Brown could invest in a new business that could be even more profitable than slave trading: privateering. His knowledge of and experience in slave trading and privateering led him to conceive of a daring plan to attack British slave trading operations in West Africa.

CHAPTER TWO

John Brown Invests
in Privateers

*A*s *noted in the last chapter*, to conceive of and implement his plan to
send a new, large privateer to Africa to attack British slave trading interests there, John Brown first had to have been an audacious Patriot, been
an experienced investor in privateers, and earned sufficient excess capital
to build a twenty-gun privateer brig. This chapter discusses each of these
factors. It also adds that as privateering became less lucrative by late 1777
because of the Royal Navy's increasing success in capturing American privateers, Brown began to reconsider how to deploy his next privateer.

Brown was a member of a family of prosperous merchants based in
Providence in the British colony of Rhode Island. John was born January
27, 1736, the fourth son of James Brown and Hope (Power) Brown. John's
father died when the boy was three. John began his working life in part-
nership with his three older brothers, Nicholas, Joseph, and Moses, and his
uncle Obadiah, who led the business. After the death of Obadiah in 1762,
the firm was named after the eldest brother, Nicholas Brown & Co. Together the Brown brothers built a thriving mercantile business prior to the
outbreak of the Revolutionary War and dominated the mercantile scene in
Providence.[1] They shipped goods around the Atlantic world to and from
the British Caribbean islands, in the coastal trade along the American Eastern Seaboard, and occasionally to Europe.

As successful as they were in the lead-up to the American Revolution, Brown, his brothers, and other merchants in Providence were not as wealthy or established as their counterparts in nearby Newport to the south. Newport merchants such as Aaron Lopez, Joseph Wanton, and Godfrey Malbone were wealthier and more socially prominent than their rivals in Providence. This made John Brown and his fellow Providence merchants scramble even harder to catch up to their Newport peers.

The Browns wisely diversified by investing in manufacturing businesses. First, in 1753, they began producing and distributing spermaceti candles made from high-quality sperm whale oil purchased mostly from Nantucket whalers. By 1763, the Browns were one of the leading spermaceti candle manufacturers in the colonies.

Two years later, the Brown brothers went into the iron manufacturing business, after iron ore was discovered in Cranston and Scituate, Rhode Island. They and several other northern Rhode Island investors (including Governor Stephen Hopkins) built in Scituate a large furnace, named Hope Furnace, after the Brown brothers' mother. Within three years, the furnace was in full operation, producing nails, iron hoops for barrels, and other products.[2]

John and Moses left Nicholas Brown & Co. in 1771 and 1773, respectively, and the firm dissolved in 1774. Each brother then went into business on his own, although they sometimes coinvested in projects. They retained their shares in Hope Furnace.

John Brown married Sarah Smith in 1760. Starting the next year through 1777, they had six children (two of them died in childhood). Their house was on South Main Street, fronting the Providence River.[3]

As the imperial crisis in the thirteen colonies unfolded, John Brown demonstrated that he was a bold Whig. He naturally objected to the British government's attempts to enforce long-ignored maritime restrictions and to impose new taxes on American imports without the consent of the American colonies. He and his brothers had been operating essentially unfettered by commercial regulations and taxes for decades. To avoid this crackdown, Brown and other New England merchants often resorted to smuggling.

In 1772, Brown seized an opportunity to strike back. He played a leading role in the taking and burning of the British revenue schooner *Gaspee*, one of the outstanding acts of colonial resistance in the years leading up to the outbreak of war in 1775.

According to the *Providence Gazette*, the *Gaspee*'s commander, Lieutenant William Dudingston, was "haughty, insolent and intolerable" and had been "personally ill-treating every master and merchant of the vessels he boarded."[4] In fact, Dudingston had been ordered to enforce British maritime legislation. The British lieutenant's imperious and heavy-handed style, however, offended many captains and merchants, who were ready for their own minor rebellion.

In the late afternoon of June 9, Captain John Lindsay, sometimes employed by John Brown as a ship commander, reported to him that the *Gaspee* had just run aground on shoals off Namquid Point near Warwick in Narragansett Bay while chasing his packet boat in shallow water. Brown quickly seized on a plan to organize an attack to get rid of the hated British warship once and for all. Brown and others estimated that the next rising tide at three a.m. the following day would float the *Gaspee* again. There was just enough time to organize the raid, execute it, and return safely to Providence without being spotted in daylight by Crown sympathizers.

Brown called for eight whaleboats and ten rowers for each boat to be brought to Fenner's Wharf on Providence's waterfront, on South Main Street near Brown's home. A boy beat a drum along Main Street calling for men to gather at Sabin's Tavern across the street from the wharf, at the northeast corner of South Main and Planet Streets. Brown put one of his top ship captains, Abraham Whipple, in charge of the operation and appointed a sea captain to command each whaleboat. The whaleboats arrived, and eager and experienced crews filled them. At ten p.m., the raiders, about eighty in number, Brown included, perhaps using coal to blacken their faces, began their journey rowing from Fenner's Wharf.

Attacking a Royal Navy warship was fraught with danger. British sailors could be expected to fight back, and if any raiders were caught, they could be charged with treason and, if convicted, hanged. One key to the operation, as Brown knew, was to surprise the men aboard the warship and stay clear of its sides, where the firing of cannon from its broadsides could scatter the Providence men and end the raid. The other key for the well-known Brown was to keep himself hidden so he could not be identified as a participant by British officers and sailors.

At twelve forty-five a.m., a sentinel on the still-stranded *Gaspee*'s deck hailed at approaching longboats. Abraham Whipple in a booming voice identified himself as the sheriff of Kent County (which was not true) and declared he had a warrant for the arrest of Lieutenant Dudingston. Just as several of the raiders tried to board his vessel, the awakened Dudingston ran onto the deck and struck one of them with a sword, cutting him. Dudingston called for his crew, most of whom were sleeping belowdecks, to come up to the top deck to defend his boat, but he only had nineteen men. There was a short exchange of musket fire from both sides. The British lieutenant crumpled in pain on the deck, struck by a musket ball in his left arm and groin. Some of the raiders swarmed aboard the *Gaspee*. Outnumbered and their commander wounded, the *Gaspee*'s crew surrendered. The raiders immediately moved the captured officers and crew ashore to nearby Pawtuxet; some raiders must have returned to the *Gaspee* to burn it to the waterline.[5]

An outraged King George III appointed a commission of inquiry to investigate what he considered lawless and treasonous behavior. But the investigation ended in total failure. No credible witness could be found to testify as to who participated in the raid, even though John Brown's name was widely bandied about. In Providence's tight-knit mercantile community, which was dominated by the Browns, any man brash enough to testify against John Brown or his allies knew that he and his family would suffer severe retaliation by local toughs. The burning of the *Gaspee* demonstrated the willingness of Rhode Island merchants, captains, and sailors to protect the maritime world they had built, even if it required violence.

Still, shortly after the outbreak of war at Lexington and Concord in April 1775, the Royal Navy was able to capture John Brown. Captain James Wallace, sent to Narragansett Bay with a small flotilla of warships to awe the populace, on April 26 seized two sloops filled with flour that had just departed Newport Harbor. To his astonishment and pleasure, Wallace discovered that on one of the sloops was none other than John Brown, one of the alleged culprits of the *Gaspee* affair. A contrite Brown claimed he had just purchased the flour and was on his way to Providence, where he was going to load it on a ship bound for the Caribbean. Wallace suspected, correctly, that the flour was destined for the New England militia then organizing outside Boston.[6] The next day, Wallace sent the beleaguered Brown to Vice Admiral Samuel Graves at Boston.[7]

A group of influential Providence men, including John's brothers, rushed to Boston to meet with representatives of the British commander in chief, General Thomas Gage. While the prisoner reportedly feared his prospects, Moses Brown successfully negotiated his brother's release on May 3. Gage, desperately seeking a peaceful, negotiated end to the increasing imperial crisis in New England, agreed to let Brown go if he pledged not to act against Britain and used his influence to persuade Rhode Island's General Assembly to send negotiators to Boston to meet with Gage. An anxious Brown agreed, achieving his release. He soon appeared before the General Assembly to encourage it to send negotiators to meet with Gage. The Lower House agreed, but the Upper House rejected the idea.[8]

Brown acted to dispel any doubts that he was not a Patriot. On June 6, he filed a suit against Captain Wallace for wrongful detention and seizure, claiming £10,000 in damages. Moses Brown scolded his brother for violating the terms of his release. In his rejoinder, John Brown unapologetically asserted that he was now "so clear in opinion that the measures now taken to force America are so wrong that it is out of my power to restrain myself from wishing success to the country in which I was born."[9]

The outbreak of war ruined the Browns' spermaceti candle business, but even more lucrative business opportunities arose. They included serving as a military contractor to the Continental Congress and investing in privateers. Brown demonstrated he was a Patriot in these endeavors but also that he was focused on increasing his wealth.

At the start of the war, the Continental army found itself startlingly short of gunpowder. General George Washington, commanding the newly established army setting siege to Boston, even resorted to subterfuge, tricking the British into believing he had more gunpowder for his troops than he actually had.

Hearing of John Brown of Providence for the first time, Washington wrote to the Rhode Island governor of the "precarious" state of his gunpowder supplies and asked him to contact Brown as a likely merchant who could obtain some gunpowder overseas. "Mr. Brown has been mentioned to me as a very proper person to consult upon this occasion," the commander in chief advised.[10]

Washington had identified the right man. With the outbreak of war, John and Nicholas Brown quickly seized the opportunity to engage in international trade to acquire gunpowder and resell it at a hefty profit. Nicholas Brown remarked in late 1775 that "brother John" had lately brought in from the Dutch-held South American colony of Surinam about 4,500 pounds of gunpowder.[11] On November 3, John Brown, from Providence, wrote to General Washington, informing him of forty-four casks of gunpowder on one of his vessels that had arrived from Surinam at Norwich, Connecticut. Perhaps trying to drive up the price, Brown informed Washington that he was "at a loss" to know what was better for "the general cause," selling it to the Continental army, to Connecticut coastal towns clamoring for it to help defend themselves against raids by British warships, or to Rhode Island, which had offered a great price.[12]

The Providence merchant ended up selling most of his powder to Rhode Island in support of its defense.[13] The lesser needs of his home colony won out against the more pressing needs of the national army. Brown did manage to supply one ton of pistol powder to Washington's army. "The General will take it, though it is a most exorbitant price," one of the commander in chief's aides responded in a November 27 letter.[14]

Seeking to expand his services as a military contractor to the Patriot cause, Brown also informed Washington in his November 3 letter that he and other owners of the Hope Furnace were revamping the works in order to start manufacturing heavy 18-pounder and 24-pounder cannon (the number of pounds refers to the relative weight of the solid iron cannonball the cannon fired). Hope Furnace "is the very best kind for making cannon," Brown informed Washington.[15]

Hope Furnace became one of three foundries in New England early in the war capable of casting cannon for warships.[16] It received a contract from Rhode Island to make sixty 18-pounder and 24-pounder cannon. This order was followed by another for sixty 12-pounders from the Marine Committee of the Continental Congress to arm two Continental navy frigates under construction in Providence, as well as thirty-two more cannon (twenty-six 12-pounders and six 6-pounders) for another Continental navy frigate, the *Raleigh*, being constructed in Portsmouth, New Hampshire. During the war, Hope Furnace cast and bored about one thousand cannon and sold them at high prices. Most were placed aboard New England privateer vessels. For example, orders poured in from privateer owners from Salem and Newburyport, Massachusetts, for 3-pounder, 4-pounder, and 6-pounder cannon.[17]

As a result of a trip to Philadelphia in December 1775, Brown persuaded the key committee of the Continental Congress managing the war effort, known as the Secret Committee, to enter into a commission agreement authorizing him to spend the astounding amount of £24,000 to import gunpowder and other military stores. In February 1776, John and Nicholas Brown entered into a second contract with the Secret Committee to procure military blankets and uniforms.[18]

John Brown suddenly became one of the most important private military contractors on the Patriot side. The profits he earned from the military contracts enabled him to invest in an even more remunerative line of business: privateering. Brown would earn spectacular profits from the privateer craze that swept Rhode Island and the rest of maritime New England in the Revolutionary War in 1776.

During the war, the Continental navy was no match for the Royal Navy, the world's strongest maritime power. While there were occasional bright spots during single-ship engagements, the largest Continental navy ships were much smaller than the Royal Navy's largest warships, which could carry fifty guns, sixty-four guns, and even ninety or more guns. And the fledgling Continental navy could never muster sufficient ships to face the Royal Navy in a fleet action. The Continental navy would eventually be assisted by the powerful allied French and Spanish fleets, but this assistance would not commence until mid-1778.

America's most effective weapon at sea by far was privateering—the operation of privately owned commerce raiders. While the incentive was private gain, the result was to advance the American war effort by enriching Americans at the expense of their enemy. From British ships, Americans captured gunpowder, weapons, food, blankets, cloth for uniforms, and other supplies desperately needed not only by the Continental army but also by state militias and citizens of the new United States.

Privateers were not pirates. Pirates operated outside of any government oversight and solely for their own personal gain. Privateers were sanctioned by a government to attack enemy shipping and were supposed to be loyal to the country that commissioned them. They were required to follow an elaborate set of rules, including respecting the rights of vessels from neutral countries, not using excessive force in capturing enemy ships, and treating prisoners humanely. A violation of any of these prohibitions could result in the loss of a privateer's rights to the prize or even its commission.

Once an enemy vessel was captured, the captain of the privateer would typically select from his ship a prize master and a small prize crew with orders to sail the captured vessel to a safe US port so the prize could be adjudicated by an admiralty court. The admiralty court would conduct a trial by jury to determine whether the prize was lawfully taken. If it was, it would be sold at public auction. After deductions for court costs, the net proceeds would be divided among the privateer's owners, officers, and crew pursuant to a formula agreed to prior to the voyage set forth in signed "articles" of agreement.[19] Sometimes the formalities of an admiralty court case could be avoided by taking the prize to a neutral country and selling the prize and its cargo there.

Surprisingly, the former thirteen colonies and Congress took their time in adopting privateering laws. While privateering was common in wars throughout the eighteenth century by all belligerent powers, there was still an unpleasant odor to taking property from private shippers. Merchants also hesitated to seize the cargos of their former friends and business associates. Moreover, declaring that American ships could act as privateers was a step toward independence, which many legislators were hesitant to take in the early stages of the war. Finally, Congress purportedly had been waging war against the king's "corrupt" ministers who had misled him. It took some time before Congress realized that in reality, its war was against all of Britain.

In November 1775, Massachusetts became the first colony to enact a law authorizing the issuance of commissions to privateers and to provide for the establishment of admiralty courts for prizes.[20] New Hampshire followed suit two months later.[21] Rhode Island enacted its own legislation authorizing privateers in March 1776, although the first report of a Rhode Island privateer capturing a British ship had occurred two months earlier.[22] Before long, New England privateers were operating in the Atlantic Ocean, initially hunting for British supply ships heading for Canada. (British merchant and military ships sailed to Canada to supply the important naval port of Halifax and the army's staging city at Quebec.)

Congress took longer to act. John Adams encouraged Congress to authorize privateering.[23] Robert Morris, writing for Congress's Secret Committee, pointed out that Parliament on December 22, 1775, had passed the Prohibitory Act authorizing the seizure and forfeiture of American ships. Morris thought Parliament would regret the vote, "especially as they have much more property to lose than we have."[24]

Finally, on March 23, 1776, Congress empowered the inhabitants of the "United Colonies" (they were not states yet) to fit out privateers under its authority and approved their issuing Continental commissions. A dual system for handling privateering arose: most privateers were commissioned under Congress's authority, while the colonies (later states) issued the commissions and established prize courts, with the right of appeal to an arm of the Continental Congress.[25]

America had the means to create a fleet of privateer vessels: experienced maritime investors, captains, crews, and their ships. American merchant ships had plied the Atlantic for more than a century, but the Prohibitory Act had closed off their main markets in Britain and its colonies in the Caribbean. Now an option became available to them other than spending idle time in ports: using their ships in privateering ventures.

Privateering was risky. Those involved could win big by capturing a rich British supply ship bound for America or a merchant vessel filled with sugar headed for London. Or they could suffer catastrophic financial losses if their vessel was taken by Royal Navy warships, and the captains and crews could be sent to terrible prisons. Despite the risks, many investors, captains, and sailors chose the path of privateering.

American merchants such as the Browns invested in privateer vessels, and their former merchant marine ship captains often commanded them. Investors typically spread the risk, each purchasing a partial share of a single privateer voyage. The privateers varied in size from 30 to 320 tons and were well armed with cannon on one or two decks and swivel guns (small-bore cannon or muskets mounted on the deck's railings). The vessels usually set out alone but occasionally joined with others.

Many who voluntarily signed the articles to join an American privateer had mixed motives of patriotism and economic self-interest. Christopher Prince, when he joined the crews of New England privateers, wrote that he had "two motives in mind, one was for the freedom of my country," and the other was to enjoy "the luxuries of life."[26]

Samuel Phillips, a neighbor of George W. Babcock's in North Kingstown, served as a major in a Rhode Island state regiment and as second in command of a party of forty-eight soldiers who at night captured British Major General Richard Prescott at a farmhouse outside Newport in July 1777, one of the most daring and successful surprise raids of the war.[27] In 1779, Phillips turned to privateering. He served as a lieutenant on four voyages, including two with Babcock, and commanded on another voyage. He was caught and imprisoned in dirty and crowded jails three times. Yet Phillips was proud of this service. Years after the war ended, he wrote, "I have ever striven hard and suffered much to help gain the independence of my country, which I ever held near and dear to me."[28]

If privateersmen were honest with themselves, they would admit that the decision to go privateering was primarily financially oriented. Continental navy and army officers bemoaned the thousands of sailors who signed on to privateering cruises rather than take less-lucrative postings enlisting in the Continental military.[29] In Providence, Esek Hopkins, the new commander in chief of the Continental navy, and in Newport, John Paul Jones, the navy's outstanding ship captain, complained that they had difficulty competing with privateers for sailors.[30]

Still, enlisting for an American privateer's voyage was patriotic too, and it also entailed the significant risk of being captured and placed in a horrid British prison where life expectancy could be short. And privateering inflicted a huge amount of damage on Britain's maritime economy, far more than the Continental navy did. Privateers intercepted supplies destined for British military forces in North America and thereby hurt the British military effort; and, when they brought the seized cargo into America, they helped the American war effort. Pressured by British merchants complaining about their losses to American privateers, the Royal Navy had to divert a substantial number of its warships to protect convoys of British merchantmen and to try to capture American privateers. Naval historian David Syrett found that the threat of capture by American privateers increased the costs of the British in supplying its military in North America.[31]

Naval historian Michael Crawford concluded that American privateers hampered the British war effort. He added, "The genius of privateering was that the pursuit of private profit by many individual privateers produced a substantial public benefit—a powerful blow to enemy commerce. When each pursued his own good, the good of the whole was advanced." Crawford saw the invisible hand of a free market economy at work, explained in a book newly published in 1776, Adam Smith's *Wealth of Nations*.[32]

Privateers sometimes engaged in fierce contests with Royal Navy warships, as well as against British and Loyalist privateers. One historian counted sixteen Royal Navy men-of-war captured by American privateers.[33] The future captain of the *Marlborough*, George Waite Babcock, as will be seen in chapter 10, never shrank from combat with the enemy, fighting five fierce battles—one against a Royal Navy sloop, two against powerful British privateers, and two against large, well-armed merchantmen.

In the early years of the war, the Royal Navy failed to devote substantial resources to protect the British merchant fleet. As a result, American privateers scoured the principal routes of British trade almost at will. They swept up and down the coastal waters of North America, combed the Caribbean waters, and seized enemy ships sailing between Britain and both the Caribbean and Canada. In 1776 alone, they captured a Quebec fleet worth £500,000 and more than half of a rich Jamaica fleet of more than sixty vessels bound for England.[34] By the end of 1776, according to Britain's own count, American privateers had taken some 350 British commercial ships.[35]

By the end of 1777, American privateers had captured about 733 British merchant vessels. The value of the seized ships was estimated by one British merchant testifying in the House of Lords to be about £1,800,600 ($330 million in 2022 dollars) and by another as not less than £2,200,000 ($403 million). By April 1777, American privateers had seized 120 ships in the Caribbean alone, and at year's end, the number seized there had more than doubled to 247.[36]

The year 1776 was the heyday for privateering in Rhode Island. From early May to the end of the year, Rhode Island issued fifty-nine Continental Congress commissions to privateers. In November, when state officials ran out of preprinted blank privateer commission forms sent by Congress, they began to handwrite them.[37]

Soon Providence became overwhelmed with surplus goods and supplies. The Reverend Ezra Stiles, minister of the Second Congregational Church in Newport, thought that from thirty-five to forty prizes had been brought into Providence by October 1776, all but two or three of which had been engaged in the sugar trade between Britain and its Caribbean colonies.[38] The newly appointed commander in chief of the Continental navy, Esek Hopkins, from his hometown of Providence, wrote on November 7, 1776, "Privateers have great luck and getting money fast."[39] John Howland returned to Providence in early 1777, after performing grueling service as a private in a Rhode Island regiment with Washington's often half-starved army. He may have regretted his decision enlisting in the land forces. He recalled, "The year 1776 was mostly employed in privateering, and many whom I had left in poor circumstances were now rich men. The wharves in Providence were crowded with large ships from Jamaica and other islands, loaded with rich products."[40]

An official list of prizes brought to Providence between April 11, 1776, and November 28, 1776, and condemned in its admiralty court, identifies forty-seven of them. The sales prices of the ships and their cargoes at auction are not all listed, but thirteen are. They reveal an average sales price of each ship and its cargo of about £9,000 (about $1.7 million). By extrapolating from that average, Providence privateers brought in captured vessels and cargoes worth more than £420,000[41] ($80 million).

A ballad published in 1694, composed for notorious English pirate Henry Every, was updated to encourage sailors to enlist on the private sloop of war *Montgomery*, which was commissioned in Providence on August 8, 1776. The song's opening paragraph emphasized the riches awaiting sailors:

> Come all you young fellows of courage so bold
> Come enter on board and we will clothe you with gold
> Come repair unto Providence and there you shall find
> A sloop called the *Montgomery* shall pleasure your minds[42]

Those "young fellows" who enlisted were not disappointed: in a month, the *Montgomery* shared in taking two prizes and took two others on its own.[43]

John Brown enjoyed more than his fair share of profits from the privateering craze in 1776, and profited in 1777 as well. They helped make him a rich man, able to secure excess cash and become an experienced investor in privateers.

From August 1776 to December 1777, before the *Marlborough* received its commission on December 13, 1777, Brown owned two privateers outright (the *Favourite* and the *Polly*) and was a partial investor in at least nine others sailing from Providence. In the same timeframe, these privateers sailed on sixteen voyages. Brown was a part owner of three of the strongest privateers to depart Providence in 1776 and 1777: the twenty-gun *Oliver Cromwell*, the twenty-two-gun *Blaze-Castle*, and the twenty-gun *Marlborough*.[44]

Brown took a keen interest in the sloop *Diamond*, probably because he owned a large share in it. The *Diamond* was small, weighing only sixty tons, and had a crew of thirty or forty men. Prior to the war, the crew would have numbered fewer than ten, but a larger crew was needed to man cannon and board enemy vessels armed with cutlasses and pistols. The *Diamond* carried just six 4-pounder cannons and ten swivel guns.[45] Still, Brown had high hopes for it.

Before the *Diamond* embarked on its first cruise in July, Brown issued orders to its captain, William Chace of Providence. To motivate Chace and his crew, Brown reported recent news of "three grand prizes brought to the eastward, one a three-decker, which with the other ship is supposed to be worth £30,000 Sterling" that was taken by "one privateer of little or no more strength than your sloop." The Providence merchant gushed, "I hope in a few weeks to have the satisfaction of going on board a prize ship from you." Brown added, "No time ought to be lost before you get on the ground for prizes," meaning the routes entering the British-held Caribbean islands.[46] Because of the "great expense as well as trouble" of outfitting a privateer for a cruise, Brown recommended that Chace remain at sea "as long as you possibly can." Any prizes, Brown ordered, were to be sent to Providence.[47]

Shortly after arriving at the Caribbean in late July, Captain Chace captured several prized, including the brig *Star and Garter*, which was sailing from St. Christopher to London and carrying 195 hogsheads of sugar, as well as other goods. When the prize arrived at Providence's wharves on August 13, John Brown no doubt experienced great "satisfaction" in stepping aboard to inspect it and its cargo. Chace also captured the *Jane*, a merchant vessel on its way from the British-held island of Dominica to London, with 310 hogsheads of sugar and 200 barrels of whale oil on board.[48]

More was to come. Captain Chace and several other American privateers fell in with a fleet of merchant ships on their return voyages from the British Caribbean to England. The *Diamond* took three more vessels. In total, it seized more than 1,000 hogsheads of sugar, 15,600 pounds of cocoa, 61,900 pounds of coffee, 12,380 gallons of rum, 17,750 pounds of cotton, and 3,800 gallons of whale oil.[49] Brown and his fellow investors had hit the jackpot. Later in August, three of the vessels captured by the *Diamond*, and their cargoes, were subjected to admiralty court procedures in Providence and sold, fetching £7,418, £8,188, and £12,138, respectively.[50] The total haul had a value of about $5.2 million in 2022 dollars.

Brown sent the *Diamond* out again in September, this time under the command of Thomas Stacy. On September 22, Stacy captured a British navy transport ship, the three-hundred-ton *Woodcock*. The British commander surrendered to Stacy despite the *Woodcock* being much larger and armed with six cannon. The British commander probably thought his crew was too small to fight off the *Diamond*. Stacy assigned a prize crew to sail the *Woodcock* to Providence, where it was sold on November 19 for £6,670.[51] On October 3, Stacy captured a brig, the 260-ton *Live Oak*, bound from Jamaica to London and filled with sugar, rum, logs, and 450 pieces of valuable mahogany.[52] Brown wound up acquiring a one-half interest in the *Live Oak* to use as a cargo vessel.

Turning north following Brown's orders, Stacy sailed for the Canadian coast. He intercepted and seized a 260-ton commercial vessel bound from Quebec to London and then an 80-ton brig filled with codfish from Newfoundland.[53]

In 1776, Brown invested as a part owner in four privateers that brought into Providence as prizes twelve commercial ships and other vessels that on average weighed 183 tons.[54] Brown also solely owned the *Favourite*, a seventy-four-ton sloop carrying ten 4-pounder carriage guns and ten swivel guns and manned by eighty men. On a voyage starting in September, it captured two prizes, including the 230-ton ship *Peggy*, with rum and sugar in its holds.[55]

By March 1777, due in part to his privateering success, Brown likely had become Rhode Island's greatest ship owner, rivaled only by his brother Nicholas. From a list compiled by Brown in that month, he held interests in twenty-four vessels. He owned one hundred percent of eleven of them, 87.5 percent of one, and fifty percent of five, with the rest held in smaller percentages. Eight of them were ships, the largest vessels used by colonial merchants, with three square-rigged masts. Six were brigs, somewhat smaller vessels than ships that had two square-rigged masts. In addition to the foremast and mainmast, a brig often carried on its mainmast a lower fore-and-aft sail with a gaff and boom. Brown listed two schooners, which had two masts that were fore-and-aft rigged (that is, they were not square rigged). Brown owned eight sloops, the smallest of the oceangoing vessels. Nine of the vessels were privateers, and three had been taken as prizes by his privateers.[56]

Warning signs for investors in privateers appeared by 1777. The heady days of easy conquests in 1776 were over. As the complaints of British merchants in London and other British ports filled the halls of the Admiralty's headquarters at Whitehall in London, Royal Navy warships were assigned to protect commercial vessels sailing in convoys and to cruise off British-controlled Caribbean islands. The Royal Navy started to have some success, seizing dozens of privateers.

The *Providence Gazette* and other New England newspapers in late 1777 increasingly reported on captures of privateers. Royal Navy frigates, typically carrying twenty-eight to thirty-two cannon and manned by two hundred men or more, were fast and more powerful than any American privateer. Even smaller Royal Navy vessels, such as sloops of war, were manned by experienced officers and sailors and could easily defeat most American privateers.

Moreover, in early December 1776, the British seized Newport. The Royal Navy, operating out of the port, established a blockade of Narragansett Bay and began seizing American ships trying to depart or enter the bay.

A captured privateer could be a financial disaster for its American investors, particularly if it was taken before it seized any enemy vessels that were later safely brought into port and sold. What is more, the privateer captain and crew would be sent to British prisons in New York or back in Britain, where many died of malnutrition and disease. A merchant associated with Lloyd's of London estimated that by the end of 1777, Royal Navy warships had captured thirty-four American privateers carrying some three thousand sailors.[57] The rate of captures of privateers, as well as trading ships, was also accelerating.

John Brown too began to feel the pain of privateers and cargo vessels in which he was a partial or whole owner being captured by British warships. In January 1778, looking back to the period from May 1777 to January 1778, he claimed that the Royal Navy had cost him most of his investments in two privateers (the *Retaliation*, of which he owned seven-eighths, and the expensive *Oliver Cromwell*, of which he owned three-sixteenths), as well as in three trading vessels (the commercial brig *Live Oak*, of which he owned one-half, and two smaller commercial vessels, of which he owned one hundred percent). Brown computed this loss at £9,200 ($1.75 million in 2022 dollars).[58]

Financially, Brown was still way ahead because of a key consideration, which has not been appreciated by maritime historians. The cost of a privateer and its cannon and stores could be quickly recouped from a single prize vessel and its cargo. The *Marlborough* itself, one of the finest and most expensive privateers built in Providence during the war, was worth about £10,000, according to Brown. This value included its cannon and stores.[59] Most of the privateers Brown invested in were worth far less. In January 1778, the average value of four privateer sloops and one privateer brig Brown invested in, including their cannon, rigging, and sails, was £3,315.[60] Yet the average sales price of each prize ship and its cargo brought into Providence and sold there in 1776, as previously noted, was about £9,000.

Still, the losses hurt Brown. He also did not like the idea of the officers and sailors of his ships, many of whom he knew personally, rotting in British prisons. In addition, Brown no doubt heard about British merchant ships having more cannon placed on them to fend off small privateers.

Brown had gained valuable experience as an investor in privateers in 1776 and 1777. His great success in military contracting and in investing in privateers also allowed him to accumulate significant capital. Brown could use this excess capital to reinvest in more privateers. But by 1777, the days of easy captures by small privateers were gone.

In response to these developments, Brown made two important decisions.

First, he decided to use his profits to invest in a new, strong, and sleek privateer to be constructed in Providence. The stronger and faster his privateer was, Brown knew, the better chance it had of avoiding capture. On the flip side, a fast and strong privateer also meant the ability to seize large enemy merchant ships as prizes. With his contacts in the shipbuilding community, Brown could have it constructed quickly. As a key owner of Hope Furnace, he could make sure his new ship would have the twenty cannon it needed.

Second, Brown decided he would send his newly built privateer to Africa and search for British prizes there. It was a stunningly original and audacious decision that likely never would have been made without his own experience in investing in slave trading voyages to Africa and interacting with Rhode Island slave trade investors and captains.

CHAPTER THREE

John Brown Decides to Send a Privateer to Africa

*F*lush *with earnings* from investments in privateering and military contracting, John Brown decided to invest in another privateering venture
to add to his fortune. It still promised the best financial returns at the time.
But by late 1777, he faced a changed landscape with increased risk if he
followed the standard path. That forced him to become creative.

Brown decided he would build a strong privateer and send it to the coast
of West Africa and attack British slave trading interests there. American
privateers had already been attacking and seizing British slave ships, but
mainly in the Caribbean. A few other Patriot leaders had the idea of sending an American warship or privateer to Africa to raid British slave trading
posts, but only Brown thought of the idea and implemented it.

The main development in late 1776 and in 1777 that concerned Brown
was the Royal Navy's increasing success in, first, providing better protection
for British merchant ships and, second, searching for and capturing American privateers. Because of this, Brown did not want to convert any of his
older ships into a privateer; most of them were bulky trading vessels that
could not outrun Royal Navy frigates. They could not even defend themselves against a Royal Navy sloop of war or even a smaller armed tender.

Brown also was wary about the risk of investing in a new and expensive privateer that would sail to the Caribbean or along the Atlantic Coast, given the threat posed by Royal Navy warships. With all the money Brown and his partners would sink into a new privateer, to have it captured would mean a substantial financial loss for them. And the ship's captain and crew would be consigned to confinement in a dank, pestilent, and overcrowded British prison ship.

Brown knew that the Royal Navy could not patrol everywhere. In fact, it was seriously overstretched. Its primary task in 1776 and 1777 had been to support the operations of the British army under Sir William Howe. Royal Navy ships, under the overall command of Vice Admiral Lord Richard Howe, in 1776 had evacuated British troops from Boston; dispatched an expeditionary force to take Charleston, South Carolina, that did not succeed; transported another expeditionary force to Staten Island, Long Island, and then to Manhattan, with the British troops defeating George Washington's army and seizing those areas; and at the end of the year transported another large expeditionary force that seized Newport. In July 1777, it transported a massive expeditionary force on a lengthy voyage to capture Philadelphia by sailing up the Chesapeake Bay in September 1777. Admiral Howe's ships further made feeble attempts to blockade America's ports. They also convoyed British army supply ships bound for North America and merchant vessels in the Caribbean trade to protect them from American privateers. When they could, Royal Navy warships searched for and attacked "rebel" privateers. Still, a large portion of the Royal Navy remained at anchor in English ports or in the English Channel, ever watchful for a French invasion.

Other factors resulted in demands on Royal Navy warships. British naval officials began to realize that the best ships for the American station, as well as patrolling the African coast, were not massive ships of the line but instead smaller frigates, brigs, and sloops. The British Admiralty had not, however, built a sufficient number of them.[1] Furthermore, the Royal Navy ships stationed in America, particularly in the northern waters, took a beating from storms. With no naval facilities in American waters adequate to refit and repair the ships, they needed to return to Britain for overhaul, which meant they were out of action for a long time.

All this meant that the Royal Navy could spare relatively few ships to patrol the edges of the British Empire, including Africa. Only small frigates, brigs, and sloops of war could be effective patrolling the West African coast, but the Royal Navy had relatively few of them, and the ones it had were needed in America. Thus, the risk of a privateer being captured on a cruise to the West Africa coast would be reduced, giving it almost free rein to attack British slave trade interests. Brown likely learned of the scarcity of British ships on the West African coast from returning Rhode Island slave ship captains, since American newspapers rarely broached the topic.

Given his concerns about the risks of investing in more privateers to prowl the western Atlantic, and his knowledge of the privateering opportunities along the coast of West Africa, Brown decided to capitalize on the latter by building a privateer with twenty guns and sending it Africa. It appeared to be a sound business decision.

A privateer sent to Africa could attack and plunder slave trading posts established by British slave traders. The posts (called "factories" because they were manned by European factors, or intermediaries, hired by British merchants) often contained warehouses full of British manufactured goods and other merchandise intended for the local slave trade. The privateersmen could carry off this booty and load the goods into the holds of their privateers. In addition, perhaps African captives kept at the slave trading posts, intended to be sold to British slave ships, could be seized and sold as prizes. Moreover, enslaved people could be captured from British slave ships whose captains would be surprised by the appearance of a powerful American privateer so far from its home port.

If Brown was really fortunate, he figured, his privateer could capture a large British slave ship filled with African captives, ready to sail for the Caribbean islands. In such a situation, the crew would be on the verge of cashing in after perhaps spending almost a year traveling to and along the African coast purchasing captives from local sellers. Brown's privateer could simply step in and snatch the slave ship and its human cargo as a prize of war. A prize crew from Brown's privateer would be ordered to sail the slave ship in the Middle Passage and try to arrive at a safe port, probably in one of the French-controlled Caribbean islands or in American-held Charleston, South Carolina, or Savannah, Georgia. There the enslaved surviving Africans on board could be sold at auction. Then Brown and his investors could really cash in.

The idea of privateers attacking enemy slave ships off the coast of Africa was not new. During the Seven Years' War, French privateers aggressively sought to capture British slave ships. A Rhode Island historian in the late nineteenth century listed nine Newport and other Rhode Island slavers captured by French privateers off the coast of West Africa during the Seven

Years' War, and that did not include the slave ship the Brown family lost in 1759.[2]

Prior to the Revolutionary War, many American privateer captains had commanded merchant ships in the carrying trade with the Caribbean, so they were familiar with the usual slave ship routes. British vessels arriving from the African coast bound to Jamaica or any of the Leeward Islands usually sailed to Antigua. From there they could sail to Nevis, St. Kitts, and Montserrat, or push on to Jamaica, some one thousand miles away. If a vessel wanted to sail to Barbados, the easternmost island in the chain of the Leeward Islands, it would sail there directly. Privateers could simply make the short sail out of French-controlled Martinique and search for prey to the windward (east) of Antigua or Barbados. Some of the slavers also used a route to Tobago.[3]

While Congress authorized the commissioning of privateers in March 1776, it was not until the late summer of 1776 that American privateers began capturing British slave ships on their return voyages to Britain. Since they were on their return voyages, they carried no enslaved people. The first captured slaver was the eighty-ton *Lancashire*, owned by an established family of slave traders out of Liverpool. The *Lancashire* had been reported as trading on the African coast in August 1775. After sailing to Jamaica and selling its African captives there, the slave ship had joined a convoy of 120 British merchant ships sailing from Jamaica for Liverpool—but many were picked off by numerous American privateers. In August, the Baltimore privateer schooner *Enterprize*, carrying ten cannon and with a crew of sixty men, captured a "Guineaman" (as slave ships were called) carrying fourteen or fifteen hogsheads of sugar and rum, as well as cash—it was the *Lancashire*. The *Enterprize* sent its prize into Chincoteague Island off the Eastern Shore of Maryland.[4]

While most British slave ships captured by American privateers were on their return voyages to England, occasionally they were taken on the first leg of the slave trading voyage, from England to Africa. That was the case with the 140-ton *Africa*, which had sailed from Bristol. On August 22, 1776, the *Rover*, an American privateer sloop commanded by Simon Forrester of Salem, Massachusetts, intercepted *Africa* off the coast of Portugal. The British slaver carried six guns and had a crew of twenty-eight. *Rover* reportedly carried eight carriage guns on its main deck and fourteen smaller swivels attached to the deck's railing, but its formerly eighty-man crew had been reduced to thirty-eight since so many of the crew had been detached to sail prize vessels to America. The *Africa*'s commander, Captain

Thomas Baker, stubbornly refused to surrender. A fierce five-hour engagement ensued, most of it at pistol range. Neither side would surrender or flee. Finally, the *Africa*'s gunpowder magazine exploded, killing all but three of the crew.[5] This incident shocked slave merchants, who began to insist that Royal Navy warships accompany them in convoys on their voyages to Africa.

While John Brown probably read about the success of the privateers *Enterprize* and *Rover*, he definitely heard about two other captures of slave ships due to their Providence connections. Captain Barzilla Smith's Massachusetts privateer schooner *Eagle* took the 140-ton British slaver *Rio Pongo* on its return voyage from Jamaica to Liverpool in November 1776. Smith sent the prize into Providence, where the ship and cargo of thirty-three tons of ivory and twelve tons of camwood, both products from Africa, and small arms, were quickly condemned and sold under local admiralty procedures.[6] About the same time, the captain of the slave ship *Britannia*, and a Royal Navy midshipman on board, were brought to Providence as prisoners. The *Britannia* had earlier in the year dropped off some 150 enslaved Africans at Jamaica, but on its return journey to Liverpool was captured by two Massachusetts privateers in October. Then it had been retaken by the British frigate HMS *Orpheus*. On its way to British-controlled New York, manned by a prize crew, the *Britannia* was again captured by an American privateer, this time the *Joseph* from Massachusetts. The twice-captured vessel was sent into Bedford, Massachusetts, while the Royal Navy midshipman who had commanded the prize was delivered under guard to Providence, to join the ship's former captain who had already been delivered there.[7]

As set forth in appendix B to this book, in 1776, American privateers captured at least fourteen slavers on their return voyages to Britain, and in 1777 four more. American privateers in 1776 and 1777 also captured or destroyed three slave ships on their way from England to Africa.

Two other seizures in fall 1776 would have caught Brown's attention because they involved captured enslaved men. The question was whether the enslaved men would be treated as "prize" property that could be sold in admiralty proceedings in Providence, with the profits shared by the privateer's investors and crew, or whether the captured men had to be freed or treated the same as white enemy prisoners of war. If it was the latter, Brown might be discouraged from attacking British slave ships.

In early September 1776, the privateer sloop *Sally,* commanded by James Munro of Providence, carrying ten cannon and manned by 103 sailors, halted and boarded a slave ship, the brigantine *Union*, sailing from St. Kitts to Liverpool. Rather than seize the vessel, Munro removed its cannon, small arms and gunpowder, and its cargo, including 611 elephant tusks and "1 Negro Boy." The ivory and enslaved boy came from Africa. John Brown owned a piece of the *Sally*, along with nine other Providence merchants. The *Union* was a slaver, whose captain, Robert Wilson, had dropped off about 195 African captives from the Gold Coast in West Africa at St. Kitts and, after being plundered by Munro, safely arrived back in Liverpool. The *Union*'s cargo (including the enslaved boy) went through admiralty court proceedings in Providence and was sold there in November, with John Brown sharing in the net proceeds.[8]

Also sold in November were "7 Negro men" who were brought into Providence as "prizes." They were enslaved Rhode Islanders who had been captured aboard the Royal Navy bomb brig *Bolton* when it was overtaken by a flotilla of Continental navy warships commanded by Esek Hopkins.[9] The Black men had enlisted from Rhode Island to serve on the British vessel or had been forced to serve by their white masters, but after the capture they were treated as property (prizes) and not as human beings (prisoners deserving rights). According to the *Providence Gazette*, all of the captives had been enslaved prior to their naval service.[10] At least three of them had been enslaved by Joseph Wanton, former governor of Rhode Island, and one had been enslaved by Newport businessman Francis Brinley.[11] Both Wanton and Brinley were Newport Tories. Hopkins, formerly one of Brown's ship captains and now commander in chief of the Continental navy, wound up purchasing one captive, Dragon Wanton.[12]

By contrast, Israel Ambrose, master of the Rhode Island privateer sloop *Snow-Bird*, captured the slave ship *Swallow*, which had previously dropped off an estimated 119 African captives in Mississippi, presumably selling them to Spanish buyers. The *Swallow* was captured on its return voyage to London. Five of the *Swallow*'s mariners were free Black men. Rather than treat these men as prize property to be sold to the highest bidder, they were treated the same as other white prisoners captured on board prizes. They were eventually brought to Newport and exchanged for American prisoners held there by the British.[13]

Based on the maritime law of privateering, a key distinction arose in this early period of the war. If Black people found on board an enemy vessel were enslaved, they could be treated as property and sold in admiralty court proceedings. If, on the other hand, Black people found on board an enemy vessel were free people, they could not be sold as property and instead had to be treated the same as enemy white prisoners. One problem for free Blacks was that they could not always prove their free status.

The year 1777 was the banner one for American privateers capturing British slave ships and their cargoes of enslaved people on their way to the Caribbean from Africa. American privateers typically operated out of French-controlled Caribbean islands, waiting for British slave ships near the end of their journeys to come within their sights. To be so captured was a bitter pill for the British slave merchants, their captains, and their crews, who had invested substantial money and time only to lose all on the brink of realizing a profit.

In 1776, American privateers did not capture any British slave ships with captive Africans on board. One knowledgeable London merchant explained that this was because of "the Americans not having before that time any market to carry the cargo of African ships to." That situation changed starting in March 1777, when French authorities governing the French-controlled Caribbean islands of Martinique, Guadeloupe, and St. Lucia permitted American privateers to bring prize slave ships to their islands and sell enslaved people there without going through formal admiralty proceedings.[14]

The change in policy employed by the governors of Martinique, Guadeloupe, and St. Lucia was heavily influenced by a young American diplomat recently stationed at Martinique, William Bingham. The young Philadelphia merchant, just twenty-four years old when he arrived at Martinique in July 1776, had been appointed by Congress's Secret Committee, led by fellow Philadelphia merchant Robert Morris. Bingham proved to be an inspired choice.

Morris gave his young protégé three directives. First, and most importantly, he was to contract secretly with French representatives for the purchase of arms and gunpowder and other military supplies that could be delivered to the desperate Continental army. Second, Bingham was to commission as many privateers to sail under the authority of the Continental Congress as he could. Third, he was to stir up tensions between France and Britain in the hopes that France would join the American side in fighting the British.[15] Bingham would achieve all three goals.

Arriving in Martinique on July 27, 1776, Bingham began operating out of the American Coffee House in St. Pierre, Martinique's compact and beautiful main city. St. Pierre was approximately two miles long and lay at the foot of a mountain chain, with a sparkling blue water harbor in its front. Martinique was a major sugar-cane producer, with fifteen thousand white

French colonials residing on the island, supported by a substantial enslaved population.

Bingham began to issue commissions to American privateers (and some French ones) sailing out of Martinique. Just as important, he persuaded the governors of the three main French-controlled islands to allow American privateers to bring their prizes to their islands to sell the vessels and the cargos on them without undergoing admiralty procedures. This risked provoking a war with Great Britain that French officials in Versailles did not want, but by early 1777, the governors were aligned with Bingham. For them, the opportunities to annoy their centuries-old enemy and profit from purchasing American prizes at a discount outweighed the small risk that such provocations could lead to war.

The timing of the policy change was perfect for American privateers seeking to capture British slave ships arriving from Africa. By 1777, the Royal Navy began to do a better job protecting British commercial vessels sailing between Britain and the Caribbean using a system of convoys. Thus, a British slaver on its return voyage to Britain could join a convoy. Royal Navy warships even protected a few British ships bound from Britain to Africa.[16] But British slave ships on their voyages from Africa to the Caribbean could not sail in convoys. The ships left the African coast at various times and various places, and no Royal Navy warships were available on the coast to find them and wait for their departures. Thus, the British slave ships on their journeys to the Caribbean remained vulnerable to American privateers as they neared their British Caribbean island destinations.

The first British slave ship with a human cargo of enslaved people captured by an American privateer was the *Bacchus,* sailing out of Liverpool under the command of Captain John Forsythe. After departing Africa with an unknown number of enslaved Africans on board, the *Bacchus* was captured by an unidentified American privateer in the Middle Passage, probably in January 1777. The captured ship and the Africans were diverted to the French-controlled island of St. Lucia. This was probably the same *Bacchus* that in 1774 had delivered some two hundred enslaved people to Charleston, South Carolina, and then had returned to its home port of Liverpool.[17]

In either late January or early February 1777, the armed sloop *Boston,* out of Boston, commanded by Captain William Brown, captured two slave ships carrying 140 enslaved people. A Boston newspaper reported, probably based on information provided by Brown or one of his officers, that one of the captured vessels was sent to North Carolina where "many of the poor slaves perished soon after their arrival."[18] The cause of the tragedy was not stated, but it could have been due to a lack of food or water. The enslaved people must have suffered terribly on the two British slave ships, and also after their captures. The decision by the American privateer's captain to sail the slaver not to a nearby French colonial port but to North Carolina, thereby adding more than 1,800 miles to the slaver's voyage, may have led to the disastrous consequences for the Africans on board. That mistake would not be repeated.[19]

One of the first large hauls of enslaved Africans on board a British slave ship captured by American privateers occurred in March 1777. The brig *Fanny*, owned by Connecticut investors and commanded by Captain Azariah Whittlesey of Saybrook, Connecticut, but fitted out in Providence, captured a "Guineaman" on its way to the Caribbean, with 292 captives on board. Whittlesey sent his prize (not identified) to Martinique, where the vessel and the African captives were sold.[20] This was at least the fourth time French-controlled Martinique was used by an American privateer to sell its African captives seized from British slavers. Martinique soon became the preferred venue for such sales. John Brown likely read the April 12, 1777, edition of the *Providence Gazette* that included the item about Whittlesey's capture.

The *Fanny* was soon outdone by another American privateer, the brig *Sturdy Beggar*, carrying fourteen cannon, ten swivel guns, and sixty men and sailing out of Baltimore. The *Sturdy Beggar* was described as "the handsomest vessel ever built in America" and "remarkable for fast sailing." Around March 25, according to a British letter writer from Grenada, an American brig (the *Sturdy Beggar*) captured the 250-ton *St. George*, carrying "450 Negroes, some thousand weight of gold dust, and a great many elephant's teeth, the whole cargo being computed to be worth £20,000 sterling." After collecting some five hundred captive Africans at Cape Coast Road, Annamaboe, and other Gold Coast ports, the slaver, owned by London investors, departed the African coast on January 1, 1777, for Grenada, almost one year after it had commenced its voyage from London.[21]

Meanwhile, Robert Morris and William Bingham agreed to enter into joint ventures funding privateers that would cruise in the Caribbean. To deal with better-armed British merchant ships, Morris recommended to Bingham that "a stout privateer" be acquired and not a small one. Morris anticipated that his "stout" privateer might capture British slave ships sailing from Africa filled with captives to the east of Barbados. He further thought in advance about where the enslaved people should be sold. In early December 1776, Morris advised Bingham to sell at Martinique all "Negroes" and "perishable commodities" seized by his privateers, but to send other captured cargo to his agents in New London, Providence, Charleston, and Georgia.[22] In this approach, as in many other areas, Morris was ahead of his fellow merchants.

One of the privateers Morris and Bingham financed was the *American Security*, captained by John Ord Jr. and sailing from Philadelphia. After it arrived in the Caribbean, it sometimes sailed together with the larger privateer *Rattlesnake*, commanded by David McCulloch. The impressive *Rattlesnake* schooner was said to mount eighteen 9-pounder guns, all brass, and carry a crew of 150 men.[23] The *Rattlesnake* had already captured a British slave ship with enslaved Africans on board. A letter writer from the Caribbean wrote on April 25, "The privateer *Rattlesnake* has taken several prizes, among others a Guinea ship with 500 slaves. This *Rattlesnake* is such a noted runner that she is said to be a terror to the English Islands" (i.e., the British-controlled Caribbean islands).[24]

Morris, reading the accounts of subsequent captures by his privateer, wrote to Bingham hopefully, "I have lately had the pleasure to hear that Ord in company with the *Rattlesnake* had taken and sent into Martinique nine sail of transport ships [and] two Guineamen, and two sails of transports into St. Eustatius. If this be true, and it seems well authenticated, we shall make a fine hand of it."[25] The newspaper report was indeed true. The two British slave ships, the 160-ton *Gascoyne* and the 250-ton *Fox*, both sailing out of London, when captured had a total of 498 Africans on board as well as elephant tusks.[26]

Bingham's account book detailed the capture and sale of the enslaved people seized from the *Gascoyne* and *Fox*. The captured slavers in all carried 284 African men, 45 women, 105 boys, and 41 girls. The captives were sold at auction at Dutch-controlled St. Eustatius. Most men brought around 800 livres each, women 660 to 725 each, boys 660 each, and girls 600 each. A pregnant woman brought 800 livres; a "meagre" woman, 200; and a sick boy, 230. An old man and a woman, "almost dead and good for nothing," were given away. The auction netted 326,988 livres after deduction of expenses and a five percent auctioneer's commission. Expenses were incurred for soldiers to guard the ships in port, bread and bananas to feed the enslaved people before the auction, a doctor for tending to them, and a Black preacher who tried to convert them to Christianity. One-half of the net proceeds, including from the sale of the captured guns, ivory, and one of the ships, was divided among the officers and crews. The other half was divided equally among Morris, Bingham, and one of their ship captains.[27]

Once an American privateer captured a slave ship filled with human cargo, the privateersmen themselves became slave traders. They wanted to sell their newly acquired "property" as quickly as possible and at the highest available price. Historian Charles R. Foy wrote of the propensity, particularly during wartime, to treat vulnerable Blacks captured on slave ships as "marketable commodities."[28] Foy pointed out that while Congress's resolutions establishing the rules for privateers and their prizes provided that "all persons taken in arms on board any prize be deemed prisoners" and treated "with humanity," privateer ship captains refused to treat Black captives on board as prisoners of war entitled to decent treatment.[29]

The privateersmen were glad to be able to sell the enslaved people on board their prizes quickly at Martinique and Guadeloupe, without going through any formal admiralty proceeding. But they were disappointed about the prices, as slave traders would be if they received lower prices than they anticipated. While newly arrived enslaved people could fetch prices in the British Caribbean prior to the war of £40 to £42 each, at Martinique, where there was an oversupply because of sales by American privateers, the sales price was about £33 each.[30]

All told, in 1777, as set forth in appendix C, American privateers captured at least twenty-six British slavers with approximately 6,334 enslaved Africans on board. Based on the average selling price of an enslaved person used by a London slave merchant when testifying in early 1778 before Parliament—£35—the value of those enslaved people who were captured was an estimated £221,690.

The work of the American privateers capturing British slave ships resulted in one unintended consequence and one startling conclusion.

The unintended consequence of the privateers' success was that British investors from Liverpool, Bristol, London, and a few smaller ports in 1777 and for the remainder of the Revolutionary War invested in many fewer African slave trading voyages. This development resulted in tens of thousands of Africans not being involuntarily forced onto slave ships to endure the horrors of the Middle Passage and spending the remainder of their lives enslaved in North America.

The startling conclusion was that as a result of American privateers capturing British slave ships and selling the African captives on board to colonial French plantation owners in the Caribbean or to American plantation owners in the South, the Continental Congress and American states were in effect supporting American participation in the African slave trade. By 1777, states commonly used Congress's preprinted commissions containing promises that the commander of the privateer and its owners would abide by Congress's rules of conduct applicable to letters of marque. State officials would fill them out in the presence of the privateer captain and owner, and then sign them. Despite the roles of the state officials, these were Continental Congress commissions. A few states still issued their own commissions, particularly Massachusetts.[31] Of course, in Martinique, William Bingham issued Continental commissions to privateers. This structure provided governmental imprimatur for American privateers to capture British slave ships, seize any property found on board the ships, and sell such property as prizes—including enslaved Africans.

It is not known if any delegates to the Continental Congress made the connection between its issuing blank commissions to privateersmen and some of those privateersmen using those commissions as authority in effect to participate in the African slave trade. If any congressional delegate would have made the connection, it would have been Robert Morris, as privateers in which he had heavily invested did capture some British slave ships whose human cargo was then sold. If they had made the connection, it is doubtful many delegates would have been bothered by it.

It is likely none of the American privateersmen or the investors financing their voyages considered returning the African captives they found on captured slave ships back to Africa. Instead, they wanted to sell the captives as soon as possible for as high a price as possible.

The wealth gained by American privateersmen from selling African captives found its way primarily into private hands. While the transfer of wealth helped the American economy, it cannot be concluded that the sales proceeds directly helped to finance the American War of Independence. While Congress shared in the profits earned by Continental navy crews that captured enemy shipping, it did not share in the profits of American privateers. It does not appear that during the war any Continental navy ship captured a British slave vessel with African captives found on board.

In Rhode Island, John Brown would have heard reports of small American privateers that attacked British slavers in the Caribbean being driven away by cannon fire from slave ships that were armed with more and more cannon. For example, according to an Englishman from St. Vincent writing on April 20, 1777, "About 20 days ago the ship *Brooks*, Capt. Noble, belonging to Liverpool, from Africa with slaves, was met by an American privateer, of ten guns, who engaged her about an hour, till Capt. Noble luckily shot away the privateer's masts, and would have brought her in, had not another privateer came to engage him, which Captain Noble thought it safer to leave than run the risk of another" sea battle.[32] The *Brooks* was a 200-ton ship, which likely was larger than the American privateer attacking it, and mounted ten carriage guns of its own. After the engagement, the *Brooks* carried on to Jamaica, unloading its human cargo of more than 450 African captives.[33]

In Providence, John Brown absorbed all these developments. Captures by both sides were reported in the *Providence Gazette*, as well as in Boston newspapers he occasionally read. Brown also conversed with his own privateer ship captains, who would learn of the latest developments from fellow privateer captains operating south in the Caribbean or north off the coast of Newfoundland.

Brown was wary about sending his brand new, expensive privateer to the Caribbean or the Canadian coast, where the risk of capture by powerful Royal Navy warships was too high for his taste. The last thing he wanted was for his new vessel to be captured on its first voyage. Yet Brown kept in mind that Great Britain's ships had more obligations than they could fulfill. They could not adequately patrol the periphery of the British Empire.

Brown began to wonder whether, and how often, the Royal Navy sent cruisers to patrol the lengthy West African coastline. He likely knew part of the story, but not all of it.

In the second half of 1775, the British Admiralty sent three warships on separate voyages to sweep the African coast of American ships. On August 25, King George III approved the seizure of "all American vessels," including those on "the coast of Africa."[34] On September 18, the Admiralty ordered the fourteen-gun sloop of war HM *Weazle*, manned by one hundred sailors, to "proceed to the coast of Africa" and "seize all ships and vessels belonging to the twelve associated colonies [Georgia excepted] that shall be found in any fort or factory on the coast."[35] On November 11, the Admiralty issued orders for the thirty-six-gun frigate HMS *Pallas*, with a crew of 180 men, to cruise the African coast, as well as the fourteen-gun sloop of war HM *Atalanta* on January 20, 1776.[36]

One of the main reasons these three Royal Navy ships were sent to Africa was to prevent the purchase of gunpowder by American ship captains from local Africans or slave ship captains from countries other than Britain. The Lords of the Admiralty in London, well aware of the American armies' desperate need for gunpowder, knew that British slavers for decades had exported to Africa massive amounts of gunpowder to trade for captives. Liverpool and Bristol merchants sent ships to Africa that unloaded more than 1.2 million pounds of gunpowder in 1774 alone.[37] Tribal leaders purchased much of the gunpowder, allowing them to use muskets in intertribal wars.

There were reports in London newspapers that several American ships did subsequently sail to the African coast in summer 1776 to purchase gunpowder from slave ships from countries other than Great Britain.[38] But most all American vessels on the African coast when British cruisers arrived at the end of 1775 were there to trade for enslaved Africans.

Typically, a substantial number of American ships were on the West African coast, thirteen on the Gold Coast alone in 1775. The Royal Navy warships under the command of William Cornwallis hoped to find unsuspecting victims who were late in hearing about the outbreak of war. The Americans had no Continental navy warships in Africa to counter the Royal Navy frigate *Pallas* and sloops of war *Atalanta* and *Weazle* cruising along the coast.[39]

Many of the American ships on the African coast in late 1775 were likely in violation of Congress's ban on slave trading. The ban took effect for slave ships departing for Africa on December 1, 1774, or afterward. Some slave voyages exceeded one year, so not all of the American slavers on the West African coast were necessarily violating Congress's slave trading prohibition. While it appears that most all North American merchants and investors abided by the slave trade ban, a few slave ship captains did not.

On December 9, 1775, the *Weazle* took the schooner *King of Barra*, commanded by Captain John Hopkins, who had on board his vessel "7 slaves and some trade goods and provisions."[40] (This John Hopkins was not the Continental navy ship captain and son of Esek Hopkins.) The *King of Barra* was an American vessel whose captain apparently had just started to trade for captives. If so, he was in violation of Congress's slave trade ban. While there is no firm information about its home port, some circumstantial evidence indicates the *King of Barra* was from Newport. The *Queen of Barra* had sailed from Newport on November 4, 1765, left Africa after embarking 158 captives, and landed the survivors at Jamaica in 1767.[41] The similarity of the names of the two vessels suggests they may have had the same Newport owners.

Captain Jacob Dunnell sailed from Dartmouth, Massachusetts, in the sloop *Nancy*, bound for the coast of Africa, on September 9, 1775. An experienced slave ship captain, he arrived on November 4 at the French-controlled island of Gorée, "at which place," he wrote, "I began my trade."[42]

Thus, Dunnell was one of the few American ship captains who departed directly from America to acquire slaves on the African coast in violation of Congress's ban. It is not known who financially backed the voyage.

Dunnell's days on the African coast were numbered. He took the same route the *Marlborough* would take two years later, sailing from Gorée down the coast to Cape Mesurado (also called Cape Montserrado and now part of Liberia). On January 10, 1776, Dunnell's sloop was captured by the British sloop of war *Atalanta*, commanded by Captain Thomas Underwood. According to Dunnell, after taking the *Nancy* and making his crew prisoners, *Atalanta* sailed down to the important British slave fort called Cape Coast Castle, where Captain Underwood "disposed of upwards of 6,000 gallons of rum, some rice and other articles on their own account, and purchased slaves; these goods were part of said sloop *Nancy*'s cargo." Dunnell added that Underwood "proceeded with the prizes down the coast, in search of the Americans, but luckily found none."[43]

If Dunnell's account is accurate, Underwood had violated the Royal Navy's express ban on its officers engaging in slave trading. The navy had a history of its officers and sailors on board warships seeking to enrich themselves by participating in the African slave trade. The British Admiralty issued orders to captains sent to the African coast to prevent this activity. In its instructions to the HMS *Pallas*, the British Admiralty stated:

And whereas complaints have been made that the Captains of His Majesty's ships have made ill use of this liberty by trading themselves on the coast of Africa, and have even transported great numbers of Negroes in His Majesty's Ships to Barbados for public sale, to the dishonor of His Majesty's service, the prejudice of the fair trader, and in breach of an act of Parliament passed in the eighth year of King George I, which prohibits under severe penalties the commanders of His Majesty's ships to receive any goods or merchandise on board in order to trade with the same. We do hereby strictly require and enjoin you, neither directly or indirectly, to concern yourself in any sort of trade whatever, as you will answer to the contrary at your peril, and in order to prevent any evasive excuses whatever hereafter we do hereby declare that if we get any information of any goods, slaves or other merchandise of any kind whatsoever being received on board the ship you command in the way of the trade, we shall esteem the same to be your own act, and shall expect you to be accountable for it, in as much as such a practice cannot possibly be carried on without your knowledge and consent.[44]

The paragraph prohibiting slave trading was typically included in the orders of any Royal Navy warship making a voyage to Africa. If slave trading by Royal Navy officers did not continue to be an issue, the order would not have used such strong language.

The *Atalanta* sailed farther down the African coast to St. Thomas, an island in the Gulf of Guinea off western Africa, where the Royal Navy frigate *Pallas* and sloop of war *Weazle* were at anchor. The *Weazle*, according to Dunnell's letter, had taken two prizes. The only information conveyed about the captured vessels was that one was a sloop called *Dartmouth* belonging to New York, commanded by a Captain Darby, and the other was a small schooner belonging to South Carolina, which had spent a long time on the coast.[45] The *London Chronicle* reported in April 1776 that "The *Atlantic* [*Atalanta*] and *Weazle* sloops of war have taken two American vessels trading on the coast of Africa, and carried them into Sierra Leone."[46]

The thirty-six-gun frigate HMS *Pallas* was active as well. Dunnell learned shortly after boarding another British ship as a prisoner of war that after cruising the coast, the *Pallas* had taken one prize, a schooner, registered at New York, commanded by one Scanett.[47] According to the *Pallas*'s captain, William Cornwallis, "several American vessels belonging to the rebellious colonies had got up the different rivers upon this part of the coast [modern day Senegal and Gambia] and were hiding there until we were gone."[48] The draft of the powerful frigate was too deep for it to sail near the coast or up the rivers into the interior. At Frenchman's Bay at the mouth of the Sierra Leone River, Cornwallis purchased a small sloop, the *St. John*, from slave traders. The *St. John* was fitted out with eight cannons and manned with sailors and marines from the *Pallas*. It was ordered by Cornwallis to search for the American slavers. On January 28, 1776, the *St. John* chased and captured the American schooner *Mary* about two hundred miles west of Libreville, Gabon.[49] The sloop also took a schooner belonging to South Carolina coming out of the Quia Port River.[50]

On May 1, 1776, the *Pallas* and the *Atalanta*, with various prize vessels manned by skeleton Royal Navy crews, sailed in company from St. Thomas across the Atlantic to Jamaica.[51] The *Weazle* soon followed, but not until it had captured on May 12 the brigantine *Hester,* commanded by John Marshall out of New York.[52]

The Royal Navy's sweep of the West African coast in late 1775 and early 1776 had disrupted American slave traders, many of whom were not even supposed to have been there under Congress's slave trading ban. Three of the seven slavers hailed from New York.

After receiving a memorial from slave merchants who complained about American privateers capturing slave ships sailing from Great Britain, the British Admiralty ordered the *Weazle* to sail in a convoy with ten London ships bound for Africa in early February 1777. The *Weazle* was further ordered to patrol the West African coast and to seize any "rebel" privateers or other American shipping.[53] Still, when the slavers arrived off the coast of Africa and the Royal Navy warship convoying them disappeared from view, the newly arrived slavers sometimes faced a rude reception from American privateers. The *London Chronicle* reported in its May 27-29, 1777, edition, "Letters from the Gold Coast of Africa say that in the month of March a large fleet of ships from Liverpool, Bristol and London arrived on that coast, and that several of them had been rummaged and plundered by the Provincial [American] privateers, who intercept almost every ship that arrives or sails from that coast."

HMS *Pallas* convoyed several ships departing England for the coast of Africa in early March 1777. The British frigate then patrolled the African coast until June 2, 1777, before heading across the Atlantic to Barbados.[54] But after that time, the Royal Navy sent no more warships to patrol and protect British slave interests on the West African coast until September 1778, seven months after the French had entered the war as an ally of the Americans. With the new French threat in particular, the British Admiralty's ships were needed more urgently elsewhere.

In Providence, Brown likely learned of the reports from returning slave ship captains to Newport and other Rhode Island ports. He likely heard of the patrols by the three Royal Navy ships in the second half of 1775, the first half of 1776, and the first part of 1777. But he also probably received subsequent reports that after that time, the Royal Navy sent no more of its warships to patrol the African coast. The British Admiralty had abandoned British slave traders and their posts along the African coast, forcing them in wartime to fend for themselves.

Brown began to consider seriously sending his new privateer, once its construction was finished, to Africa. All the pieces were falling into place.

Brown was not the first Whig to consider an expedition to Africa. A handful of others came to the conclusion that raiding Britain's weakly defended slave trading posts and forts in Africa could be profitable. But Brown was the first to actually follow through on the idea.

John Paul Jones, by war's end the Continental navy's greatest hero, made the same recommendation to Robert Morris. At the time commanding the sloop *Providence* and stationed in Newport, Jones had gained respect by re-

cently capturing sixteen enemy merchant vessels off the coast of Newfoundland. On October 17, 1776, Jones advised Morris in Philadelphia,
"An expedition of importance may be effected this winter on the coast of
Africa with part of the original fleet—either the *Alfred* or *Columbus*, with
the *Andrea Doria* and *Providence* would, I am persuaded, carry all before
them and give a blow to the English African trade, which would not soon
be recovered by not leaving them a mast standing on the coast." Jones thus
thought that the squadron of three Continental navy warships could capture
all the British slave ships on the coast. He wanted to command either the
Providence or *Andrea Doria* on such an expedition. Jones continued, "The
squadron for this service ought to sail early [so] that the prizes may reach
our ports in March or April."[55] Writing from Boston in January, Jones again
proposed an expedition to Africa to commence in the spring. This start
date would allow the prizes seized from British slavers on the African coast
to be sailed to New England ports before winter set in.[56]

Jones knew what he was talking about—as a young man he had worked
on two slave voyages. At seventeen, he hired himself out as third mate on
the slaver *King* George, at Whitehaven, an active seaport on England's
northwest coast that occasionally sent out slave ships. On May 6, 1765, the
132-ton *King George* departed Whitehaven for Africa. Late in 1765, the
King George left Africa and on Christmas Eve delivered an estimated 276
surviving African captives at Kingston, Jamaica. Jones did not take the return voyage to Whitehaven when the *King George* left Jamaica on April 26,
1766. Instead, Jones was hired as first mate on the brigantine *Two Friends*
for a slave voyage. This smaller, thirty-ton vessel, with a total crew of only
six sailors, left Kingston a few weeks later, on May 7, and arrived back at
Kingston, probably in summer 1767, carrying about eighty African captives. It must have been a miserable voyage on such a small vessel, probably
not more than fifty feet long, crammed with crew and captives. At Kingston
Jones left the vessel and hitched a ride on another ship bound for England.[57] It appears he became disgusted by the slave trade, as he never wrote
of his experiences as a slave trader nor served on a slaver again. But with
his knowledge of the African coast and the slave trade, he was in a position
to recommend to the Continental Congress's Marine Committee that it
send Continental navy warships to raid British slave trading posts and forts
on the West African coast.

Robert Morris finally responded to Jones's two letters on February 5,
1777, just when American privateers were beginning to experience great
success in the Caribbean capturing slave ships with African captives on

board. Morris explained that the Marine Committee was unable to address his proposal for an African expedition since it was on the move, after Admiral Howe's ships in September 1776 dropped off his brother's army near Elkton, Maryland, to commence its campaign to seize Philadelphia. Congressional delegates were forced to flee Philadelphia and meet again in Baltimore. Morris thought an expedition against the British posts in Florida would be best. Morris advised, "Should you prefer going to the coast of Africa, you have the consent of the Marine Committee." But he put a damper on the idea: "Remember it is a long voyage, that you cannot destroy any English settlements there, and that if you meet any of their men-of-war in those seas, they will be much superior to you in strength." The Pennsylvanian concluded, "You may, it is true, do them much mischief; but the same may be done by cruising to the windward of Barbados, as all their Guineamen fall in there. However, you are left to your choice and I am sure [you] will choose for the best."[58] (Morris failed to mention that there was a much higher risk of coming across a Royal Navy warship in the Caribbean than off the West African coast.)

Ultimately, Jones demurred, in part because in early December, a British expeditionary force seized Newport, and Admiral Howe's ships blockaded Narragansett Bay. Despite ample warning of the approaching invasion fleet, Esek Hopkins left the frigates *Providence* and *Columbus*, as well as three smaller Continental navy warships, at Providence. As a result, for the meantime, the warships were bottled up in port.

Lambert Wickes, another outstanding Continental navy captain, also thought about sailing to the African coast and attacking British slaving interests there. In early March 1777, Wickes and his sixteen-gun brig *Reprisal* were at L'Orient (now Lorient), a seaport on the Brittany coast in France. Commanding the *Reprisal*, Wickes had earlier accomplished his mission of delivering William Bingham to Martinique on September 13, 1776, but only after fighting off the HMS *Shark*. On his next mission, Wickes carried Benjamin Franklin safely from Philadelphia to France, after which he took five British prizes in the English Channel.

Franklin was in Paris at about the same time Morris wrote to Jones. Franklin and the other American commissioners in Paris suggested an African cruise to Wickes. Wickes responded, "The cruise on the coast of Guinea [Africa] I think much safer and better, but there is such difficulties attending it as cannot be got over. Our ship will not carry water and provisions enough for the cruise, as it will be necessary to take four months . . . for that cruise and we cannot take more than two months water and provisions." Wickes advised that if another Continental ship that could carry water and provisions for a four-month voyage could be sent, it could inflict real damage on British slave trading operations. While British slave ships were typically armed with cannon, they were, according to the Continental navy captain, "not in a condition to fight, as their men are generally very sickly" from remaining so long on the African coast.[59] Like Jones, Wickes did not sail to Africa. The American commissioners instead sent Wickes to the Irish Channel, where he captured eighteen more British merchant vessels. Unfortunately, Wickes's ship sank off Canada in fall 1777 with the loss of all hands.[60]

Even as late as May 1778, a French navy captain seeking a commission in the Continental navy approached Governor Patrick Henry of Virginia with the idea of a raid on British slave trading interests on the coast of West Africa. Henry wrote to Continental Congress delegate Richard Henry Lee, "I like much his scheme of attacking our foes in Africa. 'Tis very plausible and bids fair for success." Henry offered a twenty-gun warship from the Virginia state navy to join in an expedition to Africa. "Will it not distract their attention profitably?," the governor asked Lee.[61] Nothing came of this idea either.

French military strategists, in planning a naval war against Britain, also had their eyes on attacking British slave forts on the African coast. A report issued in January 1778 advised that the ten powerful warships then based at Toulon on the Mediterranean Coast could be ordered in the fall to the African coast. The French ships could then "attempt to recapture Senegal or at least to destroy the forts there and on the Gambia River, in addition to any other settlements the English may have along that coast." The unidentified author of the report advised, "According to the information we have been able to procure, the English are very weak in that region."[62] This plan was not adopted. Instead, the Toulon fleet, with additional warships, sailed to Rhode Island, where it engaged in the first joint American and French allied operation, the siege of Newport in August 1778.[63] The French did not send a naval squadron to the African coast until early 1779.

The Continental Congress, in directing the navy, never sent a warship for the primary purpose of attacking British slave trading interests on the West African coast. It is not known that any other privateer sailed to Africa for that primary purpose either. John Brown thought it was an exceptional idea. His audacity set him apart from other privateer investors.

Brown's decision not to send his new privateer to the Caribbean turned out to be a wise one. With war looming with France, the British Admiralty increased Admiral James Young's squadron in the Caribbean to about a dozen warships by the start of 1778. These ships were largely successful in protecting their convoys of merchant ships. During January 1778, when his new privateer would have arrived in the Caribbean if Brown had sent it, Royal Navy warships captured two formidable American privateers, the eighteen-gun *St. Peter* (which had made prizes of two slave ships during their return voyages to Britain in October 1777) and the twenty-two-gun *General Washington* of Boston, a "remarkable fine, very fast sailing vessel."[64]

The Royal Navy's twenty-eight- and thirty-two-gun frigates were swift, and they were more powerful than any American privateer. But Brown's new vessel might have a chance of outrunning a frigate if he built a sleek ship with sharp lines and a narrow stern. If his ship was big and strong enough, it could fend off a British sloop of war or smaller warship.

Brown decided on his plan, combining two main ideas. He would build and outfit a fast and finely contoured privateer that would carry twenty cannon. His new privateer would then sail to Africa to attack and plunder slave trading posts established by British slave traders, and British manufactured goods and other merchandise intended for the local slave trade could be seized from warehouses. In addition, perhaps African captives kept at the slave trading posts, intended to be sold to British slavers, could be seized and sold as prizes. Moreover, enslaved people could be captured from British slave ships found working on the coast. Perhaps a large British slave ship filled with African captives and ready to sail for the Caribbean islands could be seized.

Now Brown turned his attention to two factors that would be crucial to the success of the enterprise: the design and construction of the ship and, once that neared completion, the selection of the ship's commander.

CHAPTER FOUR

George Waite Babcock
is Selected as Commander

*B*y *November 1777*, shipbuilders in Providence had constructed for John Brown an impressive new privateer. The 250-ton brig, which Brown called the *Marlborough*, was built to carry twenty cannon on two decks, and when fully manned would have a crew of 125. As a square-rigged brig, it had two tall masts probably made from pine—the foremast nearest to the bow of the vessel and the larger mainmast behind it.

Providence became a relatively important center of shipbuilding during the Revolutionary War. Pursuant to orders of the Continental navy's Naval Committee, in 1776, two frigates were built in Providence, the thirty-two-gun *Warren* and the twenty-eight-gun *Providence*. John Brown served on the committee that supervised the building of the frigates.[1] He noticed the work on the frigates by two Providence shipbuilders, the draftsman Sylvester Bowers and the master carpenter Major Benjamin Tolman.[2] Brown may have retained Bowers and Tolman to build the privateer *Marlborough*.

The plans and dimensions of the *Marlborough* do not exist. It may have been close in design to another vessel that became a privateer operating out of Philadelphia, the *Oliver Cromwell*. The *Oliver Cromwell* was a 265-ton brig that typically carried about twenty cannon but once mounted as many as twenty-four. Its full complement of a crew ranged from 130 to 150.[3] The

Marlborough was a 250-ton brig that typically carried about twenty cannon but would at one time also carry twenty-nine. Its full complement for a crew was 125. Accordingly, the two ships were of similar size.

The *Oliver Cromwell* made several captures, including in late April or early May 1777, taking the British slave ship *St. George*, with about two hundred African captives on board, and selling the human cargo at Martinique.[4] On May 19, however, while on another cruise in the Caribbean, the privateer was captured by the Royal Navy's sloop of war *Beaver* after a fierce engagement lasting three-quarters of an hour.[5] The victors renamed the captured vessel *Beaver's Prize*. Three months later, Royal Navy master shipwrights stationed at Antigua carefully examined the former *Oliver Cromwell*, made drawings of it, and noted its dimensions. Its hull was 102 feet long, its deck 86 feet; the beam was 26 feet 6 inches wide, and the depth in the hold was 13 feet. The height between each of the two decks was measured at 5 feet, 4 inches.[6] The *Marlborough* likely had similar dimensions.

John Millar, a naval architectural historian, labelled the *Oliver Cromwell* a "miniature frigate."[7] The same appellation could be applied to the *Marlborough*.

In constructing the *Marlborough*, John Brown found and purchased the wood for the hull, masts, and spars, the sailcloth for the sails, and ropes for the rigging. As a naval historian explained, "Masts, spars, rope and sailcloth make up the 'engine' of sailing a ship—what enables it to go—as well as the 'brakes.' Anchors served as emergency brakes."[8]

Cannons for privateers were in short supply, but Brown could easily acquire some from his own foundry at Hope Furnace, which manufactured them. The *Marlborough* carried twenty cannon, probably sixteen on the main deck and four on the quarter-deck. The size of the cannon is not known. They were probably mostly 6-pounders, with perhaps a few 4-pounders or 3-pounders, and, if fortunate, a few 9-pounders.[9]

Brown named his new ship *Marlborough* after Sir John Churchill, the British general who led allied Protestant armies to a string of victories against the defender of the Catholic faith, King Louis XIV, and was later given a dukedom, becoming the first Duke of Marlborough. (Winston Churchill wrote a splendid three-volume history of his famous ancestor.) Brown, never a great speller, misspelled the name of his new ship as "Mallborough," which suggests that is how he pronounced the word.

Eventually, Brown had to select a commander for his privateer. It was a crucial decision that could determine the success or failure of his new vessel's maiden voyage. Brown sought a proven leader and a skilled seaman, one daring enough to sail to Africa and make the voyage a financial success and to punish British slave trading interests. Given that by late 1777, many of the established privateer ship captains were either already commanding privateer ships or languishing in British jails, Brown faced a challenging task.

Probably in November 1777, in Providence, John Brown and George Waite Babcock came to an agreement: Babcock would command the *Marlborough*. Before accepting the post as captain, Babcock must have heard Brown's pitch for his plan for a voyage to Africa and his cogent analysis. Babcock, a firm Patriot and an aggressive ship commander, agreed to the plan.

Little is known of Babcock's early life. Babcock was a common name in southern Rhode Island and remains so today. George Waite Babcock was born January 25, 1751, the eldest child of John and Lydia Babcock of Exeter, Rhode Island.[10] When George was eight years old, his father, John, died at age thirty-two.[11] His mother, Lydia, remarried Joseph Holloway of Exeter in 1761.[12]

Exeter was then, and still is, an interior rural township bordering North Kingstown to the east and South Kingstown to the south. Both were rich towns, with many fine, large dairy and horse farms, and with coastlines fronting Narragansett Bay. By contrast, Exeter was a poorer town with small, rocky farms and no access to the sea. But it enjoyed a signal advantage: easy access to the small but active port of Updike's Newtown (now called Wickford) in North Kingstown. Ten Rod Road, so named because of its 165-foot width, allowed drovers from eastern Connecticut and western Rhode Island to drive their livestock through Exeter and to the wharves at Updike's Newtown, where they could be loaded onto ships bound for the Caribbean. The road also served as a ready outlet for Exeter's landless young men to escape from toiling on their small family farms and seek jobs in the port village.

At age twenty, in 1771, George Waite Babcock married Susanna Fowler, the daughter of Simeon Fowler, also of Exeter. They were married in Exeter by Elder Solomon Sprague, a local Baptist church leader.[13] By 1774, the couple had moved to Updike's Newtown.[14]

Also in 1771, Beriah Brown of North Kingstown married Elizabeth Babcock, who may have been the sister of George Waite Babcock's father.[15] Brown was an important politician supporting the Stephen Hopkins political faction and served for decades in the influential post of sheriff of

King's County. It was a second marriage for Brown, whose first wife had died. In the early 1770s, Brown may have used his connections to improve Babcock's employment opportunities and his standing in the community. In colonial times in particular, family connections could be an important way to advance one's prospects.

When John Brown hired Babcock to command the *Marlborough*, Babcock stood five-feet-ten-inches tall, was fair skinned, and was about to turn twenty-seven.[16] Yet even at that relatively young age, he was an experienced ship officer operating out of Updike's Newtown. There is no record of his possessing any experience on a slave voyage.

Brown did indeed choose a daring captain to command his new vessel. After Babcock's command of the *Marlborough* ended in late 1778, he became known for his willingness to engage in single-ship duels. While he inflicted more damage on the enemy, his crew suffered dead and wounded as well.[17] Some privateer captains preferred to avoid the risks of such engagements.

Babcock probably first met John Brown in July 1776, when the North Kingstown resident served as a first lieutenant on the sixty-ton privateer *Diamond*, in its initial voyage commanded by Captain William Chace.[18] After the *Diamond* captured the brig *Star and Garter* in the Caribbean on July 25, Chace assigned Babcock to sail the captured vessel back to Providence and report to the Brown brothers.[19] On August 13, Babcock arrived safely in Providence with the prize and ten prisoners.[20]

Babcock sailed again as a prize master on the *Diamond*, this time commanded by Captain Thomas Stacy, on its second successful voyage for John Brown, in which Stacy captured the merchant ship *Live Oak* and two other vessels. Babcock sailed a prize back to Providence—the eighty-ton brig *Mary and Joseph*, bound from Newfoundland to Spain carrying a full load of codfish and captured on September 30, 1776.[21] Babcock received a one-quarter share, the same as five other junior officers, but less than the captain's full share.[22] In Chace and Stacy, Babcock had two competent and experienced mentors as privateer commanders.

In November 1776, Brown appointed Babcock to command the sloop *Favourite* on its second privateering voyage. The seventy-four-ton vessel, when commissioned for its voyage, carried ten 4-pounder cannon and had a crew of seventy. Brown and Babcock signed their names to the letter of marque commission on November 20 in Providence.[23] There is no report of the results of the voyage. Not every privateer voyage succeeded. It is also possible the vessel never sailed. Still, Brown remembered Babcock a year later.

Babcock remained on land throughout 1777 until late December. This decision was influenced by a major turn of events in Rhode Island. On December 7, 1776, a massive British fleet carrying 7,100 troops entered Narragansett Bay, intent on capturing Newport. With General Henry Clinton leading the invasion, Newport and the rest of Aquidneck Island easily fell to the British the next day, as did neighboring Conanicut Island (the town of Jamestown). Rhode Island and Massachusetts militia mustered by the thousands in case Clinton decided to sail up the bay to Providence. But the British general, with winter settling in, declined to do so. Patriot forces subsequently gathered on the mainland shores facing Aquidneck Island, at Bristol, Tiverton, and Little Compton, but could do little other than watch for British incursions on the mainland.

Meanwhile, Sir Peter Parker, commander of Royal Navy forces at Newport, typically posted six of his warships in the three entrances to Narragansett Bay. Five of the ships carried from twenty-eight to fifty guns. This blockade ended the easy passage of privateers from Providence and their prizes sailing in and out of Narragansett Bay.[24]

Babcock had an active 1777, primarily chasing local Tories, also called Loyalists, those who supported remaining with Britain. The American Revolutionary War was in many ways a civil war between Patriots and Tories. Babcock was right in the middle of one following the British occupation of Newport.

The area of Quidnesset, north of Updike's Newtown in North Kingstown, became a center of Loyalist activity. Several Loyalists from North Kingstown fled to Newport to enlist in Loyalist regiments that were forming there. They also gave information to the British about where to raid the farms of Patriot supporters on the coast of Rhode Island's mainland.

Babcock first came to the public's attention as a result of an accidental tragedy. At its session beginning on March 24, 1777, at the King's County Court House in Little Rest (now Kingston), the General Assembly was informed that several sons of Charles Slocum of North Kingstown were "employed by the enemies of this state in raising recruits for their service." The sons were also suspected of making visits to Newport to meet with British officers. The legislators ordered that the Slocum sons be brought before them to answer the charge. On March 26, Governor Nicholas Cooke issued a warrant to Beriah Brown, in his capacity as sheriff of King's County, to apprehend Charles, Ebenezer, and John Slocum, the sons of Charles Slocum, and bring them to the General Assembly.[25]

Taking the Slocums into custody was more than Sheriff Brown could handle on his own. Accordingly, he asked General Joseph Spencer to order Rhode Island militia to perform the task. Spencer turned to Major Thomas Clarke in Updike's Newtown. Clarke then assigned George Waite Babcock, and militia troops that Babcock could gather, to apprehend the Slocum brothers. Perhaps this was Sheriff Brown's plan all along to help Babcock become more prominent. According to conflicting reports, Babcock raised a party of either five or forty men.[26] Remarkably, one of Babcock's party was another one of the Slocum sons, who was a Patriot.[27]

On March 27, 1777, Babcock and his party of armed militia arrived at the North Kingstown store of the father of the Slocum clan, Charles. Babcock loudly called for the Slocums to come outside. Son Charles Slocum appeared at the door. He was roughly grabbed by one of the militiamen. Charles resisted, but other militiamen subdued him. His father, seeing the violent scuffle, came out of the house and tried to free his son. While the facts at this point are sketchy, during the ensuing struggle, Babcock apparently fired his pistol at the elder Charles Slocum. The ball entered a little below Slocum's heart—he died in about three hours. Despite the tragedy, the militiamen seized two of Slocum's sons and forcibly took them before the General Assembly. After permitting them to return "under a strong guard" to attend their father's funeral, the legislators ordered the Slocums to be sent to the Providence County jail.[28]

Babcock may have used excessive force in dealing with the elder Charles Slocum, if in fact he had a superior force of forty militiamen at his disposal. Slocum, despite his physical resistance, was not armed. Babcock, however, was never charged with a crime. His superior, Major Clarke, in a letter to Governor Cooke, described the shooting as an accident.[29] The British-supported *Newport Gazette* played up the incident, focusing on the tragedy of "a husband murdered" and his unfortunate "orphaned children."[30]

At the April session of the General Assembly, Babcock led a group of several North Kingstown men in successfully petitioning for the formation of a new independent company called the Newtown Rangers.[31] Babcock was selected to lead the company of approximately sixty men as its captain.[32] This would give him formal authority to control the activities of local Tories, as well as to help defend Updike's Newtown against Tory and British raids from Newport.

Soon Babcock had to contend with more Tory plots. From British-controlled New York City, in January 1777, John Hart, formerly of Little Compton, Rhode Island, was dispatched to Newport and met with its

British commander, Lord Hugh Percy. Hart's mission was to distribute counterfeit money to Loyalists in North Kingstown (who could use the fake money to pay their taxes and harm the local economy) and find recruits to enlist in Loyalist regiments being formed in Newport.[33]

In his military diary, General Percy mentioned several of Hart's clandestine trips to the mainland in February and March 1777.[34] For April 11, Percy wrote that Hart and two other men "went off this night to seize, if possible, some of the Assembly and bring them off" the mainland to Aquidneck Island. At the time, the Rhode Island General Assembly was still in session in Little Rest. Hart thus wanted to kidnap a few members of the General Assembly and have them thrown in a British prison in Newport.

Once in North Kingstown, Hart and his Tory friends altered their mission. Instead, they decided to try to capture Babcock. Perhaps he was targeted because he had formed and commanded the Newtown Rangers, with the main task of hunting local Tories. With the assistance of four sailors from a Royal Navy warship in Narragansett Bay, Hart attempted, according to Percy, "to seize Babcock in Updike's Newton, but he [Babcock] escaped. They drove [away the Patriot] guards, however, and returned back here without anybody hurt."[35]

Babcock then took the offensive. He and the Newtown Rangers intensified their efforts to intimidate and imprison Tory sympathizers. The British-supported *Newport Gazette* wrote in its edition of May 15, 1777, "The rebels have within this fortnight past began a very hot persecution at North Kingstown, Exeter, [West] Greenwich, etc. . . . About twenty of these injured and abused men, who had been for some days hiding in the bush, made their escape and arrived here [Newport] on Tuesday." In its May 29 edition, the *Newport Gazette* further reported that Babcock and his Newtown Rangers were going "from town to town, upon the Narragansett shore . . . taking up all persons who are suspected of being friendly to the" Crown.[36]

Hart's days were numbered. Information about his counterfeiting plans was passed on to George Washington and eventually reached Rhode Island officials.[37] On May 13, Hart was captured at a house in Exeter, but not by Babcock and his Newtown Rangers. Instead, the honor went to a party led by Brigadier General James Varnum of East Greenwich, back from the Continental army.[38] Carried in chains to Providence, Hart confessed to his activities distributing counterfeit money, "giving intelligence" to the British commanders in Newport, and assisting in recruiting Loyalist regiments in Newport. He was quickly tried by a military tribunal and hanged.[39]

With his nemesis dead, Babcock began to reevaluate his contribution to the war effort. Hunting down Tories did not bring him glory or put food on his table for his family. Looking around, he saw that many of his ship-captain contemporaries continued to secure positions as commanders of privateers.

With Royal Navy frigates bottling up Narragansett Bay, Babcock decided to go to Boston in search of a privateer he could captain. In 1777, he was appointed commander of the Massachusetts schooner *Gloriosa*, with ten cannon and a crew of fifty.[40] There is no record that the vessel went on a privateering cruise.

In late 1777, as John Brown searched for an experienced captain to command his privateer under construction, he recalled Babcock's services on two of his privateers, as prize master on the *Diamond* and commanding the *Favourite*. Brown also no doubt admired Babcock's decisive leadership against Tories in North Kingstown. Brown offered Babcock the command of the *Marlborough* and Babcock accepted.

Brown must have given his new hire authority to fill out the rest of the *Marlborough*'s officers, as many of them hailed from Exeter and North Kingstown. James Eldred of Updike's Newtown agreed to serve as Babcock's second in command, despite his being ten years older than Babcock.[41] Eldred's father was a man of some success, as his townsmen voted for him to serve several terms as an officer in local militia companies and as a justice of the peace for North Kingstown from the 1730s to the 1750s.[42] By 1774, James Eldred and his wife of thirteen years, Lucy, headed a household with seven young children.[43]

Eldred commanded at least two merchant ships on voyages from Newport to the Caribbean prior to the war.[44] In May 1776, and again in September 1776, the special committee charged with constructing two Continental navy frigates in Providence, the *Providence* and *Warren*, thought enough of Eldred to appoint him as a midshipman.[45] Eldred never served on either of the ships, which became bottled up in Providence once the Royal Navy entered Narragansett Bay two months later.

Eldred must have been a good sailor and officer, as he enjoyed Babcock's full confidence. The two men made a good team. Eldred's North Kingstown neighbors respected him as well. In 1778 and 1779, Eldred was appointed to serve as a lieutenant in a company of North Kingstown militia.[46]

Francis Bradfield was selected as the *Marlborough*'s second lieutenant. Bradfield also hailed from North Kingstown and had commanded merchant ships on voyages from Rhode Island to the Caribbean, as well as to the Carolinas.[47] In 1776, he was selected as the master of one of Rhode Island's two armed galleys. A few months later, in July 1776, he served as first lieutenant on the *General Greene*, a small privateer operating out of East Greenwich.[48] Bradfield was an experienced sea officer, and on his coming voyage he would be entrusted with great responsibility.

Babcock selected Nathaniel Brown to serve as the *Marlborough*'s third lieutenant. Brown probably resided in West Greenwich, another rural, interior Rhode Island town.[49]

Babcock considered whom to hire for the *Marlborough*'s voyage as captain of marines. This captain would command armed soldiers on board his ship who would fight with muskets and cutlasses in close-quarters sea battles or would be used to raid enemy posts on land. Babcock selected for this position another North Kingstown native, Christopher Brown. Brown, twenty-six, had served as ensign in the Newtown Rangers under Babcock.[50] In 1776, he ran into financial difficulties with his small-time merchant business and was briefly confined to debtor's prison.[51] Brown was the youngest son of Beriah Brown, the influential sheriff of King's County who had married one of Captain Babcock's relatives.

The *Marlborough*'s new commander also enlisted four "prize masters"—experienced ship masters who could command captured prize ships and sail them back to a safe port in North America: Ichabod Holloway of Exeter, John Bissell Jr. of North Kingstown and Exeter, and two others.[52] Holloway was likely closely related to Babcock's stepfather, Joseph Holloway. Indeed, Ichabod Holloway may have been Joseph's natural son and therefore Babcock's stepbrother.[53] Ichabod Holloway was probably related to ship captain Samuel Holloway of Newport, who died of disease on the west coast of Africa during a slave voyage in 1774.[54] Bissell, in May 1777, was appointed lieutenant in a company of militia from Exeter. In August 1777, he was one of the senior officers in a raid on Conanicut Island in Narragansett Bay that netted a Hessian soldier as a prisoner.[55]

Babcock retained as his captain's clerk twenty-year-old John Linscom Boss of Newport. With Newport occupied by the British since December 1776, Boss may have moved to reside with relatives in Richmond or South Kingstown, Rhode Island.[56]

One of Boss's tasks was to keep and update the ship's log detailing important events of the *Marlborough*'s journey. The log included columns for the date, the day's weather, the ship's course, an estimate of miles sailed that day, and a description of remarkable occurrences that day. Fortunately, Boss was meticulous in completing this task. Even more fortunately, his journal has survived and is an invaluable resource for the remainder of this book.

As did many privateers, John Brown hired a doctor to join the *Marlborough*'s crew. This doctor would administer to sailors if any of them became ill or were injured in a sea engagement or accident. The doctor would also have to treat any ill prisoners or enslaved people brought on board the *Marlborough*. The doctor was likely not well trained in his craft, and even well-trained physicians of the time were not particularly effective; but the privateer's doctor likely was familiar with basic medical cases that could arise on a ship's voyage. He must not have been an important officer or a forceful personality since in his journal, Boss mentions him only a few times and never provides his name.

Babcock and his officers did their best to recruit a crew of 125 sailors, the full complement for the *Marlborough*. He and his officers could have sailed their brig with around twenty sailors, but more men were needed to man prize vessels that were captured and to man the cannon and take up small arms in the event the *Marlborough* engaged the enemy in a fight.

No complete list of the "men and boys" (that is, the common sailors) who made up the *Marlborough*'s crew exists. Boss, in the ship's log, names some of the crew members; many of them hailed from Exeter and North Kingstown, where Babcock had resided prior to the outbreak of the revolution. (A list of the *Marlborough*'s known officers and sailors is in appendix A.) It is likely that a number of the sailors on the *Marlborough* had also served in the Newtown Rangers that Babcock commanded earlier in 1777. Thus, those who knew Babcock best agreed to serve under him.

One of the ordinary sailors was Samuel Babcock, the captain's younger brother. The two must have had a special relationship because in May 1776, Samuel successfully petitioned the Town Council of Exeter to have his older brother appointed as his guardian.[57]

It is not known if any of the crew members were Black men or boys. Neither Boss's journal nor any other records (which are, admittedly, incomplete) reveal that the crew included any Blacks. It was not uncommon for privateer crews to include several Black men and other men of color, either free or enslaved. For example, a list of the sixty-man crew of the Providence privateer *Independence*, dated September 1776, included at least three Black men.[58] If a Black man was enslaved, his master typically shared in the profits; such service occasionally could be a path to freedom.[59] Perhaps Babcock decided, if so wisely, that hiring Black men for a voyage to Africa where his crew hoped to capture enslaved Africans was a bad idea.

The articles of agreement for the *Marlborough* have not survived, so it is not known how the owners, officers, and sailors intended to divide the profits from the cruise. The agreement was probably similar to the articles of agreement for the Providence privateer *Independence*, which were entered into around September 1776. In that agreement, the owners were entitled to half the prize money, and the officers and crew were entitled to the other half. Among the officers and crew, the shares were awarded as follows: the captain, seven shares; the first lieutenant and master, four shares each; the second lieutenant and doctor, three shares each; the prize masters, gunner, boatswain, carpenter, quartermaster, master's mate, and captain of marines, two shares each; lesser officers one-and-a-half share each; all common sailors, one share each; and all boys, one-half share each. Five shares were designated as "dead shares," to be awarded to the crew members who contributed the most to making the cruise a success. Finally, "If anyone in any engagement should lose a leg or an arm, he shall receive three hundred dollars out of the effects taken."[60]

A surviving articles of agreement for the privateer sloop *Revenge*, which sailed out of New London, Connecticut, in late June 1778, was nearly identical, except that the top officers had increased shares, perhaps reflecting the competition for top officers. The captain had eight shares, and the first and second lieutenants, master, and doctor, four shares each. The *Revenge*'s articles of agreement added that the committee to determine how the dead shares would be allocated would consist of the sloop's captain, first and second lieutenants, and master.[61]

What kind of ship captain was Babcock? Based on his actions prior to his commanding the *Marlborough* and afterward, some traits are evident. Babcock was a natural leader who commanded respect. Many of the officers who served with him on the *Marlborough* would follow him to other privateers he commanded later in the war. Babcock inspired confidence in local men, both officers and common sailors. He thus attracted to his vessel the neighbors who knew him best.

Babcock's leadership style, as evidenced in Boss's journals, included consulting with his subordinate officers on important decisions. This approach helped to create a bond of trust with them. In addition, there is no mention in Boss's *Marlborough* journals that Babcock ever disciplined a sailor with flogging or other corporal punishment. This contrasts sharply with commanders on Royal Navy warships, who routinely flogged their sailors for major and minor offenses. Part of the reason for both of Babcock's traits—consulting fellow officers and not subjecting common sailors to corporal punishment—was the relatively egalitarian New England world in which they lived. The same was true in New England militia regiments, where rank-and-file soldiers sometimes even elected their officers.

In addition, Babcock was a bold and courageous leader. This was shown by his creating and commanding the Newtown Rangers and using them to ferret out and intimidate local Tories. It was also demonstrated by his decision to accept the command of the *Marlborough* on a voyage across the Atlantic Ocean to Africa to attack British slave trading interests there. After his Africa voyage, on later privateer cruises Babcock did not fear engaging enemy warships, even ones that outgunned his ship. Privateers he commanded during the war fought in five engagements in which his ship fired its broadsides and killed enemy sailors. On the other hand, Babcock was not reckless—he was daring but level headed.

Babcock must have informed each of his officers, and probably crew members, of the plan to sail for Africa to raid British slave trading posts and, if possible, capture British slave ships with captives already on board. We do not know what the officers and crew who signed up for the voyage felt about such a prospect.

Perhaps a few who were offered positions felt like a Connecticut sailor whose privateer, the *Oliver Cromwell* of New London, Connecticut, stopped in at Charleston, South Carolina. He set his passionate feelings against slavery in writing. The sailor took issue with the system of slave trading in which human beings were ripped from their homelands and transported overseas to a strange country without teaching them religion or giving them their freedom. The idea that an "enlightened people, a people professing Christianity, should treat any of God's creatures in such a manner" enraged the sailor.[62] If any officer or sailor approached by Babcock had similar feelings, he likely decided to avoid the *Marlborough*.

It was likely the case that none of the officers and crew who enlisted for the *Marlborough*'s voyage to Africa had this Connecticut sailor's humane view. Perhaps some of them tried to justify their enlistment on the ground that they would not be trading for enslaved people, they would only be taking them from established slave traders.

The reality was that the officers and crew of the *Marlborough* would, if successful, be engaged in slave trading. Once they seized African captives from a British slave ship or station, as they hoped to do, the plan was for the African captives to be sold at a profit to plantation owners and other users of slave labor. That is what any slave trader sought to do after departing the African coast for North America. In turn, John Brown and the other investors of the *Marlborough* would be in the same position as slave merchants. In addition, the government authorities that issued the commission to the *Marlborough* and handled the paperwork, from the Continental Congress and the state of Rhode Island, would be implicated in the voyage as well.

Most of those who signed up for the voyage to Africa on the *Marlborough* likely were not particularly concerned about the welfare of the enslaved people they might capture. The officers and sailors were probably like most white men of the day in North America, North or South: they bore a deep prejudice against Black people, especially Africans who practiced what they considered pagan religions, and did not believe that they deserved the same rights as white people. Even most whites in the North at this time, including many who opposed the institution of slavery, viewed Blacks as inferior to white people and not deserving of the same dignity accorded to them.

CHAPTER FIVE

The *Marlborough* Breaks Out

*S*hipbuilders in *Providence* finished construction of the *Marlborough* by the end of November 1777. Before it could be sailed to Africa, three matters had to be finalized. First, the ship needed to be provisioned, and preparations for the long voyage to Africa had to be completed. Second, the ship had to be registered with Rhode Island state maritime authorities. Third, a plan had to be adopted for escaping out of Narragansett Bay.

Both John Brown and George Waite Babcock would have overseen purchasing and hauling aboard supplies for the voyage. Brown and his fellow investors would have been responsible for paying for the supplies. It was Babcock's task to make sure the supplies were brought on board the *Marlborough* and properly stored. Dockworkers carried aboard ship wooden barrels stocked with victuals such as leavened bread (biscuit), salted beef and pork, Narragansett cheese, peas, potatoes, flour, fruit (if available), and rum or beer. Fresh water was brought aboard in special casks. Some fresh vegetables would have been loaded onto the ship as well, but they would have had to have been eaten soon on the voyage or become spoiled.

More food and water would have been brought aboard than for the usual voyage, since the *Marlborough* was heading out for a much longer cruise than privateers typically took. The *Marlborough* could be at sea for five months, while most privateer voyages at this time lasted a few weeks to at most two months. Still, there would not be enough food or fresh water to last the entire voyage. Babcock and his sailors would have to trade for, find on land, or forcibly take from enemy vessels more food and fresh water needed to sustain them for their voyage. This was a daunting prospect that few other privateersmen had to contend with during the war. Slave ship captains were, however, used to handling this risk.

In addition, casks of gunpowder for the cannon and small arms were brought on board the *Marlborough*. So difficult to find at the start of the war, gunpowder was now being manufactured at various sites in New England, including Rhode Island. Babcock would have made sure that the gunpowder was carefully stored in sealed casks to prevent accidents.

Babcock planned to bring on board his brig two small craft: a whaleboat that Boss called a jolly boat; and a barge—a relatively flat boat powered by a single mast. These small boats would be vital for transporting men and goods near the African shoreline and for sending small parties of sailors to captured prize vessels to sail them to a safe port. Babcock likely oversaw being brought aboard his new privateer pieces of lumber, tar, and other naval stores that could be needed to maintain or repair his ship or its small boats on the long voyage.

No written instructions from Brown to Babcock have survived. Whether oral or written, Brown likely advised Babcock—as Babcock would advise his prize ship captains in writing later in the voyage—to try to sell any enslaved African captives at Martinique or another French-controlled Caribbean island or at South Carolina and send any prize ships and other captured cargo to Bedford or Boston, if possible, or other safe US port.

On December 13, 1777, Brown and Babcock strolled together in Providence to the Rhode Island secretary of state's office to seek official sanction for the *Marlborough* to act as a privateer. The state official attending the office that day, as was the usual practice at the time, brought out a blank commission created and printed by the Continental Congress that authorized the vessel to sail as a letter of marque under the authority of the Continental Congress. The commission had blank spaces for the name of the vessel, name of the commander, names of the owners, type, tonnage, number of guns, and size of the crew.[1] The state official wrote in the registry that the *Marlborough* was a ship, mounted 20 carriage guns, would be manned by a crew of 125, would be commanded by George Waite Babcock, and was owned by John Brown "and others." Babcock and Brown signed the official document, which gave the operators of the vessel legal imprimatur to capture enemy shipping as a privateer. As a prerequisite to receiving a commission, because the *Marlborough* exceeded one hundred tons, a $10,000 bond had to be posted to assure that Babcock and his crew would abide by rules of conduct adopted for privateers by the Continental Congress.[2] Brown signed the bond, and his signature was witnessed by two Rhode Island officials.[3] As was the case with all executed bonds, Brown's bond was delivered to the secretary of the Continental Congress.

John Brown was the *Marlborough*'s primary owner, but the letter of marque declared that there were also other owners. A newspaper later reported that the *Marlborough* was owned by "John Brown and Company in Providence."[4] On a list of taxable property Brown prepared in January 1778, he stated that he was the owner of one-half of the *Marlborough*.[5] No known document lists the other owners, but they likely included some of the fellow Providence merchants who typically invested in privateers with him, such as his brothers Nicholas and Joseph Brown, Joseph and William Russell, Jabez Bowen, Nicholas Power, and John Innis Clark and Joseph Nightingale (making up the mercantile firm of Clark and Nightingale).

In Brown's January 1778 list of his taxable personal property in Providence, his one-half share of the *Marlborough,* including its "guns and stores," was valued at £5,000, by far his most valuable single asset. Overall, the *Marlborough*, with its cannon and stores, had a value of £10,000, which was considerably more than the other privateers in which Brown invested, with two exceptions: the privateers *Blaze-Castle* and *Oliver Cromwell,* whose exploits will be discussed shortly.[6]

Before the *Marlborough* set its sails and headed for the open sea, Brown and Babcock had to agree on a plan for sailing their new vessel out of Narragansett Bay without being pummeled by British artillery on the coasts of Aquidneck Island or captured by British warships stationed in the bay. Fortunately, they could draw on more than a year's experience of Rhode Island and Massachusetts vessels attempting to run the Royal Navy's blockade.

After a British expeditionary force on December 8, 1776, seized Newport and the rest of Aquidneck Island, as well as Conanicut Island (Jamestown), the Royal Navy immediately established a blockade of Narragansett Bay, trying not to allow American ships out or in. The two main channels of Narragansett Bay—the West (or Narragansett) Channel, and the Middle (or Main) Channel—were particularly well guarded. The typical posting of the British warships was as follows: Two ships guarded the West Channel, with a frigate stationed to the north of Updike's Newtown, and a fifty-gun ship stationed south of the port. Two frigates carrying twenty-eight to thirty-two cannon were posted in the Middle Channel between Prudence Island and the northern part of Aquidneck Island. Another warship, usually carrying fifty cannon, was stationed in the Middle Channel off the northern end of Conanicut Island. Each ship on guard in Narragansett Bay typically set out its anchor. After sunset, these blockading ships often extended their range by sending out small guard boats manned by sailors who could fire their muskets as alert signals.[7]

Some American ship captains recognized that Narragansett Bay's third channel, the one farthest to the east, then called the Sakonnet Channel (today known as the Sakonnet River), presented the most promising route to escape the blockade. Because the channel was shallow, powerful British ships and frigates could not operate there. Instead, a single warship, the fourteen-gun sloop HM *Kingsfisher,* was assigned to the Sakonnet Channel. Its usual station was far down the channel, near the entrance to Rhode Island Sound. In addition, Royal Artillery outposts on land were established at Fogland Ferry, which jutted out from Aquidneck Island about midway down the western side of the Sakonnet Channel. In support of the battery stood a row galley, the HM *Alarm,* carrying eight cannon and manned by forty men. American troops were posted at various places along the opposite, eastern coastline of the Sakonnet Channel.

It took only a short time for the Royal Artillery gunners stationed at Fogland Ferry to find the proper range. On June 4, 1777, an unidentified privateer sloop weighed anchor from Howland's Ferry at Tiverton (under the protection of American artillery) and, with a favorable wind, started down the Sakonnet Channel headed south for the sea. Several artillery shots from the British battery at Fogland Ferry were fired at the sloop, but it made a successful escape. The skilled Royal artillery gunners immediately adjusted the elevation of their cannon at Fogland Ferry battery. The next day, another sloop attempted to break out to sea through the Sakonnet Channel, encouraged by the prior day's results. But this time the battery at Fogland Ferry scored three direct hits with their solid shot, forcing the shattered sloop to turn back.[8]

John Brown already had experience as a part-owner of a large, well-armed privateer that attempted to break out of Narraganset Bay. It had been a 220-ton merchant vessel sailing from Dominica to Bristol, England, when on July 22, 1776, it was captured by John Brown's privateer sloop *Diamond* and rennamed the *Oliver Cromwell.* Based in Providence, as a privateer in November 1776, it carried sixteen 6-pounders and four 3-pounders, as well as twelve swivel guns.[9] The ship was jointly owned by Providence merchants Nicholas and John Brown, and Joseph and William Russell. John Brown had a five-sixteenths share in the new vessel.[10] As was the case with the *Marlborough*, the name of the *Oliver Cromwell* celebrated a seventeenth-century English hero greatly admired in New England for his passionate defense of Protestantism and attacks against Catholic foes. Cromwell, the leader of the Protestant "Roundheads," also had won key battles against royal forces. He had at least five New England privateers named after him.

The privateer *Oliver Cromwell* was stronger than the British fourteen-gun *Kingsfisher* stationed in the Sakonnet Channel. But the *Oliver Cromwell* experienced trouble hiring a full crew in Providence. Many sailors did not want to risk capture by the blockading British ships and spending time in the holds of a vile prison ship in Newport Harbor. Such men made their way by land to safer ports such as Bedford, New London, and Boston. By early August 1777, the shortage of sailors in the Rhode Island theater continued. The *Oliver Cromwell*'s commander, Captain Samuel Chace of Providence, could hire just twenty-three sailors, well short of his vessel's full complement of 130 men.[11] Such a small crew was enough to sail the ship but not to defend it properly. Still, Chace decided to attempt to break out of Narragansett Bay, with the goal of enlisting more sailors in Massachusetts.

On August 27, in a covering early morning fog, Chace began to sail the undermanned *Oliver Cromwell* down the Sakonnet Channel in the direction of the open sea. As it approached the end of the channel, the privateer was spotted and chased by the HM *Kingsfisher*. Chace judged that the British sloop had sufficient speed to cut off the privateer. Unable to put up a decent fight due to his small crew, and rather than have his men taken prisoners, Chace ordered his ship run aground onto the Tiverton shore. After this was done, his men safely disembarked. Shortly afterward, the *Kingsfisher* fired cannonball after cannonball into the hull of the stranded *Oliver Cromwell*.[12]

The British sloop's commander, Alexander Graeme, then sent a lieutenant and a party of sailors in a long boat to the grounded ship. In spite of Americans on shore firing muskets at them, the British tried to free the ship. Unsuccessful at that, they set the privateer on fire.[13] The *Oliver Cromwell*'s magazine exploded, destroying the vessel.[14] As a result of losing his investment in the ship and his personal property on it, it was reported that Captain Chace had "lost all he had in the world."[15]

John Brown lost money too, but at least the crew saved some of the stores, sails, and rigging. Still, Brown estimated his loss at £1,400.[16] Despite the setback, with his diversified investments, Brown was willing to invest in another large privateer, the *Marlborough*. With his new vessel, he would not make the *Oliver Cromwell*'s mistake of trying to run the blockade with a skeleton crew in the daytime.

By the end of September 1777, American merchant and privateer vessels were still languishing in Providence Harbor and other harbors off Narragansett Bay. Their owners and captains decided to wait until the arrival of poor fall and winter weather, which would give them more cover and a better chance of escaping the British blockade and reaching the sea.

Despite the success of many cruises by British frigates, the Royal Navy, because of its other worldwide commitments, lacked sufficient resources to blockade all of the ports on the long Atlantic Coast. With all of its other obligations, the Royal Navy's blockade of New England ports was, according to British naval historian David Syrett, "doomed to be ineffective."[17] The blockade was never able to halt entirely American privateers and commercial voyages, even in 1777, the year of the Royal Navy's maximum effort.[18] This was true even in Narragansett Bay, which the British controlled.

As winter approached, the increasingly rough weather shifted the advantage to American ships seeking to break out of the bay. The blockading British warships were particularly disadvantaged on dark nights with foul weather.

The night of November 30, 1777, was dark and misty. Commercial ships and privateers from Providence and four other ports on Narragansett Bay took advantage of the weather conditions to escape to the sea. One of them from Providence was John Brown's privateer sloop *Diamond*. British ships fired cannon at the American vessels, but without effect. A British frigate got under sail to go after one of the escaping vessels, but the weather was so "thick" that the British frigate gave up the chase. In Providence, Governor Cooke crowed that the last two nights had "cleared our harbor considerably."[19] A discouraged British Major Mackenzie wrote in his diary that during an exchange of prisoners, Americans had bragged that seven ships had broken out on the night of November 30 and a total of fifteen had broken out in the prior two weeks. Mackenzie called the Royal Navy "very remiss in this part of their duty."[20]

The Providence privateer *Blaze-Castle*, seeking to take advantage of the weather and a favorable wind, sailed from Providence down the West Channel between Conanicut Island and the mainland. The *Blaze-Castle* was no ordinary vessel. Originally built as a merchant ship in Bristol, England, in September 1776 it had been captured by the privateer sloop *Sally* and brought into Providence. When taken, the two-hundred-ton vessel was built like a frigate and carried fourteen cannon, but only had a crew of eighteen.[21] The *Blaze-Castle* was then converted into a privateer, carrying eighteen 6-pounders and four howitzers. It also gained a new minority owner, John Brown, who purchased a three-sixteenths interest. The *Blaze-Castle*'s primary owner, the Providence firm of Clark & Nightingale, in March 1777 had briefly contemplated employing it to attempt the capture of the *Kingsfisher* stationed in the Sakonnet Channel.[22]

Lookouts on the thirty-two-gun frigate HMS *Amazon* spotted the *Blaze-Castle* only as the privateer sped away. The *Amazon* signaled two other British ships at the southern end of the West Channel, but the signals were not seen, and they failed to react. The *Blaze-Castle* escaped to Rhode Island Sound and then to the sea.[23] With his ship's crew short of its full complement of 150 men, Captain James Munro of the *Blaze-Castle* sailed to New London to recruit additional hands. The privateer later captured five British vessels. But in June 1778, it was, in turn, captured by the thirty-two-gun frigate HMS *Unicorn*.[24]

Not all the ship captains successfully reached the open sea. On November 28, 1777, the *Amazon* captured off Warwick Neck the seventy-ton brig *Phoenix*, whose eight-man crew hoped to sail from East Greenwich to Bermuda.[25] Also on the evening of December 10, the *Peggy and Betsy*, an empty brig bound from Providence to Maryland, trying to run the blockade, accidentally ran aground in Narragansett Bay. It managed to free itself, but not until it was spotted the next morning by the *Amazon,* which gave chase. The brig's captain ran the vessel onto the Narragansett coastline below East Greenwich and then ordered his crew to gather the sails and rigging and scramble onto the shore. Soon militia gathering on the beach dragged three cannon to the area and started firing back. Undaunted, at four p.m., the *Amazon* sent a barge filled with sailors and marines who burned the beached brig.[26] This last incident showed the heightened risk of a ship accidentally running aground while trying to escape the bay at night.

John Brown would have kept track of all vessels that attempted to break the British blockade of Narragansett Bay. According to surviving British records, there were twenty-seven attempts by American vessels to run the blockade during the period when the Royal Navy made its greatest effort, from December 7, 1776, through July 29, 1778. Of these, eighteen were successful, and eight ships were either captured, ran aground, or were burned. This represents a success rate of 66.7 percent. This is a good success rate, but it still presented a substantial risk of failure for investors, ship captains, and their crews.

In fact, the number of American attempted escapes out of Narragansett Bay from December 7, 1776, through July 29, 1778, was much greater than eighteen. The British records did not record all of the escape attempts. A total of seventy-nine American commercial vessels and privateers registered with Rhode Island authorities during this period, plus four other privateers that received letters of marque and five Continental navy warships.[27] All but a handful of these vessels likely made the attempt to break out of the blockade shortly after they were registered, yet British naval forces in the bay reported capturing or destroying only eight of them. This amounts to a success rate for American vessels of more than ninety percent. The number of attempts was likely even greater, taking into account vessels from Swansea and other Massachusetts ports in Mount Hope Bay that did not always register with Rhode Island authorities. Accordingly, in reality, the British blockade was ineffective.

Rhode Island maritime records indicate that late fall and winter were the favorite times to attempt to escape from Narragansett Bay. Out of the seventy-nine registrations with Rhode Island authorities by private ship owners and captains from December 7, 1776, through July 29, 1778, sixteen were obtained in February and March 1777, and twenty-seven were obtained in November and December 1777.[28]

George Waite Babcock was able to enlist a crew of about sixty-six men from Rhode Island. The ideal crew size for the 250-ton *Marlborough* was 125, but more sailors would have to be found outside Rhode Island, beyond the British blockade. His sixty-six-man crew, Babcock figured, was large enough to sail the vessel past the blockade and to man some of his cannon, thereby avoiding the *Oliver Cromwell*'s fate. Babcock still hoped he would not have to engage a British warship with his undermanned and new crew.

Brown and Babcock settled on a good plan for breaking the blockade. They would not attempt to sail down the Middle Passage or the West Passage, as those routes were blocked by powerful frigates and fifty-gun ships. Instead, they agreed that the *Marlborough* would sail down the Sakonnet Channel, where they would confront just the sloop HM *Kingsfisher*, with fourteen guns and a crew of 125. Since the *Marlborough* mounted twenty guns of its own and had a decent-sized crew, Brown and Babcock felt the privateer would be strong enough to fight its way through the blockade if necessary. The hope was that the *Marlborough*, a new and fast brig, could easily outrun the older, barnacle-encrusted, slower *Kingsfisher*.

Babcock and Brown were aware of several factors favoring the Royal Navy sloop in an engagement. For one, the British warship was slightly

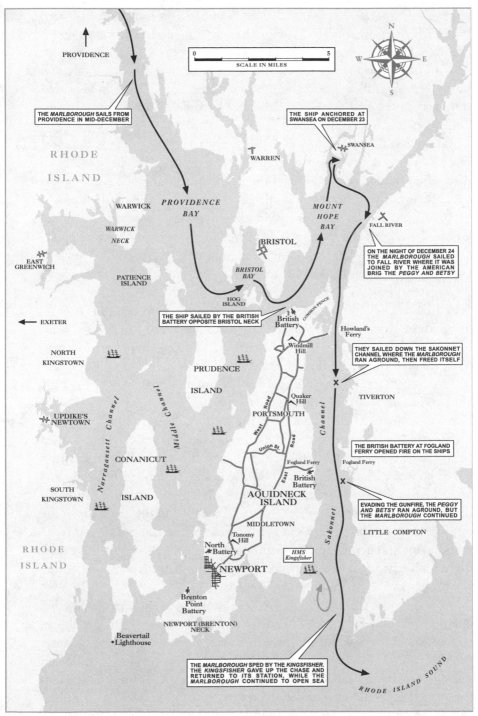

Route of the *Marlborough* out of Narragansett Bay, December 1777.

larger than the *Marlborough*, at 302 tons and 97 feet long, and had been built fairly recently, in 1770.[29] For another, the *Kingsfisher*'s 125 crew members were more experienced in sailing and gunnery than the privateersmen, who were also new to their vessel. The Rhode Islanders too were aware that several Royal Artillery posts, and the small, armed row-galley HM *Alarm*, stationed on the west side of the Sakonnet Channel, could fire deadly cannon at passing American ships.[30]

Given that the two ships were fairly evenly matched, it made the most sense for Babcock to avoid an engagement and try to speed out to sea. Even if the ships battled each other and the *Marlborough* emerged victorious, it could be so battered from cannon fire as to require refitting in Bedford.

In order to put the *Marlborough* in a position to run down the Sakonnet Channel, Babcock and his crew bid farewell to Providence shortly after obtaining the commission for a letter of marque on December 13. They unmoored their ship from a wharf at Providence and sailed it down upper Narragansett Bay, veering to the east to run across the north end of Aquidneck Island. They likely made the passage at night, with no lights aboard, to avoid the British artillery posted at Bristol Neck and Royal Navy ships on patrol. They succeeded without incident and sailed out of harm's way to Mount Hope Bay, anchoring for the remainder of the night at Swansea.

On December 23, at Swansea, John Linscom Boss lugged his bags aboard the *Marlborough*. From that day until the end of the *Marlborough*'s first two voyages, he would maintain the ship's daily journal.

Shortly after Boss came aboard, Babcock sailed his vessel from Swansea to the southeast across Mount Hope Bay, to the mouth of the Taunton River, between Massachusetts and Rhode Island. Reaching the small port of Fall River, Massachusetts, Babcock put his ship in a good position for the descent down the Sakonnet Channel. He sailed in the company of the one-hundred-ton brig *Peggy and Betsy*, bound to the Caribbean and commanded by Stephen Clay. Both commanders decided to wait for a dark night with a strong northerly wind. They did not have to wait long, as the vessels set out the next night, Christmas Eve.

At about nine p.m., as the *Marlborough* and *Peggy and Betsy* proceeded down the shallow Sakonnet Channel, the *Marlborough* became grounded. Brown's spanking new and expensive privateer faced total disaster before it could even leave Narragansett Bay. If the vessel remained grounded when the sun rose, British sailors in small boats sent from Aquidneck Island and the *Kingsfisher* could surround it and try to capture it and free it, or, failing that, set it on fire. Captain Clay decided to remain with Babcock, perhaps thinking he could take aboard the *Marlborough*'s crew if Babcock decided to abandon his ship.

Meanwhile, Babcock and his crew did not panic. Babcock sent out some crewmen on small boats to pull vigorously on lines tied to their ship, known as hauling. Another technique to free a ship from a sandbar was to lighten its load by dumping cannon or supplies overboard. Babcock did not undertake that course. To do so would have likely ended his voyage to Africa. After three hours of desperately heaving and hauling, the *Marlborough*'s crew was able to free the brig from the sand bank. Greatly relieved, Babcock and his crew continued sailing down the channel. It was now early Christmas morning, and there were only a few hours of darkness left.

As the two American vessels headed down the channel toward the open sea, their commanders anticipated the next potential danger, the Royal Artillery battery midway down the channel stationed at Fogland Ferry and the nearby armed galley HM *Alarm*. British artillerymen spotted the silhouettes of the two oncoming ships. At about one a.m., artillery fire from Fogland Ferry came alarmingly close to the American vessels. Both the *Marlborough* and *Peggy and Betsy* adopted evasive maneuvers and hugged the opposite eastern shore, but in doing so, the *Peggy and Betsy* ran aground. Babcock did not stop to return the favor and help Captain Clay, realizing that time was of the essence. Babcock knew the officers on board the fourteen-gun sloop *Kingsfisher* anchored at the southern end of the channel would see or hear the artillery fire and prepare to intercept his new vessel.

Near the end of the Sakonnet Channel, the officers of the *Kingsfisher* had indeed seen "the flashes and heard the reports of several guns from Fogland Ferry."[31] But in addition to the darkness and stormy weather, the *Marlborough* had another distinct advantage—it was already underway with its sails out, and it had not yet been spotted by the *Kingsfisher*. It would take thirty minutes for the Royal Navy sloop to raise its anchor and set its sails to pursue its intended prey.

At about two a.m., the commander of the *Kingsfisher*, Captain Graeme, finally saw the dim outline of his quarry. But by the time his ship got underway, it was already behind the privateer. Graeme noted in his ship's log that the "chase" (the *Marlborough*) was "just ahead"—probably within several hundred yards. Graeme ordered crew members manning his bow gun to fire a shot at the fleeing "rebel vessel." In response, Babcock fired three shots from the *Marlborough*'s stern guns. All of the cannon balls splashed harmlessly in the water.

Then the *Marlborough*, a superior sailing vessel, made its escape out of the Sakonnet Channel, speeding away into the darkness toward Rhode Island Sound, with "fresh breezes" providing the wind power. "[C]hase leaving us fast," Graeme recorded in his log at two-thirty a.m.[32] By three a.m. on Christmas, Graeme wrote, "the chase most out of sight." The Royal Navy captain issued orders to halt the pursuit and return back to the *Kingsfisher's* normal station.[33]

British army officer Major Mackenzie was not surprised at the *Marlborough's* escape. In his daily diary, he called the *Kingsfisher* a "remarkably bad sailor," while "the rebel vessels are generally light and clean when they attempt to go out." Mackenzie also described the HM *Alarm* as "ill-fitted out, weakly manned, and a bad sailor."[34]

Captain Clay, who earlier in the night had increased his own risk of getting caught by remaining with the temporarily grounded *Marlborough*, was not so lucky. After becoming grounded and unable to free the *Peggy and Betsy*, its ten-man crew abandoned the vessel. The next day the British battery at Fogland Ferry and the *Alarm* row-galley fired cannon shots at the brig, hulling it several times and disabling it. The Americans brought down to the Tiverton shore two artillery pieces that drove off the galley. Finally, on December 27 and 29, British parties in long boats succeeded in rowing to the brig and setting it on fire.[35] Babcock had barely avoided that sad fate.

Babcock was out of Narragansett Bay but was not yet ready to sail for Africa. He wanted more sailors to man his vessel. He first set his course for Tarpaulin Cove, a protected inlet off Naushon Island, one of the Elizabeth Islands in Vineyard Sound. Tarpaulin Cove was frequented by privateers, and generations earlier, by pirates. The ship and crew spent Christmas there; at this time, Christmas was more a day of quiet religious observance than a holiday of celebration.

Before departing, Captain Babcock scribbled a note about his encounter with *Kingsfisher* and sent it to Providence to run as an advertisement in the December 27 edition of the *Providence Gazette*. Babcock's main goal was to encourage more sailors to join him at Bedford on his privateering cruise. He announced that his ship "will certainly sail" by January 4. With bravado, he added, "having fought her way out by the British ship and galley at Fogland . . . had Capt. Babcock been fully manned, he would undoubtedly have taken the enemy's ship and carried her into port." Babcock's braggadocio might have turned away some sailors, who may have been concerned about the privateer captain's willingness to attack a British warship.

The next day, Babcock sailed his privateer to Holmes Hole (now Vineyard Haven) at Martha's Vineyard, hoping to "get some more hands."[36] Babcock and several of his officers spent three days at Holmes Hole recruiting sailors.

Babcock next sailed to "Old Town" (Edgartown) on Martha's Vineyard and spent three more days there recruiting. In addition to the efforts at Bedford, he and his officers found some success on the island, bringing on board thirty new crew members by January 2.[37]

The commander had collected a total crew of ninety-six officers and sailors.[38] He was short of the intended crew of 125 for the vessel, but he would make do with what he had.

The ninety-six New England men and boys were ready to set forth on their journey crammed into their small wooden world. If the *Marlborough* had been preparing for a slave trading voyage, a crew of about nineteen men would have been expected to sail the brig.[39] Now in wartime, the size of the crew was much larger—extra sailors were needed during a ship-to-ship engagement to man the cannon and serve in boarding parties. Crew members were also needed to man captured prize vessels to sail them back to a safe port in North America. The extra men and boys made for living conditions in close quarters. The hammocks where the common sailors slept belowdecks must have been close together indeed. Babcock enjoyed more room in his captain's cabin at the ship's stern, and nearby his subordinate officers would have shared smaller quarters.

It was also an unabashedly male world aboard ship; there were no women. Maritime historian Marcus Rediker succinctly captured the confining life on a ship: "Shipboard life constituted a binding chain of linked limits: limited space, limited freedom, limited movement, limited sensory stimulation, and limited choices of leisure activities, social interaction, food, and play."[40]

Babcock completed final preparations for the long journey to the West African coast. On December 31, he sent a barge full of empty barrels to the docks at Old Town to be filled with fresh water. The next day, a local pilot guided his privateer out of the harbor and past dangerous shoals.

On January 2, 1778, captain's clerk Boss wrote in his journal, "We set sail from Old Town in Martha's Vineyard bound to sea. With a fair wind and a prosperous gale and 96 men and boys on board."[41] Each sailor must have been filled with both excitement and uncertainty about what lay ahead of them. Their extraordinary voyage had begun.

CHAPTER SIX

The *Marlborough* Arrives in Africa

*B**abcock's Marlborough* made good time plying through the Atlantic under full sail in fair weather, headed for the African coast. A standard route made by New England slave ships bound for Africa was to first head southeast toward Bermuda, picking up the North Atlantic Current and turning south, probably at between 20 and 25 degrees north latitude.[1] The slave ship would then follow the trade winds on a southeasterly course taking it close to northern Portugal, where it would drop down to northern Africa and the Madeira Islands to pick up the Canary Current. The *Marlborough* was able to take a more direct route, ending up to the south of the Madiera Islands. Based on mathematical calculations found in his ship's journal, Boss must have plotted the course for the *Marlborough*. The distance from Martha's Vineyard to the west coast of Africa where slave trading was concentrated, based on the *Marlborough*'s route, was roughly three thousand eight-hundred miles. (See map on pages 158–159.)

Before departing Providence, John Brown must have discussed with Babcock where the *Marlborough* should be sailed on Africa's long coast and what to do there. They undoubtedly agreed that the *Marlborough* should head to Senegambia, which contained the northernmost slave trading ports on the West African coast that were the closest to Providence. Senegambia had become the first British colony in Africa in 1765, but it had never attracted white settlers, and, other than having a few forts that supported British slave traders, it was a colony in name only.[2] Senegambia was a term used by the British to refer to their settlements on Saint-Louis Island at the mouth of the Senegal River and on James Island on the Gambia River, as well as to the general region of what are now the modern states of Senegal, Gambia, Guinea-Bissau, and Guinea. The outbreak of the Revolutionary War, and particularly the depredations of American privateers in the Caribbean, had reduced the British slave trade in Senegambia but had not eliminated it. From 1771 to 1775, British slave ships had embarked about twenty thousand Africans from Senegambia, while in the war years from 1776 to 1780, they had embarked from the region half that number.[3]

Brown knew that some islands off the coast of Senegambia had private, substantial posts that supported the British slave trade. These posts served two primary purposes. First, they had warehouses filled with merchandise and naval supplies. Second, they were places where captives could be collected and held in pens. Both purposes aided arriving British slave ships. The merchandise could be used to purchase captives to sell to ship captains, the naval supplies could help ships stay afloat, and captives gathered in bulk made buying them more efficient for ship captains.

Brown and Babcock likely discussed the *Marlborough* limiting its reach to these islands. There were plenty of British slave trading posts and slave ships for Babcock and his men to attack on or near British-controlled islands.

To venture into the interior of Africa, the crew of the American privateer would have to take small boats up rivers, since the *Marlborough*'s draft was too deep for almost all of them. By doing so, the Americans would lose the advantage of the ship's powerful twenty cannon. They would also expose themselves to potentially deadly diseases. It was well known that crew members on slave ships often contracted deadly fevers while boating up rivers. White slavers did not know that mosquito bites caused many diseases, but they did know that traveling into the interior of Africa could result in acquiring deadly ones. In one instance, a slave ship operating off Cape Mesurado lost all but three crew members from disease by sending its men up rivers in search of African captives to purchase.[4] Brown and Babcock likely agreed that the privateer and his crew should avoid as much as possible traveling up any rivers.

Planning to arrive on the African coast and operate there in February and March would also have the benefit of avoiding Africa's harsh summers. Summer increased the risk of thunderstorms and squalls wrecking a ship, and mosquito-borne illnesses were at their worst.

Brown probably also recommended that Babcock stop for resupply at Gorée Island, then under the control of the French and the key French slave trading post in Senegambia. It would have been a logical first stop for an American slave ship heading south down the west coast.

On January 13, Babcock's first crisis began to take shape. Samuel Babcock, the ship commander's younger brother, became ill. Captain Babcock, the ship's doctor, and the rest of the officers diagnosed Samuel as suffering from smallpox that evening. Some of the sailors, prior to the voyage, had already had the dreaded disease or had been inoculated for it and were therefore immune from catching it again. But more than half of the sailors had not had the disease or been inoculated. If the smallpox virus spread to the unprotected crew the natural way, by human contact, it could kill dozens of sailors and cut the voyage short. With the ship crowded with crew members performing their tasks, it would be difficult to contain the contagion.

On land, a traditional approach was to isolate smallpox victims in a so-called pest house to avoid contagion. Captain Babcock decided to isolate the stricken Samuel from the rest of the crew. "[F]or the preservation of those that never had it," he ordered Samuel to be placed by himself halfway up the foremast on a small flat platform called the foretop. It must have been a wrenching decision for Babcock to take this harsh step, but he decided to risk sacrificing one sailor in order to spare others, even if that one sailor was his own brother.

After Samuel Babcock spent a night at the foretop alone, and seeing him suffer in front of the entire crew, the captain reconsidered his prior order. He directed a sailor, identified only as Mr. Smith, to care for Samuel at the foretop but "to be careful not to spread the smallpox in the ship." The next day, Boss wrote in his journal, crewmen "Thomas Carpenter & Thomas Brown stationed in the foretop to watch and take care of S. Babcock there to stay night & day & Smith to go up and down."[5] Presumably, Smith climbed up and down the rigging of the mainmast bringing water and food as needed. The three men must have previously had smallpox.

The patient's illness lingered. Spending all that time in the foretop, exposed to the weather, must also have weakened him. In the early morning of January 24, Boss wrote in his journal, "Samuel Babcock departed this transitory life in hopes for a better." His lifeless body was "decently sewed up in Captain Babcock's hammock," a high honor. At eight a.m., in a driving rain, Boss "read prayers over his body" and "it was committed to the watery deep."[6]

Captain Babcock's precautions did not entirely contain the smallpox outbreak. In the afternoon of January 20, crewman David Wilcox displayed symptoms of the disease. The next day, John Larkin did too. They contracted it "the natural way," by exposure to a crewman who had the disease, the most deadly way to catch the virus. Wilcox died nine days later, but Larkin survived.

Babcock then considered an alternative measure, inoculation. If adopted, it would mean that each crew member who had never had smallpox would have live *Variola* virus deliberately implanted into an incision on his hand or arm. The disease from inoculation was generally mild, but not always. Occasionally someone who contracted the illness through the procedure died of it. More importantly, those who fell ill could spread the disease to others in the more deadly natural way.[7]

While a North Kingstown resident in April 1777, Babcock had been inoculated in a pest house in Exeter. But because he did it without permission from the Exeter Town Council and was not then an Exeter resident, the council fined him six dollars.[8] Babcock must have regretted not bringing Samuel with him, even if that might have doubled his fine.

Babcock made his decision: "for the benefit of the cruise," all sailors who had never had smallpox were ordered to be inoculated.[9] This meant forty-nine men and boys were inoculated.

On January 27 and 28, inoculated crew members broke out with smallpox. Most of them had mild cases of the disease. They were likely quarantined to the extent possible, so as to prevent others from catching the illness. Still, a few others who had not been inoculated complained of having smallpox symptoms.[10]

The inoculations finally contained the outbreak, but not without cost. Two crewmen who underwent the procedure died on February 1 and 2: sailor Jedidiah Collins and "gunners boy" Stephen Congdon. The last victim was John Davis, who claimed he had contracted smallpox as a young boy in the west of England. As a result, he was not inoculated. Davis must have been mistaken. He died on February 12.[11]

Fortunately for the surviving crewmen, no other sailors died of the disease, and the crisis ended. Captain Babcock had passed his first command test. But with the five deaths, his crew was reduced to ninety-one "men & boys."

Every day on the voyage to Africa, the *Marlborough*'s crew looked for British or Loyalist vessels to capture. Most of the "sails" (that is, ships) they saw on the horizon disappeared from view. Babcock was able to run down a few of them. Bearing a commission from the Continental Congress, he had the right to stop, board, and examine the vessels to determine if they were from neutral countries and therefore protected from seizure. Babcock typically sent his first lieutenant, James Eldred, and a small party of armed men over in a small boat to the vessel. Eldred would examine the ship's logbook and papers for evidence of ownership. He was always on guard against the use of false papers. If anything appeared suspicious or if he had any doubts, he would bring the papers back to the *Marlborough* for Babcock's review. If Eldred had good reason to suspect that the ship and cargo were owned by British subjects or American Loyalists, he could seize the vessel consistent with the *Marlborough*'s privateering commission. Babcock could then place a prize master and crew on board the captured vessel and send it back to Massachusetts for trial at an admiralty court.

Babcock was able to add a crew member from one of the ships he stopped to examine. On January 20, Babcock stopped a vessel that turned out to be a Spanish ship out of Havana and headed for Cadiz, Spain. As usual, Babcock dispatched Eldred, accompanied by a few other armed sailors, to board the vessel. Babcock and Eldred became persuaded the ship was indeed Spanish. Eldred even handed Babcock the ship's log, written entirely in Spanish, which none of the Americans could read. The vessel was not seized as a prize (indeed, the Continental Congress at this time was desperately trying to lure Spain into an alliance with France to oppose Britain). However, Eldred came across an American prisoner on board the Spanish ship. Why the American was on the Spanish ship as a captive was not explained. In any event, it struck Eldred as wrong, and he freed the prisoner and brought him on board the *Marlborough*. The grateful man signed the ship's articles and joined the crew.[12]

The *Marlborough* began sailing south over warmer and warmer seas. It likely picked up the Canary Current, which sweeps ships toward the northwest coast of Africa.[13] The ship's officers who took the standard midday observations found that they were making good time. On average, the ship sailed about 120 miles per day. Fortunately for them, no storms impeded their progress or threated their destruction.

The crew aboard the *Marlborough* was kept busy by the officers. Seamen took shifts in the mastheads keeping watch. They set out more sail in weak to moderate breezes and "reefed," or took in sails, when the wind increased in intensity. When a sail was placed in the desired position, crew members would "bend" the sail, that is, fasten it to its proper wooden yard or stay that was secured to a mast. Master Boss's journal entry for January 16 (which ran from noon of January 16 to noon of January 17) reveals how hard sailors had to work:

The first part moderate breezes. At 3 p.m. hands to bending the mainsail and at 5 p.m. [took] the foretop sail and reefed it. Also reefed the main and mizzen top sail. At 2 a.m. had small showers of rain. At 7 a.m. let one reef out of the main and foretop sail and set top gallant sail. At 10 a.m. set the sprit sail. At 11 a.m. let both reefs out of the main and foretop sails.[14]

Sailors were also assigned to numerous chores, including mending the sails. The ship's carpenter was kept busy maintaining the longboats and barrels containing provisions and fresh water. He also had the tasks of fitting out the barge and setting its mast.[15]

In the early morning of January 26, just twenty-three days out of Martha's Vineyard, a lookout stationed high on a mast spotted the Madeira Islands. These are the first major islands to the northwest of Africa. They are about 350 miles from the northwest coast of Africa and 520 miles southwest of Portugal. The Portuguese began to settle the islands in about 1425. The main island of Madeira was known throughout the Atlantic world for its wines. Less well known was that the Portuguese brought enslaved Africans to the Madeira Islands to work on plantations later in the fifteenth century—one of the first uses of African slave labor by Europeans. Slave ships sometimes stopped to refit and resupply at the islands, but Babcock carried on, perhaps because Portugal was somewhat allied with Great Britain.

On January 28, the *Marlborough* sailed south between the islands of La Palma and La Gomera in the Canary Islands. Two other Canary Islands well known to sailors were spotted in the distance: Tenerife and Fuerteventura.[16] The archipelago of islands, claimed by Spain, were formed by volcanic eruptions millions of years ago and still had mountains rising thousands of feet above sea level that Babcock and his crew would have easily viewed from far away. Tenerife, in particular, was important as a way station for ships traveling across the Atlantic to Africa, but Babcock did not stop at Tenerife either and continued to sail on to the southeast toward the African coast.

During the afternoon of January 30, Babcock conducted lessons training his men on how to fire the cannon stationed on the ship's main deck. He was getting his crew ready for a possible confrontation with a British warship, a well-armed slave ship—or even Barbary pirates known to lurk off the coast. Later, Babcock had his carpenter construct several fake wooden cannon that when pushed out of portholes would make his brig look to an enemy vessel even more powerful than it really was.

On January 31, at three p.m., the *Marlborough* crossed the Tropic of Cancer, the line marking the sun's northernmost zenith in the earth's orbit. Traditionally, it was one of two times when, for a short period, power would transfer from the captain and his officers to veteran sailors who had previously crossed the line. Veterans planned and oversaw crossing-the-line ceremonies that the uninitiated would have to endure. (A crossing-the-line ceremony would also be held when a ship crossed the equator and perhaps the Tropic of Capricorn.)

For example, in February 1777, John Palmer of the Connecticut privateer *Revenge* wrote in his log book, "this day we crossed the Tropic line and we had full employ of shaving the hands [of sailors who had not crossed the line before] and swearing [at] them."[17] In this case, there were two common features of the traditional ceremony, shaving and swearing. There was also shaving and ducking in water. Sailor Timothy Boardman, on the Connecticut privateer *Oliver Cromwell*, "Crossed the Tropic. Shaved and ducked about 60 men."[18] Connecticut mariner Eleazer Elkin, for his first time crossing the line, was strapped to a chair where he "was daubed all over my face with tar, slush and hog dung. They shaved me with an old rusty knife." Buckets of water were then thrown in Elkin's face. The celebrations typically ended in the captain permitting grog rations to be issued to the crew.[19]

The sailors on the *Marlborough* did not show much inventiveness during their crossing of the Tropic of Cancer. According to master Boss, the crew celebrated with "considerable sport." Two common seamen dressed in sail canvas, perhaps representing King Neptune and his consort, Queen Amphitrite. They demanded from Captain Babcock a bottle of rum for the crew and also required all the sailors crossing the Tropic of Cancer for the first time to pay for it. Babcock agreed, going along with the fun, but not losing much, if any, money either.

Officers and men were thrilled to see the African coast. But the convergence of land and sea was also a dangerous place for ships. Most shipwrecks occurred in sight of land. Many ships had wrecked on shoals off the dangerous African coast, where the barren Sahara desert met the Atlantic Ocean. Treacherous shoals and sandbars extended several miles from the shoreline, challenging even the most experienced ship captains. Babcock and his officers were aware of the danger, but still their instruments did not always enable them to fix their position and avoid shallow water.

At four a.m. on February 1, a potentially fatal disaster occurred. In the Bahia de San Cipriano, off the coast of Western Sahara south of what is now the port of Dakhla, lookouts from Babcock's ship yelled to officers below that they had spotted breakers on the coast. It was too late. Shortly afterward, the *Marlborough* struck a shoal and ran aground. The American privateersmen faced the prospect of their ship being crushed by incoming waves. If that happened, as seemed likely at the time, many of the men would die before they could even get to the shore. But by desperately hauling—with crewmen on small boats pulling vigorously on lines tied to their ship—the brig lurched free from the shoals. As had occurred when the *Marlborough* had run aground in the Sakonnet Channel in Narragansett Bay, Babcock did not throw any cannon or other heavy items overboard to lighten his ship. The sailors looked at the damage and were relieved not to find any punctures in the wooden hull.

"This happy deliverance of God happened," Boss wrote in his log, "on the Coast of Barbary where live the cruel Moors."[20] Boss and other crew members must have feared that if local Berbers captured them, they themselves would be imprisoned and enslaved. Barbary pirates, as they were called, over the decades had seized and enslaved thousands of British (including American) sailors and held them for ransom. The irony that Boss and his fellow crewmen were heading to a land where human beings were commonly captured and enslaved, and that they hoped to benefit from that fact, was not mentioned.

Babcock issued orders for his officers from then on to take soundings, which suggests he and his officers had failed to do that previously. By carefully testing the depth of the bay, the *Marlborough* safely passed a headland jettying out into the ocean, probably what is now Cabo Barbas (Cape Barbas).

At six a.m. on February 4, lookouts for the first time spotted the African mainland coast. It was probably what is now part of Mauritania. Captain Babcock ordered First Lieutenant James Eldred, Boss, and ten other crew members, all armed, to take the ship's barge to the shore to gain intelligence of their location and of any British warships in the area. While those left on the *Marlborough* threw out fishing lines and quickly caught snapper and grouper, Eldred and his party went ashore. They were glad to step on land once more. But they found the location uninhabited, except for "wild beasts" and tracks of humans and camels. After the exploration party returned to the *Marlborough*, Babcock ordered his crew to sail down the coast a bit farther. This time Babcock commanded the barge that went ashore, but again no people were found.[21]

Finally, at eight a.m. on February 7, the crew saw in the distance a fort on an island off the coast. It was Saint-Louis Fort (or Senegal Fort) on Saint-Louis Island in what is now the country of Senegal. Saint-Louis Fort,

Babcock knew, was held by the British. Saint-Louis originally was a French colony that had served as a center for France's slave trading in Senegal, but a British naval force that included two ships of the line surprised and seized it on April 30, 1758, during the Seven Years' War. At war's end, Saint-Louis was not returned to France under the peace treaty between the countries.[22] It had been the first stop in Africa by British warships patrolling the African coast in 1775.

At the time, Saint-Louis had a population of more than 3,000, which included about 400 Europeans (French and Portuguese), called habitants; about 1,850 enslaved Africans; and about 800 free Africans, including those of mixed race.[23] The governor of the British posts in Senegambia, John Clark, had arrived at Saint-Louis from London in late 1776.[24] A small garrison of British regular soldiers manned the fort. Saint-Louis Fort guarded the mouth of the Senegal River, which was used to transport captured Africans to Saint-Louis Island for the slave trade and also allowed the British to control the lucrative gum trade on the mainland.[25] (A modern study examined the largest British slave trading posts in Upper Guinea, which comprised Senegambia, and to the south, Sierra Leone and the Windward Coast. The study concluded that Saint-Louis was the number two slave trading port in all of Upper Guinea, handling approximately twelve percent of the trade.)[26] Around the fort lay a hospital, a church, a few brick houses for the small white and mixed-race population, and numerous huts in which the Africans lived.[27]

Babcock felt that the substantial fort was too strong for his single ship and small crew to overwhelm. Instead, he tried to trick the British so he could gain valuable intelligence.

Approaching the fort but staying outside of cannon range, at eleven a.m., Babcock ordered that a single cannon be fired and a British jack be raised on the mainmast. Babcock had a British flag on board for just this type of occasion. Using false colors and flags was a common ploy for privateers to deceive the enemy. Babcock hoped the move would reduce the concerns of the British officers commanding the fort so they would send out a small boat with men whom the sailors on the *Marlborough* could seize and interrogate for intelligence. The suspicious British commander in the fort, however, never responded. Frustrated, at six p.m. Babcock had his cannoneers fire another round and ordered the British flag to be brought down. His effort to trick the British had failed.[28] Nonetheless, Governor John Clark shot off a note to his superiors in London, complaining of being abandoned to the mercy of American corsairs.[29]

Early the next morning, on February 8, the *Marlborough* sailed away and headed down the coast toward the Cape Verde peninsula, which now contains the city of Dakar in Senegal. The next day John Linscom Boss penned in his journal a drawing of Cape Verde, an important natural feature for sailors.

At about nine a.m. on February 9, the crew saw their first Africans. Six of them in two canoes ventured out to the strange vessel, probably to trade. But they refused to come on board the *Marlborough*, perhaps because they did not recognize the ship and feared its captain and crew could try to enslave them. Or they may have been confused that the *Marlborough* did not appear to be a traditional slave ship interested in trade. In any event, Babcock decided to leave them behind.[30]

Two hours later, the crew spotted one of its main destinations, Gorée Island. High on a bluff, overlooking Gorée Bay, was a fort flying a large French flag. It was Fort St. François, the main fortification on the French-controlled island. In the turquoise waters of the bay was anchored a French snow flying a colorful pennant on its mainmast. Boss was so pleased by the scene that he drew a sketch of it in the *Marlborough*'s log, one of only two sketches he did in the log.[31] Captain Babcock expected he would receive a welcome reception and key intelligence.

Gorée Island (Isle de Gorée), though tiny, had served as a hub for France's African slave trade. It became among the first outposts established by Europeans to facilitate the transportation of enslaved Africans across the Atlantic Ocean. The French established on the island their principal slave trading posts off coastal West Africa during the fifteenth and sixteenth centuries. As European countries struggled for control of the slave trade, Gorée changed hands among the Portuguese, Dutch, French, and British numerous times from 1588 to 1814.

France controlled the island for most of the eighteenth century. However, at the end of December 1758, during the Seven Years' War, it was captured by a British expeditionary force consisting of five ships of the line and 700 soldiers commanded by Commodore Augustus Keppel; it was defended by 250 French troops and 400 local armed men. As part of the postwar settlement, Gorée Island was returned to French control.[32] By 1778, about 150 Europeans resided on it, surrounded by about 1,200 enslaved Africans. White inhabitants feared slave revolts more than another European war.[33] Gorée, by 1778, had ceased serving as a major slave trading center. In the 1770s, French exports of enslaved Africans from the island amounted to just 820 per year.[34] The Loango Coast and Benin to the south were far more important for French slave traders.

Gorée Island was strategically located at the westernmost extension of the African continent, between what are now the countries of Senegal and Gambia. It was a natural place for a main stop after a voyage from Great Britain or North America to the West African coast. Thus, Gorée Island became an important center for resupply to load fresh water, meat, fish, and wood. The narrow island held two forts.[35]

The *Marlborough*, entering Gorée Bay at one p.m., fired a signal gun and hoisted "Continental Colours," indicating the ship hailed from the new United States. At about three p.m., two important visitors arrived on a small boat from the fort: the island's lieutenant governor, Charles-Joseph-Bonaventure Boucher, and the owner of the French merchant vessel (the snow in Boss's drawing) anchored in the bay.

The French ship owner, whose name Boss does not provide, conveyed information to Babcock that greatly relieved his anxieties. The Frenchman said he had sailed from the Gambia River to the south two weeks earlier and did not see or hear of any British warships in the vicinity. No doubt the lieutenant governor passed on information that he too was not aware of any British warships patrolling the African coast. A key assumption underlying the *Marlborough*'s voyage had been confirmed as fact.

Boucher had other interesting news. He reported that three days earlier, two Continental navy frigates had visited his fort. Babcock had just missed them. They turned out to be the twenty-gun ship *Alfred*, commanded by Captain Elisha Hinman of New London, Connecticut, and the thirty-two-gun frigate *Raleigh*, commanded by Captain Thomas Thompson from Portsmouth, New Hampshire. They had only captured a London sloop that was not a slaver. Based on his conversation with Boucher, Babcock determined that the Continental ships must not have remained on the African coast and instead must have already sailed for the United States.[36]

Babcock then asked Boucher to supply him with a local pilot to guide the *Marlborough* safely into the Gambia River, almost one hundred miles south of Gorée. Babcock was planning to surprise, attack, and destroy James Fort, a major British slave fort on an island up the Gambia. It was the key to the British slave trade in Senegambia. (The same modern study mentioned above indicated that James Fort was the top slave trading port in all of Upper Guinea, handling approximately twenty-four percent of the trade by all countries in that region.)[37] The Gambia was one of the few rivers in Upper Guinea that was deep enough for warships to sail. Whether the 250-ton *Marlborough* could have sailed to James Fort is uncertain, as a British slave ship captain reported that the Gambia River could only be navigated

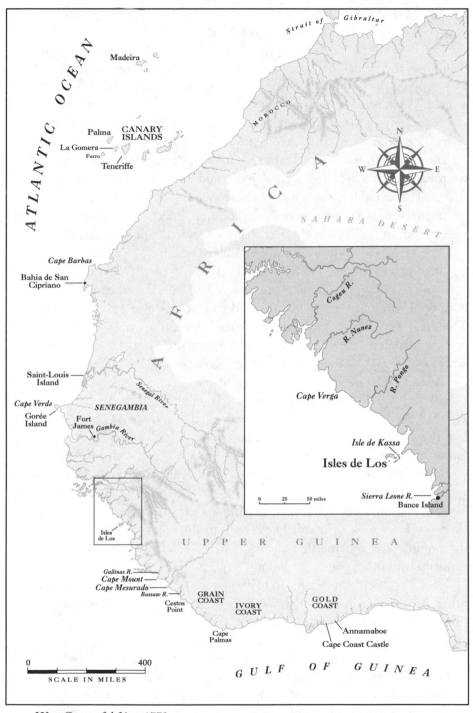

West Coast of Africa, 1778.

by vessels that drew ten feet of water or less, that is, vessels under 150 tons.[38] However, in 1779, French warships would accomplish the feat and destroy the fort.[39] The New England captain hoped for a positive response to his request, as the French had been surreptitiously assisting the Patriot cause by supplying the Continental army with guns and supplies. But Boucher refused. What is more, he informed Babcock that his ship could remain at Gorée for only up to twenty-four hours, enough for his men to obtain fresh water. The Americans would receive no official favorable treatment.

The governor, Alexandre-Davis-Ar.mény de Paradis, was under orders from Paris not to take any action that could provoke a war with Great Britain. France did not want to start a new war with its historic enemy until its new fleets of warships were ready. In addition, Boucher and the governor were no doubt sensitive to the fact that British warships operated off the coast of Africa more often than did French navy ships.

Unknown to the two French officials at Gorée, several days earlier, on February 6, 1778, in far-away Paris, France had signed a treaty of alliance with the United States and had decided to enter the war against Britain. The great American victory at the Battle of Saratoga helped persuade French officials that the Americans could sustain their war of independence and allayed fears that the revolution might collapse and leave France fighting Britain on its own. Still, knowledge of the alliance was kept secret. A French fleet would not be ready to depart Toulon for North America until April 13. And it was not until May 20, after the fleet cleared Gibraltar and left the Mediterranean, that its commander, Charles Henri Théodat, Comte d'Estaing, directed his ship captains to open their sealed orders, revealing for the first time the stunning news of France's declaration of war against Britain.[40]

After the meeting on board the *Marlborough* off Gorée Island, the French visitors took their small boat back to the main fort, honored by a three-gun salute ordered by Babcock. The *Marlborough*'s captain had to come up with other plans that did not require French assistance.

John Blondfield, an American agent, wrote to Benjamin Franklin and other American commissioners in Paris of Babcock's meeting with the French at Gorée. He wrote:

> By a vessel last evening from Gorée, the [French] governor [of Gorée] who came passenger told me that two armed vessels, one belonging to Congress and the other a privateer ship [the *Marlborough*], had called there the latter end of February. [The governor's] orders from [France] obliged him to order

them [both American ships] out of port giving them only twenty-four hours to refresh and water. . . . They [the officers of the *Marlborough*] applied for a pilot to take them into the River, intending to destroy the English settlement, which was refused them. As Gorée would or could not harbor them they stood to the southward since when he had heard from them. In all probability they must have made great havoc in them seas [as] there is no British men-of-war on that station.[41]

It is interesting to compare the effort and results of Babcock and the *Marlborough* on the coast of Africa to those of the two Continental navy ships, the *Alfred* and *Raleigh*, and their captains. In short, Babcock would prove himself to be a daring commander, and the privateer *Marlborough* would indeed create "great havoc" with British slave trading interests off Guinea-Bissau. By comparison, the two Continental navy captains and frigates made little impression. It was a stark example of how privateers could be a more effective instrument of war than regular navy ships. In both cases, much depended on the boldness of the commanders.

The *Raleigh* and *Alfred* had departed the seaport of L'Orient in northwest France on the Brittany coast on December 29, 1777, for their return voyage to America by way of Africa and then the Caribbean. Benjamin Franklin, Silas Dean, and Arthur Lee, the American commissioners in Paris, in a November 25 letter, had recommended to Captain Thompson that because "the British factories [i.e., slave trading posts] and commerce on the African coast are at this time without any force sufficient to protect them" that the two Continental warships should, before proceeding to the Caribbean, sail to the African coast and "greatly annoy, and distress, the enemy in that quarter."[42]

In wanting the Continental navy captains to disrupt the British African slave trade, the American commissioners had anticipated the desires of Continental Congress delegates in Philadelphia. Congress's Committee for Foreign Affairs wrote to the American commissioners in Paris on December 2, advising that Continental navy ships in France could try to raid the coast of Africa and sell any prizes to French or Dutch African settlements.[43] But it would take many weeks for that letter to reach Paris.

Hinman and Thompson did not make much of an effort on the Senegal coast, capturing just one small trading sloop on February 2, 1778. (Interestingly, Thompson's *Raleigh* had three Black sailors in its crew and added one more from the crew of the captured sloop.)[44] After arriving at Gorée Island four days later, on February 7, the two Continental navy captains commenced their Atlantic crossings. Upon arriving in the Caribbean, on March 9, Captain Hinman, his 180-man crew, and the *Alfred* were captured after an engagement with the Royal Navy frigate *Ariadne*, with twenty guns, and sloop of war *Ceres*, with sixteen guns. Meanwhile, Thompson and his *Raleigh*, too far away to assist, escaped the fray. Thompson was later relieved of his command because of his failure to try to prevent the *Alfred*'s capture.[45]

An American privateer that went to the African coast a few months prior to the arrival of the *Marlborough* had some initial success, but too much success led to a disaster. The sixteen-gun privateer *Alligator* took three British commercial vessels off Cape Verde and the Madeira Islands in late December 1777, one of which was described as an "English ship from the coast of Guinea." Following each capture, the *Alligator* sent some if its sailors to man the prize ships, reducing the size of its own crew. The prisoners from the three ships realized that many of the members of the *Alligator*'s remaining crew hailed from Britain and Ireland. On January 2, the prisoners and several crew members who conspired with them rose up and seized the ship from its American officers and crew.[46]

Buoyed by the intelligence of the lack of British warships to the south, Babcock decided to sail down the coast toward Cape Saint Mary and the Gambia River in Gambia. Without a pilot to guide the *Marlborough* up the Gambia River, Babcock set aside any further notions of attacking James Fort. On February 10, after refreshing the vessel's water supplies and firing a three-gun salute, the *Marlborough* departed Gorée Island. Babcock carefully sailed his vessel for several days to the southeast. He frequently sent one of his lieutenants ahead in the ship's "jolly boat" in order to take soundings to ensure the *Marlborough* would not again become grounded.[47]

Babcock and his men were now operating in a distinct maritime culture on the west coast of Africa. European sailing ships sometimes anchored at the mouths of rivers and hesitated to venture farther up the rivers for fear of running aground on hidden sandbars. Canoe transport linked the ocean-sailing ships to villages dotting the shoreline and rivers. Canoes were often operated by grumettas, African maritime laborers who were sometimes free and worked for hire but were also sometimes enslaved by local African rulers and merchants or local Europeans. The highly skilled "canoemen" brought African captives to slave ships, and also fresh water, fruit, and other provisions, all for trade.[48]

The *Marlborough*'s crew scanned the horizon for telltale sails. The officers and sailors had worked hard to come to this point off of Africa. They were anxious to start capturing prizes so that all could share in the profits.

They figured that most of the vessels in the area would be British slavers, who frequented this part of the African coast, particularly vessels from Liverpool. By this time, most all of the North American slavers had ceased making African slaving voyages.

In the early afternoon of February 18, in clear weather with light breezes, the *Marlborough*'s crew spotted in the distance a vessel under sail. The potential prize was sailing inside of the Rhode Island vessel, closer to the land. Babcock ordered his crew to begin the chase. The *Marlborough*'s prey tried to slip away, continuing to hug the coast, but Babcock and his sailors closed the gap between the two vessels. At six p.m., however, Babcock ordered his ship to come to anchor. The *Marlborough* was in only seven fathoms of water, the tide was going out, and darkness soon would be upon them. At daylight the next morning, a sail was spotted in the distance to the north close to the coast. The smaller vessel knew that the *Marlborough* could not venture in the shallow water and hoped to wait until the American privateer departed.

Babcock had another idea. He ordered his first lieutenant, James Eldred, to take "10 men well-armed" in the ship's barge and try to capture their prey. At six a.m., the barge, powered by a sail on a single mast, stood in toward the coast and disappeared from view.[49]

On board the *Marlborough*, the crew anxiously waited for a sign that Eldred's mission was a success. There was the risk that the vessel could outgun the small barge and put up a fight. At ten a.m., an incoming tide drew the privateer vessel into a bay where the crew set its anchor.

Finally, after what felt like an eternity, at eleven-thirty a.m., a sail in the distance was spotted coming toward them. This was a sign that Eldred had succeeded and that a prize crew was sailing the captured ship to the *Marlborough*. At one p.m., the elated crew could also see the ship's barge heading toward their vessel. An hour later, Lieutenant Eldred was back on board the main ship.

The new prize, which anchored nearby, was the schooner *Sally*. It was captained by William Moore, an Englishman. His vessel mounted six 1-pound cannon, but he did not resist when Eldred and his ten armed men approached his schooner and demanded that he surrender. It may be that Moore did not resist because he felt he could not trust his crew to put up a determined fight. His schooner was manned by eleven African grumettas he hired to assist him in his slave trading enterprise.

In addition to the eleven grumettas, Eldred found on board the *Sally* three enslaved people. Captain Moore had bargained for them with local traders and had stowed them on his schooner. The captives must have been very concerned and confused about their seizure by new captors. Eldred also discovered on Moore's vessel an assortment of British manufactured goods intended to be traded for more African captives: cloth, calico, and handkerchiefs. Investigating further, Eldred found small arms that could be used to defend the ship against a slave insurrection or other threats. Babcock sent Boss to take an inventory of the goods and to supervise their transfer to the *Marlborough*.

The three enslaved Africans, Babcock's first captives, were also transported to the *Marlborough*. Babcock must have ordered the carpenter to prepare an area belowdecks that could be secured with a firm hatch or door to prevent their escape from the ship or their harming any of the crew. The hatch would have had grates to allow air into the hold. At this point, the senior officers on the *Marlborough* began to have some of the same concerns as if they were sailing on a regular slave ship.

Indeed, they had become in effect slave traders. They had the same goal as a slave ship captain would have: get the captives on his vessel to the Caribbean as quickly as feasible in order to sell them to local French colonial planters and earn a handsome profit. Babcock and his officers had no interest in purchasing captive Africans from slaver traders on the coast. But by capturing enslaved Africans on British slave vessels, they suddenly put themselves in a position close to that of European and American slave buyers. The Africans held hostage on the *Marlborough* saw little difference between Moore or Babcock; they were both white men intent on treating them as mere commodities to sell at a profit.

Babcock brought on board Moore's eleven grumettas, but he did not treat them as enslaved captives. For one, to have done so would have raised the ire of local people, whom Babcock did not want to arouse, and it would have violated his privateering commission. Within a week, these local sailors were freed.[50]

Babcock and his men made clear distinctions in dealing with native peoples. They did not enslave every African they took prisoner. They needed the cooperation of local people to supply them with food and fresh water. To antagonize native leaders would also have put their own safety at risk. Historically, white slave ship captains cooperated with coastal local leaders who supplied them with captives as well as food and water. Babcock was focused on harming British interests. It appears he adopted the policy of treating all local Africans as free people who could not be enslaved unless they had been enslaved and treated as cargo by a British slave ship owner.

For Babcock, his most important role was as privateer captain. He held a commission from the Continental Congress that imposed significant limitations on what he could capture and sell. He was not a pirate. America was at war with Great Britain, and Babcock was therefore permitted to seize and sell cargo on British ships. An enslaved captive found on a British ship, shallop, or other vessel that was treated as cargo on an enemy vessel would also be treated by Babcock as cargo under his privateering commission. In some respects, rather than their skin color, what mattered most to Babcock about the people found on enemy vessels was their status, whether or not they were treated as British property.

In addition, a captive found on a non-British vessel, if it could be established as the property of British traders, could also be taken. Such human cargo could be captured and sold pursuant to admiralty court proceedings, if those proceedings established that the cargo was British property.[51]

What of a captive found on a non-British vessel that was not British property but was intended to be sold by African slave merchants or local rulers to British traders? This appears to have been an ambiguous area of the law of privateering. Babcock simply treated such captives as property permitted to be seized by him under his Continental commission.

The grumettas found on the *Sally* did not constitute human cargo. Grumettas were sometimes free men who hired themselves out. Frequently, they were enslaved by African merchants or rulers and leased out to British slave traders; in those cases, the grumettas were neither cargo nor British property. A grumetta enslaved by a British slave trader could be British property, but making that determination was not easy. It is likely that John Brown, given his familiarity with the African slave trade, explained these distinctions to Babcock prior to the *Marlborough*'s voyage.

While Babcock and his crew were pleased to make the first capture of a vessel on their cruise, they benefitted mostly from the information conveyed by Captain Moore.

This was not the first time William Moore had been captured by an American privateer. He had previously commanded the slave ship *St. George*, which probably had left Cape Coast Castle, in what is now Ghana, in mid-January 1777.[52] On March 25, just as it neared its destination at Grenada, the *St. George* was seized by the Baltimore privateer *Sturdy Beggar*. The slave ship, the property of London merchants, carried about 450 African captives, gold dust, and ivory, all which was said to be worth £20,000. The *Sturdy Beggar* brought the prize into Port Dauphine at Martinique, where the human and other cargo was sold.[53]

Moore was released and sailed back to Africa, where he was trying to rebuild his career as a small-time slave trader. He had likely invested his life's savings in his schooner and its cargo.

Despite being a British citizen, Moore sought lenient treatment from Babcock by telling him all the local information he had that might assist an American privateer operating off the African coast. The British sea captain probably hoped that if he cooperated and Babcock's cruise was successful, Babcock might return his schooner and grumettas to him.

Moore informed Babcock of a British ship out of London flying a French flag, and other vessels, all slavers presumably, that he had seen off the coast of what is now Morocco where the Atlas Mountains rise. Moore added that he was aware of a schooner, also British, that had sailed up a nearby river (probably the Cogon River in present-day Gambia) that mounted eight 1-pound cannon. Most tantalizingly, Moore spoke of a "rich factory" (that is, a slave trading post) operated by British slave merchants on one of the islands at the Isles de Los, known as Factory Island (Isle de Kassa in present-day Guinea).[54]

Immediately, Babcock asked Moore to pilot the *Marlborough*, first to the Cogon River and then to Isle de Kassa. The Rhode Island captain knew that Moore's local knowledge was vital and that no one on his ship possessed it. Babcock explained to Moore that if his advice "proved true," Moore would benefit, but warned that if his advice was "bad," he would fare much worse. Not hesitating, despite his English background, Moore responded that he would assist Babcock "to the best of his knowledge."

Babcock and his three lieutenants discussed among themselves Moore's intelligence. They decided to use their barge and the shallow-drafted *Sally* to try to capture the British schooner up the Cogon River. Moore agreed to guide Babcock's small flotilla of vessels so as to avoid dangerous shoals. The privateer's crew began preparations for the journey. Babcock ordered that six swivel guns from the *Marlborough* be carried over to the *Sally* and that his carpenter secure the guns onto the railing on top of the sides of the *Sally*'s upper deck. In just an hour the work was completed. At four p.m., the crews of the schooner and barge, along with the addition of Lieutenant Eldred and eleven armed men, departed for the Cogon River with the mission of capturing the slave vessel Moore had brought to their attention.[55]

On board the *Marlborough* that night, wrote Boss in his log book, the crew "remained in suspense." Finally, at five a.m. the next day, February 19, Boss and others on the vessel "saw flashes of guns" and then heard loud bangs. Babcock ordered a lantern to be "hoisted" up a mast and a cannon to be fired to signal his ship's location. An hour later, the men aboard the *Marlborough* spotted the *Sally* returning with a prize in tow.[56]

The prize turned out to be the schooner *Fort Rose*, commanded by Richard Roberts. Twelve Africans were found on board. Nine were grumettas employed by Roberts and three were enslaved. The schooner carried slave trade articles similar to those that Moore had carried on the *Sally*. All the goods—and the African grumettas, captives, and Captain Roberts— were brought on board the *Marlborough*. As with the *Sally*, the grumettas were temporarily confined but eventually released.

Roberts may have been based at the Isles de Los. An account book from an unidentified slave ship captain indicates that the captain sold Roberts slave trade goods at the Isles de Los in January 1775.[57]

Babcock ordered Ichabod Holloway, five men, and one boy to board the *Fort Rose,* and John Bissell and the same number of sailors to board the *Sally*. Holloway and Bissell were experienced ship officers. They were ordered to follow the *Marlborough* in their prize vessels. Boss commented in his journal that the two light vessels could prove "of great service to us in the rivers" where more slave ship prizes could be found in shallow waters.

Roberts, undoubtedly a British subject, subsequently aided Babcock by giving him intelligence about the British agent at Isle de Kassa in the Isles de Los.[58] Both Roberts's and Moore's decisions to cooperate with the Americans showed they cared more about making money as slave traders than being loyal to Great Britain and helping their country win its war against the American "rebels." Roberts and Moore likely committed treason against King George by giving Britain's enemies valuable intelligence. These would not be the only times slave traders on the African coast, who typically worked with British slave ships and traders, chose to assist the *Marlborough*, to the great benefit of Babcock and his crew.

Next, Babcock turned his eyes south toward the Isles de Los. If Captain Moore was correct, a British slave trading post on one of its main islands, Isle de Kassa, was vulnerable to an assault by his men and could be a rich prize. The privateer captain decided he would raid Isle de Kassa. The small flotilla of three vessels set sail at ten a.m. on February 19 and headed southeast along the coast.[59]

CHAPTER SEVEN

The Attack on the Isles de Los

*W*ith all sails set, the *Marlborough* headed southeast for Isle de Kassa, in the chain of islands known as the Isles de Los. The slave ship captain William Moore advised Captain Babcock on the best route. At six p.m. on February 19, lookouts in the mastheads spotted in the distance the Fouta Djallon highlands at Cape Verga on the coast of what is now Guinea. Babcock shortened his sails for the night, but at sunrise set all his sails again.[1]

As Babcock and his crew approached the Isles de Los, they probably knew little about their destination. They likely were aware of the basics. The Isles de Los comprised six islands almost two miles from Cape Sangara and Tumbo Island, near what is now Conakry, the capital of the Republic of Guinea.

Portuguese sailors in the fifteenth century, discovering evidence of the worship of idols on one of the islands, called the collection of islands the Islands of Idols.[2] Centuries later, this name was somehow corrupted to Isles de Los.

Babcock and his men likely knew there was a major British slave trading post located on one of the islands. That island was called Factory Island, though its formal name then (and now) was Isle de Kassa. It was the easternmost of the chain of islands called the Isles de Los and was closest to Cape Sangara on the mainland and Tumbo Island.

Factory Island was approximately five miles long and about a half-mile wide in many parts (but as little as 350 yards wide at its narrowest point). It was thickly wooded, except around the town in the middle of the island that contained a major slave trading post. On its east coast, facing the African coast, it had sandy beaches on which longboats could land their cargoes. It was here that white employees known as factors, representing merchant firms in Britain, established their main slave trading posts. This was how Factory Island got its name.[3] Who the factors were who were stationed at Isle de Kassa at this time is not known. They likely were either former sailors who had been hired from slave ships or agents sent directly from Britain.

The British slave trading post at Isle de Kassa was an important embarkation site for enslaved people, as well as a frequent stop for ships sailing down the west coast of Africa.[4] It served a dual purpose for its British managers. The first, and primary, purpose was to acquire and hold captives, and then sell them to slave ship captains. The slave trading post's second purpose was to service passing slave ships in need of maintenance and repairs and replenish their fresh water and other stores.

Most of the work at the slave trading post at Isle de Kassa was related to purchasing captives. At the one major town midway down the coastward side of the island, British agents at the post kept a large inventory of manufactured and other trade goods in warehouses. The inventory would be loaded onto shallops and other small boats, and sometimes schooners, and used to trade on the mainland for African captives with local African rulers, local African small merchants, and sometimes European merchants. The African captives mostly hailed from the interior, up nearby rivers, such as the Rio Nunez, Rio Pongo, Dembia, Forékariah, and Scarcies. When the slaving vessels returned with their captives, the British factors would herd them into barracoons or other places of confinement, until slave ship captains showed up offshore in their vessels to buy the enslaved people.

To assist them, the white factory managers hired grumettas, who were either free or enslaved African workers. If they were enslaved by other Africans, their masters would be paid for their services. Grumettas were also used by African rulers and merchants to bring captives from the mainland to Isle de Kassa in shallops, canoes, and other small boats. Sometimes they also brought local goods, such as camwood and ivory. Negotiations would then be conducted for a barter exchange.[5]

For the slave merchant houses back in Liverpool, Bristol, and London that invested in and sent out slave ships to West Africa, purchasing enslaved people in bulk at a slave trading post or fort was more efficient than sailing down the coast and stopping occasionally to buy a few captives at a time from locals. By being able to purchase numerous captives all at once from a slave trading post, a slave ship could spend less time on the African coast, thus saving money by expending less for food and lowering the risk of deadly diseases that could decimate African captives and the white crew.

As an island, Isle de Kassa offered several advantages. First, it was known for its excellent fresh water, which was reportedly rare on the African coast, and for having ocean breezes (which kept the mosquitos away).[6] This meant that whites did not have to venture onto the mainland, which was known to harbor poor drinking water and deadly diseases for them. Second, islanders planted vegetables, raised livestock, and acquired fruits, all of which they could sell to visiting ships in need of fresh provisions. Finally, for large sailing ships, the island offered a safe anchorage in deep waters.

As with most British slave trading posts, the one at the Isle de Kassa had only a few Europeans manning it. Many of the grumettas the agents at Isle de Kassa hired likely hailed from nearby villages on the island. The locals on the island, part of a larger tribe on the mainland, profited from the slave trading post's business. They could be expected to help defend the post even though it was a slave trading enterprise.

The Isles de Los had long supplied enslaved people for British slave merchants. In 1754, a reported 1,640 captives were shipped from the Isles de Los on board Liverpool vessels alone.[7] A study of slave trading ports places the Isles de Los fifth among all slave trading ports in Upper Guinea, shipping just over nine percent of the total African captives sent from the region.[8]

The Isles de Los continued to serve as an active slave trading center even after word of the American Revolutionary War got back to the British factors manning the slave trading post at Isle de Kassa. For example, in late summer 1777, the *Charlotte* arrived at St. Domingo in the Caribbean with 255 captives who had embarked on the ship from the Isles de Los. In about February 1776, the *Sally*, out of Lancaster, England, arrived at Grenada with 150 African captives from the Isles de Los.[9]

Babcock might have been aware that in 1776, two British slave ships that had picked up most of their captives at the Isles de Los had been captured by American privateers on their return voyages to Liverpool. Before their captures, the 350-ton slave ship *Isaac* had transported across the Atlantic from the Isles de Los to Tortola more than 360 Africans, and the 250-ton slaver *William* had purchased more than 300 captives at the Isles de Los and dropped off the survivors at Jamaica.[10]

The British slaver *Diana,* from Liverpool and carrying sixteen cannon, had departed the Isles de Los on January 30, 1778. This was the eighth slave trading voyage since 1769 for the ship's commander, James Eckley Colley. It would also be his last. The *Diana* had purchased about three hundred Africans at the Isles de Los, thus depleting the supply of available captives when the *Marlborough* arrived there on February 20. While sailing in the Caribbean, the *Diana* was captured by an American privateer, with 278 enslaved people still on board.[11]

The main slave trading facilities on Isle de Kassa were in the middle of the island, facing the mainland, and were operated by Barber & Co. of Liverpool. The driving force behind this company was Miles Barber of Lancaster and later Liverpool and London. According to a French intelligence report from the mid-1780s, Barber had started his slave trading enterprise after making an agreement with King Tom, the same ruler whom Babcock would soon meet. King Tom, a local chief of the Koya Tenme tribe, allowed Barber to build a slave trading post on the island, granting him a monopoly. Barber soon built a major slave trading post there and began establishing subsidiary operations on the mainland. The report indicated that Barber and King Tom first entered into their agreement in 1754, but it is more likely that the date was later, perhaps around 1763.[12]

Barber must have relied on his agents and slave ship captains for negotiating and interacting with King Tom and other local Africans. There is no evidence Barber ever visited Isle de Kassa or anywhere else in Africa.

European slavers depended on African rulers to provide them with captives to keep the slave trade going, to allow them to establish and maintain their slave trading posts, and for security. King Tom was one of those rulers, and he would serve in such a capacity for decades to come. (British visitors often gave local leaders a royal appellation, and the local leaders sometimes went along with it, as did King Tom in this case.)

African rulers on the coast drove hard bargains with white slave traders. Typically, rent had to be paid for the privilege of using the land on which a slave trading post was built and operated, and a small duty had to be paid on goods imported or exported through the post. In return, the African landlord offered to protect his tenant from attack.[13] Such an arrangement was likely entered into between King Tom and Barber & Co.

Henry Smeathman, an English botanist, visited Sierra Leone in 1773 and crossed paths with King Tom. According to Smeathman, King Tom "by some established right receives a certain duty for every ship trading here" for African captives, and for the ship purchasing "wood and water. I am told he is only a deputy from the real king, who lives higher up in the country [i.e., the interior] or, as some say, [King Tom] is the collector of his customs."[14]

A map published in 1777 based on a survey performed by William Woodville, one of Miles Barber's slave ship captains, indicates that Barber had developed the site on Isle de Kassa into a substantial operation. Barber employed Woodville as a slave ship captain in 1775 on a voyage to the Isles de Los, which is presumably when Woodville prepared his map of the five islands making up the chain.[15] A map of the Isle de Kassa, labeled Factory Island, shows "Mr. Barber's Factory" in the middle of the island, with a collection of what appears to be eight buildings, near "Factory Point" and "the Port" on the east side of the island.[16] Babcock and his men would soon land at the area called the Port, which John Linscom Boss called the harbor. The map also shows at the northern part of the island a collection of houses called King Tom's Town. This was likely where King Tom had one of his main residences.

The Englishman Smeathman visited Barber's slave trading post the day before arriving at Sierra Leone. The traveler described the Isles de Los as "little mountainous islands covered with trees and shrubs" that were "delightfully pleasant" to behold. He wrote about what he saw from his vessel in the bay:

> We found four ships here, two large ships & two snows; the former of which, if not all, belonged to Miles Barber. Esqr., an eminent and enterprising merchant in Liverpool. Besides these there were 4 or 5 sloops & schooners, which are employed in running up the numerous rivers & creeks on the coast, where the large ones cannot or it is not convenient for them to go.[17]

Unfortunately, Smeathman did not step on shore and so did not describe Barber's buildings on land.

In the mid-1780s, a French traveler visited British slave trading posts at Isle de Kassa and other locations in Upper Guinea. He described Barber's slave trading post as a "very fine" establishment set "in the middle of the west coast" of the island.

The French traveler did not describe Barber's facilities in detail, but he did generally describe British slave trading posts such as Barber's as having excellent "magazines, warehouses and docks." The magazines would have held gunpowder and arms. The warehouses would have stored the merchandise, mostly produced in Great Britain, used to trade for enslaved people, food for the workers and captives, and ships' stores. The docks for large ships may not have existed at Barber's slave trading post in 1778, since a dock at the site was not mentioned in Smeathman's journal or in Boss's ship's log and was not marked on Woodville's map.

The French traveler also described British slave trading posts as containing workshops, in which free or enslaved Africans worked as carpenters, brickmakers, sailmakers, ropemakers, blacksmiths, coopers, and other trades.[18] At Bance Island, where a large slave trading fort had been established by London merchants, a 1763 report indicated that thirty-eight grumettas engaged in twelve different occupations.[19] Barber's slave trading post likely had similar operations, if on a smaller scale, in order to sell these services to passing slave ships.

As did other British slave trading posts on the west coast of Africa at the time of the American Revolution, the post at Isle de Kassa likely had other buildings. A barracoon, or pens or a house for holding the captives, and a house used for sick captives were likely present.[20] Living quarters for the grumettas and their families would have existed. One or a few comfortable houses for the white slave trading post managers would have been constructed as well.

A French intelligence report, undated but probably from around 1784, provides a detailed description of Miles Barber's "considerable" factory he had built at Isle de Kassa. The report said the facilities included two slave pens; a wharf for loading and unloading ships; a house for the European agents; a warehouse storing merchandise, another storing wines, and a third storing gunpowder; a building for the manufacture of ropes (cordage for rigging ships); a workshop for carpenters and another for blacksmiths; a large ship anchored in the bay; and a brig and a large number of shallops used for trading for captives in the various nearby rivers on the mainland. The report added that rice and other crops were grown on some plots, and livestock and poultry were raised, all of which were sold to passing ships.

According to the report, "The slave trade is done by the grumettas, who are trustworthy and intelligent slaves belonging to" Barber. The grumettas then numbered, according to the report, 450 to 500. The report continued that the grumettas "penetrate up the rivers and into the interior" to places difficult to access, all to find more captives to purchase. The report named eleven locations where Barber had floating factories and other posts on the mainland and other islands.[21]

In March 1778, Barber's facilities were probably similar to those described in the 1784 intelligence report, but on a smaller scale and without a wharf. In addition, Barber likely had fewer grumettas and locations outside Isle de Kassa in 1778 than he had in 1784. Still, his operations when Babcock and his men saw them were substantial.

It is likely there was another item at the slave trading post at Isle de Kassa not mentioned by the French observers: shackles and other iron restraints. A white manager at the Bance Island slave trading post in 1751 ordered one hundred shackles, one hundred handcuffs, one thousand fastening devices called forelocks, and six strong chains.[22] A grumetta blacksmith was retained to repair these items as needed. The slave trading post at Isle de Kassa probably had a similar setup.

Between 1763 and 1775, Barber invested and coinvested with other slave merchants in vessels that debarked from the Isles de Los with some 5,900 African captives on board bound for North America.[23]

Babcock and his crew sailed toward Isle de Kassa with great anticipation. Now, after all their preparations and sailing thousands of miles, they were within reach of attacking, sacking, and plundering a major British slave trading post, whose warehouses surely must be filled with all sorts of merchandise. If they could seize some enslaved Africans held for trade, all the better, in their minds.

At eight-thirty a.m. on February 20, on what would be a fine and clear day, the *Marlborough*'s lookouts spotted the Isles de Los about five leagues away. At ten a.m., the American ship's crew heard several cannon shots. The cannon was likely fired by the British agents as a warning to other vessels in the area that an enemy ship could be approaching. Babcock decided to take all his sailors off the prize schooners *Sally* and *Fort Rose*, except for a skeleton crew of two men each.[24] He wanted as many able-bodied sailors as possible on board the *Marlborough* in the event a battle was in the offing.

Babcock headed for the harbor at Isle de Kassa, on the island's east side, facing the African coast.[25] Just before his arrival, a small sailboat was spotted to the southeast. Babcock issued orders to chase the small boat. The potential prize sailed toward the *Marlborough*, probably not suspecting it was a privateer. The oncoming vessel turned out to be a small sloop of about five tons operated by free African sailors (Boss did not say how many in his log). It may have been supplying visiting slave ships with food and other articles. In any event, Babcock ordered the Africans stowed on board the *Marlborough*; he would determine their fates later. His crew also seized from the sloop a small amount of cloth, tobacco, and guns. This vessel may not have been British, but Babcock took it and its goods as a prize anyway, probably based on his suspicion that the vessel was supporting the British slave trade at Isle de Kassa. Babcock ordered one of his men, named Cleveland (possibly a ship's mate), and one other crewman to sail the small new prize, which could be useful operating in shallow water.

At three p.m., the *Marlborough* entered the harbor at Isle de Kassa. The New Englanders scanned the horizon for potential prizes. In the harbor was the French ship the *Seine*, a sloop also flying French colors, a schooner flying no colors, and several shallops and other small vessels also flying no colors. The presence of the French ship indicated that the proprietors of the slave trading post at Isle de Kassa had no qualms about trading with the French.

Then crewmen on the *Marlborough* saw in the distance a barge heading toward them flying the Union Jack. But as soon as the men in the barge saw the *Marlborough*'s Continental colors, the barge turned around and headed back to its post. Babcock fired several cannon at the barge, but the cannonballs splashed harmlessly in the water.[26]

Babcock ordered the crew to bring the *Marlborough* to within a quarter mile of the village at the harbor and drop anchor. No doubt Babcock was nervous about his ship running aground on a sandbar. Meanwhile, the schooner *Fort Rose* sailed close to the land near the village and came under fire from a cannon and small arms. The battle over the slave trading post at Isle de Kassa had begun.

While the opposing sides were blazing away at each other, one of Babcock's prize masters, S. Kelley (his first name is not known), with a small party of armed men, used the ship's barge to seize a nearby shallop at anchor and claim it as a prize. More shallops were seized. Boss later stated that six African captives were taken from these "first shallops."[27]

Babcock determined that the village was operated by British agents running a slave trading enterprise so that it was an appropriate target. Therefore, at five p.m., he ordered his gunners to open fire. For about one hour, the *Marlborough*'s broadsides of about ten cannon pummeled the village, likely forcing most African villagers—men, women, and children—and others at the slave trading post to run to the tree line for cover.

Babcock figured that the ship's cannon had suppressed some of the fighters on the shore. He ordered Ichabod Holloway to take six men in the ship's barge to capture a schooner that was spotted near the land. Boss accompanied Holloway. While still under sporadic fire from the shore, Holloway, Boss, and the other five armed sailors boarded the schooner ready for action, but they met no resistance.

At seven p.m., Holloway and his small party, sailing their barge and the newly captured schooner, arrived back at the *Marlborough*'s side. The vessel proved to be the *Betsey*, a "rich prize," according to Boss, with a large quantity of various dry goods, including tobacco.[28] The seized goods were likely intended to be exchanged for African captives. Boss did not report finding any captives on board.

An hour later, Babcock organized an amphibious force to invade the island. He ordered fifty men to arm themselves and take the two captured schooners and the barge to the shore under Captain Christopher Brown, commander of the marines.

Tensions rose as Brown and his three boats approached the beach, the Americans fearing they would meet resistance from British factors and their local African allies. They need not have worried. After the boats ran aground on the sand, the armed men jumped into the shallow water and ran ashore unmolested.

Babcock's decision to send a substantial body of his men ashore was a courageous one—for an unexpected reason. Babcock and other ship captains off the coast of Africa knew that the land was a place for whites to catch deadly diseases from sources they did not understand. Royal Navy officials, for example, instructed ship commanders headed for the African coast "for the preservation of the health" of the ship's officers and sailors not to permit their men to "lie on shore" or to "do any work on shore which the Natives can be hired to do for a small expense."[29] Time would tell if Babcock's decision would have fatal consequences.

Meanwhile, Captain Brown marched his men up to the buildings bordering the shore and placed sentinels at key locations. With darkness coming and the village not entirely secured, Babcock decided to wait until morning to raid the British warehouses.

During the night, a few of the local villagers took potshots with their muskets at Brown's men from the nearby woods and other houses. These villagers likely worked as intermediaries at the British slave trading post, helping to transport captives to and from slave ships anchored offshore and guarding captives held in confinement. Some of them may also have been employed as craftsmen.

Intermittent firing rang out through the night. Boss explained in his journal that Brown's sentinels, when they heard or saw "skulkers" in the dark, called out to them, and if they did not respond, shot at them "as foes." Babcock's men patrolling the coastline on the two schooners also shot at locals onshore (which must not have been very accurate). Boss, in his ship's

The *Blandford Frigate* by Nicholas Pocock, 1760. A ship called the *Blandford*, from London and bound for Jamaica, carried more than 400 African captives in the Middle Passage in 1744. (*Bristol City Museums*)

Advertisement from a Charleston, South Carolina, newspaper announcing the arrival of the British slave ship *Bance Island* in 1760. British slave ships brought most of the enslaved Africans to what would become the United States. The Laurens referred to is Henry Laurens, who likely imported more African captives in colonial times than any other American. He later became President of the Continental Congress. (*New York Public Library*)

Drawing of Esek Hopkins as commander-in-chief of the Continental Navy, 1776. In 1763-64, Hopkins commanded a slave trading ship from Rhode Island owned by the Brown brothers that turned into one of the deadliest slave voyages in colonial times. (*New York Public Library*)

John Brown, merchant from Providence, Rhode Island. Watercolor on ivory, by Edward Green-bone, 1794. (*New-York Historical Society*)

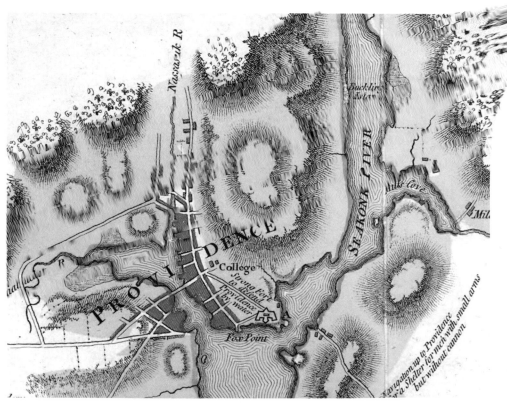

Detail of map showing Providence, Rhode Island. The wharves John Brown would have used were located on the waterfront south and east of the bridge spanning the Providence River. From "A Top-ographical Map of Narragansett Bay," by Charles Blaskowitz, London, 1777. (*Library of Congress*)

The *Blandford Frigate* by Nicholas Pocock, 1760. A ship called the *Blandford*, from London and bound for Jamaica, carried more than 400 African captives in the Middle Passage in 1744. (*Bristol City Museums*)

Advertisement from a Charleston, South Carolina, newspaper announcing the arrival of the British slave ship *Bance Island* in 1760. British slave ships brought most of the enslaved Africans to what would become the United States. The Laurens referred to is Henry Laurens, who likely imported more African captives in colonial times than any other American. He later became President of the Continental Congress. (*New York Public Library*)

Drawing of Esek Hopkins as commander-in-chief of the Continental Navy, 1776. In 1763-64, Hopkins commanded a slave trading ship from Rhode Island owned by the Brown brothers that turned into one of the deadliest slave voyages in colonial times. (*New York Public Library*)

John Brown, merchant from Providence, Rhode Island. Watercolor on ivory, by Edward Greene Malbone, 1794. (*New-York Historical Society*)

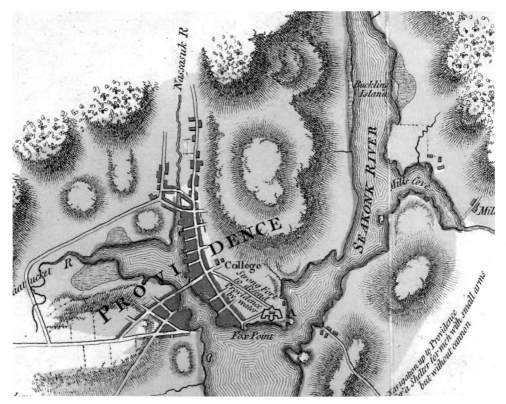

Detail of map showing Providence, Rhode Island. The wharves John Brown would have used were located on the waterfront south and east of the bridge spanning the Providence River. From "A Topographical Map of Narragansett Bay," by Charles Blaskowitz, London, 1777. (*Library of Congress*)

The 12-gun privateer brig *Independence*, on the left and commanded by Thomas Truxton, captures a larger and better armed British merchant ship sailing from the Caribbean, in 1777. Watercolor by Irwin Bevan (1852-1940). (*Naval History and Heritage Command*)

The *Blandford Frigate*, by Nicholas Pocock, 1760. In the top drawing, a British officer, the frigate's captain, purchases enslaved and manacled men, in exchange for guns and other trade goods, from a group of African traders. At the bottom, the *Blandford* sails in the Middle Passage with a Caribbean Island in sight. (*Bristol City Museums*)

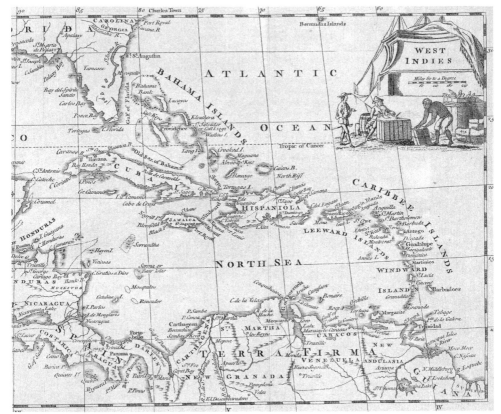

British island possessions in the Caribbean shown include Barbados (in the Windward Islands, lower right), Antigua (in the Leeward Islands, north of the Windward Islands), and Jamaica (in the center south of Cuba). French island possessions shown include Martinique (also called Martinico), St. Lucia (the northernmost of the Windward Islands) and Guadeloupe (one of the Leeward Islands). In 1777 and the first half of 1778, British slave ships bound for a British colonial island possession were often captured by American privateers and brought to a French colonial island possession and sold there (along with the human cargo). London, circa 1770. (*John Carter Brown Library, Brown University*)

John Paul Jones, shown here as a captain in the Continental navy, began his sailing career as a junior officer on board two British slave trading ships. During the American Revolutionary War, he recommend that he be authorized to raid British slave trading interests on the west coast of Africa. (*U.S. Senate*)

Outstanding model of the Pennsylvania privateer *Oliver Cromwell*, which was captured by the Royal Navy in 1777 and renamed *Beaver's Prize*. This vessel was nearly the same size as the *Marlborough* and both vessels may have been designed and built by the same American shipbuilders. (*Copyright Peter Tamm Sen. Foundation/Internationales Maritimes Museum, Hamburg*)

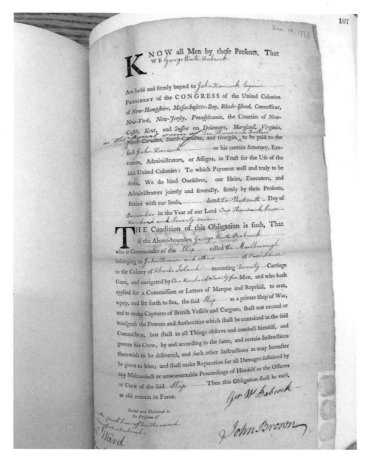

The privateer commission for the brig *Marlborough*, signed by John Brown and George Waite Babcock, December 13, 1777. The form of the commission was provided by the Continental Congress and submitted to Rhode Island admiralty officials in Providence. (*Rhode Island State Archives*)

Black privateersmen enlisted to serve on many American privateers, but there is no evidence one sailed on the *Marlborough*. While the painting is original to the American Revolution, art experts later determined that the black skin was painted on in modern times, probably in the early 1970s. (*Christian McBurney*)

British warships in the Middle Channel in Narragansett Bay, having dispatched small boats filled with solders ready to land on shore and occupy Newport and the rest of Aquidneck Island. *The Attack on Rhode Island, December 8th, 1776*, a watercolor by Irvan Bevan (1852-1940). (*Mariners' Museum*)

Africans traded with passing European and American ships selling them water, food, and enslaved people. African traders used canoes, including large ones, to make contact with the sailing ships. In this drawing, African canoemen and traders battle the surf in West Africa, with what could be a slave ship lurking in the background. (*Wilhelm Sievers*, Afrika, Eine Allgemeine Landeskunde, *Leipzieg, 1891*)

African canoemen transporting enslaved Africans to slave ships at anchor in the bay at what is now Elmina, Ghana. (*Anshawm Churchill*, Collection of Voyages and Travels, *vol. 5, London, 1732*)

A scene in an African village from an eighteenth century drawing. Detail from *A Prospect of Bense* [Bance] *Island and Fort, from William Smith*, London, 1745. (*Houghton Library, Harvard University*)

Excerpt from the *Marlborough*'s log kept by John Linscom Boss, showing one of only two drawings in the log. This drawing shows the scene Boss viewed upon arriving at the harbor at Isle de Gorée. On the left side he wrote "Gorea Fort," with an image of the French fort sitting high on top of cliffs, and on the right side he wrote, "the French snow in the Bay." (*Morristown National Historical Park*)

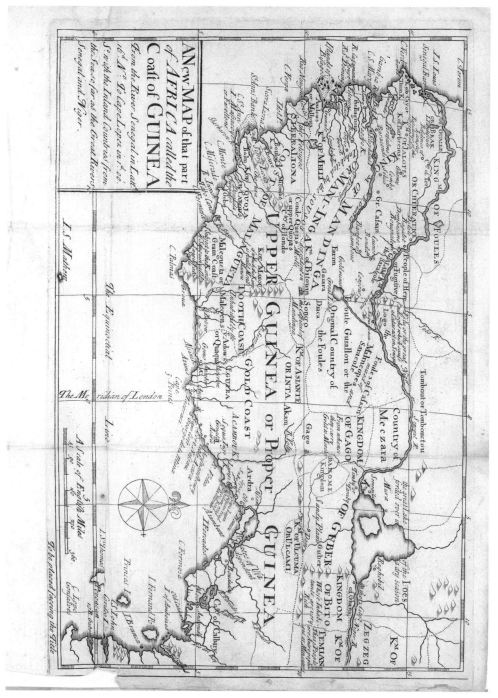

"A New Map of that part of Africa called the Coast of Guinea." London, J. Wren publisher, 1754. A map of western Africa showing the coast from present-day Guinea-Bissau to Gabon, indicating the locations of tribes, kingdoms, settlements, and rivers. On the coast, in the upper left is written "I.S. Louis" for St.-Louis Island, and in the center is "Idol Is." for Isles de Los. (*John Carter Brown Library, Brown University*)

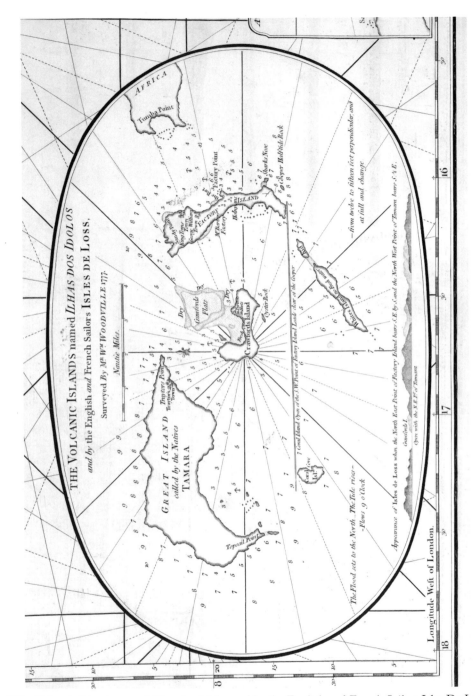

"The Volcanic Islands named Ilhas dos Idolos and by the Englich and French Sailors Isles De Loss, Surveyed by Mr. Wm. Woodville 1777." Factory Island is on the right side, facing Trumbo Point in the African mainland. The hills of Factory Island are shown at the bottom, from the viewpoint of a sailor. Woodville, the map maker, captained a slave ship owned by Miles Barber that visited Isles de Los in 1775 and he commanded another slave ship that was captured by an American privateer in 1777. From the *African Pilot*, circa. 1794-1804. (*Library of Congress*)

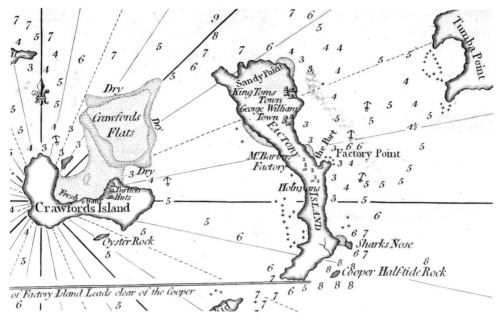

Detail from the Woodville map, showing Factory Island (Isle de Kassa). Factory Point and "Mr. Barber's Factory," with buildings shown, are in the middle of the island. King Tom's Town is at the north of the island. (*Library of Congress*)

View of Factory Point on Factory Island (Isle de Kassa), showing the slave trading facilities first developed by Miles Barber and Company. At the time of the watercolor, done in 1793, the factory was owned by John and Thomas Hodgson, slave merchants from Liverpool. The British slaver *Sandown* is shown, as well as boats manned by Africans. (*Sandown Ship's Log, National Maritime Museum*)

Most enslaved Africans transported to North America were captured in wars or military raids. This watercolor from a British slave ship log of 1793-1794 shows members of the Fulani, a primarily Muslim people, guiding a coffle of captive Africans, likely prisoners captured in battle or on raids, to the coast at Sierra Leone to trade with European slave traders. Fulani warriors carry spears and bow and arrows, while the captives are secured. (*Sandown's Ship's Log, National Maritime Museum*)

An African slave trading scene. The number 5 is the location of the slave ship. The number 6 is where a small boat is being rowed by hired grumettas, taking African captives to the slave ship. On shore, next to number 7, family and friends lament the loss of a loved one. The drawing is by the Frenchman M. Chambeau and was published in Amsterdam and Marseille in 1783. (*John Carter Brown Library, Brown University*)

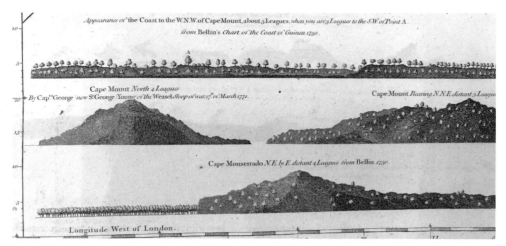

Another map from the *African Pilot*, this one showing the outlines and heights of hills at Cape Mount and Cape Mesurado that ship captains used to identify their locations. The *Marlborough* made two significant captures of British slave ships, one at Cape Mount and the other near Cape Mesurado. (*Library of Congress*)

Shackles used to secure enslaved captives. These are similar to ones the author has seen that were described as leg shackles and were recovered from the shipwreck of a British slave ship. (*Smithsonian National Museum of African American History and Culture*)

Receipt, signed by George W. Babcock, confirming that John Anderson, the physician aboard the *Fancy* on its voyage from Africa to North America, received a fee for his services in the form of "three Prime Slaves." (*Redwood Library & Athenaeum*)

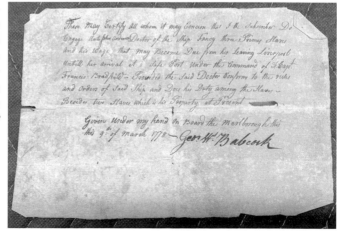

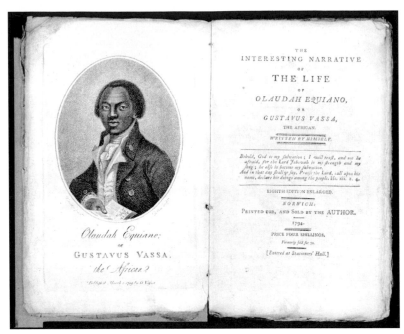

Portrait of Olaudah Equiano, or Gustavus Vassa, opposite the title page of his autobiography, London, 1794. Equiano holds a copy of the Bible open to the book of Acts. According to his autobiography, Equiano was born in what is present-day Nigeria and was sold into slavery in childhood. His book contains one of the few descriptions of the horrors of the Middle Passage. He later earned his freedom and became a leader in the British antislavery movement. (*Library of Congress*)

George W. Babcock purchased this house, left, at 1515 South Road in East Greenwich on August 11, 1778, and moved his family there. His share of the profits from the *Marlborough*'s African voyage likely made this purchase possible. It is now known as the Silas Jones House, after its first owner, who built it in 1762. Babcock sold the house in March 1782. (*Bruce MacGunnigle*) Right, the home of Samuel Phillips, at 34 Pleasant Street in Wickford, Rhode Island, with a view of Narragansett Bay. He built the impressive house in 1773. Phillips served on the privateer *General Mifflin* under Captain Babcock's command as a second lieutenant in 1779 and first lieutenant in 1781. On his five privateering voyages, he was captured and imprisoned in dank jails three times. The house is named the Major Samuel Philips [*sic*] Jr. house, in recognition of Phillips's service as a major in a Rhode Island state regiment in 1778. (*Christian McBurney*)

Captain George W. Babcock's orders to Francis Bradfield, commander of the prize *Fancy*, written on board the *Marlborough* at Cape Montserrado, March 7, 1778. With a list of the officers and crew to sail the ship *Fancy*, with 310 enslaved Africans on board, to North America. (*Cornell University Library*)

Newspaper advertisement, dated January 1, 1777, announcing the planned sale of the prize British ship *Lydia*, captured by the Baltimore privateer *Harlequin*, commanded by James Handy, in Baltimore. (*Naval History and Heritage Command*)

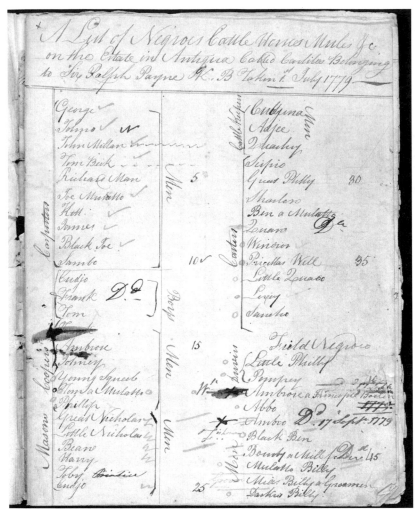

"A List of Negroes, Cattle, Horses, Mules, etc. on the Estate in Antigua Called Carlisle Belonging to Sir Ralph Payne, K. B. Taken 1st July 1779." A total of 452 enslaved men, women, and children are listed by their first names. (*Beinecke Rare Book and Manuscript Library, Yale University*)

Detail from *A Prospect of Bense* [Bance] *Island and Fort*, London, 1745. Bance Island was the largest private British slave trading post on the Upper Guinea coast, exceeding even Miles Barber's operations at Factory Island. (*Houghton Library, Harvard University*)

log, described the New Englanders as keeping up "a constant fire." By the morning, two villagers—one African man and one French boy—lay dead from musket balls. Several other villagers were wounded.[30] None of Babcock's crew were harmed.

With the situation secure, at four a.m. on February 21, sailors on the *Marlborough* used a rope and its anchor to pull their ship closer to the village, stopping when the ship settled to within "pistol shot" range of the shore. That done, at seven a.m., Babcock ordered his men to be ready for the *Marlborough* to receive the merchandise from the British warehouses.

Back on shore, Captain Brown ordered his men to break into the warehouses in search of trade goods—the spoils of victory. They found an amazing quantity of merchandise stuffed into several wooden warehouses.

What must have caught Brown's attention initially were stacks of cases of gin. Gin was commonly used for gifts to African leaders, but given the large amount held in storage, gin must have been the British merchant company's trade good of choice for acquiring captives. With Rhode Island slave ship captains no longer appearing in Senegambia with rum to trade, it may have been that the British slave traders thought they could fill the alcohol gap with gin. The gin could have been made in Britain, but Dutch gin was also popular then.

With perspiration dripping down their faces because of the high heat and humidity, Brown's men began to carry the cases of gin, ivory tusks, camwood, and a variety of dry goods, as well as chests of arms and gunpowder stored in the warehouses, to shallops and other small boats seized nearby. The smaller vessels were used to transport the goods to the nearby and waiting Rhode Island privateer. When the small boats arrived alongside the *Marlborough*, sailors aboard the ship lifted the cargo onto it. Crew members then took care to stow the cargo belowdecks in the main hold.

Despite the steady work of the privateersmen, the British warehouses still bulged with trade goods. Brown realized that moving the booty to the *Marlborough* was a huge task that would take his men days to complete.

Inside one of the buildings, Brown's men found a single captive African. He was presumably chained and left behind by the quickly departing British slave traders. Brown seized the enslaved man and sent him on board the *Marlborough* under a guard.[31] The slave traders may have had time to march any other enslaved people held at the post to the north, beyond Babcock's grasp. Boss does not include in his description of this raid any references to barracoons or other pens where imprisoned Africans were held until sold to a passing slave ship, but they must have been present.

At eleven a.m., with the temperature increasing, a man appearing to be a local chief approached the *Marlborough* in a small boat. After the man signaled his peaceful intentions, he was allowed on board. He introduced himself as King Tom. As previously mentioned, he was the well-known figure who had worked with Miles Barber and his slave traders at Isle de Kassa, as well as with many European and American ship captains, for decades. Seeing that Babcock, with his armed ships and numerous armed crewmen, held the upper hand, King Tom came to negotiate. He must have figured that he might be able to avoid the entire village next to Barber's slave trading post being put to the torch if he cooperated with these newly arrived white men. He further must have determined that if his men helped the newcomers, the quicker the Americans would depart. He was also open to any schemes that could increase his wealth.

King Tom offered to have some of his men assist Babcock's sailors in carrying the captured British goods to the *Marlborough*. Babcock agreed, and King Tom went ashore to order some villagers to help transport the merchandise.[32]

Babcock and King Tom met again onshore in what locals called a palaver—an unhurried negotiation. First, Babcock negotiated for King Tom's men to find fresh water and fill casks for his ships. The African leader, always interested in making money dealing with Europeans or Americans, consented. Babcock handed King Tom a letter for him to have delivered to the white men who operated the British slave trading post. These men had retreated to a larger village on the Isle de Kassa, probably King Tom's Town. In his letter, Babcock offered the British agents a deal. If they would "surrender all English property in their hands," he would "treat them with honor" and not destroy their vessels, warehouses, and other buildings. If, however, they did not abide by his demands, Babcock would "burn, sink and destroy" all of the slave outfit's vessels and buildings.[33] The palaver then ended.

By his demands, Babcock indicated he was more interested in taking as much of the slave trading post's trade goods as possible on his ship for the voyage back to America than in destroying and burning the vessels, warehouses, and other buildings of the slaving enterprise. This was one of those instances where the private interest from profiteering superseded the national interest that a Continental navy ship might adhere to.

Returning to his flagship, Babcock had two unexpected visitors: Thomas Hereford and Stephen Hammond, white men who claimed they originally hailed from Rhode Island. They described themselves as "traders," meaning slave traders. They pleaded with Babcock not to burn or destroy their houses and personal property. Babcock "assured them" that he would spare their property. If the claim that they were Rhode Islanders was true, they must have made their living selling captives to British slave trading posts on the Isles de Los and to British slave ship captains. Babcock must have suspected that Hereford and Hammond had violated the Continental Congress's ban on Americans participating in the British slave trade. In fact, Hereford had entered into two joint ventures with Liverpool merchants, dispatching two slave trading ships from the Isles de Los filled with African captives in 1773 and 1775. Because Babcock kept his promise and did not destroy his facilities, Hereford entered into another joint venture with Liverpool merchants that resulted in more Africans being carried on a British slaver from the Isles de Los to the British Caribbean in 1779.[34] In this instance, by dealing with British merchants, Hereford clearly violated the ban on trading with the enemy.

Another American voluntarily visited Babcock. He was a white man named Paul Cross, and he apparently hailed from South Carolina.[35] In his journal, Boss described Cross as a "freeborn American."[36] Cross was an established slave trader in Senegambia who resided at Cape Mesurado. He was a private trader who acquired African captives from the coast or up the rivers and sold them to passing slave ships, mostly British ones from Liverpool. He would also sell to British slave trading posts and forts. Cross had substantial slave trading operations. He traded at Cape Mount, the Gallinas River, the Sestos River, and the Isles de Los. According to one report, by 1773, Cross had fifty or sixty grumettas (many enslaved) working for him along the West African coast.[37]

Cross's presence at the Isles de Los suggests that he was at or on his way to Isle de Kassa to engage in business with Miles Barber's slave trading post. Alternatively, Cross could have intended to meet with Hammond and Hereford, with whom he occasionally did business.[38]

Despite his deep connections to British slave trading interests, Cross offered his services to Babcock as a pilot. Given Cross's intimate knowledge of the coastal region in Senegambia, Babcock accepted the offer. Babcock and his crew were fortunate to have Cross's assistance.

As Babcock's men continued to load their privateer with goods, in the distance, a small shallop appeared sailing for Isle de Kassa. Babcock issued orders for Captain Kelley (who was referred to as captain, probably since he had previously commanded merchant vessels) in the prize *Sally* to capture the shallop. As Kelley approached the shallop, its small crew abandoned the vessel. Kelley took what he could from the shallop, including six valuable "elephant's teeth" (ivory tusks) and the vessel's sails, and returned to the privateer.[39] It is not clear whether Kelley's seizure complied with the Continental Congress's commission to seize only enemy property. Kelley and Babcock likely again took the position that the goods were either British property or intended to be traded to the British slave traders at Isle de Kassa and could therefore be lawfully seized.

Meanwhile, King Tom returned on board the *Marlborough*. His men, used to working with Europeans and American slavers, accompanied King Tom to take away empty water casks. King Tom informed Babcock of news that the British agents had rejected Babcock's demand and that they had departed the island for the mainland. The news must have disappointed Babcock. Still, perhaps he respected the agents for not cooperating with the enemy (unlike Captains Moore and Roberts). In turn, Babcock requested King Tom to keep villagers away from the warehouses and not to plunder them, as they risked Captain Brown's sentinels shooting them.[40]

While King Tom frequently served as an intermediary to British slave traders and Royal Navy commanders who patrolled the West African coast, he sometimes found them irksome. Historian Randy Sparks tells the following story of King Tom:

> The captain of a Liverpool ship trading to Sierra Leone obtained a girl from King Tom, the ruler of the country, "to use as a mistress for the time being." He was to return her before he sailed, as was "usually done," but instead he "took her away with him." When George Young [a future Royal Navy admiral] arrived there a short time later on a navy vessel, "the king . . . complained . . . to me very heavily, and begged me to apply to his brother George (meaning our king) to get her restored to him." The records do not reveal whether or not she returned.[41]

A major theme of Sparks's book on slave trading is that local African leaders who worked with British slave traders and facilitated the slave trade were independent actors who were not pawns of the British.[42] That was certainly the case with King Tom. He did not have any special loyalty to British traders. He acted out of self-interest, and he had local tribesmen to support him. He likely figured that the British slave trading post would not be restored anytime soon, and that he might as well earn some profits by dealing with the American privateersmen who for the moment held sway with their large ship and powerful cannons.

Babcock, and his officers and men, were not used to seeing Black men in leadership positions. But the Americans were in Africa now, where Africans dominated.

The next day, February 22, was another hot one. The work of carrying, transporting, loading, and stowing continued.

Babcock realized he was running out of room aboard the *Marlborough*, so he decided to use the prize schooner *Betsey* as well. Ichabod Holloway soon had his sailors working with the schooner's sails and otherwise fitting it out for a cruise across the Atlantic Ocean. In a promising development for Babcock, King Tom's men returned the casks filled with fresh water, which was crucial to the health of Babcock's sailors on their long voyage home.[43]

February 23 was more of the same for Babcock's officers and sailors, but it was a red letter day for Captain William Moore. In return for providing Babcock with useful intelligence about British ships in the area and the exposed British slave trading post at Isle de Kassa, and helping to pilot the *Marlborough* safely to the island, Babcock kept his promise and returned the schooner *Sally* to Moore. Given that Babcock was desperate for another vessel to take on board more plunder, the decision may have given the Rhode Island captain some pause. But perhaps he considered the vessel too small for a transatlantic voyage. He also returned to Moore his crew—eleven grumettas—but retained as captives the three enslaved people taken from Moore's vessel.[44]

Babcock's decision to give the *Sally* back to Moore facilitated Moore's future slave trading business. It also establishes that the Rhode Island captain was a man of his word and was more interested in profiting from plundering the British than in trying to limit the African slave trade.

It is not known if Moore later faced reprisals from British authorities or British slave traders (including those at Isle de Kassa) for cooperating with the Americans. Given America was at war with the Crown, Moore's conduct amounted to treason. But in West Africa at this time, white slave traders typically were obsessed with making money and were not overly concerned with national allegiances.

By eight a.m. on February 24, the *Marlborough* was so full of goods and captives that it could take nothing more on board. This frustrated Babcock, who from the top deck of his vessel, could see more goods to load sitting on the beach, with some of his men guarding them. Babcock signaled for Salomon Prevoit, the commander of the French ship *Seine*, to visit him on shore. Up to now, Prevoit had remained in the harbor and simply watched the proceedings.

When the Frenchman arrived, Babcock asked if he could purchase a sloop from him. As a citizen of a neutral power not at war with Britain, Prevoit had not participated in the plundering of British property. He probably wanted to avoid being seen as assisting Babcock in any way. If his conduct was used as part of an excuse for Britain to declare war on France, Prevoit would face serious repercussions back in France. In addition, Prevoit was likely in the harbor at Isle de Kassa to trade with the British for African captives. Miles Barber traded with French slave traders, even when British law discouraged it. Prevoit must have figured that the British agents would eventually return after the Americans left. The French commander declined to sell Babcock his sloop.

The disappointed Babcock loaded as much as he could on a captured shallop and on the *Betsey*. With the *Marlborough* stuffed to the brim with valuable goods, Babcock ordered all of the ship's cannon to be loaded and primed.[45]

At four p.m., while Babcock was onshore inspecting operations, lookouts on the *Marlborough* spotted a brig in the distance. Lieutenant Eldred, informed of the promising development, called loudly to get Babcock's attention and signaled for him to return to his vessel. In short order, Babcock was back on the *Marlborough*'s quarterdeck and issued orders to his crew to prepare for sailing. The ship in the distance could be the solution to his shortage of vessels, and it also could be a valuable prize in its own right. Before departing, he ordered Holloway, commanding the *Betsey*, and John Bissell, commanding the *Fort Rose*, to remain behind and make sure the villagers did not plunder the remaining merchandise and their small craft still onshore. As Babcock prepared to chase the unknown brig, he had to order the cable line to his anchor cut, as the anchor "was fast in a rock at the bottom." But with darkness approaching, Babcock postponed sailing until morning.[46]

At six a.m. the next day, February 25, the *Marlborough* got underway. Finally, after seven hours of sailing, the unidentified brig was spotted to the north. After a favorable shift in the wind, Babcock became confident he could capture "the chase," as a targeted vessel was called. The speedy Rhode Island ship, even with a full load of cargo on board, began to reduce the distance between the two vessels.

As the *Marlborough* closed with the chase, Babcock saw it was a brigantine armed with eight cannon and four cohorns. He ordered all of his men to battle stations. At four p.m., the *Marlborough* sailed up alongside its prey. This was the key moment. According to Boss, Babcock used his speaking trumpet and "hailed her and ordered her to strike, which they [the opposing crew] did without a gun being fired on either side."

Babcock sent Eldred over in the ship's barge, along with his second lieu-
tenant, Francis Bradfield, and several other sailors to serve as a prize crew.
The two officers sent back to the *Marlborough* the brigantine's captain, Peter
Whitfield Brancker from Liverpool, and some of his crew, as prisoners.[47]

Brancker's brigantine, named *Pearl*, proved to be a rich prize. It held in
its holds 102 tons of camwood, 6 ivory tusks weighing 700 pounds, 80
pounds of gum, and an astounding 30 tons of rice.[48] Built in Liverpool in
1763, the *Pearl* had been extensively repaired with ten guns added in 1776.
The 236-ton vessel by itself was a nice prize for the New Englanders.[49]

The *Pearl* had departed Liverpool for Africa on May 19, 1777.[50] On the
first leg of the voyage, Brancker had successfully fended off an American
privateer. A London newspaper reported in its January 14, 1778, edition,
"The *Pearl*, Brancker, from Liverpool, is safe arrived on the coast of Africa,
after beating off an American privateer of 12 guns."[51] The privateer mentioned could have been the *Alligator*, which would later be overwhelmed
by an uprising of its prisoners.[52]

There were several indications that the *Pearl* was not on a slave trading
voyage. First, no enslaved people were reported being on board it. Instead,
Brancker had traded for the African goods found on his vessel. Thus, on
this voyage at least, he was not interested in trading for African captives.
Moreover, Brancker's crew was just ten men, including himself.[53] The small
size of the crew is another indication that the *Pearl* was not as slaver—a
slave crew would have been more than double the size. Given the risk from
American privateers of sailing a British slave ship in Caribbean waters in
1777, Brancker must have made the decision that he would send a ship to
trade with African merchants, but not for captives.

With mainly African-sourced goods on board, and given the length of
time his brigantine had already spent in Africa, Brancker was likely only days
away from sailing back to Liverpool before his ship was captured.

While Brancker was not on a slave trading voyage on this occasion, he
must have been enticed by what he found in Africa in late 1777 and early
1778. From 1779 to 1783, during the Revolutionary War, he commanded
three slave ships sailing out of Liverpool that disembarked African captives
at Jamaica. From 1784 to 1791, he commanded four more such voyages.[54]
After his sailing days ended, Brancker became a slave merchant and later
an active defender of the African slave trade. In 1798, the Liverpool council
presented him with a small gift valued at 100 guineas in gratitude for his
work in Parliament opposing a bill that would have abolished the slave
trade. In the same year, he invested in a slave ship that carried 296 captive

Africans from Whydah. He became mayor of Liverpool in 1801, and in 1807 was on a list of the "Company of Merchants Trading to Africa."[55]

Babcock issued orders for the *Marlborough* and *Pearl* to return to Isle de Kassa. In a short time, by seven p.m., the two ships were at anchor in the island's harbor. The remaining captive crew members of the *Pearl* were brought to the *Marlborough*, where they were secured belowdecks, with extra guards posted by Captain Brown.[56]

The next morning, February 26, Babcock issued orders to begin preparations to depart the Isles de Los. Ten sailors were sent ashore to cut wood, which would be needed for fuel to keep the men warm on the trip back to chilly New England. Master J. Peters found two anchors at the slave trading post that he brought on board the *Marlborough*; one replaced the anchor that was lost, and the other was held as a spare. Food was sent to the *Pearl*'s prize crew: two casks of beef, two casks of bread, and six "gugs" of gin, as well as casks of fresh water.

Babcock also decided to transfer as much of the dry goods as possible from the *Pearl* to the *Marlborough*. He must have determined that while his ship was already crammed with cargo, he did not want to risk losing any valuable goods. The lightly armed and manned, and slower, *Pearl* stood a better chance of being captured by British warships than the speedier, well-armed, and decently manned *Marlborough*.

Babcock set February 28 as the day of departure. At eight a.m. February 27, he released his free prisoners: all the white crewmen aboard the captured vessels and all the free African sailors. He had them put in two shallops, loaded with one cask of beef and one of bread, and sent them ashore. Babcock could have held on to the white sailors in order to try to exchange them for American sailors rotting in British prisons, but he must have decided he did not want to have his food and water resources reduced by them and worry about security aboard his vessel.

In addition, Babcock released Richard Roberts, the former captain of the *Fort Rose*, and gave him a prize schooner. The former prize *Sally*, commanded by the recently freed William Moore, escorted Roberts and his new schooner up a nearby river. Roberts received the favorable treatment because, according to Boss, he "gave us intelligence concerning the factor at the Isles de Los." Unlike Captain Moore, however, Captain Roberts did not get back his vessel.[57] Babcock also kept on board the *Marlborough* the three enslaved Africans he had captured from Roberts.

Babcock was harsh with the British slave traders at Isle de Kassa, who had abandoned the village and failed to cooperate with him in exchange for his preserving their property. Babcock decided to burn all of the slave trading post's buildings, as well as the town's stores, as it was all "English property." However, there was no mention of torching all the huts and other residences of the village as well. At nine a.m., Babcock sent Captain Brown with fifteen "well-armed" men ashore to cut more wood, set fire to the wood, and begin burning the designated property. In an hour, according to Boss, the town stores and "the buildings were all in flames." Boss thought the British factors would "lament their misconduct in not saving the town by surrendering the town and all English property in their hands when the captain wrote them a very entreating letter."[58]

The destruction of the slave trading post at Isle de Kassa was the outstanding act of the *Marlborough*'s voyage to Africa. A common sailor from Martha's Vineyard, Silas Daggett, in his Revolutionary War pension application submitted in 1818, recalled his service on board "the ship *Marlborough*" under Captain Babcock. He briefly described what he considered to be the highlights of the voyage: the ship and its crew "proceeded to the coast of Africa, captured a number of English vessels, and destroyed a large factory and fort at the Islands De Los."[59]

For the British firm or firms that owned and operated the slave trading post at Isle de Kassa, the financial loss was crippling. Not only did Babcock and his men seize and take away a massive amount of trade goods, but they burned the warehouses and other buildings that had supported the firm's slave trading business. However, which firm or firms suffered the losses from the attack by Babcock and his men are not known for sure.

Peter Brancker later informed British sources that the firm that had suffered the loss at Isle de Kassa was Andrew French & Co. of London. Its principal was Andrew French, originally a merchant from Galway, Ireland.[60] The company was mostly involved in the carrying trade to the Americas and Europe[61] and is not otherwise known to have been involved in the slave trade. Brancker wrote, "the settlements on the Isles de Loss, belonging to Messrs. Andrew French & Co. of London, had been plundered, burnt, and destroyed by the crew of" the *Marlborough*. Brancker estimated the British mercantile firm's loss at £70,000, which in today's currency is almost $13 million.[62]

It is likely that the slave trader Miles Barber had leased his substantial slave trading facilities to Andrew French & Co. The relationship between Barber and Co. of Liverpool and Andrew French & Co. is suggested by the fact that Miles Barber and his three partners went bankrupt in 1777. From 1773 to 1776, Barber began trading with three British partners with voyages concentrating mostly on the Isles de Los.[63] But it appears that in 1777, the depredations and threats from American privateers in the Caribbean had pushed their financial conditions over the edge. Barber and his three partners had had their investments in slave ships rendered worthless after the ships were captured by American privateers in late 1776.[64] Barber is not reported to have shipped any Africans from the Isles de Los after 1776 and for the remainder of the Revolutionary War. Accordingly, based on these facts, Barber likely leased his facilities at Isle de Kassa to Andrew French & Co. By 1777, Barber had moved to London, where Andrew French & Co. was headquartered. It is also possible that the two firms had entered into a joint venture, with Andrew French & Co. operating the site.

If Barber's slave trading post and its buildings were leased to Andrew French & Co., as is strongly suspected, then both firms would have suffered losses. Andrew French & Co. lost its merchandise seized by Babcock, while Barber and Co. suffered from the destruction of the slave trading post's structures. If instead the two companies had been in a joint venture, then they would have jointly suffered the loss. In any event, it would take some time before the facilities at the slave trading post on the Isle de Kassa could be rebuilt and again participate in trade for captive Africans on a large scale.

In 1906, a French historian, Jules Machat, published a book on the history of France's role in the African slave trade. Machat relied heavily on official French navy records. In discussing the impact the American Revolutionary War had on the slave forts of West Africa, he wrote that an Englishman named Barber from London had his factory at the Isles de Los destroyed by "Bostonians."[65] This Barber was no doubt the slave merchant from Liverpool and London, Miles Barber. Slave trade historian Hugh Thomas agreed, writing that Barber's slave trading post at the Isles de Los "was sacked by Americans during the War of Independence."[66] The term "Bostonians" that Machat must have read in the French navy records was sometimes used by the French to mean any American privateersmen. French navy officers who recounted the information can be forgiven for not accurately describing the New England region from where most of the privateersmen on the *Marlborough* had hailed.

Navy historian Benjamin Armstrong argues that the early American navy's use of maritime raiding and irregular warfare was an important operational and strategic concept that paralleled the development of American fleet operations and commerce raiding. Armstrong gave as the first example of the United States' naval irregular warfare the raid by John Paul Jones, when commanding the Continental navy sloop *Ranger*, of Whitehaven harbor in Scotland, and the Earl of Selkirk's estate, in late April 1778.[67] Armstrong could have included the raid on Isle de Kassa by George Waite Babcock and his crew on board the *Marlborough* in February 1778. In fact, Babcock's raid caused far more monetary damage than did Jones's raid, although the latter caused more shock in Britain, since it was the first raid on a British seaport since the Dutch wars in the seventeenth century. Babcock's raid was also an example of privateers supplementing the work of the Continental navy in attacking British commerce.

Babcock and his men continued to keep an eye out for potential prizes and the British agents. At three p.m., still on February 27, a lookout spotted a canoe headed from Isle de Kassa to the mainland. It could have contained the slave trading post's European operators. Babcock dispatched Lieutenant Eldred and several armed sailors on board a newly captured barge powered by sail to try to "cut off" the canoe before it reached land. Eldred got his barge close enough to the canoe to order his men to fire at it, but to no effect. The fast canoe outpaced the barge and escaped. Eldred ordered his men back to the *Marlborough*. On the return trip, a sailor cleared his musket by snapping his flintlock. The spark caused a cartridge to explode. In turn, several cartridge boxes caught fire. The fire burned Eldred's leg and scorched one of the sailors, but none of them was severely harmed.[68]

As he prepared to depart Isle de Kassa, Babcock finally agreed on a trade with Salomon Prevoit, the French merchant captain. A few days earlier, Prevoit, from his ship the *Seine*, had demonstrated his interest in a trade by sending Babcock extra casks of fresh water. The gift got Babcock's attention. Babcock sold the Frenchman four of his enslaved people and fourteen hogsheads of tobacco. In exchange, Babcock received more casks of fresh water and various dry goods of equal value. According to Boss, the value of the trade on each side was "1800 Barrs, each Barr equal to 3/6 Sterling."[69] An iron bar was the monetary unit used in Africa to value enslaved Africans.

Babcock was now a slave trader. This trade does indicate, however, that he was more interested in returning to America with dry goods than enslaved people. But he and his men had no interest in freeing their captives without profiting from them.

For his February 28 entry in his ship's log, Boss wrote that the *Marlborough* had ten enslaved people on board, not counting the four just delivered to Prevoit. Boss stated that six of the remaining ten had been "taken out of the first shallops and 1 at the Isles de Los."[70] Boss meant here that six of the prisoners had been captured at Isle de Kassa in small sailing boats by Captain Kelley using the barge and perhaps by the *Pearl* and *Fort Rose*. The masters of the shallops were probably in the harbor preparing to sell their human cargo to the British factors. As previously mentioned, Captain Brown had found one enslaved man in chains on shore. That left three other enslaved people taken from vessels before the *Marlborough* arrived at Isle de Kassa.

Boss separately wrote that the *Marlborough*'s men had seized three shallops of those stopped at Isle de Kassa. Babcock gave one of them to "the traders" (probably the slave trading Rhode Islanders Hereford and Hammond) and traded the other two to Captain Prevoit.[71]

While Babcock wanted the *Marlborough* to stay longer on the African coast to hunt for British slave ships, he began to think of sending some of his prizes to North America. He ordered the brig *Pearl*, commanded by Ichabod Holloway, and the *Betsey*, now captained by S. Kelley, and their skeleton crews to sail to North America. Babcock probably thought they were too slow and susceptible to being captured by British warships. If the *Marlborough* accompanied them, it could sail only as fast as the slowest of the two smaller vessels. Most of the crew and the seized valuable goods, and all of the enslaved people, were aboard the twenty-gun *Marlborough*. Still, the *Betsey*, also stuffed with cargo, and the *Pearl* were valuable prizes in their own right and could be sold at a handsome profit in North America. Sending them back to North America immediately would also avoid a drain on the *Marlborough*'s food and fresh water supplies.

After sending more casks of water to the *Betsey* and *Fort Rose*, Babcock was ready to depart the harbor at Isle de Kassa. The Rhode Island captain had at his command a small flotilla: in addition to the *Marlborough*, *Pearl*, and *Betsey*, it included the schooner *Fort Rose*, commanded by John Bissell, and the new sail-powered barge seized in the small bay outside Barber's slave trading post. At about four a.m. February 28, 1778, Babcock "fired a signal gun" to alert his flotilla to prepare to get underway. All of Babcock's vessels began to sail out of the bay and to the south. It was an impressive sight, considering Babcock and his men were a relative handful of privateersmen from southern New England. The slave trader Paul Cross served as a pilot at Babcock's side, recommending the best route for the ships. By late afternoon, Babcock saw that his newly acquired barge had trouble keeping up with the other vessels, so he had it hoisted aboard his flagship. At six p.m., the flotilla was almost twenty-one miles southeast of the Isles de Los.[72]

After traveling with topsails only in the night, at five a.m. the next day, March 1, Babcock ordered all sails set on both the *Marlborough* and *Fort Rose.* The brigantine *Pearl* and the schooner *Betsey*, manned by prize crews from the *Marlborough*, veered away to the west, bound for North America. By eleven a.m., the *Marlborough*'s lookouts had lost sight of them. Babcock and his remaining crew, sailing farther south along the west coast of Africa, continued on their remarkable, and so far extremely successful, voyage—at least from their vantage points.[73]

CHAPTER EIGHT

The Capture of the
Fancy "All Slaved"

The morning after departing the Isles de Los, lookouts high on the fore-tops of the *Marlborough*'s masts lost sight of the *Pearl* and *Betsey* sailing west for North America. The *Fort Rose,* under John Bissell, continued to accompany Babcock's flagship. As the *Pearl* and *Betsey* disappeared into the horizon, the crews on the *Marlborough* and *Fort Rose* hoped their friends on board the two vessels would make it to a safe port without being intercepted and captured by an enemy warship. A safe voyage also meant all the crew in Babcock's small flotilla would share in the profits.

Meanwhile, for several days nothing remarkable occurred. The *Marlborough* and *Fort Rose* sailed south along the African coast and approached Cape Mount (or Cape Mont, now Grand Cape Mount in Liberia), a slave trading port dominated by the British that shipped in the Atlantic slave trade about the same number of African captives as did the Isles de Los.

Babcock was following a common route down the coast of West Africa by slave traders who relied on numerous private purchases as opposed to making a single stop and purchase at a slave trading post. For example, in 1795, two sloops from Rhode Island (one from Warren and the other from Providence) stopped to purchase captives first at Gorée and then at the Isles de Los, before continuing south to Bance Island in the Sierra Leone River and next to Cape Mount.[1]

The night of March 5, 1778, the *Marlborough* and *Fort Rose* came to anchor six miles southeast of the Gallinas River (now in Sierra Leone). Babcock was well aware that slave traders, both white and Black, using shallops
and other small boats, often operated near the mouths of major rivers. But
no potential British prizes were spotted. The next morning, as Babcock
and Bissell continued down the coast, two small craft were seen sailing toward the *Marlborough*, one a barge and the other a small schooner. Their
commanders must have thought the Rhode Island vessel was a slave ship
arrived from England and looked forward to selling them Africans they
carried in the steaming holds of their vessels. Babcock easily captured the
two small craft.

On board the barge was one Englishman, six grumettas working for
him, and four enslaved people. The schooner held two Englishmen, eight
grumettas, and nine enslaved people. Boss wrote in his journal, "We took
them on board and put the major part of them in irons for our own security
and so proceeded to Cape Mont."[2] With such a large cache of prisoners,
both free and unfree, Babcock took the precaution of chaining most of the
new captives. He was likely aware that most slave revolts occurred while
the slave ship was still sailing along the African coast or had just started its
journey to North America. A sense of danger hung over the *Marlborough*.
Still, based on the traditional approach taken on slave ships, he probably
allowed the female and child captive Africans to roam freely. He now had
a total of twenty-three enslaved Africans on his crowded flagship.

Later the same day, March 6, at two p.m., a ship was spotted at anchor
just off Cape Mount. Babcock issued orders to sail directly at the potential
prize. As the *Marlborough* came closer, the crew could see that the vessel in
the distance flew a British flag and mounted either ten or fourteen deck
guns.[3] It was no match for the *Marlborough*. Within two hours, the *Marlborough* sailed up alongside the enemy vessel, with all men at their battle stations. Using his speaking trumpet, Babcock yelled at the captain of the
opposing ship to strike his colors and surrender. The captain, Joseph Fisher,
obliged without firing a shot. Babcock sent on his barge Lieutenants Eldred
and Francis Bradfield, with six armed men, to take control of Fisher's vessel.

The captured vessel was the brig *Kitty*, seventy tons and just nine weeks
out of Liverpool. Captain Fisher held a letter of marque, meaning that even
though he was primarily a slave trader, he was also commissioned to seize
prizes. With ten cannon on the main deck and four cohorns and swivel
guns mounted on the ship's sides, the *Kitty* had respectable firepower.
Fisher determined, however, that he was outgunned and outmanned by the

American privateer and thus surrendered without fighting. Boss reported that the *Kitty* had on board "a cargo of dry goods suitable for the trade," meaning the slave trade. Babcock ordered his ship to anchor nearby the captured vessel. He then took a small boat to view the *Kitty* for himself.[4]

In addition to Fisher, Babcock captured twenty-five men on board the *Kitty*. The new captives were probably all crew members. Since Boss did not say how many of them were enslaved, it is likely none were and that the *Kitty* had not yet had time to acquire any.[5]

The *Kitty* had completed a successful slave voyage in 1775. It landed an estimated 287 enslaved Africans at Jamaica and returned to Liverpool two days after Christmas 1775. On that voyage, twenty-one crewmen had departed Liverpool, but seven died on the voyage. The *Kitty* was employed for another slave voyage in 1773 and 1774, during which twenty of thirty-three crewmen died.[6]

Babcock lacked room on his ship to house the twenty-six new prisoners securely. The Rhode Islander came up with a plan: he took one of his shallops, placed all of the new prisoners on it, with water and provisions for them, and anchored it a short distance from the *Marlborough*. If the prisoners tried to sail the shallop away, Babcock could easily recapture them.[7] Babcock also put a prize crew aboard the *Kitty*.

That night, Babcock had all the adult enslaved males secured "in irons" belowdecks on the *Marlborough*. In addition, he placed armed sentinels at every hatchway. These tactics were standard practices for slave traders. Babcock was prepared for an insurrection that evening, but it never happened.

Babcock must also have been concerned about the risk of locals attacking his ship and trying to free the prisoners—or more likely, to hold them for ransom. He ordered his small flotilla to sail, with the addition of the *Kitty* and the shallop bursting with white prisoners, to the south at four a.m. the next day for Cape Mount.

That evening, after coming to an anchor, Babcock allowed on board some local Africans called caboceers—agents of African chiefs who supplied captives from the interior to European and American slave traders on the coast. They had come to the *Marlborough* to reclaim some of the shallops Babcock had seized the prior day. Not wanting the alienate the caboceers, Babcock agreed to return their small craft. There is no indication, however, that he returned the trading goods his men seized aboard the shallops. Babcock hosted his guests for the evening and allowed them to sleep on board his brig.

Babcock's decision to treat the caboceers with respect paid off handsomely. According to Boss, on the morning of March 7, "a Black king called

Robin Gray" arrived in a canoe at the side of the *Marlborough* and was allowed to come on board. Gray was an African slave trader at Cape Mount who would have frequent dealings with slave ship captains for decades on the Windward Coast. In 1790, Nathaniel Cutting of Boston, on the slave ship *Hercules*, met "King Gray," as he called him, and witnessed him and the captain of the *Hercules* negotiate for the sale of an African captive. Cutting said that European slave traders had given Gray the title king out of "deference & respect" to him for the "great authority & influence" he had in the region. Cutting noted that Gray was not African royalty but instead had "by great shrewdness & valour . . . made himself the chief of a considerable extent of territory" near or at Cape Mount. Cutting was told that Gray was then about eighty years old but that by his agility and manner of speech, he acted much younger. That would have made Gray about sixty-eight when Boss saw him in 1778. Boss did not describe Gray's clothing, but Cutting did: "King Gray came on board . . . dressed in a purple silk coat trimmed with silver lace, a fine white shirt & striped Holland trousers." Gray sometimes arrived barefooted.[8]

Gray conveyed to Babcock stunning news: a large British "slave ship all slaved ready to sail to the West Indies" was anchored about a two-hour sail away at Cape Mesurado, just south of Cape Mount. By "all slaved," Boss meant that the ship was filled to its capacity with African captives, had enough fresh water and provisions for the Atlantic crossing, and was about to depart the African coast for the westward journey to the Caribbean.

Gray's information excited the Rhode Islanders. If they could capture the slave ship and sell the captives on board in North America, every officer and sailor could strike it rich. Babcock decided to set sail immediately. The captain sent Gray's canoe ashore, while, as Boss described it, Babcock "kept" Gray on board the *Marlborough* for the trip to Cape Mesurado.[9] The language implies that Gray came along against his will, but that is not clear.

After completing operations to secure the prize *Kitty* and its prisoners, at two p.m. on March 7, Babcock ordered his small flotilla to commence sailing to the southeast, in a northwest wind. Around two hours later, about twenty-five miles north of Cape Mesurado, Babcock saw the slave ship, still at anchor. Babcock could see that the vessel flew a British flag and had portal openings for sixteen guns.

Babcock had in his sights the *Fancy*, a ship built in Liverpool in 1773 and now under the command of William Allanson. Liverpool slave merchant Thomas Case owned the vessel through the company bearing his name.[10]

The *Fancy* had already made three successful slaving voyages from Liverpool. In each of the first two voyages, the *Fancy* had carried some 290 captives from Africa, selling them at Jamaica in 1774 and St. Kitts in 1775. More recently, Captain Allanson had taken command of the *Fancy* on his first slaving voyage and had departed Liverpool for Africa on April 1, 1776. He arrived in Jamaica with about 328 captive Africans at the end of 1776. After the return voyage, Allanson sailed into Liverpool's harbor on March 14, 1777.[11]

When Babcock found the ship, Allanson was in the middle of his second slave voyage commanding the *Fancy*. Allanson had departed Liverpool on June 30, 1777, with a crew of thirty-two.[12]

The *Fancy* was no ordinary slaver—Allanson also held a letter of marque authorizing him to attack American shipping.[13] It mounted fourteen guns—eight 6-pounders and six 4-pounders. The *Fancy* also had two wooden cannon, in an effort to show potential enemies that the ship was stronger than it really was.[14]

In a history of Liverpool privateers during the Revolutionary War, the following item was included: "The *Fancy*, Captain Allanson, on the passage from Jamaica to Liverpool, had an engagement . . . with an American privateer of 10 guns and 50 men." In this engagement, guns fired from the larger armed British slaver killed three American sailors and forced the American privateer to submit. Allanson "obliged the captain to produce his papers, which were French, and then let him go about his business."[15] The date of this encounter is not known. After discovering that the privateer carried official French papers, Allanson allowed it to depart. At the time, France was probably not yet at war with Britain, and Allanson did not want to risk provoking one by capturing a French vessel, even if American sailors were manning it. This information strongly points to the encounter occurring in early spring 1777. Thus, the *Fancy* had recently been tested in combat.

While Babcock and his crew were ready for a bloody encounter, the odds still greatly favored them. The *Marlborough*, at 250 tons, was much heavier than the *Fancy*. The reports on the *Fancy*'s tonnage are conflicting, at either 167 or 120 tons.[16] And the *Marlborough* carried more cannon, twenty to fourteen, and had a larger crew, seventy-six to twenty-eight. (Babcock did not know that the *Fancy*'s crew had likely been reduced by one or a few men who were then on shore.)[17] In addition, the *Marlborough* was under sail and could maneuver to fire its broadsides to the best effect, while the *Fancy* was stationary at anchor.

With all hands at battle stations, Babcock sailed up to the stern of the slave ship, avoiding its broadsides. Again using his speaking trumpet, Babcock ordered Allanson to strike his ship's colors. Realizing he was outmanned, outgunned, and outmaneuvered, Allanson chose not to play the role of tragic hero. To the relief of the *Marlborough*'s crew, the slave ship pulled down its colors, the sign of surrender. The American privateer anchored nearby.[18]

Captain Babcock sent James Eldred, with a party of six armed men, to board the slave ship. Once on board, Eldred quickly sent twenty-six white sailors and two free Africans as prisoners to the *Marlborough*. At six p.m., Babcock took a small boat over to the captured ship and learned that it had more than three hundred enslaved Africans on board, as well as fourteen tons of rice and a substantial number of elephant tusks. The rice was a most welcome find, as it could be used to feed the captives on the voyage in the Middle Passage. Any rice left over from the voyage and the ivory could also be sold at a profit. Babcock returned to his flagship, accompanied by his new prisoner, Captain Allanson.[19]

Unfortunately, Boss did not describe in his ship's log the sights and sounds of the *Fancy* and all of the people on board. It must have been a unique—and horrifying—experience.

Henry Smeathman, a self-taught English naturalist who visited Barber's slave trading post on Isle de Kassa in 1773, described his "extraordinary" experience approaching and going on board the slave ship *Africa* anchored in the harbor. The slaver had about four hundred African captives on board. Smeathman's experience may have been similar to that of the officers on board the *Marlborough*.

As he approached the slave ship on a small boat, Smeathman was first struck by its appearance, particularly the barricade structure (called a barricado) on the ship's main deck that housed the male captives and was kept separate from the quarter deck above it. On the quarterdeck was built a round house structure, from which the crew could try to put down any insurrection. Hanging on the sides of the vessel were African grumettas hired or enslaved to assist both white and Black slave traders. When Smeathman came within hearing distance of the ship, he was "struck . . . with a confused noise of human voices and the clanking of chains," which sounds shook him with "inexpressible horror." Smeathman then spotted the "black faces of women and children slaves who are kept upon and under the quarterdeck, apart from the men on the main deck." He saw about sixty to eighty women and children on the quarterdeck, sitting and wandering on the part of it nearest to the main deck, without chains. Most of the children were naked, while the women "had a piece of cloth wrapped around them which covered their bodies from as high as their navels to the knee . . . ." When he got close enough to the women and children, he was shocked by the strong smell and loud noises, as well as seeing the "inexpressible anguish" of the mothers as they watched over their children or fed infants at their breasts. During his tour of the slave ship, Smeathman wrote that he "became absorbed in a thousand melancholy reflections and bore a very small part of the conversation."[20]

Smeathman did not mention seeing the adult males, but he must have heard them belowdecks. In a letter to a friend in July 1773, Smeathman vividly described a scene in the holds of another slave ship, with a backdrop of rain.

> Alas! What a scene of misery and distress is a full slaved ship in the rains! The clanking of chains, the groans of the sick, and the stench of the whole is scarcely supportable [with] two or three slaves thrown overboard every day dying of fever, flux, measles, worms all together. All the day the chains rattling or the sound of the armorer riveting some poor devil just arrived in galling heavy irons. . . . Here the Doctor dressing sores, wounds & ulcers, or cramming the men with medicines and another standing over them with a cat [a whip] to make them swallow.[21]

Boss did not mention from where the captives on board the *Fancy* came. The *Marlborough*, from the time it arrived at Gorée, had been operating in what was then known as Senegambia, an area roughly including what is now Senegal, Gambia, Guinea-Bissau, and Guinea.

Islam had spread to Senegambia in the ninth century, and by the eighteenth century was the dominant religion. However, many Africans continued to practice traditional religions. They became the target of Muslim raiders, including the Mande-speaking Malinke. Africans who failed to convert to Islam were most at risk of being sold into slavery. Historian Marcus Rediker, in *The Slave Ship: A Human History*, writes, "With the expansion of the aristocratic, militaristic, horse-riding Malinke, many members of the small cultural groups were taken and sold to the slavers." He continues, "In Senegambia more than anywhere else in Guinea, Islamic/Saharan and European/Atlantic forces met, clashed, and cooperated, ultimately transforming the region. Over the course of the eighteenth century, about four hundred thousand enslaved people in this region were sold to the slave ships and sent to the New World, about half of them in British and American ships."[22] Most of the victims were non-Muslims, as under Islam's strictures a Muslim was not permitted to enslave another Muslim.

Historian Sean E. Kelley, in *The Voyage of the Slave Ship Hare*, writes more about the wars that led to the availability of captives for enslavement for white slave traders:

> In Upper Guinea [which included Senegambia], the most common mechanism for enslavement was the continuing series of Muslim holy wars. The jihad in the Futa Jallon . . . was responsible for the major surge in exports in the 1760s and 1770s; the Futa Jallon sent an ever-growing number of coffles to traders on the Gambia, the Isles de Los, and the Scarcies and in Sierra Leone. The triumph of Ibrahim Sori over his most potent enemy in 1776 brought some relief over the constant strife in the Futa Jallon itself, but the now stable state continued its slave raids, with Islam providing the justification.[23]

Based on the history summarized above, it is likely that many of the *Fancy's* captives were non-Muslims who had been captured in raids by Muslim warriors.

Sometimes a war was started in order for the more powerful tribe to gain captives to sell on the coast. On occasion, a raid was conducted on the appearance of a slave ship off the coast. The aggressive tribes often sought to trade captives for muskets and other firearms made by European manufacturers, giving them an edge against neighboring interior tribesmen who lacked firearms.[24]

Enslaved people were also obtained from sources other than wars and raids—from conviction in tribal courts for adultery and other crimes, bankruptcy, or even witchcraft (the latter typically arose as a result of a dispute with a local leader). Others were kidnapped by itinerant travelers and carried to the coast.

African rulers and traders procured the bulk of the captives from the interior, had them marched to the coast (sometimes for hundreds of miles), and sold them to African traders—to Blacks, whites, and men of mixed heritage. The traders on the coast then dealt with slave ship captains and operators of slave trading posts.

The individual stories of the captive Africans on board the *Fancy* are lost to history. Stories of the enslaved people—their feelings and emotions at becoming enslaved, being taken far away from their homelands, enduring the Middle Passage, and then sold like cattle in North America—are missing. Indeed, this part of the story will be missing throughout this book because, unfortunately, few first person written accounts of enslaved people who endured captivity in Africa, the Middle Passage, and being sold into slavery in North America have survived. Most of the writings about the slave trade that exist are from European and American whites who did not care about the stories of their captives. Indeed, the whites did not even record their names. All the slave trading whites wanted to do was to sell the captives like a commodity; in that world, names and personal histories held no importance to slave trading whites.

One of the few exceptions to a lack of first person accounts by African captives is that of Venture Smith. According to his narrative,[25] Smith was born Broteer Furro, probably around 1730, in a place in the interior he recalled as Dukandara in "Guinea," a term referring generally to West Africa. His father, prince of the tribe of Dukandara, exercised authority with honor and generosity. His mother was one of his father's three wives. His family's world was turned upside down when an army of some six thousand warriors overwhelmed his people. Smith's father fought with arrows, but the more-numerous attackers had guns. Venture, his father, and the women of their family were captured, tied together, and led away. As a six-year-old, Venture then witnessed the torture and murder of his father by the raiders for refusing to disclose the location of his buried treasure.

Venture was forced to serve as a waiter for the leader of a scouting party for the marauding army, which continued its destructive trek toward the coast. Venture was marched some four hundred miles, he thought, some of it carrying on top of his head a large, heavy, flat stone used for grinding corn. The marauding army took more prisoners, whose hands were tied behind their backs and who were also forced to walk to the coast.

By the time the army arrived at the key coastal slave trading center of Annamaboe (in present-day Ghana), its soldiers were worn out and short of supplies. The powerful tribe operating Annamaboe was probably the Fantee, who were experienced slave traders. Fantee warriors attacked the tired marauders, defeated them, and seized Venture and his fellow captives. Venture then recalled, "All of us were then put into the castle, and kept for market. [Then] I and other prisoners were put on board a canoe . . . and rowed away to a vessel belonging to Rhode Island, commanded by Captain Collingwood, and the mate Thomas Mumford." Venture said he was sold for a mere "four gallons of rum, and a piece of calico." Mumford decided to call him Venture because he considered purchasing him to be a business venture. The vessel was probably the *Charming Susannah*, which had departed Newport in late 1738 and returned in September 1739.[26]

During the Middle Passage, Venture survived a smallpox epidemic that ravaged the ship. He recalled the slave ship embarking with about 260 captives on the coast of Africa, but "not more than two hundred" survived the voyage. If true, it was a tragically high death rate of more than twenty-three percent. The ship arrived at the island of Barbados in the Caribbean, where most of the enslaved were sold to local planters. Venture, now eight years old, and three others endured another journey by sea and were taken to Rhode Island. Venture must have been a "privilege" slave, who was part of the compensation of the slave ship's officers. By comparison to the Middle Passage, Smith called the trip from Barbados to Rhode Island "a comfortable passage."

Venture Smith was enslaved in three locations in the North: Narraganset, Rhode Island; Stonington, Connecticut; and Long Island, New York. As an adult, Smith became known for his great size and strength. His physique and unwillingness to suffer insult made him a problem for his enslavers. He was sold several times before, through hard work and perseverance, he was able to purchase his freedom in 1765. He later purchased the freedom of his wife and children. As a free man, he pursued a variety of entrepreneurial activities: farming, lumbering, fishing, and working as a small-scale trader along the Connecticut River and the east end of Long Island Sound. Smith died on September 19, 1805, at age seventy-seven.

Venture Smith's story covers by far the most common way Africans were captured in their homelands for the slave trade: wars or raids. This was likely the case with most of the captives on board the *Fancy* as well.

George Waite Babcock and his crew did not know any of the stories of the captive Africans on their ships. The New Englanders could not speak any of the local languages. Perhaps they preferred not to know their personal histories, as they would have had the effect of humanizing the captives, making it more difficult to treat them as commodities who could be sold for a profit. Crew members may have also kept away from the captives out of fear, knowing that they might want to start an insurrection on their ship and that some of the men were tall and strong warriors.

Of course, each of the captives on board the *Fancy* had his or her own story. Each one had family and friends on the mainland. Some of the captives may have been related to each other, lived in the same town, or fought in the same army. Prior to their captures, they had hopes and dreams for their futures. Now all that was, tragically, in the past.

On the morning of March 8, 1778, Babcock made some important decisions. He put his second lieutenant, Francis Bradfield, in command of the *Fancy*. Babcock further sent two mates, nine common sailors, and three boys from the *Marlborough*'s crew to sail the *Fancy*. It is likely that several of the men included Captain Brown's guards to look after the large number of enslaved people. Babcock put John Bissell in charge of the *Kitty*, with a skeleton crew of seven men and two boys. He also transferred from the *Marlborough* to the *Kitty* four enslaved people: two adult males and two adult females. That left Babcock with the bulk of the crew, seventy-five men and boys. He also retained perhaps thirty captive Africans on board the *Marlborough* (as well as a handful of grumettas).[27] Boss did not explain why Babcock decided not to transfer all of his captives to the *Fancy*. Perhaps Babcock felt that the *Fancy* was too crowded or that he wanted to diversify the risk that either the *Marlborough* or the *Fancy* would be captured.

In addition, Babcock released most of the white prisoners he had seized on the African coast. He gave them small boats "to go wither they pleased." These included Captain Allanson and his crew and Captain Fisher and his crew. Babcock supplied them with beef and bread. According to Boss, Babcock was concerned about having so many prisoners on his ship who could try to seize it.[28] Babcock did not release any captive Africans; he planned to have them sold back in the New World.

In the afternoon, Babcock sent his boatswain, John Finn, and several carpenters under him on board the *Fancy* "in order to bring 4 carriage guns carrying 6-pound shot, which we hoisted in and mounted." In addition, four cohorns and swivel guns were transferred from the *Kitty* to the *Marlborough*.[29] Boss was pleased—this meant the *Marlborough* now carried twenty-four cannon and four smaller cohorns and swivel guns. At four p.m., guards were posted on the privateer "as usual," wrote Boss. The Newport native also noted that "Several Black Kings" came on board the *Marlborough*.[30]

The next morning, March 9, Babcock sent two valuable items aboard the *Fancy*: a speaking trumpet (for yelling across open water at passing vessels) and a compass. Babcock must have had a spare of each; perhaps he anticipated this need, knowing that prize crews could benefit from them. At eight a.m., Babcock ordered his small flotilla to continue sailing south, led by the *Marlborough* and followed in order by the *Kitty, Fancy,* and *Fort Rose.* The *Marlborough* fired off a cannon as a signal to depart, which was repeated by each of the other vessels in the American flotilla. Only an hour later, five canoes intercepted them, carrying fruit, which Babcock gladly purchased. By eleven a.m., Cape Mesurado lay two leagues to the southeast. At three p.m., the flotilla anchored, with each ship occupying the corner of an imaginary square.

Babcock and the Black Kings agreed on a deal. Babcock would deliver them goods in exchange for refilling his fresh water casks. The Black Kings and a few sailors took some empty casks on the privateer's barge and headed for the shore.[31]

In addition, the local slave trader and pilot Paul Cross accompanied the African leaders to the shore, taking them in the *Marlborough*'s jolly boat. Cross added to the passengers a number of African men whom Boss called "pawns." Cross specialized in "pawning" transactions—unique economic arrangements with potentially dreadful consequences. In a pawning transaction, a Black African trader seeking to expand his operations typically borrowed funds or goods from a slave ship captain. To secure repayment of the loan, the trader sometimes used his own children (typically, sons) as collateral. They were called pawns. If the terms of the repayment were not satisfied, then the pawns were forfeited and enslaved.[32] As an example of Cross's experience in handling pawns, in 1771, he acquired twenty-three captives for the Liverpool slave ship *Little Will*, fourteen of whom were pawns.[33]

Boss, in his journal, described the men Cross had placed on board the jolly boat as "Pawn Slaves." Thus, it appears that some of the enslaved people that Boss recorded the *Marlborough* as capturing were, in fact, pawns. Babcock must have asked Cross to return the pawns to their families. Babcock did not enslave them. Why Babcock took this step is not clear. He probably thought that it was not fair for him to take the pawns to North America without giving their families a chance to redeem them. It may have been a combination of showing goodwill to the Black Kings whose cooperation he sought and maintaining good relations with local families. Any family who unfairly lost a pawn, typically a relative, could become enraged and demand retaliation, something Babcock wanted to avoid. Some slave ship captains did not show the humanity Babcock did toward pawns.

Babcock must have been a bit nervous seeing his most important two small boats depart his ship manned by people who were not part of his crew.

At six a.m. on March 9, Francis Bradfield arrived on board the *Marlborough* with the doctor of the *Fancy*, John Anderson. It was common for British slave merchants to employ physicians on their slave ships.[34] Anderson's background is not known, but he likely was raised and trained in Scotland. Anderson was prepared to strike a deal with his American captors. He had been hired out of Liverpool by the *Fancy*'s owners to serve as the medical doctor for the ship's crew and its African captives. He was due a good wage from the ship's Liverpool owners: three of the enslaved captives (called privilege slaves). But he likely would not get paid now that the voyage had ended in failure. What is more, Anderson already owned two of the Black people aboard the *Fancy*. He probably used the two men to assist him in feeding and caring for the African captives, as well as being his personal servants. Now he could lose them too if he did not strike a deal with the Americans. Anderson realized that he had some bargaining power: his medical services were still needed to help keep the African captives on the *Fancy* alive and as healthy as possible. He was willing to serve his American captors, despite his status as a British citizen and their prisoner, so long as he was paid proper compensation.

Bradfield and Babcock too recognized that Anderson's services could be useful on the long voyage to North America. The Americans were not experienced in handling African captives on a slave ship. The two officers must have thought that Anderson, with his experience feeding and caring for African captives on slave ships, could keep as many captives as possible healthy, and, as a result, the captives could command good prices when sold. The New England crew members might benefit from a doctor on board the *Fancy* as well.

The parties arrived at an agreement. Anderson would serve as a physician on the *Fancy* on its voyage back to North America and in exchange would receive as payment "three Prime Slaves" from the captives on board the *Fancy* and would be permitted to retain his two enslaved men. This was essentially the same deal Anderson had with the *Fancy*'s British owners. On a strip of paper, using his feather pen and ink, Babcock wrote out the short agreement, which survives to this day:

> These may certify all whom it may concern that I the subscriber do engage unto John Anderson, Doctor of the ship the *Fancy*, three Prime Slaves as his wage that may become due from his leaving Liverpool until her arrival at a safe port under the command of Capt. Francis Bradfield; provided the said Doctor conforms to the rules and orders of said ship and does his duty among the Slaves—Besides two slaves which is his property at present. Given under my hand on Board the *Marlborough* this 9th of March 1778. Geo. W. Babcock[35]

While the African captives on board the *Fancy* were not aware of the deal, the arrangement was promising for their health. Now they would at least have a physician experienced in the slave trade caring for them and not just Americans who were novices in the slave trade.

The next morning, March 10, the weather was fair. The *Marlborough*'s sailors were pleased to see African men in canoes paddling toward their ship and bringing more fruit with which to barter. The traders accepted tobacco from the New Englanders for their fruit. Meanwhile, Anderson and Bradfield came on board the *Marlborough* at one p.m. to dine with Babcock. The men must have discussed the health and needs of the captives on the captured British slave ship. They also likely discussed Babcock's plans for the *Fancy* to make its own way to North America and where to land and dispose of the enslaved people on board at the most favorable prices.[36]

Anderson returned to the *Fancy* before Bradfield, "on account of messing [feeding] the slaves," according to Boss. Boss here referred to the role of the *Fancy*'s doctor supervising the feeding of the more than three hundred captives on his vessel, typically twice a day. Perhaps at Anderson's recommendation, Babcock ordered some livestock to be sent to the *Fancy* in preparation for its Atlantic crossing.

Sending the *Fancy* to North America on its own ahead of the *Marlborough* was risky. The *Fancy* now was manned by a relatively small crew, and, after Babcock removed four of its 6-pounder cannons, only four 6-pounders and six 4-pounders remained. Accordingly, the *Fancy* could be attacked and taken by a relatively small, armed Royal Navy sloop or a decently armed privateer operated by Loyalists out of one of the British-controlled Caribbean islands. If, instead, the *Fancy* sailed in company with the *Marlborough*, the *Fancy* and its valuable human cargo would be better protected from enemy raiders.

Babcock, however, did not want the *Marlborough* to leave the West African coast immediately. He desired to capture more British slave ships. In addition, he wanted to sail the *Marlborough* back to Boston, while it made more sense for the *Fancy* to sail to the Caribbean or the American South and sell the African captives there. Thus, the two ships would take different routes back to North America. The biggest risk of capture by a Royal Navy warship or Loyalist privateer was close to the *Fancy*'s expected destination. The *Marlborough* was not really needed to protect the *Fancy* on its voyage in the Middle Passage.

Having decided that he would not have the *Fancy* sail in convoy with the *Marlborough*, Babcock must have concluded that more captives on board the *Fancy* would survive the Middle Passage if the *Fancy* departed for North America immediately and did not linger on the hot African coast. Prolonged confinement belowdecks in steamy, crowded conditions were breeding grounds for deadly diseases, such as dysentery. Many of the captives had already been worn down by long marches and depression from leaving their loved ones. The more enslaved people who survived and could be sold in North America, the greater would be the profits shared by Babcock and his crew. Babcock was probably also worried that if the *Fancy* remained on the coast, it would deplete the fresh water and food stores the enslaved Africans and white crew on the *Fancy* would need for the Atlantic crossing.

Boss wrote in the ship's log that sailors on the *Marlborough* "took several small Blacks on board the *Fancy*." Babcock must have sent several of the enslaved children to the *Fancy*. Why, it is not known. Perhaps he felt they would be better cared for there. Or perhaps the children were part of the compensation that would be paid to the *Fancy*'s commander, Bradfield. Children were less of a threat to slave ship crews than adults and were therefore often allowed to walk on the quarterdeck or main deck.

At two p.m. on March 10, Paul Cross returned with the *Marlborough*'s jolly boat, carrying with him the Black Kings, who bore upsetting news. The ship's barge, which had been sent with empty fresh water casks to be refilled by Africans, had run aground on a sandbar. During the accident, two African men manning the barge were reported to have drowned—one was named the Duke of Marlborough, who may have been a leader. The loss of the barge and water casks was a blow to Babcock, and perhaps he also felt badly about the deaths of the two men while performing a mission for him. A few hours later, the Black Kings departed the *Marlborough* on canoes for the shore, probably to try to arrange for another way to provide fresh water to the American ship.

Babcock also had to address a rare personnel problem among his officers. Captain Bradfield sent his boatswain, John Finn, back to the *Marlborough*. According to Boss, Finn had behaved "bad on board the *Fancy*" by "abusing the doctor and officers" on the slaver. Babcock resolved the issue by sending Finn aboard the *Kitty*, under John Bissell. After another active day off the coast of West Africa, Babcock ordered his sentinels to their posts, and everyone else on board the American privateer flagship tried to get some sleep during the steamy night.[37]

The next morning, March 11, more canoes arrived alongside the *Marlborough*, carrying fruit, as well as goats and fowl, to exchange for tobacco. At eight a.m., the small American flotilla again got under sail, heading south. Before departing, Babcock ordered each of his ships to fire a three-gun salute to honor the Black Kings, a sign of respect for them. By noon, Cape Mesurado was behind them, about three leagues to the north.

The *Kitty*, with trade goods on board, did not follow Babcock's flotilla. Instead, in Boss's words, Captain Bissell "shaped his course for America" to the northwest. Boss did not say what port Babcock ordered the *Kitty* to head for, but he did note that Bissell had on board "4 slaves—2 men and 2 boys."[38] These enslaved people likely came from the *Fancy*. The *Kitty* would be the third of Babcock's vessels to sail for the United States, following the *Pearl* and *Betsey*, but the first with enslaved Africans on board.

At one p.m., a lookout high on the *Marlborough*'s masts saw to the leeward a sunken boat exposed at the surface, with a man in the boat. Babcock ordered a few of his sailors on one of his remaining small boats and the *Fort Rose* to investigate. It turned out to be the *Marlborough*'s missing barge, and on board was the Duke of Marlborough, one of the two African men thought to have drowned. Boss was not clear in his journal, but it appears that the man was still alive and therefore was rescued. Boss showed more concern for the barge, stating that it was "Providence" for them to have found and reacquired their barge, "which we wanted very much." After dumping the water from the barge, Babcock sent a spare small boat to the *Fancy* "as he [Bradfield] had no boat," probably because Bradfield had earlier sent Babcock the *Fancy*'s barge.

Preparations were made for the *Fancy* to sail to North America and to decide on the plan for selling the enslaved captives on board. At five p.m., Babcock sent Lieutenant Nathaniel Brown to the *Fancy* "to get an exact account of the number of slaves." Babcock wanted the precise number in order to understand what he and his men could expect to receive as their shares of the net proceeds when the Africans were sold. He did not want his men and him left behind cheated. When Brown returned, he informed Babcock that the *Fancy* had 310 enslaved people on board.[39] Based on the then average price for an enslaved African sold in the British Caribbean, £35, the total value of the *Fancy*'s human cargo was £11,000.

If the 250-ton *Marlborough* was crowded with about seventy-five white sailors and twenty-four African captives, plus all of its cargo stowed in its holds, the *Fancy* was positively jammed with a human cargo of 310 enslaved people plus the crew of 12 sailors. Ship carpenters would have made this possible by making belowdecks a six-foot-wide, two-and-a-half-foot-high shelf ringing the vessel. Bulkheads would have also been built to make a large compartment for the enslaved males and a smaller compartment for the enslaved females and children. Each enslaved male was typically chained at an ankle to another captive; sometimes they were chained at both a wrist and an ankle. Often the iron shackles rubbed skin off the men.

Assuming the *Fancy* was 120 tons, it had aboard 2.68 people for each ton of the ship. On average, a one-hundred-ton British slave ship carried

2.5 enslaved people per ton. At 120 tons, that converted to 300 enslaved people. But the *Fancy* had 310.[40] The African men, and sometimes the women and children, on board the *Fancy* were packed tightly belowdecks. The heat on the African coast, combined with the body heat of some three hundred people inside the hull of the ship, must have led to great suffering and raised temperatures to dangerous levels. (By comparison, in the eighteenth century, a ship used to take poor white immigrants from Europe to North American on average carried 1.25 passengers for every registered ton.)[41]

Bradfield and the *Fancy* departed the West African coast and headed for the Middle Passage on March 12.[42] Now the only ships Babcock controlled were the *Marlborough* and *Fort Rose*.

Babcock decided that the *Fort Rose* was not worth sailing back to America. He gave the schooner to Paul Cross, whose services as a pilot at the Isles de Los and afterward had been invaluable to Babcock and his men. (Babcock also gave him an American commission, which was not found among Cross's papers. While the commission would have been useful if Cross came across another American privateer, he likely destroyed it, for fear a Royal Navy officer would find it and punish him for assisting the Americans.) Babcock further asked Cross to return the free grumettas the Americans had captured back to the shore.[43] Since Cross continued to work on the West African coast and wanted to retain good relations with local people, he likely complied with Babcock's request and did not try to enslave the pawns.

After the *Marlborough*'s crew removed most all items of value from the *Fort Rose* and transferred them to their ship, including five 3-pounder cannon, Babcock placed on board the small vessel one cask of bread and one cask of beef, some gin, two-thirds of a hogshead of tobacco, and some brass kettles for trading.[44] The *Marlborough* now carried twenty-nine carriage guns and four cohorns and swivel guns.

A pleased Cross sailed off in the *Fort Rose* at two p.m., but then his vessel was intercepted by a canoe from the mainland. An alert gun was fired from the canoe, a signal for Cross to come alongside the canoe. Babcock ordered the *Marlborough* to sail to the *Fort Rose* to determine what was happening. Cross returned to the *Marlborough* and informed Babcock that the local Africans in the canoe had informed him that "there was a sloop and boats gone into the Bassaw River this morning."[45] (The Bassaw River is now called the St. John River and is in what is now Liberia.) Babcock suspected that the sloop was a Liverpool slave trading sloop he had been told about earlier by local Africans and had been hoping to capture. Babcock ordered the *Marlborough* to sail into the wind ("haul wind") and head for the entrance to the Bassaw River.

By four p.m., lookouts spotted a sloop and several boats in the river. Only an hour later, the *Marlborough* was within gunshot distance of the sloop and its boats. Babcock ordered his ship's anchor out and two guns fired at the sloop as a warning. By then, Babcock knew this was not the Liverpool slaver before him, but he wanted to capture the vessels in any event. Babcock sent Eldred and a few armed sailors on a small boat to demand that the sloop's captain surrender his vessel. Thirty minutes later, Eldred returned in his small boat with a Mr. Richards, with a written message from the sloop's captain requesting to know the terms of capitulation. Eldred confirmed to the Rhode Island captain that the sloop was a slave trader and had grumettas on board. Babcock then dictated a response to a crewman, N. Daggett, who wrote it down. Babcock said he realized the small sloop was not worth keeping, so if its captain surrendered, he would be entitled to keep his sloop and grumettas who worked for him, but if he did not cooperate, he would have to "abide by the consequences." In other words, if he cooperated, the goods on his vessel would be seized but he would be allowed to retain his sloop and African workers. Richards was kept on board the *Marlborough* while Daggett delivered the message.

The sloop's captain, Ireland Grace, agreed to surrender on Babcock's terms. Grace was an experienced slave ship captain: he had commanded at least four slave ship voyages from Liverpool, beginning in 1771. On a 1776 voyage financed by Miles Barber's partner Samuel Sandys, Grace purchased captives primarily from the Isles de Los.[46] After returning to Liverpool from his last voyage in 1777, he apparently could not find employment as a slave ship captain, probably as a result of the decline of the British slave trade caused mainly by the depredations of American privateers. Grace then sailed to Africa, becoming a low-level slave trader.

After delivering the message, Daggett returned to the *Marlborough* with, as Boss described in his journal, Captain Grace "and his girls." Grace's "girls" were most certainly African girls he held as captives. It would have been madness for Grace to have sailed with his own daughters on a slave trading vessel, where they would have had a high risk of catching a deadly disease and have to witness the horrors of slave trading. Daggett returned to Grace's sloop and had one of its guns fired, indicating he was in control of the vessel.[47]

The arrival of the young enslaved females aboard the *Marlborough* brought the total number of captives on the privateer to twenty-seven.

The next morning, March 13, Babcock boarded the captured sloop and ordered everything of value to be removed to the *Marlborough*. Consistent with the surrender terms, he returned to Captain Grace the sloop and the grumettas he employed.[48]

In the afternoon, Babcock ordered the *Marlborough* and *Kitty* to continue sailing south, while Paul Cross took his final leave and sailed north on the *Fort Rose*. Babcock's decision to give the schooner to Cross would help Cross's future slave trading business. As with Captain William Moore, the decision showed that Babcock was more interested in profiting from British plunder and showing that his conduct was honorable to another white man than trying to limit the African slave trade. Cross continued to work with British slave ship captains and traders until his death in 1784. He once told a colleague in 1781 that he had been "Blest with my share of success" and estimated the value of his captives at £2,400.[49]

For increased security, Babcock put four of the British sailors captured on the *Fancy* in a long boat. The *Marlborough* probably towed it with a cable. At six p.m., Babcock generously asked the prisoners in the longboat to come aboard the *Marlborough* to dine with his crew; only two of the four men accepted.

The American flotilla started to sail again at four a.m. the next day, this time toward the coast. Three hours later, a canoe with three Africans was spotted heading from the shore toward the *Marlborough*. One of the Africans came on board the privateer and informed Babcock that the Liverpool slaver he sought to capture had sailed three days ago to the west. This news, which Babcock took as true, was disappointing. He was not aware of any other prospects for captures. The threat of American privateers in the Caribbean had apparently already resulted in fewer British slavers than usual working on the coast. Meanwhile, perhaps to thank them for their efforts, crewmen on board the *Marlborough* threw several pipes of gin over the privateer's side and watched as two of the Africans leaped into the water to catch the submerged offerings.[50]

What motivated Robin Gray, other "Black Kings," and local Africans to cooperate with Babcock and his men is unknown. They likely respected whatever side had the most power or that could pay them the most. Alternatively, perhaps resentment had built up against the British and their dominance in the African slave trade and what they perceived as arrogance.

Local African leaders were far from being lackeys of British slave ship captains and commanders of British slave forts. As intermediaries in the slave trade, and given the large numbers of followers they could call on, compared to the infrequent slave ships and their small crews, they held substantial power. White slave ship captains, factors at slave trading posts, and slave traders knew they had to court and cooperate with local African coastal leaders to succeed in the slave trade. Boston traveler Nathaniel Cutting noticed this feature when American and European slave traders dealt with Robin Gray in the early 1790s. African leaders did not have any particular allegiance to a European country; they were out to make money for themselves. Occasionally, they would demonstrate their power and independence by acting against British interests.[51] This could have been one of those occasions.

At two p.m. on March 14, Babcock held a meeting with his principal officers. According to Boss, "it was concluded that our water and provisions were expending very fast and with no hopes of getting more." In addition, the officers expressed concern that it was "a time of the year very dangerous on this coast," meaning the threat of tropical storms. Accordingly, it was "unanimously agreed to proceed directly for North America."[52] Babcock did not hesitate and redirected his vessel, which had been sailing to the south and southeast for the last several months, to the north. They were just four leagues from what is now called the Cestos Rock off Cestos Point, Liberia. Boss wrote in his journal, "Shaping our course by God's permission for America, hoping for a safe and short passage." Boss further noted that as the *Marlborough* departed the coast of West Africa, it had on board seventy-five men and boys as sailors, "& 18 men and boys and 9 girl slaves, in all 103 souls."[53]

The Fates of the *Fancy*, *Pearl*, *Kitty*, and *Betsey*, and Their Captive Africans

*U*p *to now*, Captain Babcock, the officers, and the sailors of the *Marlborough* had performed important services for the Patriot cause. They had dealt a heavy blow to the British slave trade on the West African coast, which was a substantial part of the British economy. When slave merchants in Great Britain learned of the raid, the news would also tend to discourage them from investing more in the slave trade, at least while the Revolutionary War continued.

At this stage of their voyage, commencing with the return trip across the Atlantic Ocean, Babcock and his men had to address the ugly consequences of what they had wrought. In order to make the voyage a huge financial success, they had to sell in North America the enslaved Africans on board the *Marlborough* and its prize vessels. The New Englanders, when they departed the African coast, had a total of 341 captives on their vessels—310 on the *Fancy*, 4 on the *Kitty*, and 27 on the *Marlborough*. The New Englanders were essentially slave traders at this point.

Naturally, Babcock and his crew wanted each of the prize vessels *Fancy*, *Kitty*, *Pearl*, and *Betsey* to have an uneventful Atlantic passage and arrive at a safe port. There, the valuable merchandise that was taken from Isles de Los and prize vessels and then stuffed into every nook and cranny of the vessels, and even the ships themselves, in addition to the enslaved people who survived the Middle Passage on board the *Fancy* and *Kitty*, could be sold and the profits shared by officers and crew. Of course, John Brown and the other investors would obtain their shares too.

The survival and health of the African captives carried on Babcock's ships depended on the voyage in the Middle Passage. The shorter the time for the journey, the more likely that fewer enslaved people would become seriously ill and die on board. Each day in the Middle Passage increased the risk of food and water shortages, illnesses, and dysentery and other contagious diseases. The average duration of a voyage from all regions of Africa to the Americas was just over two months.[1]

As previously mentioned, Rhode Island slave voyages had a mortality rate for Africans forced to endure the Middle Passage of about twelve to fifteen percent. The *Marlborough* only had twenty-seven captives on board and the *Kitty* just four. Since their boats were not crammed with enslaved people belowdecks, they could expect a much lower mortality rate. That was not the case with the *Fancy*, however.

A prize vessel on its voyage to a safe port always faced the risk of recapture by an enemy warship. Two developments increased the risk of capture even more since the time the *Marlborough* had escaped out of Narragansett Bay early Christmas morning in 1777.

First, the *Marlborough*'s officers and crew did not know that France and the United States had secretly concluded a Treaty of Amity and Commerce, signed February 6, 1778. Under the treaty, France recognized the independence of the new United States and offered military and financial assistance to the Americans. On March 17, 1778, four days after being informed of the treaty by the French ambassador in London, Britain declared war on France. The British Admiralty, which knew about the treaty beforehand from spies working in Paris, sent even more ships to the Caribbean to protect against the threat the French navy posed to the British-controlled sugar islands. As a result, Royal Navy warships presented a greater menace than ever to Babcock's prize vessels sailing in Caribbean waters.

In another ominous development for American privateers, Parliament authorized British and Loyalist privateering. At first, the British government hesitated to issue letters of marque to private British ships, perhaps out of concern that sailors would throng to more-lucrative privateering, leaving the Royal Navy short of manpower. But in early 1777, as American privateers inflicted a heavy toll on British merchant ships, the British outlook changed, and letters of marque were authorized to be issued to British privateers in late March 1777. In January 1778, letters of marque were authorized to be issued to Loyalist privateers in the British-controlled Caribbean islands. By early 1778, the seas in the West Indies were swarming with British and Loyalist privateers.[2] They soon scored some significant successes against lightly armed American privateers and their even-more-vulnerable prize vessels.

What happened to the *Marlborough*'s prize vessels on their voyages to North America? Only a few snippets of information are available on three of the other four.

The May 30, 1778, edition of the *Providence Gazette* contained the first mention of the *Marlborough*'s African voyage. It also mentioned two of its prize vessels:

> By advices from the West Indies, we learn that the privateer ship the *Marlborough*, Capt. Babcock, of this port [Providence], some time since landed a number of men on the Island of Delos [the Isles de Los], on the coast of Africa, from whence he took a large quantity of valuable dry goods. He had taken a vessel laden with 140 tons of camwood and 40 tons of rice; and a schooner (which has arrived at Martinique) with 8 chests of arms, 200 brass kettles, 9,000 weight of tobacco and 6 chests of beads. He also captured and destroyed a number of drogers on the [African] coast.

The first vessel mentioned "laden with 140 tons of camwood and 40 tons of rice" must have been the brig *Pearl,* and the second vessel mentioned (the schooner) must have been the *Betsey.* The two vessels had sailed for North America in tandem on March 1, after the *Marlborough*'s crew had sacked the British slave trading post at the Isles de Los, but before Babcock and the remaining New Englanders had captured the *Fancy* or the *Kitty.*

The *Providence Gazette*'s mention that the schooner (that is, the *Betsey*) had arrived at Martinique is good evidence that the prize vessel was not captured on its trip to the Caribbean. The *Betsey* must have arrived at Martinique in late April, having had about a fifty-day journey through the Middle Passage.

It is not known what happened to the *Betsey* after its arrival. Perhaps its captain, the former merchant ship commander S. Kelley whom Babcock appointed as prize master, sold the *Betsey* at Martinique, forcing him and his crew to sail to Rhode Island on another vessel. Perhaps the *Betsey* was captured on its voyage from Martinique to New England. There is no known surviving record of the *Betsey* being sold at auction, with the proceeds being shared by Babcock and his crew, but that does not necessarily mean such documents never existed. Surviving records of the disposition of privateer cargos and their prize vessels are far from complete. The author also has not found any records of S. Kelley, either before or after his Africa voyage.

In all probability, a sailor on board the *Betsey* provided the detailed information about the *Marlborough*'s voyage to the *Providence Gazette*. This suggests that part or all of its crew made it back to Rhode Island by May 30, 1778, and therefore that their vessel was not captured. (This would also explain why the *Fancy* and *Kitty* were not mentioned in the May 30 squib; the *Betsey* departed the African coast before their captures.) Another possibility, however, is that a sailor on another American vessel obtained the information from talking with a member of the *Betsey*'s crew at Martinique or was given a letter from a member of the *Betsey*'s crew. Such a sailor could then have returned to Rhode Island on another ship and passed the information or letter to the Providence newspaper.

The May 30 notice in the *Providence Gazette* did not mention the fate of the *Pearl*, commanded by Ichabod Holloway. The *Pearl* and *Betsey,* although they departed the African coast in tandem, likely became separated.

The fate of the *Pearl* is described in the following item that appeared in the May 9, 1778, edition of the *Jamaica Gazette* published in Kingston:

> The brigantine *Pearl,* Capt. Braker [Brancker], from the coast of Guinea, bound for Liverpool, with a valuable cargo of gum, elephants' teeth, and camwood, on board, was on the 24th of Feb. taken off the Isles de Los, by an American privateer of 20 guns, commanded by one Babcock; the said brig [the *Pearl*] has been retaken by the *Alexander,* Captain Bain, and *Nancy,* Capt. M'Larthy, letters of marque from Greenock, and brought into Port Royal on Wednesday last.[3]

Captains Bain and M'Larthy, commanding two British privateers off of Jamaica, on or about May 7, 1778, captured the *Pearl* some sixty-eight days after it left the African coast and brought their prize into Port Royal, Jamaica.[4] The privateers originally hailed from Greenock, a small but active port on the west coast of Scotland. The *Pearl*'s former commander, Peter

Brancker, accompanied Ichabod Holloway on the *Pearl*'s voyage home as a prisoner but was freed as a result of his former brig's recapture. Under the rules of maritime law, however, he and the owners of the *Pearl* had no more rights to the brig; the *Pearl* was now owned by Captains Bain and M'Larthy and their crews (at least after proper condemnation by an admiralty court). Brancker must have, however, negotiated a deal to repurchase the *Pearl*, as both he and his ship arrived back at Liverpool in September 1778.[5]

Babcock made the right decision to empty the *Pearl* of much of its valuable cargo and load it onto the *Marlborough*, and to man the *Pearl* with a skeleton crew. Whether Holloway's ending up near Jamaica and not a safer port such as Boston was intentional or because of bad navigation is not known. John Brown had typically ordered the commanders of his prize vessels that did not have enslaved people on board to sail to a safe New England port, and Babcock likely instructed Holloway to do the same.

For Ichabod Holloway and the rest of the six American privateersmen, their captures meant the real prospect of facing the next several months and perhaps years in horrible British prisons, either at New York, Halifax in Canada, or in Britain. Based on the high death rates in those prisons, particularly in New York, a few of them could be expected to die there.

Instead, after their capture on the *Pearl*, Holloway and his six crew members had an extraordinary adventure. With no prisons available in the British-controlled Caribbean islands for American privateersmen, and with a possible major confrontation looming with the French fleet recently arrived in North America, there was apparently nowhere to keep the *Pearl*'s prize crew. The six captive Americans, who had reportedly suffered much "ill-usage" after their capture, and their British captors agreed that the Americans would sail to British-held New York City in a Loyalist schooner, the *John and Sally*, laden with rum, on condition of working as sailors to pay for their passage. When they reached the New Jersey coast on August 1, 1778, however, Holloway and his men decided to break their agreement. They overpowered the schooner's master and crew, confined them, and brought the schooner safely into nearby Egg Harbor, New Jersey—conveniently, a popular place for Patriot privateersmen to bring their prizes.[6]

Holloway and his men now had a substantial prize in which to share. The *John and Sally* and its cargo could be claimed by them alone and did not have to be shared with the rest of the *Marlborough*'s crew. Holloway claimed that the value of the vessel and cargo was as much as $12,000. However, Holloway became angry, believing that the prize vessel and cargo were sold at auction in New Jersey's admiralty court for about two-thirds of their fair market values. In February 1779, he submitted a petition to the Continental Congress asking for it to rule in his favor; Holloway remained in a tavern in Philadelphia, waiting for a decision, all the while paying for his keep and spending more than he wanted.[7] The author did not find any documents indicating how the petition was resolved.

Ichabod Holloway survived the war. According to the 1782 census of Rhode Island, he headed a household in Exeter that included his wife, a female child, and a Black person (the census does not indicate whether the individual was enslaved or free).[8] But by 1787, he had fallen on hard financial times—his creditors gave him five years to pay his debts.[9]

The following report about the fate of the third prize, the *Kitty*, commanded by John Bissell, appeared in London newspapers in July 1778: "The *Kitty*, Fisher, of Liverpool, is taken on the coast of Africa by the *Marlborough* American privateer of twenty-six guns."[10] Another item, in the August 20, 1778, editions of London newspapers, gave the same information but added that the prize *Kitty* was "carried into Martinico."[11] If accurate, this report indicates that Bissell made it to French-controlled Martinique and likely sold his vessel, cargo, and four enslaved people there. It typically took about two months, sometimes a few weeks more or a few weeks less, for news to make its way from the British Caribbean to London. That would have placed the *Kitty*'s arrival at Martinique roughly between late May and mid-June 1778.

There is other circumstantial evidence that the *Kitty* was sailed across the Atlantic safely and therefore was sold as a prize. The commander of the *Kitty*'s prize crew, John Bissell, survived the war. Prior to his voyage to Africa, he was listed in a 1777 military census as residing in North Kingstown. In the Rhode Island 1782 census, Bissell is reported as heading a household of four white people in the same town.[12] After the war he filed an application for a veteran's pension, describing his service with the Rhode Island state militia. In the application, he stated that he served one month with a North Kingstown militia outfit in August 1778, during the French and American joint campaign against British forces in Newport. Bissell's brother David also applied for a veteran's pension. In his application, David stated he had served on the *Marlborough* under Captain George W. Babcock on a voyage to Africa and had made the voyage with John Bissell.[13] Thus, John and David Bissell must have reached a safe port in May or June 1778. If so, they were also likely to have been able to sell the *Kitty* and the four enslaved people. If their vessel had been intercepted and captured by a British warship or Loyalist privateer, the Bissells likely would have spent a considerable amount of time in British prisons, and John would not have been able to serve in the local militia during the Rhode Island Campaign of August 1778.

The fate of the four enslaved people on board the *Kitty* is also not known. Rather than being sold, they may have been transferred to one of the owners of the *Marlborough* or to a few of the officers of the ship as partial payment for their services. This was not an uncommon practice for slave voyages. The Brown brothers had followed this practice with the *Sally*'s voyage in 1764. As indicated above, Ichabod Holloway, commander of the *Pearl*, had a Black individual residing with his family in 1782. It is possible that person had been a captive on the *Kitty*.

What was the fate of the *Fancy*, commanded by Lieutenant Francis Bradfield and carrying 310 African captives when it departed the coast of West Africa? In short, its fate is unknown, and any conclusion would be speculation. On March 7, 1778, the day after the *Fancy*'s capture off the West African coast, Babcock sent Bradfield written orders stating what port to take the captured ship to and where to land his human cargo. Remarkably, Babcock's orders to Bradfield still exist. They were purchased in an auction by a private buyer in 2007 and then donated to the Cornell University Library.[14] They make for interesting reading.

The orders, dated March 7, 1778, are addressed to Francis Bradfield and are signed "Geo. W. Babcock."[15] Babcock begins his orders, "Your being appointed Captain of the Ship *Fancy* having on board Slaves, 12 tons camwood, 27 hundredweight of Ivory, and 14 tons of rice, etc., I do recommend and require that you take the greatest precaution and embrace every wind in making the best of your way to a safe port in the Southern States, if possible." This is a clear directive for Bradfield to give precedence for sailing to South Carolina or Georgia—likely Charleston or Savannah. Charleston was the most likely destination, as it was the port that took in by far the most African captives among the thirteen colonies.

Babcock did not provide in his orders the number of enslaved people on board the *Fancy*. He would not know that the exact number was 310 until five days after he wrote these orders.

Babcock's orders were consistent with the second report about the *Marlborough*'s voyage that appeared in the *Providence Gazette*. The June 13, 1778, edition contained a squib with the observation that Babcock had ordered "a large Guineaman, having on board 300 slaves . . . to South Carolina." Presumably, the editor of the Providence newspaper obtained the information from one of the *Marlborough*'s returning officers.

In his March 7 orders, Babcock directed Bradfield on how to proceed once the *Fancy* arrived in South Carolina:

> And if you should arrive at South Carolina or thereabouts then libel your vessel [i.e., begin admiralty proceedings] and seek the best market for your Slaves & Cargo & Vessel that will tend to the advantage of the owners & ship's company and take up bills of credit of the shortest dates & best houses, otherwise in Continental money. After you have disposed of the same proceed the safest way home or make safe remittances home to the owners or agent. Otherwise make the best of it according as you find things circumstanced.[16]

These are clear directions from Babcock for Bradfield to sell all of the African captives on board the *Fancy* in South Carolina. First, Bradfield had to follow the admiralty court procedures in South Carolina. To sell the captives, Bradfield likely would have retained a firm in Charleston that had experience buying and selling newly arrived enslaved Africans.

Bradfield arguably did not fall under Congress's resolutions banning the importation of enslaved people. Those resolutions did not cover "property" seized on prize vessels.[17] Thus, presumably any enslaved person seized aboard a prize ship could be sold just the same as any other item of property. Babcock must have held this view, as would have most all other privateer captains.

Royal Navy captains sometimes behaved the same way, and occasionally even worse. For example, Captain John Colpoys of HMS *Seaford* captured the Massachusetts privateer brigantine *General Washington*, carrying eighteen guns and manned by a crew of eighty-five, on January 18, 1778. Ten of the American sailors were Black men. After bringing his prize into Barbados the next day, he sold all ten at a slave market.[18] It is probable that at the time of the privateer's capture, some or even all of the victims had been free men in America.

Babcock wanted Bradfield to sell to the "best houses" in South Carolina, meaning those firms that had the strongest credit ratings. This is because the Rhode Island captain wanted Bradfield to take a bill of exchange (Babcock called it a bill of credit)—a promise to pay or exchange goods in the future—as payment for the sale of the enslaved people, as well as of the other cargo and the vessel itself. The holder of a such a bill of exchange would have to rely on the ability of the firm that issued it to make good on its promise to pay. If the firm had a strong reputation, then the bill of exchange could be sold back in New England for a small discount. In Providence, John Brown would be able to obtain merchandise in satisfaction for the bill of exchange or be able to sell the bill of exchange. Babcock preferred that Bradfield not take Continental paper money unless it was necessary, probably out of concern that the money was easier to lose or have stolen, and that Continental currency was consistently depreciating in value.

Bills of exchange were commonly received by ship captains upon the sale of their human cargo. In one well-documented voyage of a Rhode Island slave ship, the *Hare* in 1754 and 1755, its captain sold fifty-six captives at Charleston, South Carolina. He received in exchange, in part, a shipload of rice. But rice being far bulkier than human beings, it would have taken several shiploads to equal the value of one shipload of African captives. The difference was largely made up with bills of exchange. At this time, the bills of exchange were generally guaranteed by British banks or financial houses, making them even more secure as payment.[19] No American bank yet existed to do the same task.

Babcock added in his orders:

> If you should by chance fall in with the West India Islands, proceed directly for the first and safest port among the French. Then to act as above. Directed in consequence of the sales take bills upon the best houses in France. Then inform your owners or agent of your transactions by the first opportunity and after doing as you think best directing as much as possible to your instruction, but leaving it with you to act as you think best—proceeding directly for America unto your agents or owners.[20]

John Linscom Boss wrote in his journal that on March 12, Babcock issued orders to Bradfield for the voyage across the Atlantic. This was five days after the March 7 date of the above orders. Boss wrote that the second lieutenant was ordered "to proceed for one of the Southern States or French West Indies."[21] As noted in chapter 2, the most popular port for American privateers to sell enslaved people on board captured prizes taken in the Caribbean was French-held Martinique. The islands of Guadeloupe and St. Lucia were other possibilities. However, because of the outbreak of war between Britain and France, of which Babcock on March 7 had no idea, the French-controlled islands were now exposed to attack by the Royal Navy. On the other hand, Captain Bradfield may have preferred sailing to a French island in the Caribbean because to sail on to distant Charleston would take another month, thus exposing his ship to increased risks of capture. Because of the trade winds, the voyage to Charleston would have to pass through the Caribbean, then infested with Royal Navy warships and British and Loyalist privateers.

Babcock concluded his orders addressing the risk of embezzlement by Bradfield or other members of his crew: "To account for the same, trusting to your fidelity for the same, requesting you to take great precaution that no embezzlement of goods, stores or anything else be made by any person [or] forfeiture of the whole prize money according to the ship's articles."[22]

This author has not discovered any records in Martinique, Charleston, or anywhere else mentioning the *Fancy*. Few of South Carolina's admiralty records from the Revolutionary War have survived.[23] No reference to the *Fancy* has been found in Charleston newspapers of this period; the port's newspapers rarely mentioned privateer prizes. Few official Martinique records from the Revolutionary War exist.

There is no known newspaper report indicating the *Fancy*'s fate. Often, an officer or crew member of an American privateer would let a newspaper printer in an American port know about important developments in a privateer's voyage. This was particularly true if the privateer's crew had something to brag about, such as the seizure of a large British merchant vessel and its return to a safe port. The absence of a report about what happened to the *Fancy* could mean the vessel was captured and its crew was imprisoned and thus unable to return to America.

The absence could also mean that the officers and crew were ashamed of their roles in sailing the *Fancy* across the Atlantic and attempting to resell the enslaved people on board. At the time in the North, including in Rhode Island and Massachusetts, there were increased stirrings in opposition to slavery and the slave trade in particular. The changes in mindset among the people were being reflected in state laws limiting the slave trade and the treatment of Black prisoners captured by American privateersmen. What Babcock and his men were doing at this stage of their voyages was hardly distinguishable from that of an experienced slave ship captain. Not wishing to be the target of criticisms from some quarters, it appears no one on the *Fancy*—or the *Marlborough*—provided information to any newspaper printers about the fate of the *Fancy* and its African captives.

My personal belief is that the *Fancy* was captured by a British or Loyalist privateer in the Caribbean. I base this view mainly on the lack of certain records. For example, I have found no evidence that Babcock, Brown, officers and sailors of the *Marlborough* crew, or their families, benefitted from a cash windfall from the sale of the captives on the *Fancy*. I also have not

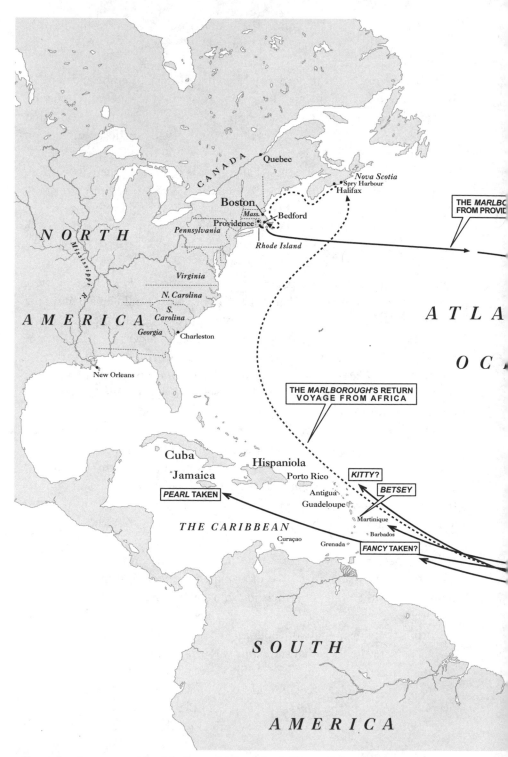

Transatlantic voyages of the *Marlborough*, *Fancy*, *Pearl*, *Kitty*, and *Betsey*.

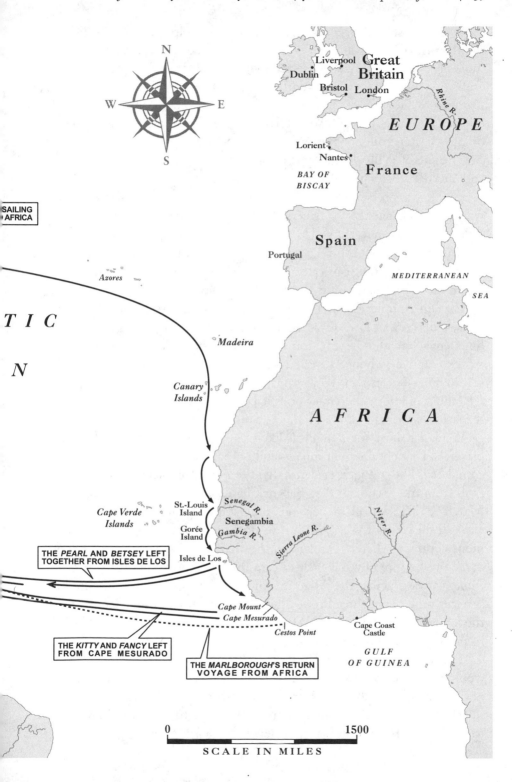

N

W E

S

SAILING
AFRICA

Azores

T I C

N

BAY OF
BISCAY

Liverpool
Dublin
Bristol
London

Great
Britain

EUROPE

Lorient
Nantes

France

Portugal

Spain

MEDITERRANEAN

SEA

Rhine R.

Madeira

Canary
Islands

AFRICA

Cape Verde
Islands

St.-Louis
Island

Gorée
Island

Senegal R.

Senegambia

Gambia R.

Sierra Leone R.

Niger R.

THE *PEARL* AND *BETSEY* LEFT
TOGETHER FROM ISLES DE LOS

Isles de Los

Cape Mount
Cape Mesurado

Cestos Point

Cape Coast
Castle

GULF
OF GUINEA

THE *KITTY* AND *FANCY* LEFT
FROM CAPE MESURADO

THE *MARLBOROUGH'S* RETURN
VOYAGE FROM AFRICA

0   1500

SCALE IN MILES

found in British navy records that a Royal Navy ship captured the *Fancy*. While my inability to locate such records is not determinative, it makes it more likely that the prize was seized by a British or Loyalist privateer operating in the Caribbean. In addition, if the *Fancy* had made it to South Carolina or Georgia, given the size of its human cargo, the landing and sale of the captives probably would have generated comment by newspapers or letter writers. But none of that has been found.

The fate of William Allanson, once the slave ship captain of the *Fancy* and later Babcock's prisoner, does not provide any clues about what happened. He was probably on the *Fancy* when it arrived in the Caribbean and was either exchanged by the Americans if they reached a safe port or released if the ship had been recaptured by the British. Allanson apparently was smitten with the idea of capturing a slave ship himself. In about March 1779, Allanson, commanding a privateer out of Liverpool named *Tartar* and cruising in the Caribbean, captured the French slave ship *Nairac*, commanded by Captain Antoine Babinot and carrying eight carriage guns, two swivel guns, and a crew of forty-three. Allanson took *Nairac* after a vigorous, one-hour engagement. The 250-ton ship had on board an astounding 697 African captives, whom Allanson sold in Jamaica.[24] After war's end, Allanson commanded six slave voyages from Liverpool.[25]

Tidbits of information must be relied on to try to piece together possible scenarios of the fates of the *Fancy*, its crew, and its human cargo.

While I believe the *Fancy* was likely captured by a British or Loyalist privateer, I cannot discount the possibility that the voyage was successfully completed. The strongest evidence that the *Fancy* completed its voyage derives from the document that Babcock handed to Dr. John Anderson on March 9, 1778, when Babcock and Anderson were on board the *Marlborough* off the coast of West Africa. The document is essentially an employment contract, whereby Anderson, the British physician for the *Fancy*, agreed to be hired by Babcock to care for the captives and crew on the *Fancy*'s voyage across the Atlantic. Anderson's wages for completing his services were to be "three Prime Slaves." On the back of this document is the following inscription: "Rec'd June 28, 1778. The Contents in Full." This receipt was signed by Anderson.[26]

The agreement between Babcock and Anderson states that Anderson would be paid only if the *Fancy* arrived at a "safe port under the command of Capt. Francis Bradfield." The receipt confirming that Anderson was paid in full by Babcock, therefore, is some evidence that the *Fancy* did make it to a safe port. It is the strongest evidence that exists today.

The June 28, 1778, date of Anderson's receipt may tell another story. Captain Bradfield should have completed the *Fancy*'s voyage to South Carolina or Georgia sometime in late May. If the *Fancy* had arrived at a safe port, Anderson should have been paid immediately. Why did it take more than a month for him to receive the "three Prime Slaves" as his wages? It could be that the *Fancy* was captured but Anderson was released since he was a British citizen. Anderson might then have made his way to Rhode Island to pick up his payment from Babcock. It might have taken until June 28 for that to occur. On the other hand, if the *Fancy* had been captured, it is not clear why Anderson would have been paid his fee.

Rhode Island census records disclose that Francis Bradfield, the *Fancy*'s captain, survived the war. The 1774 census indicates that he resided in North Kingstown, heading a household that included two adult white women and a white female child. One of the adult women was probably Bradfield's wife and the girl was likely their child. The other adult woman was probably the mother of Bradfield or of his wife. A Rhode Island military census also indicates Bradfield was still in North Kingstown in 1777.[27]

In a 1782 Rhode Island census, Bradfield is still listed as residing in North Kingstown. His household had increased to eight people—six adult white males and females, and two Black people (whether enslaved or free is not reported).[28] Thus, Bradfield survived his ordeal with the *Fancy*. Accordingly, Bradfield either brought the *Fancy* to a safe port, or his vessel and its 310 enslaved people were captured by the British and Bradfield survived his imprisonment.

The listing of two Black people in Bradfield's household in 1782 is intriguing. As mentioned above, it was a common practice for slave ship captains to be awarded several captives as part of their compensation for a successful voyage. The 1774 census did not report any Black people in Bradfield's household. While it cannot be known for certain how the two Black people became part of his household, it is possible Bradfield acquired them as enslaved people from the *Fancy*. But he could have also acquired them from the *Marlborough* or the *Kitty*, both of which also carried African captives back to New England. Or Bradfield could have acquired them in another manner.

There is another source of information that might explain the *Fancy*'s fate. It is from the log of the fifty-gun British ship HMS *Portland*. Commanded by Captain Thomas Dumaresq, in April 1778 it began to cruise off the coast of the British-controlled Caribbean island of Antigua. At the time, it had been at anchor for several days in the harbor at St. Johns. The

Portland's captain, in his logs, typically reported American ships captured by British warships and Loyalist privateers and brought into St. Johns.

For the evening of May 6, 1778, the *Portland*'s log includes the following item: "Sailed ye *Fancy* and *Suprize* and at noon [May 7] they came in with an American schooner from Guinea with 100 slaves."[29] This item appears to indicate that Loyalists from Antigua sailed privateers called *Surprize* and *Fancy*, and that they had captured an American schooner that had reportedly sailed from Africa with one hundred enslaved people on board.

Was the American schooner with African captives on board actually the prize *Fancy* commanded by Bradfield? An indication that it might not be the captured vessel was that it was described as a schooner. Schooners had two masts with sails parallel to the length of the ship. The *Fancy* was larger than a schooner, with three masts that had sails perpendicular to the length of the ship. However, the *Portland*'s description could have been an error. In addition, the *Fancy* had 310 African captives on board when it departed the coast of West Africa, and this vessel was described as having only one hundred.

On the other hand, some facts suggest this captured slave ship might have been the *Fancy* from the coast of West Africa. First, the timing was right. After departing the West African coast on March 11, Bradfield's *Fancy* would have arrived in the Caribbean in early May, about the same time as the other three vessels Babcock sent from the West African coast to the Caribbean in early March. The slave ship that HMS *Portland* reported as captured was taken on May 6. The *Pearl* was captured May 7, the *Betsey* probably arrived at Martinique about May 10, and the *Kitty* likely arrived at Martinique in mid-May.

Second, there were few other American slave ships returning from Africa sailing at this point, if any. The Continental Congress's ban on importing African captives or engaging in the slave trade with any of Britain's colonies remained in effect throughout the war. Other than the *Fancy*, this author is not aware of any slave ships sailed by Americans in this time frame.

Third, the *Portland*'s log states that one of the two Loyalist privateers was named the *Fancy*. It is possible that the author of the ship's log simply mixed up the vessel that was named the *Fancy*. The author has not found a record of a Loyalist privateer with that name operating out of Antigua in May 1778. We know that the slave ship *Fancy* was on a voyage either to the Caribbean or to South Carolina (via the Caribbean) in this time frame. The *Fancy* was not a popular name for ships at this time. It would be a remarkable coincidence that the privateer would also have been named *Fancy*.

Fourth, there is no reference to the *Fancy* successfully completing its voyage in contemporary American records or newspapers. If the *Fancy* had succeeded in arriving at a safe port and selling its human cargo, this would have been interesting news that American newspapers likely would have wanted to print. But they never did. In addition, the author did not find any mention of payments relating to the *Fancy* in archives relating to Captain Babcock and the prize money he paid out to his sailors from his privateering voyages.

If the American vessel identified in the *Portland*'s logs as a slave ship was the *Fancy*, the most startling fact is not the report of the May 6 capture, but the statement that only one hundred enslaved Africans were on board at the time of its capture. Given that Bradfield had reported to Babcock that precisely 310 enslaved people were on board the *Fancy* on March 11, can the discrepancy be resolved? There are two plausible explanations.

One is that the scribe for the *Portland*'s log simply got the number of enslaved people wrong. The scribe may have been provided incorrect information.

The other plausible explanation, horrible to contemplate, is that some two hundred captive Africans perished on board the *Fancy* on its voyage to North America. Slavers wanted as many of their captives to survive the Middle Passage as possible so as to increase their profits and avoid a financial loss. The average death rate among African captives on board a slave ship making the Atlantic crossing for healthy voyages hovered around five percent. Slave traders could never reduce the rate consistently below that, perhaps because they packed the enslaved people so close to each other belowdecks.[30] But sometimes the death rate on a particular voyage reached shockingly high rates, as was the case with the *Sally*'s voyage sponsored by John Brown and his brothers in 1763–64.

American privateersmen who captured slaves ships on the high seas had the same motive to keep as many captives alive and healthy as possible, but they were at a distinct disadvantage. The *Fancy*'s prize crew was too small and inexperienced for safely transporting African captives on a voyage in the Middle Passage.

For example, an experienced crew would have allowed the enslaved adult men on the *Fancy* to be brought from the lower decks to the main deck to spend hours walking in the fresh air and stretching their legs on a daily basis, even if they were chained to each other. As long as the captives did not threaten the crew, they could remain on deck. Such a practice would have reduced the risk of the tightly packed captives catching and communicating deadly diseases when they were crammed belowdecks. Eventually, if the male captives appeared unlikely to rebel, they could have their chains removed, which reduced the risk of infection. Perhaps Bradfield did not allow the Africans such liberties, despite the *Fancy's* doctor, John Anderson, recommending it.

Due to the poor quality of the food and water on a voyage, bouts of dysentery were common, and the "bloody flux," as it was called, could break out in epidemic proportions. The increasing exposure of the captives to dysentery increased the rates of contamination of supplies and the incidence of death. Dysentery accounted for the majority of the deaths on slave voyages.

High mortality rates on voyages were occasionally due to outbreaks of smallpox, measles, or other highly communicable diseases that were not related to time at sea or the conditions of the food and water. Of course, the crew of the *Marlborough* had had an outbreak of smallpox in January 1778 but had defeated it through inoculation. That approach would be very difficult to repeat with African captives.

In addition, crewmen should have been sent into the holds of the ship belowdecks at least once a week to clear the blood, mucus, excrement, and other filth that accumulated on the wooden planks where the captives slept. If that was not done, the Africans, already packed together, would have been even more vulnerable to deadly diseases.

The problem was not only an inexperienced crew but the small size of the crew Babcock sent aboard the *Fancy*, just "12 men and 2 boys," according to Boss's journal entry for March 7.[31] That crew size was fine for a regular prize vessel, but the *Fancy* was not an ordinary prize vessel. It had more than three hundred African captives on board. Normally, a slave ship carrying such a human cargo would have had a crew of at least twenty-five to thirty sailors. One experienced British slave ship captain stated, "The general rule is to have 10 sailors for every 100 slaves which the ship can carry."[32] The larger crew was needed to handle the enslaved people on the main deck, feed them and clean their sleeping areas, and, mostly, to prevent or defeat insurrections. On the *Fancy's* three prior African voyages, the crew had started with at least thirty-five officers and sailors.[33] With his smaller crew, and with few or none of them (other than Dr. Anderson) having experience handling African captives, Lieutenant Bradfield may have felt he had to keep the 310 captives on his vessel cooped up belowdecks for days on end, with disastrous results.

The close physical proximity of African captives crowded belowdecks for weeks and months created an ideal environment for infectious disease.

Once disease broke out in the cramped quarters of the lower deck of a slave ship, it could spread quickly. This could happen even with an experienced crew of the proper size, but the risk of it occurring with a small, inexperienced crew was greater. In addition, many of the *Fancy*'s captives had already spent a long time sweltering in the deep holds of the ships for weeks and months on the coast of Africa and were thus weakened and exposed to a higher risk of disease.

There are few narratives left by Africans who survived the Middle Passage. One was by Olaudah Equiano, who was kidnapped from his village in what is now Nigeria and forced onto a slave ship that sailed in the Middle Passage in the 1750s. Equiano later bought his freedom and became a prominent abolitionist in London.[34]

Equiano described the sensation of being put below the main deck with the other captives: "I received such a salutation in my nostrils as I had never experienced in my life; so that with the loathsomeness of the stench, and crying together, I became so sick and low that I was not able to eat, nor had I the least desire to taste anything." He felt a little better when he found fellow Igbo people aboard, but he was convinced that the white men were evil spirits. Similarly, he was amazed by the workings of the ship and thought it moved by magic. Eventually, the ship weighed anchor and his Middle Passage commenced.

Down in the small hold, assaulted by hot and foul air, with captives crammed together, many of them grew sick and died. Equiano described "the whole a scene of horror almost inconceivable" with the "loathsomeness of the stench" and "the shrieks of the women, and the groans of the dying." Thankfully, because Equiano was a minor, he was not chained and had some freedom to move about.

The white crewmen could be cruel to enslaved people who refused to cooperate with their plan to sell them at their destination. On one occasion, after three captives tried to jump overboard and end their lives rather than accept their enslavement, one of them was recaptured and flogged mercilessly. Likewise, the African captives inside the ship's hull were cruelly denied fresh air. Equiano, like other captives, was whipped for refusing food. All this Equiano experienced on what was apparently a normal voyage in the Middle Passage. The *Fancy*'s voyage may have been much worse.

There is no record left by the enslaved people on board the *Fancy*. Many of them may have come from the same tribe or even grown up with each other. One recent author on the African slave trade had the following to say about how captive Africans might have responded to their terrible plight on a slave ship: "Degraded and humiliated by their circumstances, individuals overcame differences to concentrate on the common need, survival. The slave ship could forge a fictive kinship between those aboard ship, with 'shipmate' likened to a fraternal relationship. Shared suffering created a special bond among shipmates."[35]

If the enslaved people did make it to South Carolina or Georgia, they were probably somewhat better off than if they had instead been disembarked at a British- or French-controlled Caribbean Island. The death rates of enslaved people in the Caribbean were much higher than on the North American mainland. This was particularly true during the Revolutionary War when, first, American privateers captured scores of ships filled with provisions for the British Caribbean colonies and, later, when the Caribbean became the site of a struggle between the British and French fleets. Either way, the survivors would still have been consigned to a lifetime of involuntary labor, bondage, and rules enforced by the whip.

CHAPTER TEN

The Fates of the *Marlborough,* Its African Captives, and George Waite Babcock

*O*n *the voyage back* to New England, Captain Babcock and his crew wanted the *Marlborough* to arrive safely, preferably at a Massachusetts port where the valuable trade goods stuffed in every nook and cranny of the vessel could be sold and the profits shared by the officers and crew, as well as John Brown and the other investors. For the same reasons, they wanted the twenty-seven African men, women, and children on their ship to survive the Middle Passage.

Babcock and his officers and men also hungered for more captures of enemy vessels on their return voyage. At the same time, they feared coming in contact with a powerful Royal Navy warship.

Captain's clerk Boss, based on the markings in his ship's log, was apparently knowledgeable about navigation. Captain Babcock may have been too, but it is not clear which one of them assumed the primary role of navigator. Of course, Babcock ultimately decided what course his vessel should take. Most slave ships from the west coast of Africa sailed northwest until they found the latitude of the Caribbean Islands and then sailed due west until they spotted one of them. Babcock also had the *Marlborough* sail to the northwest, but he wanted to avoid the Caribbean. He must have decided to head north toward the northern part of North America, and then west, hoping to arrive off the New England coast. Given the inexact science of maritime navigation at this time, Babcock's goal would not be easy to accomplish. Navigators were fairly proficient at calculating latitude but still struggled with longitude. The invention of the chronometer, and its perfection in the 1760s, solved the problem, but its use was not yet common.[1]

The first important event occurring on the return journey was the death of Christopher Brown, captain of the marines, at just twenty-six. Brown had spent a lot of time onshore at Isle de Kassa. He likely contracted an illness on land, which first manifested itself on March 12. On March 18, the ship's doctor pronounced his fever to be "putrid." It was hardly a specific diagnosis, but it was a sign the illness was taking a grim turn for the worse. Two days later, Brown died. Boss wrote of Brown, "He lived regarded & died lamented." Early the next morning, the crew "committed the body of Capt. Brown to the watery deep, with the honors of war by firing 3 volleys of small arms and colors half-mast high."[2] When Babcock returned to North Kingstown he would have to inform Sheriff Beriah Brown of the death of his son. Christopher Brown left a wife, Penelope. Beriah Brown would have a fieldstone placed in his family cemetery marking his son's death.[3]

On June 4, Thomas Evans, a boy who likely hailed from England and was hired as a sailor on the *Marlborough* at the Isles de Los, died of an unknown illness.[4] The New Englanders were fortunate that only Brown and Evans died of disease after visiting the coast of West Africa.

The crew kept a sharp eye out for potential prizes: enemy ships from Britain or its possessions. But from April 4 to May 9, the crew spotted and stopped only commercial or government vessels from neutral or allied countries: Denmark, Spain, Holland, and France. The French captain warned the Americans that a Royal Navy frigate carrying twenty-four guns was cruising off Cape Cod.[5]

On May 11, at two p.m., a lookout on the *Marlborough* spotted yet another sail in the distance. The *Marlborough* set its course to intercept it. As the *Marlborough* drew closer, its men could see that the vessel they were chasing was a ship of about two hundred tons appearing to carry eighteen cannon. Thus, its captain and crew could be willing to fight, even though the *Marlborough* was fifty tons heavier and carried twenty-nine cannon. Four hours later, the Rhode Island privateer had chased down its prey, which fired one of its cannon in a weak effort to ward off its pursuer. Then "to our joy," wrote Boss in his journal, a British flag was raised on the vessel.

The British colors meant the *Marlborough* could legally claim it as a prize. The *Marlborough* drew up alongside the vessel, and Captain Babcock, using his speaking trumpet, demanded that the ship strike its colors. The ship's master immediately complied.

Eldred and several men who would help sail the prize, including prize master William Wallace, took the jolly boat over to the British vessel and boarded it. The prize turned out to be the *John* sailing out of Leith, Scotland, and commanded by John Ogilvy. The *John* carried beef, pork, flour, hams, cheese, sugar, and port wine and was headed for British-controlled New York City. Eldred also observed that four of the *John*'s cannon were fakes made of wood.[6] Babcock and his men were much pleased—both the vessel and its cargo made the seizure a valuable prize. Babcock also needed the provisions to help feed his crew and the twenty-seven enslaved Africans on the *Marlborough*.

In the afternoon the next day, another sail in the distance was spotted, and Babcock ordered the *Marlborough* to give chase, with the *John* to follow. But the Rhode Islander's luck had run out—the vessel turned out to be owned and operated by Frenchmen. Its captain made a request of Babcock. He had several British "gentlemen" he had taken prisoner, presumably by capturing their ship, and he asked that Babcock take them on board the *Marlborough*. Babcock agreed, and the prisoners, in swelling seas as a storm was brewing, were transferred in a small boat to the privateer.[7] Between them, the *Marlborough* and *John* now had a total of thirty-six white prisoners on board.[8]

Two days later, after the storm had subsided, Babcock ordered that some of the foodstuffs carried by the *John* be transferred to the *Marlborough*. According to Boss, the *Marlborough*'s crew "was much in need of" the extra provisions.[9] The *Marlborough* continued sailing to the northwest, with the *John* following.

Finally, at five a.m. on May 25, land was spotted in the distance. The men had figured they were just north of Penobscot Bay in Maine. Seeing just a few "fish houses" where "drying fish" was set out, Babcock sent several crewmen on small boats to the shore, to what Boss described as "this wild . . . part of America." For the next several days, the men refilled fresh water casks and gathered firewood to bring back to the ship. Babcock also had more food supplies transferred from the *John* to the *Marlborough*.

As the *Marlborough* and *John* lay at anchor in a bay, an American schooner flying "Continental colors" sailed toward them and also came to anchor. The schooner was a privateer, with a crew of twenty-one out of

Salem, Massachusetts. Its captain informed Babcock that he was in Spry Harbour, Nova Scotia, not Maine. The news lowered the spirits of the Rhode Islanders. It appears Boss's navigation had taken the *Marlborough* considerably farther to the north than Babcock had intended. The port of Halifax, Nova Scotia, about fifty miles to the southwest, was used by Royal Navy warships. Mostly only local fishermen worked on the barren coast. Still, the Salem captain also warned Babcock that several Royal Navy warships were then cruising the waters from Halifax to Cape Cod.[10]

Several days later, still in Spry Harbour, a lookout on board the *Marlborough* spotted a sail in the distance. Babcock ordered his crew to give chase. In an hour, the fast American privateer had pulled up alongside the vessel, but it still failed to slow down. After Babcock ordered one of his cannon fired, the vessel surrendered. Babcock sent Lieutenant Nathaniel Brown and six men to take control of the ship, the brig *Bridget* out of Newburyport, Massachusetts, a merchant vessel carrying tobacco. It had been recently captured by the sixty-four-gun British warship *Raisonable*. Its small British prize crew, commanded by a Royal Navy midshipman, was sailing it to Canada, probably to Halifax. The *Bridget* had originally been owned by Brigadier General Jonathan Titcomb and Colonel Ralph Cross of Salem. But according to the maritime laws of the United States, by retaking the brig from the Royal Navy, it was now the property of John Brown and the officers and crew of the *Marlborough*. The British prisoners were secured. Brown took command of the *Bridget* and followed the *Marlborough* and *John* down the Maine coast.[11]

Two days later, on June 1, Babcock ordered Brown to leave the *Marlborough*'s company and sail the *Bridget* to a safe port. Boss explained in the ship's log, "she was a faster sailor than us or the ship *John* at present" (the latter two vessels were laden with captured goods).[12] It is not clear if that statement was true, given that the *Marlborough* had run down the *Bridget*, but perhaps the *Marlborough* had had the benefit of a favorable wind.

Curiously, in recording the events on the homeward voyage, Boss made few references to the twenty-seven enslaved people on the *Marlborough*. It was likely the enslaved children and women during the day were allowed to walk around the main deck of the ship freely. It was also likely that the enslaved adult males spent most of their time chained belowdecks and each day were allowed only infrequent visits on the top decks to stretch their legs and breathe fresh air. If the captive men did not create disturbances on the top decks, perhaps they were allowed to remain there longer. At night, the adult men, as well as perhaps the women and children, were secured belowdecks, the hatchway was closed, and a sentry was posted at the hatchway. These were normal practices for slave ships of the times, and as a result, Boss may not have felt they were worth mentioning.

The first reference to an enslaved person on the *Marlborough*'s return voyage was on April 4. Boss wrote of one of the enslaved girls falling off the ship and into the churning sea. He wrote, "This afternoon one of the Black girls fell overboard, but by the assistance of one of the men swimming to her with a spar, and the boat" going after her, the child "was taken on board again without any damage other than drinking a little salt water."[13] According to Boss's account, one of the white sailors jumped overboard to rescue the girl, and Babcock or another officer apparently ordered a small craft to be lowered and sent to pick up the two swimmers. Sometimes African captives intentionally hurled themselves into the sea rather than submit to the ordeal of slavery. In this instance, Boss described the girl as falling overboard, which suggests it may have been an accident.

Boss's second reference to one of the Africans was on May 28. The clerk wrote in his journal, "This day buried one woman on land" (in Nova Scotia), who had died of disease.[14] Since the only women on board the *Marlborough* were Africans, the woman who died must have been enslaved. She was the only captive African known to have died on the *Marlborough*'s voyage to New England.

The final reference to an enslaved captive on the voyage home occurred in connection with an attempted uprising on the ship *John* by the white prisoners. At two p.m. on June 3, as the *Marlborough* sailed near the port of Boston, Babcock saw the *John* sailing erratically or not on the agreed-upon course. He ordered two guns fired as a signal for the *John* to sail to the *Marlborough*. The *John* did not heed the request. Babcock then ordered the *Marlborough* to sail directly at the *John* and for the privateer's bow gun to be fired at the *John*. At this, the *John* cooperated and allowed Babcock and some armed men to board. According to Boss, "a slave told the captain" about the existence of "a plot among the prisoners." In response, Babcock sent two of the white prisoners to the *Marlborough* and had another, probably the ringleader, "put in irons, hand & feet."[15] It was not clear if the enslaved person who gave the information to Babcock was one of the *Marlborough*'s captives or one who had been captured on the *John*.

Finally, on June 6, the *Marlborough*'s crew spotted a familiar sight: the island of Nantucket five leagues to the northwest. At nine a.m. the next day, a Sunday, Babcock, accompanied by some of his crew and the "gentlemen prisoners" from the French sloop, went ashore to Nantucket.

Babcock did not intend to end his journey there, and with the British still holding Newport and the Royal Navy blockading Narragansett Bay, he had no intention of trying to return the *Marlborough* to Providence either. Instead, he wanted to conclude his voyage at Bedford, which at the time was best known as the port to which many New England privateers brought their prizes and captured goods to be sold. In addition, Bedford was a few days' walk to Providence and the rest of Rhode Island, from where most of the crew hailed.

At Nantucket, Babcock sought to hire a pilot to guide his ship through the treacherous Nantucket shoals. He also wanted to determine if there was word of a British warship cruising in the area. The "gentlemen prisoners" were allowed to stay at a local inn, at their own expense. The next day, Babcock and the gentlemen prisoners returned to the *Marlborough*, with a Mr. Pease, a local pilot.

At four a.m. on June 9, the *Marlborough* made its way into Nantucket Sound. Babcock sent a small boat ahead to inquire about the presence of Royal Navy warships. He received the answer that HMS *Unicorn*, a British frigate carrying twenty-eight guns, was cruising in Buzzard's Bay. Even though he was almost to Woods Hole on Cape Cod, Babcock played it safe and decided to turn his ship around and return to Nantucket.[16]

It was fortunate for Babcock that he was so careful. The *Unicorn* had left its usual station in the Sakonnet Channel in Narragansett Bay the morning of June 7, and the next day its crew had captured a Salem merchant vessel returning from the French-controlled island of Guadeloupe. Luckily for Babcock and his men, the *Unicorn*'s captain wanted to proceed to Halifax. His ship sailed past Nantucket on June 9. The following day, the *Unicorn* spotted and chased the *Blaze-Castle*, one of the other impressive privateers from Providence that was a match for the *Marlborough*. The *Blaze-Castle* carried eighteen guns, ten fewer than the *Unicorn*. John Brown owned three-sixteenths of the *Blaze-Castle*. Its captain, James Munro, had previously taken five prizes, and manning them with prize crews had greatly reduced the size of his crew. When the British warship caught up to the *Blaze-Castle*, the few remaining crewmen reportedly refused to fight, compelling Munro to surrender without firing a shot.[17] The *Marlborough*'s crew had barely avoided a confrontation with the *Unicorn*.

At three a.m. on June 10, 1778, the *Marlborough* again made its way to Nantucket Sound heading toward Bedford, with a small boat sent ahead as a lookout. The passage was uneventful. At six p.m., the *Marlborough* and *John* anchored in Bedford's harbor. Babcock immediately sent Eldred to the town on a small boat, carrying with him "5 of the gentlemen prisoners to get lodgings for them in order to clear the ship of them." Next, Babcock, "[s]ent all other prisoners on shore after having provided a house for them and set a guard over them."[18] Since Boss did not mention any of the twenty-six surviving enslaved people in his journal after this point, they all must have remained on board.

Two days later, on the afternoon of June 12, Boss penned his last entry in the ship's log for the *Marlborough*'s African voyage: "This afternoon I set foot once more on American land." Boss met with a local doctor "by whom I learn that my father was well a few days past & I hope it is well with the rest of the family—who I soon depart to see. So ends this Journal."[19]

Babcock, in turn, learned that on May 11, his wife had given birth to their first child. The boy too was named George Waite Babcock.[20]

The arrival of the *Marlborough* at the wharves of Bedford must have created a stir. The Rhode Island vessel was, after all, the first privateer to venture to Africa and return safely to port. Many of Bedford's sailors and dockworkers likely had an inkling of the *Marlborough*'s extraordinary voyage prior to its arrival based on the squib about the privateer sacking the British slave trading post at the Isles de Los appearing in the May 30, 1778, edition of the *Providence Gazette* (and reprinted in Boston's *Continental Journal* on June 10).

The next item published in area newspapers about the *Marlborough* was the following snippet in the *Providence Gazette*'s June 13 edition:

> Since our last the privateer ship *Marlborough*, Capt. Babcock, of this place [Providence], arrived in port from a successful cruise, having taken 28 prizes. Six of the most valuable were manned and three of them have arrived; the others were sunk and destroyed. She brought in with her a ship laden with dry goods, wine, port, etc. and a brig with provisions. A large Guineaman, having on board 300 Slaves, was ordered to South Carolina. The *Marlborough* has large quantities of effects on board, taken from the enemy.

The *Providence Gazette* must have obtained the information from an officer or member of the crew of the *Marlborough* as he passed through Providence on his way home to Exeter or North Kingstown to the south. The six prize vessels that Babcock manned were the *Fancy*, *Pearl*, *Kitty*, and the *Betsey* that had been seized off the West African coast, and the ship *John* and brig *Bridget* that had been captured on the *Marlborough*'s return voyage. The reference to three of the prizes having arrived safely in port must have been to the *John*, the *Bridget*, and probably the *Betsey*. The "ship laden with dry goods" was the recently retaken *Bridget* from Newburyport, while the "brig with provisions" was the *John*. Of course, the "large Guineaman" with "300 Slaves" on board "ordered to South Carolina" was the *Fancy*.

The report of the *Marlborough* taking twenty-eight prizes in one cruise would have made it one of the largest hauls of any privateer during the war. But the count from Boss's journal was closer to twenty. They included five ships and brigs, four schooners, two sloops, one barge, and at least four small shallops.

Boston's *Independent Chronicle*, in its June 18 edition, published a different item about the *Marlborough*'s return. No doubt another ship's officer or crew member provided the newspaper's editor with the information. It reads:

> Capt. George Wait[e] Babcock, in the privateer ship the *Marlborough*, belonging to Mr. John Brown and Company of Providence, has taken two prizes, one is arrived, and the cargo is 84 casks loaf sugar, cheese, pork, beef, flour oatmeal, porter, claret and sherry wines, etc. etc. etc. The other is not arrived, but Capt. Babcock thought proper to select 300 cases of Geneva [gin], 150 half [cases of the same], 20 butts [of the same], 1,000 small arms, a quantity of British goods, 1,000 weight of ivory teeth, etc. with which he is arrived in a safe port.

This report was later reprinted in several Connecticut and Boston newspapers and summarized in Maryland and Pennsylvania newspapers.[21] The prize that had arrived with eighty-four casks of sugar was the *John*. The "other" prize that had not yet arrived in a safe port (and never would) was the *Pearl*. No mention was made of the *Bridget*.

Yet another Boston newspaper, the *Independent Ledger*, in its July 6, 1778, edition, published a slightly different report about the *Marlborough*'s African voyage: "Arrived also the *Marlborough*, a Providence privateer, with a prize. She has been on the coasts of Africa, had taken 20 British vessels, destroyed a British fort, and [destroyed] all the trade in that quarter of the coast." The report about the *Marlborough* destroying all the trade in that quarter of the West African coast was a reference to the African slave trade.

In London and Liverpool, in July, the *Marlborough*'s captures of the *Fancy*, *Pearl*, and *Kitty* off the coast of Africa were mentioned in a number of newspapers.[22] One report, repeated in several London newspapers, even provided the privateer's name.[23]

Upon his return, Babcock's first item of business was to dispose of the white prisoners he had taken from his prizes, including the Royal Navy sailors, as well as the "gentlemen prisoners" from the French sloop. No doubt Babcock wanted to transfer his prisoners as quickly as possible in order to reduce his expenses of feeding and quartering them and the hassle of securing them. Babcock probably sent one of his men to Providence with news of his prisoners the same day they landed at Bedford.

On June 9, the Rhode Island Council of War ordered Babcock to deliver his prisoners to a Rhode Island official so the state could try to exchange them for American prisoners—most of them privateersmen and other American seamen captured on the high seas and languishing on steamy and pestilent British prison ships in Newport Harbor. There were periods of time in 1777 and 1778 when the prisoners kept at Newport suffered from a high rate of death and disease because of too little and poor-quality food, overcrowding, and mixing healthy prisoners with sick ones.[24]

Babcock complied with the order. After the *John* arrived in Boston, several days after the *Marlborough* reached Bedford, Babcock gathered all thirty-six of his white prisoners and sent them to Barnstable on Cape Cod. The commanding general of Rhode Island state forces at Tiverton, Rhode Island, Ezekiel Cornell, sent to Barnstable a lieutenant and seven soldiers on horses, who escorted the prisoners to Tiverton. General Cornell then moved the prisoners five miles into the interior to prevent them from being rescued by a British raiding party from Newport.[25] Later in the month, these prisoners were exchanged, some likely for unarmed civilians from Bristol and Warren, Rhode Island, who had been captured in a British raid on May 25 and stowed away in a filthy British ship in Newport Harbor.[26]

After William Wallace, the prize master of the *John*, arrived at Boston, he traveled to Providence to meet with John Brown. The two men then went to Boston and began efforts to sell the *John* and its merchandise in the maritime court for the Middle District in Massachusetts.[27] A newspaper advertisement in the June 18 edition of Boston's *Independent Chronicle* announced that Babcock had filed a libel in the maritime court, the first step in selling seized items, "against the ship *John*, of about two hundred tons burthen, James Ogilvy late master; and against sundry articles of merchandise, firearms, powder, etc. taken on the high seas from British subjects." The records surrounding the disposition of the white prisoners and the newspaper notice of the libeling of the *John* and its merchandise are the only two surviving records indicating how the various prizes, goods, and people seized by the *Marlborough* on its voyage to and from Africa were disposed of and handled.

Conspicuous by its absence in the *Providence Gazette*, *Massachusetts Spy*, and *Independent Ledger* newspaper reports is the mention of the twenty-six enslaved people presumably still aboard the *Marlborough*. Babcock and the rest of his officers and men might have wanted to avoid what they figured would amount to bad publicity. They might not have wanted to expose their human cargo out of concern that some New England residents would be shocked and heap opprobrium on the *Marlborough*'s crew for not being willing to set their African captives free, particularly those then present in Massachusetts. While some New England elites and a few others still held some enslaved people, most New Englanders did not, and the continuation of slavery in the New England states was becoming uncomfortable for many. Rhode Island and Connecticut had also outlawed the importation of enslaved people. In addition, Babcock and the rest of his officers and men likely did not want to advertise their human cargo so as to avoid the risk of hampering their efforts to sell the African captives, in case they wanted to violate state laws that prevented such sales.

At this stage of the voyage, Babcock was acting like a slave trader, and his men on the return voyage had served the role of a slave ship's crew. But they also had to deal with laws and rules regarding their status as privateersmen acting under the authority of a commission from the Continental Congress.

Sailing the *Marlborough* to Massachusetts presented potential legal obstacles. The state had directly confronted the issue of what to do with enslaved people captured by American privateers who were passengers on a prize vessel. On September 16, 1776, the Massachusetts legislature had passed the following law:

> Whereas this Court is credibly informed that two Negro men, lately taken on the High Seas, on board the sloop *Hannibal*, and brought into this State as prisoners, are advertised to be sold at Salem the 17th instant by public auction, Resolved, That all persons concerned with the Said Negroes be and they hereby are forbidden to sell them or in any manner to treat them other ways than is already ordered for the treatment of prisoners taken in like manner; and if any Sale of the said Negroes shall be made, it is hereby declared null and void. And that whenever it shall happen, that any Negroes are taken on the High Seas, and brought as prisoners into this State, they shall not be allowed to be sold, nor treated any other ways than as prisoners ordered to be treated, who are taken in like manner.[28]

The legislation did not require that enslaved passengers be freed. Rather, the act declared that the captives had to be treated the same as enemy white prisoners of war. Presumably, the legislation applied to any type of prisoner—whether the Black person was a passenger accompanying his or her master or was a member of the crew of the seized ship.

The original House of Representatives' draft resolution had included the phrase, "the Selling and enslaving of the human species is a direct violation of the natural rights alike vested in all men by their Creator and utterly inconsistent with the avowed principles on which this and the other United States have carried their struggle for liberty even to the last appeal."[29] But this language met with opposition and did not survive in the final bill that was passed.

At least two times attempts had been made by Boston merchants to skirt the law. The May 8, 1777, edition of Boston's *Independent Chronicle* announced an auction the following week on the Long Wharf for a prize vessel and all its property, including "three Negro Boys." Presumably, the youngsters had been traveling as passengers or serving as part of the vessel's crew prior to its capture. If so, it would have been a blatant violation of the law to sell them as enslaved people.

In the June 26, 1777, edition of the same newspaper, an advertisement announced the sale at "General Hancock's Wharf" of goods taken from a prize vessel seized by a local privateer. Among the items sold were "two Negro men and one Negro woman," whose labor contracts were to be sold for a period of seven years, after which they "are to be freed by the Purchaser." These three Blacks were thus sold as indentured servants for a term of years and not as permanent enslaved people. This approach may have been adopted to avoid the 1776 legislation.

In November 1777, a Black woman named Cuba, who had been taken into Boston on board a prize vessel, pleaded with Massachusetts state authorities to prevent her captors from selling her as an enslaved person. She had been seized from a British vessel by Captain Seth Harding, commander of the Connecticut state navy ship *Oliver Cromwell*. Cuba must have been a passenger on the captured ship.

Cuba was represented by a Boston attorney who filed a petition with the Massachusetts Council on her behalf. Using the convention of speaking in the third person, the petition stated that Cuba "is rejoiced she is in this Land of Liberty where she hopes to spend the rest of her life in comfort and freedom," but that "the officers of the *Oliver Cromwell* want to make her their own property." The petition added that the Connecticut vessel's lieutenant, John Chapman, "after abusing the Council . . . in a most scurrilous manner, swore he did not believe God ever made a Negro and that in spite of all courts and persons whatsoever, he would have her sold as a slave and sent to Jamaica next week." Harding and Chapman kept Cuba confined in a house in Massachusetts. The petition implored the Massachusetts Council to order "that she should be considered and treated as being within the true intent and meaning of the Act" passed on September 16, 1776, "respecting Negroes taken on the high seas and brought" into Massachusetts and released.[30]

The council resolved the case in Cuba's favor. On December 3, 1777, it issued an order directing "the Judge of the Maritime Court [to] certify that the said Negro woman comes within the meaning and intent" of the September 16, 1776, resolve.[31] Accordingly, Cuba could not be libeled in a Massachusetts maritime court and sold as an enslaved person.

Captain Babcock and his officers would likely have been aware of the ruling in Cuba's favor, as the ruling had been issued prior to the *Marlborough*'s departure from Providence in late December 1777. The Massachusetts law was clear on its face that the *Marlborough*'s enslaved Africans seized on enemy vessels as passengers or sailors could not be sold within the state.

It is not clear how the Massachusetts legislation applied to African captives on board the *Marlborough* who were seized as cargo on British slave trading ships and other vessels suspected of trading with the British. These captives were not passengers or sailors; rather, they were treated under admiralty law as property, a commodity. Babcock may not have wanted to be a test case.

Rhode Island, by contrast, had not addressed the legal status of an enslaved person captured by an American privateer. There were several laws that were somewhat relevant. In 1774, Rhode Island's General Assembly had banned the importation of enslaved people. The act was specifically intended to prevent enslaved people from being brought into the colony (now a state) and sold. If any were imported, they would be automatically freed and the person responsible for importing them could be subject to a penalty of £100 for each violation. There was a narrow exception intended for the benefit of Rhode Island slave traders: enslaved people could be brought into Rhode Island if they had been brought from the coast of Africa and could not be sold in the Caribbean. But in such a case, the owner of the enslaved people had to give a bond of £100 for each enslaved person so brought into Rhode Island, which the state would keep if the enslaved person was not exported out of the state within one year.[32]

It was not clear how Rhode Island's nonimportation act applied in the case of enslaved people captured aboard enemy ships and claimed as property from a prize. The issue, it will be recalled, previously arose in connection with a capture by Esek Hopkins, the former slave ship captain for the Brown family and then the commander in chief of the Continental navy. In 1776, Hopkins led a small squadron of Continental navy ships that came across two small Royal Navy vessels and captured one of them, the bomb brig *Bolton.* On board the *Bolton* were seven enslaved people who had been serving as members of the vessel's crew. They probably all had been enslaved by merchants and others from Newport and the surrounding area, where the *Bolton* had been operating prior to its capture.

The September 14, 1776, edition of the *Providence Gazette* included a notice of libel by Hopkins "against Seven Negro Slaves late in the service of the King of Great Britain" on board the *Bolton.* The captives were tried and condemned as property on October 1 in the maritime court in Providence.[33] It does not appear that anyone sought to apply the nonimportation act to the sale of the seven enslaved people.[34]

Based on Hopkins's example, it appeared there was a path for Babcock to have sold the enslaved Africans carried by the *Marlborough* in Rhode Island. He may, however, have hesitated out of concern over the risk of being forced to pay £2,600 for a bond covering the twenty-six enslaved people on his ship.

There were other obstacles to bringing the Africans to Rhode Island. For one, Newport and the rest of Aquidneck Island, and Conanicut Island, were still occupied by the British. The Royal Navy continued to blockade Narragansett Bay. Thus, to get the twenty-six enslaved people from Bedford to Rhode Island safely, he might have had to have marched them to Providence in a coffle—a group of enslaved people chained together so as to minimize the risk of their running away. He could have used another approach, such as securing the captives onto carts. Either prospect was likely considered too public and unappealing. In addition, given the tremendous blow to Rhode Island's economy from the British occupation of Newport and the Revolutionary War, there was little demand for enslaved people in the state. There is no record that Babcock attempted to commence admiralty proceedings in Providence to sell the enslaved people as property from captured prizes.

The lack of any records or correspondence addressing attempts to sell the enslaved people on the *Marlborough* could have been due not to the laws of Rhode Island and Massachusetts but to the desire of Babcock and his officers to avoid publicity about the nature of their human cargo: they may have wanted to avoid the shame of being associated with slave traders. This conclusion is somewhat supported by the facts that no report of the enslaved people on board the *Marlborough* was ever made in a New England newspaper and that no attempt was apparently made to dispose of the human cargo in admiralty proceedings in Rhode Island or Massachusetts.

John Brown, of course, had no qualms about trading in African captives. Some other Rhode Island merchants, sea captains, and sailors felt the same. But more and more Northerners were concerned about slavery in their midst and about the African slave trade in particular.[35] Knowing this, Brown may have decided to avoid making waves in Rhode Island and Massachusetts, particularly if he never intended to sell the captives there.

Brown could have had the twenty-six captives on his vessel sailed to Charleston, South Carolina, or another Southern port, to sell. A sale in the South would not have presented any legal complications or met with any appreciable opprobrium from local citizens. And he likely would have obtained much higher prices in the South than in New England. However, it would have increased costs to make such a voyage—hiring a crew for the voyage and spending more funds on food for the crew and the enslaved people. In addition, there was the danger the vessel would be captured by a Royal Navy warship.

It is not known how Brown and Babcock disposed of the twenty-six African captives aboard his vessel. It is a distinct possibility that they were quietly sold, in Rhode Island and/or Massachusetts, in New Jersey, or in a Southern state. If so, Babcock would have illegally avoided maritime court proceedings and instead directly shared the net sale proceeds with his crew and John Brown and the other investors in the *Marlborough*. The most likely scenario is that Babcock and Brown sent a smaller vessel with the twenty-six African captives on board to sell them in South Carolina or Georgia, either privately or through admiralty court proceedings. The least likely scenario is that Babcock simply freed the enslaved people.

Babcock was flush with cash when he arrived back in Rhode Island, and he used some of his earnings from privateering to buy a house for his growing family. On August 11, 1778, he purchased for £540 what is now called the Silas Jones House in the village of East Greenwich. Like Updike's Newtown a short distance to the south, East Greenwich was a small but thriving port (at least prior to the war) with access to Narragansett Bay. East Greenwich had the advantage of being more protected than Updike's Newtown from a raid by the British or Loyalist forces then occupying Newport.

George, Susanna, and their newborn son moved into the medium-sized, gambrel-roofed, and comfortable house, sitting on twenty-two acres of land.[36]

Captain Babcock continued to command privateers. This was his calling until war's end. On his voyages, he had a habit of not backing down when confronted by heavily armed enemy vessels.

John Brown and the other Rhode Island investors sold their interests in the *Marlborough* to a group of Massachusetts investors led by Boston's James Swan and Tauton's James Godfrey. With Swan's assistance, "George Waite Babcock, mariner of Exeter, R.I.," obtained a commission from the Massachusetts government to command the *Marlborough* on September 8, 1778.[37] James Eldred agreed to serve as first lieutenant and John Linscom Boss as captain's clerk, keeping the ship's log. Departing Boston on September 13, 1778, for a fourteen week cruise off the banks of Newfoundland, Babcock and the *Marlborough* did not repeat their great success in Africa. Still, it was a profitable voyage and included its share of drama.

The voyage began inauspiciously when the Boston privateer was run down by the *Hope*, a sixteen-gun Royal Navy sloop, on the morning of September 21. Babcock refused to yield, despite facing a Royal Navy warship manned by an experienced crew. A fierce engagement ensued, with the *Marlborough*, according to Boss, extracting its "bloody pay" by "firing broadsides from each" of the ship's sides. Firing broadsides from both sides of a ship was unusual, although not unprecedented. Boss wrote in his journal that "the engagement lasted 2 glasses [in this case two hours] without any suspension" until the enemy sloop "ran from us."*

The *Marlborough* suffered two dead and five wounded. One of the wounded sailors was John Larkin, who had survived the smallpox on the ship's voyage to Africa.[38] According to a report printed in a Halifax, Canada, newspaper, the "close action . . . continued near two hours" until the *Hope*, with its sails and rigging badly damaged, made its escape. The

---

*On a large sailing vessel, the ship's company was typically divided into two shifts or "watches" made up of eight half hours each. One half hour was called a "glass." The helmsman used a thirty-minute hourglass and would sound the ship's bell a consecutive number of times for each "glass" of the current watch. On occasion, a glass was set for one hour, rather than thirty minutes. For an example of one that was sixty minutes long, see Log of the Continental Navy Ship *Ranger*, Captain John Paul Jones, in Crawford et al., eds., *Naval Documents*, 12:838-54. For a reference to a "one hour, or half hour glass," see *Journal of the Virginia Navy Board*, April 6, 1778, in ibid., 44.

newspaper reported that the British sloop had suffered one man killed and two wounded. The sloop's captain was among the wounded. According to the Halifax newspaper account, he "received a shot thorough his body, but is thought to be doing well."[39]

Babcock, after his men mended the sails and repaired the rigging from cannonball damage, had to decide whether to return to Boston so his wounded crew members could be cared for. He decided not to return. As it turned out, all the wounded men survived the voyage.

On his cruise, Babcock and his crew captured three vessels, each bound for Jamaica. On November 4, the brig *Nautilus* out of London and Cork, Ireland, was burned after its merchandise, sails, rigging, and prisoners were removed and stored on the *Marlborough*.[40]

A week later, on November 11, the *Marlborough* came across the transport vessel *Nancy* out of Glasgow, Scotland. The *Nancy* carried ten cannon and had a crew of fifteen men and eight boys. They put up a fight against the *Marlborough* for about thirty minutes and managed to fire a broadside at it. The *Nancy* did not surrender until after receiving four broadsides from the *Marlborough*. It does not appear the battle caused any serious injuries. The prize had on board a valuable cargo of dry goods and provisions. Babcock ordered a fifteen-man prize crew to sail the *Nancy* to Boston.[41]

The third prize, the one-hundred-ton brigantine *Lord Claire*, sailing out of Cork, when captured carried a cargo estimated at £30,000. All three captures, as well as the names of the *Marlborough* and Babcock, were again noted in London newspapers.[42]

During the last several weeks of the voyage, as winter set in, the *Marlborough* was pummeled by "strong gales" until it finally returned to Boston on December 20, anchoring near Boston Harbor's Long Wharf and firing a salute.[43] The fourteen-week cruise would be the last time Babcock would sail on the *Marlborough*. The ship's ultimate fate is not known. Its name may have been changed by new owners.

Babcock learned after his return to Boston that on December 2, a British warship, the fifty-gun *Experiment* commanded by Captain James Wallace, had captured the *Nancy* and its prize crew and ordered them sent to British-held New York City. Then, on January 5, 1779, the *Nancy* was retaken by the Continental navy sloop *Providence*, commanded by Captain John Peck Rathbun, who had a prize crew sail it into the harbor at Plymouth, Massachusetts.[44] As with Babcock, Rathbun hailed from Exeter, Rhode Island. It was remarkable that both men were outstanding ship commanders who came from the same small landlocked town. Babcock unfortunately litigated the matter, insisting that the officers and men of his ship *Marlborough* were entitled to one-half of the proceeds from the sale of the *Nancy* and its cargo. His position was counter to well-established law. Babcock lost his appeal and had to pay $390 in costs to Rathbun and others.[45]

Babcock received a commission on March 31, 1779, to command the privateer *General Mifflin,* which mounted twenty 6-pounders. Even though Babcock was spending more time in Boston, in an agreement relating to this cruise that he signed and was dated March 31, 1779, Babcock was described as residing in East Greenwich.[46] The privateer, owned primarily by Boston merchants, had a crew of 130. James Eldred again signed on as first lieutenant, and Nathaniel Brown signed on as second lieutenant, reprising their roles on the *Marlborough*'s voyage to Africa. Major Samuel Phillips of North Kingstown served as another second lieutenant. John Linscom Boss also enlisted on the voyage and again kept the ship's log, which is used here as a source in a history book for the first time.[47]

Babcock's fame during the Revolutionary War, such as it was prior to this book, was gained primarily from his commanding the *General Mifflin* on this voyage from Boston, which commenced on April 9, 1779.

The *General Mifflin* ultimately set its course for the coast of Ireland, the departure point for many British military supply ships to the British army in North America. Some Continental navy and privateer captains had great success bringing the war to Britain's doorstep, such as John Paul Jones and Gustavus Conygham. On May 1, Boss recorded in his journal, "All hands exercising cannon and small arms firing," and added, "and taking very good shot."[48] The crew would need to be prepared in the coming days.

On May 2, 1779, in one of his only surviving letters, Babcock reported to Beriah Brown in North Kingstown, his agent for this voyage and brother-in-law, that he had just captured the British brig *Providence,* loaded with 230 casks of wine, several hundred miles east of Nova Scotia. Babcock informed his relative that he had taken tens casks for the crew's consumption.[49] The *Providence* was a supply ship from Ireland bound for British-held Quebec. Babcock ordered an officer and nine men to sail the prize to Boston.[50]

On May 9, the *General Mifflin* ran down a massive British military storeship, aptly named the *Elephant,* from New York bound for London. Babcock ordered the British commander to strike "her English colors," but instead, according to Boss's journal, a "hot" engagement ensued for thirty minutes before the British ship finally surrendered. The storeship's commander, Lieutenant Robert Long, and six of his men, were killed in the sea battle, and ten more were wounded. Boss reported only one of the *General*

Mifflin's crew suffering injury, "a French lad" who was slightly wounded in the thigh. (Boss also wrote that a small iron ball from grapeshot fired by the enemy ship "passed within a foot of my head" and smashed into the side of his vessel, resulting in "splinters flying in my face." He was unhurt.)[51] Three days later, the *Elephant*, with fourteen men from the *General Mifflin* as a prize crew, was ordered to sail to Boston.[52]

The *General Mifflin* also took two commercial brigs, one named *Betsey*. Babcock again made the London newspapers.[53]

On May 17, as the sea churned with high waves, lookouts on the foretops of the *General Mifflin*'s masts spotted a ship sailing its way. It was the British privateer *Tartar*, sailing out of Cork with the goal of capturing American privateers. It carried twenty-six guns and was manned by about 180 men. By contrast, the *General Mifflin* had twenty 6-pounders and about 107 sailors on board. Babcock's crew had been reduced after twenty-three officers and sailors had been used to man prize vessels. Despite being outgunned and outmanned, Babcock set sail for the enemy vessel. The *General Mifflin* and *Tartar* met at eleven a.m. In the ship's log, Boss related what happened:

Babcock hailed the *Tartar* and demanded the vessel strike its colors, but there was no reply. "In a moment began a bloody engagement generally within pistol shot." The fighting lasted two-and-a-half hours and was as "smart" at the beginning as it was at the end. At one p.m., with both ships still firing away, some of Babcock's men tried to board the *Tartar*, but it moved away which prevented the Americans from boarding. The *General Mifflin* "kept a continual fire" on the *Tartar* from both of its broadsides. Even Boss fired three pistol shots at the enemy vessel. Finally, after two unanswered broadsides from the *General Mifflin*, the *Tartar* struck its flag.[54]

According to Babcock's captain of marines, Jonathan Mix, the *Tartar* was filled with "wild Irishmen." An account sent to Benjamin Franklin in Paris said that during the "desperate attack to board" the *Tartar*, "the English captain was killed and the ship directly surrendered." An account by the lieutenant of the *Tartar* stated that his ship had sprung a leak in the rough seas and that as a result, it could not open its lower deck gun ports and could bring only six guns against the *General Mifflin*. If true, the *Tartar* must have been heeled to the side from which the *General Mifflin* approached.

In his journal, Boss stated that in addition to the death of the *Tartar*'s commander, Osbourne Greatrix, seventeen of the *Tartar*'s men were killed in the action and twenty wounded. On the American side, James Sprague was killed, John Babcock (who was probably a relative of the *General Mifflin*'s commander) was mortally wounded, and a boatswain was slightly wounded. Both the *General Mifflin* and the *Tartar*, according to Boss, were "greatly shattered."[55] Another reliable account stated that the *Tartar* lost about eighteen dead and seventeen wounded, including its captain and captain of marines, while the *General Mifflin* suffered about two dead and seven wounded.[56]

After taking the *Tartar* and its 162 survivors, Babcock faced a dilemma. Before the battle, he had about fifty prisoners on board the *General Mifflin* from prior captures. Now he had 212 prisoners on his ships, but he was short of the food necessary to sustain them on a voyage across the Atlantic. He made the humane decision to send 190 of the prisoners on the *Betsey* to nearby Ireland. He did it on the condition that the same number of American prisoners be released from British jails. Babcock received signed promises from the master of the *Elephant,* the master of the captured brig, and the first lieutenant of the *Tartar* that they would release an equal number of American prisoners. (The British ship commanders who signed the document lacked the authority to enter into the agreement, which Babcock probably knew.) The prisoners set sail for Galway.[57]

At Passy in France, American diplomat Benjamin Franklin expressed his pleasure with the conduct of "the brave Captain of the *General Mifflin*."[58]

Babcock decided to have his ship and the *Tartar* sail to Nantes, France, to repair both battered vessels. First, he had Nathaniel Brown, Samuel Phillips, and forty-eight other of his men sail the leaky *Tartar*.[59] However, on their way to France in the English Channel, on June 23, the Americans spotted a fourteen-ship convoy. Soon three British warships were chasing the *General Mifflin* and two others chased the *Tartar*. Both American vessels escaped, but it was a close call. One British cannonball splashed only yards from the *General Mifflin*'s stern.[60] Lieutenant Brown became separated from the *General Mifflin* and decided to sail the *Tartar* back to Boston. On his way, he captured an enemy brig laden with fish.[61] Arriving at Boston on July 31, the ship and crew must have received a rousing reception on Boston's waterfront.[62]

Meanwhile, in July, the *General Mifflin* made it safely to Nantes (coincidentally, France's dominant slave trading port).[63] With the repairs to the *General Mifflin* completed, Babcock and the ship departed France on August 14, 1779. On this return voyage to Boston in September and October, Babcock captured four more prizes.[64]

On the voyage, Babcock got into yet another deadly engagement with a heavily armed enemy vessel. According to a journal kept by a common sailor, Jonathan Carpenter, on September 7, the *General Mifflin* had a "smart engagement" with an unidentified Loyalist privateer carrying eighteen guns. The enemy vessel "shot away our foretop mast and wheeled and then ran," escaping. The damaged *General Mifflin* did not follow. The engagement cost Babcock's crew three men killed and from seven to twelve men wounded (reports differed).[65] One of the killed was fourteen-year-old John Waite Holloway, Babcock's half-brother.[66] Holloway was the third of Babcock's relatives to die on privateering voyages he commanded.

A sailor from North Kingstown and Exeter mentioned the engagement in his application for a military pension years later. He claimed that after the "severe battle," the Loyalist privateer had signaled its surrender, but before any of Babcock's men could board it, the enemy vessel sailed off and escaped.[67]

The *Boston Gazette* reported the *General Mifflin*'s return to Boston on October 23, after "10 weeks from France."[68] Babcock and the surviving sailors had departed Boston more than six months prior to their return. On arriving back at Boston, Babcock learned that his luck had not been all good. The valuable *Elephant* military storeship, with fourteen of Babcock's men sailing it, was retaken by a Scottish privateer, and another prize vessel with a prize crew was retaken on the voyage back to Boston.[69] The captured crewmen were likely hauled off to dank prisons in England.

Babcock took the *General Mifflin* out for another cruise, this time out of Providence, on May 7, 1780. A new Providence newspaper, the *American Journal and General Advertiser,* reported in its May 17 edition that Captain Babcock and his privateer had arrived at Providence on May 16. (The British had evacuated Newport in October 1779, so that Narragansett Bay was again open for American shipping.) The report continued: "Capt. Babcock has captured and brought in with him a large letter of marque ship, laden with 500 puncheons of rum, etc. She was bound from Jamaica for New York. The prize mounts 19 guns, and has 75 men. She engaged the *Mifflin* a few minutes, but the captain, having his arm broke by a shot, struck his colors."

The prize vessel, the three-hundred-ton *Glasgow,* commanded by John Harrison, was bound from Jamaica to New York City but also had a commission to take prizes. After the contest ended successfully, Babcock decided to return with his valuable prize immediately to Providence, where the vessel and its cargo were tried in maritime court on June 8, 1780.[70]

Writing of this capture at sea on May 10, Babcock bragged to Beriah Brown, "had I known of this ship being so handy to me, I assure you none of your volunteers should have parted me. I could then with triumph say that I could fit you out with a ship that you need not be afraid to venture in."[71] Babcock implied that some sailors who Brown had approached to enlist in the voyage had begged off, fearing Babcock's reputation for engaging armed enemy warships.

After seeing his prize safely into Providence, Babcock departed Narragansett Bay for another cruise, this time to the south. The *General Mifflin* returned to Boston on July 29, 1780, after taking several more prizes.[72] On yet another cruise, the privateer captured a twenty-gun ship bound from New York to Newfoundland sometime in August and brought the prize to Boston on October 11.[73]

On the *General Mifflin*'s voyages up to this point, there is evidence that its crew consisted of many Rhode Islanders from North Kingstown and Exeter.[74] His townsmen continued to trust Babcock.

On about September 11, 1780, departing Boston, Babcock once again took the *General Mifflin* out to sea. This time he was described as a "mariner of Boston."[75]

At first, it appeared Babcock was having his usual luck. At daybreak on November 23, he came across a convoy of transport vessels from Cork carrying provisions to the British army ensconced in Charleston. Babcock spotted the British military transport *Brothers* that probably was larger than his vessel but did not carry as many guns. Babcock ordered the *General Mifflin* to fly British colors. After the vessels closed, Babcock ordered the British colors to be taken down and the Continental colors, with thirteen stripes, hoisted up. After the two ships fired four or five guns at each other, the transport tried to escape, but Babcock ran the vessel down. The *Brothers*'s captain later wrote, "He still kept firing upon us, he being so much superior, and coming up fast, his grapeshot tumbling about the decks . . . I thought it most prudent to strike."[76] The next day, November 24, the *General Mifflin* took another transport, the *Experiment*, which carried camp equipment for the British army.

The situation changed dramatically when two powerful Royal Navy warships that had been convoying the Cork fleet, the HMBS *Raleigh*, supported by HMS *Hyaean* nearby, appeared on the scene. First, the two British warships recaptured the two transports and their prize crews. Then, according to a British observer, "at half past eight the *Raleigh* came up close alongside of *Mifflin*, all clear and ready for action, and ordered him [Babcock] to strike, which he accordingly did, without a gun fired on either side." It must have mortified Babcock to surrender when the enemy vessel used the standard tactic he had employed many times. The *General Mifflin*, along with its two prizes, were brought into British-occupied Charleston.[77]

Ironically, the *Raleigh* was the former Continental navy frigate *Raleigh*, which under Captain Thomas Thompson had preceded the *Marlborough* to Gorée in February 1778. The *Raleigh* afterward had been captured and taken into the Royal Navy as the bomb ship *Raleigh*.[78]

Sailors captured on the *General Mifflin* off Charleston spent time in miserable British prisons. James Tennant of South Kingstown, Rhode Island, was imprisoned for a year at Charleston before being released.[79] Many others likely shared a similar fate. One prisoner was Christopher Raymond Perry, also of South Kingstown, the future father of navy heroes Oliver Hazard Perry and Matthew Galbraith Perry. He was imprisoned for three months on the infamous prison ship *Jersey* moored off Brooklyn. Perry barely survived a debilitating fever before he was exchanged.[80]

Remarkably, five of the *General Mifflin*'s crewmen aboard a prison ship in Charleston Harbor managed to escape soon after their capture. Their return to New England was facilitated by selling enslaved people. One evening aboard the prison ship in Charleston Harbor, the five crewmen observed a schooner that anchored near the prison ship. The schooner had several enslaved people on board. When the sentry was distracted, the Americans took the opportunity to escape from the prison ship and board the schooner. The Americans quickly overwhelmed and confined the sentry and the enslaved people and immediately sailed the schooner out of the harbor. They put into Patriot-held Wilmington, North Carolina, where they sold their enslaved captives. They then used the money from the sale to purchase a cargo of naval stores, which they transported on board the schooner to Newport, where they arrived on January 3, 1781.[81] The naval stores were likely resold at a nice profit to the French fleet then based in Newport.

Babcock had the good fortune of being exchanged in short order. He may have received good treatment from his captors because of his release of 190 prisoners after he captured the *Tartar* off the coast of Ireland.

After Babcock's loss of the *General Mifflin*, he never again commanded a large privateer. This development was due in part to a shift in the privateer war. By mid-1778, the Royal Navy, British privateers, and Loyalist privateers began to win their naval war with American privateers. By 1781, most of the large American privateers had been captured. Henceforth, Babcock would only command small privateers.

Records show Babcock on March 17, 1781, as part owner of the Rhode Island privateer schooner *Happy Return*. Two other part owners were James Eldred and Nathaniel Brown, his former officers on the *Marlborough* and the *General Mifflin*. On April 7, 1781, Babcock and another of his former officers on the *Marlborough*, Ichabod Holloway, were listed as part owners of the Massachusetts privateer schooner *Betty*.[82]

In 1781, Babcock and his family had their permanent residence in East Greenwich, Rhode Island, but he must have spent a lot of time in Boston too, searching for new commands. Records for the privateer *Happy Return* indicate Babcock hailed from Boston.[83]

From Boston, on June 11, 1781, Babcock took command of a small vessel, the ten-gun *Venus*, built in Weymouth, Massachusetts, and with a crew of eighty men. Boston investors owned half of the vessel, and Providence investors (including John Brown and two of his brothers) owned the other half. Babcock had written the Browns encouraging them to invest in the vessel, arguing that the ship was "cheap" and "I do flatter myself to do something with her and with the greatest spirit." John Brown still had confidence in Babcock. But only a short time after departing the port of Boston, on July 16, the *Venus* was captured by the thirty-two-gun frigate HMS *Danae* off the coast of Nova Scotia.[84] Babcock and his men were brought to Halifax. Most were released shortly thereafter, arriving back in Boston on August 13. They were treated "with uncommon humanity and kindness, not only when on board" the *Danae* but also after "their arrival at Halifax." For this unusually humane treatment, the prisoners publicly thanked their captors.[85] Babcock may have again reaped the benefits of his previously sending 190 prisoners to Galway after taking the *Tartar*.

Babcock returned to his home in East Greenwich, reuniting with his wife, Susanna. The Rhode Island 1782 census shows just two white adults living at his East Greenwich home.[86] Thus, it appears that their son, George, had died.

At this point, it seems the Babcocks decided to move to Boston. George Waite Babcock had operated as a commander of privateers out of Boston since 1779. In March 1782, he sold his house in East Greenwich. When he next appears in official Massachusetts records, he is described as hailing from Boston.[87]

By 1782, the war was essentially over, but Babcock and many other New England privateersmen sought to extract as much plunder as possible before a formal treaty was signed. Babcock's next vessel was the smallest one he ever commanded, the schooner *Hero*, carrying nine guns and with a crew of just twenty-five men. On July 1, 1782, he and his crew, along with the crews of four other small privateers, ninety-two men in total, raided and plundered the prosperous Nova Scotian coastal town of Lunenburg, about fifty miles southwest of Halifax. Perhaps Babcock recalled his raid of the Isles de Los four years earlier. Several 4-pound shots fired from the *Hero* forced the last defenders in a blockhouse to surrender. Babcock then went ashore and, based on one account, assumed command of the operations on land.[88]

The Nova Scotians, most of whom relied on fishing for subsistence, were often victimized by American privateersmen, who, according to one New Englander's account, "fell to plundering with a pleasing and natural vivacity." Food stores were seized, as well as "good West-India rum."[89] Next, the raiders threatened to destroy the houses of Lunenburg residents, unless they received a ransom of £1,000. The townsmen paid the ransom. Before departing, the privateersmen spiked the town's cannon and carried off most of the small arms held by the populace. The raid was hardly Babcock's finest hour, but it did result in the Massachusetts House of Representatives congratulating him and the other privateer captains. In London, at least seven newspapers covered the raid, prominently mentioning Babcock's role.[90]

It appears that by 1784, Babcock faced serious financial difficulties. In June 1783, he lost a court case against John Linscom Boss and had to pay his former captain's clerk a judgment of £150.[91] The surviving records do not make it clear what the source of the dispute was—it could have been a disagreement about the sharing of prize money for a 1782 voyage, with Boss as one of the investors.

In June 1784, Babcock lost another lawsuit, this one brought by the estate of a Bedford man, requiring Babcock to provide as security for the payment of the court judgment certain real estate he owned in Bedford—a wharf and land fronting water on Orange Street.[92] Perhaps in an effort to raise money to pay the debt, some land that Babcock still owned in Updike's Newtown, North Kingstown, was sold in August 1784. The sale was by John and Elizabeth Babcock, who each held a power of attorney for George W. Babcock. In the deed, "George Weight [*sic*] Babcock" is described as "late of Newport," indicating that he was a Newport resident at that time.[93]

The mention of George Waite Babcock in the North Kingstown deed is the last that the historical record preserves about him. Nothing is reported of him or Susanna in any later official or unofficial records that have survived and are known. Babcock is not mentioned in the 1790 federal census as heading a household in Rhode Island, Massachusetts, or any other state. These are indications that sometime after 1784 and before 1790, either Babcock died or moved and changed his name. He may have taken the latter course to avoid creditors. Some history books have misidentified Babcock in post-1782 events.[94]

Babcock's disappearance from official records has contributed to his not being appreciated as one of America's top privateer captains during the Revolutionary War. Considering his spectacular voyage to Africa and his later privateer successes, Babcock should be recognized as one of the outstanding American privateer captains of the war. Yet he is rarely mentioned in history books covering the Revolution's naval war. He is sometimes not even mentioned in books detailing the history of American privateers.

As a result of this book publicizing his prominent role in attacking British slave trade interests in Africa, his reputation as a privateer captain should improve. But due to his treatment of African captives on board the *Marlborough* when it returned to Massachusetts and the other African captives on board the *Fancy* and other vessels he captured in Africa, serious questions will be raised about his legacy.

John Linscom Boss married Sarah Boss, his second cousin from rural Richmond, Rhode Island, on February 21, 1779.[95] By 1782, Boss headed his own household in Newport.[96] The couple had nine children, eight born at Newport, but only two of them survived past age forty.[97] The eldest son, John Linscom Boss Jr., was elected twice to Congress from Rhode Island as a Federalist, serving from 1815 to 1819. But he also died relatively young, at thirty-eight, in August 1819.[98]

John Brown continued to invest in privateers and get richer. In early July 1778 in Providence, he received his share of twenty-nine thousand gallons of Madeira wine from a prize vessel taken by one of his privateers and sailed into Boston. Brown sent a gift of some of the wine—"the Best in the whole Cargo"—to George Washington.[99]

In 1779, Brown began construction of a twenty-gun privateer ship, which he named *General Washington*. However, after its commissioning in August 1780, Brown ignored the care he took with the *Marlborough* and sent the *General Washington* to search for British merchant vessels in the British Caribbean and off the coast of Newfoundland. Instead, in October 1780, the *General Washington* was taken by a British 74-gun warship.[100]

After the war, Brown invested in three transatlantic slaving voyages, in 1785, 1786, and 1795.[101] In 1784, he became the leading opponent of a proposal to ban Rhode Island's participation in the slave trade. He defended the trade, often in direct conflict with his abolitionist brother, Moses. Even after participation of Rhode Islanders in the slave trade had been prohibited by the state's General Assembly in 1787, John would exclaim, "in my opinion there is no more crime in bringing off a cargo of slaves than in bringing off a cargo of jackasses."[102]

In 1797, as a result of sponsoring an illegal 1795 slave voyage to Cuba, Brown was the first Rhode Islander, and probably the first American, to be tried under the federal Slave Trade Act of 1794. Though he was acquitted of criminal charges, his ship the *Hope* was forfeited and placed at auction. In 1799, Brown and others paid a call on Samuel Bosworth, the surveyor of the port of Bristol, warning him not to take part in an auction of another slave ship (not owned by Brown) the next morning. Bosworth ignored the threat, and while walking to the auction the next day, the federal official was kidnapped and deposited two miles down Narragansett Bay. This intimidated federal and state officials and effectively halted enforcement of the Slave Trade Act. Illegal slave trading in Rhode Island did not end until the implementation of the federal Anti-Slave Trade Act of 1807 on January 1, 1808.[103]

Slave trading was never central to Brown's expanding mercantile business. He was the first Rhode Island merchant to break into the lucrative trade with China. The ship he sent out in 1787 was a converted privateer from the Revolutionary War, the *General Washington*, which he had repurchased after its capture.[104] Brown built two other ships for the China and India trade, the 950-ton *President Washington* in 1790 and the 624-ton *George Washington* in 1793.[105] His shipping contacts in India and China produced great riches for Brown, making him Providence's leading merchant. His home on Benefit Street was described by John Quincy Adams in 1789 as "the most magnificent and elegant mansion I have ever seen on the continent."[106] Today, it is the main house shown by the Rhode Island Historical Society.

In addition to his mercantile activities, Brown was active in civic duties. He served in the Continental Congress from 1784 to 1785 and as a US representative in Congress from 1799 to 1801. He was active in the First Baptist Church in Providence and served as treasurer of Rhode Island College (now Brown University) for 21 years.[107]

What happened to the captives on board the *Fancy*, *Marlborough*, and *Kitty*? At this time we do not have a clue, as no written record of what became of them is known to exist.

CHAPTER ELEVEN

American Privateers Reduce Britain's African Slave Trade

G*eorge Waite Babcock* and the rest of the crew of the *Marlborough* were part of a broad-based attack on Britain's African slave trade by American privateers capturing British slave ships. The success of American privateers in capturing British slave ships was remarkable considering that the new United States was facing the most powerful navy in the world.

These attacks considerably reduced the British slave trade from 1776 to 1778. They led British slave merchants in Liverpool, Bristol, and London to agonize about whether they should continue to invest in the business as long as the war continued. Many decided to hold back. As a result, the British slave trade from 1777 to 1778 declined in some cases by more than seventy percent, and perhaps more than 60,000 Africans avoided being forced onto British slave ships and carried to the New World.

The Revolutionary War's impact in reducing the British slave trade to the Caribbean had several causes, but arguably the most important one from 1776 to 1778 was the role of American privateers attacking British slave ships. Other important causes in that time frame included American privateers capturing British merchant ships from British Caribbean islands carrying sugar in the third leg of the triangular trade, and them seizing British ships filled with provisions intended to feed the white and Black population of the British Caribbean islands.

This is the first book to detail and emphasize the role of American privateers in disrupting the British slave trade. A few other historians have mentioned the topic but not in a comprehensive manner.[1]

This chapter focuses on the period from August 1776 to August 1778, during which American privateers had their greatest success and impact. It was also before the French navy became actively engaged in the war. Once the powerful French navy appeared on the scene in North America and West Africa, British slave traders had even more to worry about than American privateers. Britain declared war on France on March 17, 1778, but it was not until late July and early August 1778 that French ships faced Royal Navy warships (in Narragansett Bay in Rhode Island). American privateers continued to prey on British merchant ships for the remainder of the war and to pose a threat to the British slave trade, but they never duplicated their spectacular successes of 1776 and 1777.

Babcock and the *Marlborough* damaged the British slave trade more than any other American privateer. On April 4, 1778, Richard Miles, the governor of the important British slave trading fort at Cape Coast Castle (in what is now Ghana), informed members of the Company of Merchants Trading to Africa, based in London, of the *Marlborough*'s four major captures. Miles wrote:

> I am sorry to inform you that two ships, the *Kitty*, Fisher, and the *Fancy*, Allanson, both of Liverpool, have been taken, the one at Cape Mount, the other at Montserrat [Cape Mesurado], by an American privateer called the *Marlborough* mounting 24 guns and commanded by George White [*sic*] Babcock. . . . From all we can learn the privateer must have left the Coast, having taken two prizes (names unknown) before she fell in with these ships.[2]

The two unidentified British vessels that Miles mentioned had been captured by the *Marlborough* were the *Pearl* and *Betsey*. News of the captures on the west coast of Africa by the American privateer, and the lack of British warships on the coast to challenge American privateers, must have caused trepidation in slave trading circles in Liverpool, London, and Bristol.

Thomas Case, the *Fancy*'s owner, became bankrupt in 1778. This was Case's second loss to an American privateer. On November 17, 1777, an American privateer captured the *Whim*, a seventy-ton snow out of Liverpool partly owned by Case and his brother, with 214 African captives on board.[3] It is likely that Case went bankrupt largely as a result of these two steep losses.

Babcock and his crew went one step further than capturing British slave ships: they plundered and destroyed a major British slave trading post at the Isles de Los. Naval History and Heritage Command historian Dennis Conrad agreed that the *Marlborough*'s operations on the African coast had "dealt a heavy blow to the English slave trade."[4] Babcock's attack on Barber's "factory" at Isle de Kassa deepened Miles Barber's bankruptcy, ended the participation of Andrew French & Co. in the slave trade, and heightened the concern of British slave merchants about investing further in slave trading posts in Africa or slave trading ventures during wartime.

Two Continental navy warships, the thirty-two-gun *Raleigh* and the twenty-gun *Alfred*, preceded the *Marlborough* at Gorée. Their presence created some angst at British posts in Upper Guinea, but they accomplished little in terms of disrupting the British slave trade. The substantial impact the *Marlborough* had on the British slave trade compared to the minimal impact of the two Continental navy ships reflects the overall impact American privateers had compared to the Continental navy. That impact is also revealed by the reactions inside Great Britain from 1775 to 1778.

News of the outbreak of war in the American colonies at Lexington and Concord in April 1775 and Bunker Hill two months later had an immediate impact on British participation in the African slave trade. One consequence was a riot in Liverpool in late August and early September 1775. Indeed, it grew into one of the largest and most destructive riots in England in the second half of the eighteenth century.

The immediate cause of the Liverpool riots was the attempt by John and Thomas Yates, owners of the slave ship *Derby*, to cut sailors' wages. The Yates brothers reasoned that since the outbreak of the American Revolution had already reduced the number of ships sent on African voyages, thus resulting in an increase in unemployment among the thousands of Liverpool sailors who worked in the trade, they could reduce wages. The sailors reacted angrily, cutting down the rigging of the *Derby* and a few other ships still willing to sail to Africa. The riots spiraled into armed attacks that left several sailors dead and the houses of a number of Liverpool slave traders, including that of Thomas Yates, ransacked. While there were several underlying causes of the riots, one writer gave as the cause news of American privateers taking a few British slavers in late August 1775: "The African merchants, having lost one or two ships [to American privateers], reduced the men's wages."[5]

The Liverpool riots caused the first recognition that the conflict with America had threatened Britain's valuable transatlantic slave trade. An observer in London reported later that September, "The African trade has felt the blow already. The West India trade staggers, and is doomed to fall next. No trade can long stand the present unwise contest."⁶ A writer in the September 29, 1775, edition of the *Liverpool General Advertiser* lamented, "Our once extensive trade to Africa is at a standstill; all commerce with America is at an end. . . . Survey our docks; count there the gallant ships laid up and useless. When will they be again refitted? What will become of the sailor, the tradesman, the poor laborer, during the approaching winter?" Liverpool's merchants and tradesmen submitted a petition to Parliament, warning that war with America would lead to the "ruin" of trade with Africa and the Caribbean.⁷

The war's adverse impact on the African slave trade was addressed in parliamentary debates in December 1775 over a proposed law permitting the Royal Navy to seize all American vessels. Nathaniel Bayley presciently objected on the ground that "as soon as it was made lawful to take American vessels," American privateers would begin to seize British commercial ships. He noted that British manufacturers exported some £470,000 of products to Africa, which, along with other trade, would be jeopardized by passage of the bill. But the majority coalition in the House of Commons led by Prime Minister Lord North, which supported an aggressive response to the American rebellion, prevailed, and the Prohibitory Act was passed.⁸

When news arrived in London in September 1776 that the American privateer *Rover* had attacked the Bristol slaver *Africa* off the coast of Portugal and that the British vessel had blown up, deep concern arose in financial circles. The *London Chronicle*, which reported the loss, added, "From the above information, the merchants and underwriters propose an immediate application to the Lords of the Admiralty for regular convoys."⁹ Two months later, a Bristol slave merchant wrote to Governor David Mill at Cape Coast Castle, "there has not been one Guineaman fitted out of this place since the *Africa* in July last."¹⁰

American privateers began capturing British slave ships with no enslaved people on board in August 1776. Appendix B lists twenty-six such ships captured from August 1776 to August 1778. More than half of them were seized in 1776. American privateers began capturing British slave ships with enslaved Africans on board in January 1777. Appendix C lists forty-one such ships, with an estimated eleven thousand enslaved people on board, captured from January 1777 to August 1778. George Waite Babcock and the *Marlborough*'s crew contributed to both types of captures in early 1778.

Many African voyages were insured by underwriters in London. By the third quarter of 1776, those underwriters took note of the depredations of American privateering. Insurance rates for merchant ships increased, not steadily, but in leaps and bounds. A Venetian diplomat wrote to his government in late September 1776, "American privateers have captured British ships trading with Portugal, Africa, and Italy . . . insurance [rates] which were once one and a half percent jumped to ten and a half percent and are staying there."[11] In January 1777, after a convoy of thirty commercial vessels had left Jamaica but only one had arrived in London, insurance rates increased to an astounding twenty-eight percent.[12] A London observer noted that during the Seven Years' War between Great Britain and France and Spain, "insurance never exceeded 7 percent."[13] For slave ship voyages, which required higher insurance rates than other types of commercial voyages, insurance rates more than doubled to almost thirty percent.[14]

Eventually, insurance rates stabilized, but they remained high. They varied based on whether the British commercial vessel traveled in a convoy protected by Royal Navy warships. While the convoy system was fairly effective on voyages between Britain and the Caribbean, the overstretched Royal Navy could not always spare sufficient ships for convoy duty. According to the Duke of Richmond, speaking to the House of Lords in February 1778, "the price of insurance to the West Indies and North America is increased from 2 and 2½ percent to 5 percent, with convoy, but without convoy, and unarmed, the said insurance has been made at 15 percent, but generally ships in such circumstances cannot be insured at all."[15]

The convoys provided marginal assistance to those in the African slave trade. Few convoys could be made on the voyage from Britain to Africa. And convoys were not possible at all for British slave ships departing the west coast of Africa for the Caribbean, because of the disparate locations and times of departures of the ships when they were finally "all slaved."

In addition to rising insurance rates, slave merchants faced increased shipping costs. This occurred in part because seamen's wages, after the Liverpool riots, actually increased from thirty-five shillings to about sixty-five to seventy shillings per week.[16] The wage increase was primarily due to the fact that so many sailors enlisted into or were impressed into the Royal Navy, thus driving up demand for remaining sailors, and the risk of capture by American privateers on board commercial vessels.

British slavers in Africa and the Caribbean began to publicize the havoc American privateers were wreaking on the African slave trade. One British observer, in a letter dated May 23, 1777, from Martinique, advised a slave merchant in Liverpool, "if your town has any Africa vessels near ready, they [should] put plenty of guns & men into them, as it is Guineamen [the American privateers] chiefly wish to intercept."[17] Arming slave ships with more cannon, small arms, and ammunition increased costs further.

The following letter, written in November 1777 by a British slave agent trading on the Gold Coast of Africa, was published two months later in the *London Chronicle*:

> For these two months past we have had about 12 sail of ships, with slaves on board, sailed from this and other ports of Africa, bound to the West Indies, eight of which we have already had advice of being taken by the American privateers, and carried into either Guadeloupe, Martinico, or some other of the French ports; and our Governor [i.e., a British official] had done all in his power to get them delivered up, but the messenger he sent has returned a few days ago, as he could get no answer.[18]

In a February 19, 1778, letter, Richard Miles, writing from Cape Coast Castle on the Gold Coast, complained, "I have only to observe that almost every Guineaman from this port [Cape Coast Castle] the last year has been taken close upon the West Indies Islands by the Americans, and by a small vessel arrived here from Antigua 7 days ago, I learn these seas are still crowded with privateers." Miles added that on one of the captured British slave ships, the *Fox*, not only were the African captives taken by the American privateersmen, so was some of his own personal property on board the vessel.[19]

In February 1778, Parliament's House of Lords held an inquiry focused on the wartime losses suffered by British merchants in the African slave trade caused by American privateers. One witness, John Shoolbred of London, spoke for British slave merchants. He "declared himself an African merchant and an underwriter" of insurance premiums. (Shoolbred did not mention that in April 1777, he lost the slave ship *Hawke*, with 454 African captives on board, to an American privateer.)[20]

Prior to testifying, Shoolbred had reviewed the account books at Lloyd's, the insurance association. His testimony to the House of Lords was summarized as follows: "that the African trade had been materially injured in consequence of the American war; that upwards of 200 sail were generally engaged in that trade, previous to the war; that not a fourth of that number, not above 40 ships, were now sent out; that 15 of the ships and cargoes had been taken by the Americans."[21] According to Shoolbred's numbers, the war had reduced British slave voyages by eighty percent.

Shoolbred, an experienced London slave merchant, blamed American privateers for most of the decline in the British slave trade. He testified that they had captured 37.5 percent of all British ships sent to Africa on slave trading voyages.

Shoolbred estimated the monetary losses suffered by British merchants in the African slave trade caused by American privateers. Based on slave ships carrying on average 257 captives each worth £35, every ship taken by the Americans resulted in a loss of about £9,000.[22] Based on a loss of fifteen slavers to American privateers, the estimated total loss of cargo amounted to £135,000. His estimates did not include the value of a fully rigged ship ready for the African slave trade that would also be seized by the Americans.

Shoolbred noted that an American privateer did not take a slave ship with African captives on board until March 1777, which was well after American privateers had been ravaging other types of British commercial vessels. The London merchant explained the late date on account of "the Americans not having before that time any market to carry the cargo of African ships to." He did not expressly state that starting in March 1777, American privateers could bring prize slave ships to French-controlled Martinique and sell African captives there, probably because he knew his audience was already aware of it.

Shoolbred concluded, with bitterness, that "most of the African vessels that had been taken were made prizes of within sight of the [British Caribbean] islands, by American ships that had not been out but a few hours" when the slaver up to that time had avoided "every natural risk of the voyage."[23] In other words, British ship captains and their crews had survived all the myriad risks of a long slave trading voyage, only to be captured by American privateers just as those voyages were about to be completed and great profits earned. Of course, this is exactly what had happened with Shoolbred's own *Hawke*.

Relying on Shoolbred's statistics, the Duke of Richmond observed that "of 200 ships annually employed in the African trade before the commencement of the present civil war, whose value, upon average, was about £9,000 each, there are not now 40 of said ships employed in said trade, whereby there is a diminution in this branch of commerce of 160 ships, which at

£9,000 each, amounts to a loss of £1,440,000 per annum." After mentioning increases in insurance premiums and sailors' wages, the duke railed, "the present diminution of the African trade, the interruption of the North American trade to the West Indies, and the captures made of the West India ships, have greatly distressed the British colonies in the West Indies."[24]

Liverpool, as the port most active in the Africa trade, suffered the most from the reduction in the trade. A historian of Liverpool wrote, "The slave ships were lying idle in the docks, the war having almost ruined the man traffic, to the great grief and pecuniary loss of many excellent citizens of Liverpool and their friends—certain native chiefs on the coast of Africa."[25]

Historian Andrew O'Shaughnessy wrote that as a result of the decline in the slave trade in the early years of the Revolutionary War, "twelve out of thirty leading slave companies in Liverpool" ceased "operation before 1778."[26] British slave trade historian Nicholas Radburn calculated that "three-quarters of Liverpool's slaving merchants in 1776 had left the trade by 1784, whereas one-half the investors in slave ships in 1784 continued the business in 1790."[27] Radburn found that the number of bankruptcies among Liverpool slave traders had risen dramatically in 1777 and 1778. He discovered that the following numbers of Liverpool slave traders had become bankrupt in the following years: 1772, three; 1775, two; 1777, nine (including Miles Barber), and 1778, three.[28] While no study has been done examining the causes of the bankruptcies, it can be noted that the years 1772 and 1775 saw a credit crisis in the slave trade market in the British Caribbean that reverberated in Liverpool,[29] and that 1777 and 1778 were the years that the American privateers had their greatest impact on British slave traders.

Appendix E shows the names of the Liverpool slave trading merchants who went bankrupt from 1772 to 1783, and the year they became bankrupt, as well as any slave ships in which they invested that were captured by American privateers from 1776 to 1778. In several instances, the Liverpool merchant became bankrupt in the same year he lost his investment in one or more slave ships (or, if the capture was late in the year, in the following year when word of the capture would have arrived in Britain). Thomas Case, who lost the *Fancy* to the *Marlborough*, has already been mentioned as an example. Miles Barber was another. As yet another example, Samuel Sandys went bankrupt in 1777, after he lost his investment in three slave ships because of captures by American privateers, two in November 1776 and one in February 1777. In addition, John Yates became bankrupt in

1777, after he lost his investment in three slaves ships that were captured by American privateers, one in August 1776, one in July 1777, and one in October 1777 (the last was the *Derby*, which had sparked the Liverpool riots of late August 1775).

Out of twenty-one Liverpool slave trading merchants who became bankrupts from 1772 to 1783, twelve were bankrupted in 1777 and 1778, the years in which American privateers had their most success in capturing British slavers. There is not a definite correlation between the bankruptcies and captured slave ships; more study would have to be done to establish it. But there does seem to be a probability that in some cases, bankruptcies were caused by captures of slave ships in which the bankrupt merchant had invested. In any event, the actions of all American privateers from 1776 to 1778 helped to depress the entire British slave trading industry, thus making it more difficult for Liverpool slave merchants to pay the substantial debts they owed to creditors.[30]

London slave traders were late to the African trade, becoming heavily invested starting around 1772. By 1778, several of them had become bankrupt, resulting in losses totaling £710,000 ($130 million in 2022 dollars).[31]

There were stories of American privateers causing personal financial failure of those associated with the slave trade. For example, Archibald Dalziel, a Scottish-trained surgeon on slave ships, moved on to becoming a slave merchant. After arriving in Africa in 1763, he wrote to his family in Scotland, "I have at last come into the spirit of the slave trade & must own (perhaps to be to my shame) that I can now traffic in that way without remorse."[32] Later in the same decade, he served four years as governor of the British slave trading fort at Whydah off the coast of what is now Benin. On a slave trading voyage sponsored mainly by him from Jamaica to Africa in May 1778, he and his slave ship fell prey to an American privateer. After his release, he returned to London in August 1778, only to find that this capture had pushed him into bankruptcy. He subsequently left the slave business and became the captain of a privateer and only returned to slave trading after the war in 1783.[33]

David Mill, from 1770 to 1777 the governor of the key British slave trading fort at Cape Coast Castle on the Gold Coast of West Africa, worked for sixteen years on the African coast for various British slave trading interests. He was reported to have amassed a fortune of about £10,000, mainly from slave trading. He had "all of his property" that he had accumulated on board the slave ship *Hawke* when it was seized by an American privateer on its way from Africa to Antigua in April 1777. After Mill learned that the prize was taken to the French-controlled island of Martinique, he desperately tried to reacquire his property by offering to pay a steep ransom for it, but he failed.[34]

There were other personal stories of American privateers capturing British slave ships causing economic hardship, even if financial failure did not result. Richard Brew had been one of the most active British slave merchants on Africa's Gold Coast from the 1750s until his death from disease in August 1776. He left behind huge debts. The British slave ship *St. George* carried not only hundreds of African captives but also Brew's personal property that was intended to be used to repay his creditors in Britain. Another slaver, the *Fox*, also had on board hundreds of captives, twenty of whom were intended to be sold to pay Brew's creditors. Both ships were captured by American privateers, thus confounding his creditors even more.[35]

William Davenport, a slave trader from Liverpool, saw his slave trading business more than quadruple from 1766 to 1776, but the commencement of the Revolutionary War altered this trajectory. After investing £7,787 in slave voyages in 1776, he invested £2,051 in 1777, and then nothing in 1778. The year 1778 marked the lowest ebb of Davenport's thirty-eight-year career as a slave merchant.[36] He was a co-investor in two slave ships that were captured on their voyages back to Liverpool, one by a Continental navy sloop in October 1776, and the other by an American privateer in August 1778.[37]

An important indication of the impact the American Revolutionary War had on the African slave trade was the steep decline of prices for African captives in Africa. In 1788, the great English abolitionist Thomas Clarkson published the first history of the slave trade, based in part on interviews with many British slave ship captains and merchants and examining slave ship financial records. He wrote that during the war, the price of a captive for the slave trade on the west coast of Africa fell to as low as £7, while an enslaved African sold in the British Caribbean could bring as much as £45.[38] The low price in Africa must have been due to low demand. With many fewer African slave voyages being made from Great Britain and North America, prices paid by slavers in Africa plummeted from an average of about £23 in 1775 to as low as £7 in the next several years.[39]

Richard Miles, the governor of Cape Coast Castle on the Gold Coast, mentioned the "very low prices" for African captives sold to British slave ship captains in 1778. On January 15, 1778, in a letter to John Shoolbred in London, Miles listed five British slave ships and the prices they paid in Africa (most all in 1777) for more than two thousand captives. Miles arrived at an average price per captive of £13.8.[40] In another letter written on the same date, Miles informed the Company of Merchants Trading to Africa in London that he was confident that local powerful Fantees and Shantees would sell captives on the "cheap" based on the "very low prices they had laid their slaves in at this last year [1777]."[41] Miles liked the low prices but feared they would induce many slave traders to jump back into slave trading and result in increasing "the price again as high as ever."[42] Miles need not have worried, as the price per captive for two British slave ships trading near Cape Coast Castle in the first part of 1778 ranged from just under £13 to £14.[43]

The average prices of enslaved people sold in Jamaica and other Western Caribbean Islands from 1770 to 1784 overall were not volatile, ranging from a low of £43.1 to a high of £46. From 1775 to 1779, the average price was £43.8.[44] These prices were similar to the Caribbean as a whole (although prices in Jamaica and the rest of the Western Caribbean were consistently about twenty percent higher than in the Eastern Caribbean because of increased transportation costs).[45]

Prices for enslaved people may have remained high because the price of sugar increased during the war years.[46] That increase may have occurred in part as a result of American privateers capturing so many British merchant ships carrying sugar back to Britain that a sugar shortage arose in Britain, driving up prices, and because of increased insurance rates for the ones that were not captured. The prices of African captives and sugar were related since the primary economic role of enslaved people laboring on British Caribbean plantations was to produce sugar from cane. Planters, particularly in Jamaica, remained eager to replace enslaved workers who had died with newly arrived African captives.

Sometimes local conditions resulted in a temporary sharp drop in the prices for African captives, which further disrupted British slave trading markets. Naturally, British ship captains arriving from Africa to the British Caribbean sought to sell their human cargo for as high a price as possible. But any British-controlled island near Martinique or Guadeloupe in 1777 saw prices for African captives sold drop markedly. The sale of prize African captives by American privateersmen to buyers in Martinique and Guadeloupe, according to Nicholas Radburn, "depressed demand in the Windward Islands, which relied in part on visiting French buyers from Martinique and Guadeloupe to keep up slave prices."[47] For example, one of William Davenport's slave ship captains disembarked about four hundred African captives at the British-controlled island of Dominica in May

1777, but the factors responsible for their sale wrote to Davenport that they "never had so much trouble in a sale" because of the ready availability of prize slaves at Martinique and the low demand in Dominica. As a result, the average sales price was just £26, a substantial drop from the £33 price the same slave ship captain had received on his previous voyage to Dominica in November 1775.[48]

A British letter writer from Grenada in late March 1777 complained that sixty African captives who were sold at Grenada by a British slave ship captain for "£39 and £40 sterling each," and then were captured on board a transport vessel by an American privateer, were taken to Martinique and "there sold at from £20 to £25 sterling each."[49] A letter writer from the British Caribbean informed Liverpool's mayor in May 1777 that privateersmen selling captured enslaved Africans from "Guineamen" at Martinique received "about 18 sterling per head."[50] A British merchant from St. Vincent in May 1777 noted that there were then nine privateers and twenty of their prize British vessels in Martinique and lamented that as a result of the sales of prize enslaved people at Martinique, "Negroes are cheaper there than in Africa."[51] That claim was true only if the average prices of captives sold in Africa prior to the war are taken into account.

Some historians have gone too far in describing the extent to which the African slave trade was reduced during the Revolutionary War. The first historian of the slave trade, Thomas Clarkson, wrote in 1808 that the Atlantic slave trade was reduced so drastically by 1779 that the war amounted to a "practical experiment" in the abolition of the slave trade.[52] More recently, an author in the *New Cambridge Modern History* observes that "the British slave trade was itself brought to a standstill during the American War."[53] However, while the British slave trade declined dramatically during the war, it never entirely disappeared.

The disparity in prices in Africa and the British Caribbean did present enticing opportunities for a few bold British slave merchants and sea captains. As Clarkson explained, by purchasing captives on the west coast of Africa for £7 and selling them in Jamaica for £45, "the adventurer, who escaped the ships of the enemy, made his fortune."[54]

That was the case with Captain John Muir commanding the small brig *Adventure*, who purchased some 370 Africans for an average price of just under £11.[55] In a letter dated February 27, 1778, and written from the British-controlled island of Tobago, Muir wrote, "We arrived here with a valuable cargo of slaves, which has turned out to great advantage."[56] According to a British slave trader in Tobago, Muir sold 300 of the 345 of his surviving captives for an average of £43 each. He added that at Tobago, "parcels of 20 or 40 or 50" captives "must always command an immediate sale from £43 to £50 sterling."[57] Even so, Muir was relieved to have avoided capture by American privateers. In his letter, Muir added, "The Americans have taken almost every ship from Africa for some time." He then told about his vessel fending off an American privateer carrying twelve guns during a fierce engagement in which men on both sides were killed, including, remarkably, several African captives fighting alongside Muir's crewmen.[58]

By 1782, after a difficult four-year struggle, the Royal Navy had acquired the upper hand in its great contest with the French navy. In addition, the Royal Navy and British and Loyalist privateers were winning the war against American privateers. Thus, some British slave merchants became more comfortable investing in African slave voyages. Because of the huge profits that could be made on what one Liverpool slave trader called "golden voyages," slave ship captains began mercilessly cramming even more captives into slave ship holds.[59] For example, Peter Brancker, the former commander of the brig *Pearl* that the *Marlborough* had captured off the African coast, in 1783 arrived at Kingston, Jamaica, in command of the slave ship *George* from Liverpool and disembarked 607 captives, despite his vessel weighing just 229 tons.[60]

British slave trade historian Nicholas Radburn wrote about the impact that low prices on the African coast during the Revolutionary War had on ship captains crowding Africans into smaller and smaller spaces in 1782 and 1783:

In June 1782, Liverpool firm Bake & Dawson sent the *Mosley Hill* to Bonny [on the coast of what is now Nigeria], where the captain, John Hewan, made what [Alexander] Falconbridge called "an extraordinary purchase" of 797 people because he found slaves "remarkably cheap from the dullness of the trade." Hewan forced the Africans into spaces of just 3´8˝square per person. There was, Falconbridge stated, "no interval of room between their bodies" and they "suffered so much" that there was "nothing but shrieking and yelling the whole night."[61]

Still, despite the occasional "golden voyage," the British African slave trade did decline during the years of the Revolutionary War from 1775 to 1783, and significantly. It declined by as much as eighty-five percent in some years. In the early years of the war, a major cause of the decline, if not the primary cause, was the captures, and threats posed, by American privateers.

In May 1777, British slave merchants submitted a petition to the Board of Trade, complaining about the Company of Merchants Trading to Africa and the governors of its slave forts along the African coast. The petitioners' complaints included the following report: "During the last two years, the [British Caribbean] colonies did not receive 16,000 [enslaved captives] annually from all parts of Africa, even when any of those purchased there escaped being taken by American privateers on their passage to the West Indies."[62] Those in the slave trade business knew that in the years prior to the war, on average, more than forty thousand African captives were shipped annually to British Caribbean islands. This contemporary report indicates that the slave trade had already markedly decreased in the period from the second half of 1775 to the second half of 1777, and offered as a primary cause the activities of American privateers.

British slave merchants learned of American privateers capturing substantial numbers of British slave ships on each leg of the triangular trade. In addition to slave ships captured on their return voyages to Britain, with their holds filled with sugar, molasses, and other products, and seizures of slave ships overcrowded with African captives on their voyages to British-controlled Caribbean islands, in 1776 and in 1777, American privateers also intercepted several slave ships on their voyages from Britain to Africa, with mostly British manufactured goods in their holds.

As a result, British merchants were forced to reassess whether they wanted to continue making large investments in African slave ventures and risk American privateers capturing their ships, which could result in staggering losses to them. The wise financial move was to hold back from making substantial investments in long slave voyages until the risk of loss was reduced, perhaps until the war ended, or at the earliest when the Royal Navy was able to assert its superiority. Many slave merchants thus decided to cease or reduce substantially such investments. While the African trade never stopped, the significant losses of slave ships to American privateers from August 1776 through August 1778 justified the decisions of British slave merchants to cut back dramatically the number of their African slave voyages.

American privateers also posed a threat of sailing across the Atlantic and attacking British slave trading forts and factories in Africa. The officers and men of the *Marlborough* demonstrated that the threat was real, which further dampened British interest in slave trading voyages.

American privateers also disrupted the British slave trade by capturing hundreds of sugar ships and other commercial ships trading in the British

Caribbean. In 1776, American privateers captured more than half of a rich Jamaican fleet of more than sixty vessels bound for England.[63] By April 1777, American privateers had seized 120 ships in the Caribbean alone, and at year's end, the number seized had more than doubled to 247.[64] Plantation owners in the British Caribbean relied on the profits from their sales of sugar and molasses with British merchants to repay their debts and generate credit to purchase goods, as well as more African captives. But the onset of the Revolutionary War led to a sharp decline in exporting sugar and molasses.[65] London and other British merchant houses that had their vessels seized by American privateers also understandably reduced the number of their voyages to the British Caribbean. When ships did make it through, they passed on to plantation owners increased shipping and insurance costs.[66] As a result, with lower profits, British plantation owners had less available cash to purchase the African captives that were able to make it through the gauntlet of American privateers.

American privateers, by capturing provision ships from Britain and Ireland bound for the British Caribbean, disrupted the ability of plantation owners to feed their enslaved laborers. Neither the Continental Congress nor British Parliament permitted American merchants to supply British Caribbean colonies with food. This disrupted the long-standing carrying trade, in which American merchants carried food to the British Caribbean. The ban forced Britain to send ships, many from Ireland, filled with provisions, particularly for the Leeward and Windward Islands, which produced little of their own food. But American privateers seized as prizes many of these provision ships. This situation created temporary food shortages in the British Caribbean colonies.

One commentator from Grenada in April 1777 wrote in a widely published letter: "Everything continues excessive dear here. . . . A fleet of vessels came from Ireland a few days ago; from sixty vessels that departed from Ireland not above twenty-five arrived in this and the neighboring islands; the others (as it is thought) being all taken by the American privateers. God knows, if this American war continues much longer, we shall all die with hunger."[67]

The prices of provisions roughly doubled in 1776 compared to 1775.[68] Planters had to decide whether to use their shrinking funds to buy food for their enslaved workers or remit sugar to Britain to pay their debts to British merchants.

By capturing provision ships, American privateers reduced the demand for African captives in the Leeward and Windward Islands in particular.

More captives would mean more mouths to feed. One report in fall 1776 stated, "The want of provisions is still so great at Barbados that the inhabitants have resolved to buy no more slaves. The *Juno*, which arrived there from Africa, was obliged to go to Tobago to sell those [captives] she had on board."[69] On September 30, 1776, in Jamaica, John Shickle wrote to an absentee landlord whose plantation he oversaw, "I have not bought any new Negroes as you ordered" because "provisions are so scarce."[70]

The triple attack by American privateers—capturing British slave ships and raiding African slave trading posts, capturing British sugar ships, and capturing British provision ships—had a profound effect on the British slave trade. The African trade was reduced substantially.

From 1770 to 1775, according to a comprehensive database of transatlantic slave voyages, on average each year, ships from British ports embarked about 43,000 captives from Africa bound for the British Caribbean colonies. The years in that span with the highest numbers were 1774 with about 47,000 captives and 1775 with about 45,000. Then the number of captives embarked on British slavers began to decline markedly, to about 38,000 in 1776, 22,000 in 1777, 10,000 in 1778, and 7,500 in each of 1779 and 1780.[71] According to these figures, the decline of embarkations from 1775 was the following: to 1776, 16.5 percent; to 1777, 52 percent; to 1778, 78 percent; and to 1779 and 1780, 83.5 percent.

Applying those same annual totals and using 1775 as the base year, the following estimated annual decline in the shipment of African captives on British ships across the Atlantic to the British Caribbean ("Africans Not Carried") can be calculated:

YEAR	CAPTIVES CARRIED	AFRICANS NOT CARRIED
1776	38,000	7,000
1777	22,000	23,000
1778	10,000	36,000
1779	8,000	38,000
Totals 1776–1778	70,000	66,000
Totals 1776–1779	78,000	104,000

The decline in the British slave trade can be confirmed by examining the number of clearances for African voyages from British ports. As mentioned above, John Shoolbred, a London slave merchant and insurance underwriter, testified in February 1778 before the House of Lords "that the African trade had been materially injured in consequence of the American war; that upwards of 200 sail were generally engaged in that trade, previous to the war; that not a fourth of that number, not above 40 ships, were now sent out."[72] According to Shoolbred, the African slave trade in Great Britain had declined from a high point in 1775 to the end of 1777 by an astounding eighty percent.

A small part of the decline of ships sent to Africa was due to the fact that British slave ships could no longer carry African captives to South Carolina, Georgia, or other destinations in the thirteen mainland colonies. This part of the slave trade had been banned by Congress starting December 1, 1774, and by the British Parliament a year later. However, the bulk of the decline of Britain's African voyages was attributable to fewer British slave ships ending up in the British Caribbean.

Thomas Clarkson, the English abolitionist who examined British slave trading records in the 1780s, calculated the following clearances for Africa from Britain from 1772 to 1779. The chart shows the percentage decline in ships departing from British ports compared to the baseline year of 1775.

YEAR	LIVERPOOL	TOTAL BRITISH PORTS	PERCENTAGE DECLINE FROM 1775
1772	100	175	
1773	105	151	
1774	92	167	
1775	81	152	
1776	57	101	33.6%
1777	31	58	61.8%
1778	26	41	73.0%
1779	11	28[73]	81.6%

Two modern historians of the slave trade, James A. Rawley and Stephen D. Behrendt, estimate the following average annual slave voyage clearances from the three main British ports:

PERIOD	BRISTOL	LIVERPOOL	LONDON	TOTAL	PERCENTAGE DECLINE
1772–75	24	92	39	155	
1776–82	4	30	10	44[74]	71.6%

The decline in the average annual clearances from the period 1772 to 1775 to the period during the Revolutionary War of 1776 to 1782 is 71.6 percent.

Bristol practically ceased participating in the trade. Britain's smaller slave trading ports were also affected. For example, from 1757 to 1776, eighty-six vessels cleared from Lancaster to Africa, but with the onset of the Revolutionary War, slave trading from Lancaster effectively ended.[75]

Another historian calculated that in 1771, 192 ships clearing for the African coast carried forty-seven thousand enslaved people to the Caribbean.[76] This amounts to an average of 246 captives on each ship, which is consistent with a separate study.[77] Applying the same percentages as in the above paragraph and using 1774 as the base year results in the following estimated decline in the shipment of African captives on British ships across the Atlantic Ocean:

YEAR	CAPTIVES CARRIED	AFRICANS NOT CARRIED
1775	37,000	4,000
1776	25,000	16,000
1777	14,000	27,000
1778	10,000	31,000
1779	7,000	34,000
Totals 1775-1777	76,000	47,000
Totals 1775-1778	86,000	78,000
Totals 1775-1779	93,000	112,000

The following is a chart of "new" captives brought against their will from Africa who were retained on four Caribbean islands.[78]

YEAR	ANTIGUA	BARBADOS	DOMINICA	JAMAICA	TOTAL
1775	1,127	879	5,687	13,870	21,563
1776	476	407	3,032	15,016	18,931
1777	286	34	1,996	5,049	7,365
1778	9	7	305	4,419	4,740

As indicated in the above chart, plantation owners in Antigua and Barbados virtually stopped purchasing African captives by 1778. Jamaica experienced more than a two-thirds decline in "new" captives retained on the island; it grew a substantial amount of its own food and thus did not suffer from a shortage of provisions as much as Antigua and Barbados. The decline from 1775 to 1778 was 78 percent.

The reduced numbers of British slave ships arriving during the Revolutionary War at Jamaica, Britain's most important sugar-producing island, has been studied by historian Trevor Burnard. He writes, "In the three years before the war, 231 slaving ventures landing 60,480 slaves arrived in Jamaica. Between 1777 and 1782, however, only 95 ships with 34,526 slaves arrived in Jamaica."[79] Because of the lower supply of African captives brought to Jamaica, planters could not restock their plantations with new enslaved workers at the same rate as they previously had done, despite mortality rates for enslaved people remaining high. According to Burnard, "slaves who died from overwork and malnutrition were not replaced." Burnard concludes that the "rapid decline in the supply of African enslaved people to Jamaica" during the war was responsible for a significant decline in the enslaved population in Jamaica, which in turn threatened the planters' livelihoods.[80]

Historians who have briefly addressed the steep decline in the British African slave trade during the Revolutionary War explain that such a decline is common in any war. But that explanation is incomplete.

When war broke out between France and Britain in the eighteenth century, prior to the American Revolution, the British slave trade declined somewhat. After all, France had the second-most powerful navy in the world and had its own pesky privateers. But the decline in the British slave trade during the American Revolution far exceeded the decline in these prior wars. This was true even before the French navy began active operations against the Royal Navy in late July and early August 1778. Appendix D lists for each year the number of African captives carried on British and US slave ships to the British Caribbean in the forty years from 1752 to 1792. The Seven Years' War lasted from 1756 to 1763 (1754 to 1763 in North America). In 1752 and 1753, British ships on average carried about twenty-one thousand captive Africans to the Caribbean islands each year. Those numbers actually increased in 1754 and 1755. The annual average declined a small amount, to about nineteen thousand, from 1756 to 1759. After that, as the Royal Navy began to assert its dominance over the French navy, British slavers carried substantially more than in the years prior to when the war broke out—almost twenty-nine thousand in 1761. The numbers declined somewhat in 1762 and 1763, perhaps as a result of Spain becoming allied with France in 1761, but never below the 1752 and 1753 totals.[81]

Thus, Britain's war with its former thirteen colonies, including with America's resourceful privateers, was different from prior wars. As indicated above, British shipments of African captives to the British Caribbean islands fell from about thirty-seven thousand to forty-five thousand in 1775 to about twenty-two thousand in 1777, ten thousand in 1778, and eight thousand in 1779. The dramatic impact the Revolutionary War had on the African slave trade has not been appreciated either by historians of the American Revolution or by most historians of the African slave trade.[82]

Others argue that the Revolutionary War merely deferred the slave purchases of British Caribbean planters. The numbers do not, however, support this argument either. While there were undoubtedly many deferred purchases, the British slave trade did not return to the levels it consistently achieved in the six years from 1770 to 1775 until 1791. From 1770 to 1775, on average each year, ships from British ports embarked about thirty-five thousand captives from Africa bound for the British Caribbean colonies. In 1784, the year after the war ended, due to deferred demand, there was an increase in captive Africans embarked by British slave ships, from about twenty thousand in 1783 to thirty-seven thousand in 1784. But in the six years from 1785 to 1790, the average of captive Africans embarked by British slave ships each year was twenty-seven thousand, well below the 1770–1775 average of thirty-five thousand. In 1791 and 1792, the embarkation numbers began to match those from 1770–1775, but that was for a different market for African captives from the Revolutionary War years more than fifteen years earlier.[83]

A number of factors caused the steep decline in the British African slave trade described above, in addition to the actions of American privateers. Determining the number of Africans not carried attributable to each cause is an impossible task. Nonetheless, I believe that the main cause of the steep decline from 1776 to the first half of 1778 was the captures, and threats of captures, by American privateers. That was certainly the crux of the testimony and debates in Parliament in early 1778, as discussed above. British slave merchants refused to invest in expensive slave voyages to the same extent they did prior to the war, primarily out of concern that their ships would be captured by American privateers.

Appendices B and C to this book contain the first comprehensive listing of British slave ships captured by American privateers during the Revolutionary War. Reviewing these results, it is understandable why British merchants would have been discouraged from making further investment in slave voyages.

As set forth in appendix B, from August 1776 to August 1778, American privateers captured twenty-six British slave ships with no captives on board. Nineteen were taken on their homeward voyages from the British Caribbean to Britain, while five were captured on their voyages from Britain to Africa, and two (the *Kitty* and *Betsey* by the *Marlborough*) were taken on the West African coast. In addition, as also set forth at the end of appendix B, American privateers removed everything of value from two other British slave ships on their voyages back to England and captured several other slavers that were later recaptured by the Royal Navy.

These slave ships, when captured, typically had on board a full cargo of sugar, sugar-related products, or African-sourced products, and sometimes even cash proceeds from the sales of African captives. Accordingly, the captures harmed the financial condition of British slave merchants not only from the loss of the ship but also from the loss of the cargo and cash.

The cargo taken on homeward-bound voyages could never match the value of the African captives sold in the Caribbean. Thus, ship captains usually brought home with them bills of exchange written by slave trading houses that the captains received from the sale of African captives. If bills of exchange were lost as a result of the capture of the slave ship by an American privateer, those bills of exchange could be reissued, but that process took time and further disrupted the activities of British slave merchants.

As set forth in appendix C, from January 1777 to August 1778, American privateers captured at least forty-one British slavers with approximately eleven thousand enslaved Africans on board. Based on the average selling price of an enslaved person at this time in the British Caribbean of £35 used by John Shoolbred, the value of those enslaved people who were captured was an estimated £385,000. These captures were particularly painful for the British slave merchants, captains, and their crews, given how close the slavers were to arriving at their destinations and selling their human cargo. The damage inflicted by American privateers by these captures was remarkable.

American privateers were capable of capturing more slave ships in the first part of 1778, but due to American privateers capturing so many of them in the prior two years, and British slave merchants sending out fewer ships on slave voyages, there were fewer of them to capture.

In addition, appendix C describes the seizures made by two French colonial privateers, each claiming commissions from the Continental Congress, of two other British slave ships with a total of about 294 African captives on board, and captures made by American privateers of two more British slave ships carrying about 160 African captives from one British Caribbean island to another.[84] The French colonial privateers would not have operated against British ships without commissions from the Continental Congress. Their actions would have added to the concerns of British slave merchants.

Appendix C also provides four examples of armed British slave ships fighting violent sea battles with American privateers and fending them off.[85] While the slavers prevailed in these instances, the idea of having to engage in deadly combat would have further increased the apprehensions of British slave merchants.

The threat of capture by American privateers remained after the French formally entered the war on the side of the United States in mid-1778. Now British slavers had two potent forces to worry about: American privateers and the formidable French navy.

A separate, if less important, cause of the decline of the British slave trade was that the captures of British slave ships by American privateers dramatically reduced the size of the British slave ship fleet. Before the Revolutionary War, some two hundred British ships typically engaged in the slave trade. Appendices B and C show that at least sixty-seven British slave ships capable of making transatlantic slave voyages were seized by American privateers, including three by the *Marlborough*, from August 1776 to August 1778.

Slave ships were specially fitted out with expensive alterations. Carpenters needed to be hired to build rows of decking in the holds. Bulkheads were typically constructed in lower decks to separate adult men from the women and children, and the captives from the crew. For ventilation into the holds, gratings had to be built on the ship's sides and on the hatches used to secure the captives belowdecks. Carpenters were also often paid to build a barricado on the main deck, surrounding the hatches leading to the holds and separating the main deck from the higher quarter deck, as protection against a possible uprising by the captives. A small door was typically built to allow one captive at a time to get through to the main deck.[86]

The role of American privateers in reducing the British slave trade was remarkable considering that the new United States was facing warships from the most powerful navy in the world. Overall during the war, the Continental navy captured about two hundred British merchant vessels; for every one taken by the Continental navy, more than ten were taken by American privateers.[87] When it came to capturing British slave ships, the gap was much wider. The Continental navy captured only two British slave ships from August 1776 to August 1778, both without African captives on board, and one of them was later recaptured by a British frigate. American privateers substantially outperformed Continental navy warships when it came to disrupting the British slave trade.

The *Marlborough*'s sacking and plundering of Barber and Co.'s well-known slave trading post at the Isles de Los may also have pushed private owners of British slave trading posts and forts to reduce their spending to maintain their facilities. The once-thriving James Fort on the Gambia River and Fort Bance on Bance Island near the mouth of the Sierra Leone River, for example, were virtually ignored by their owners during the early part of the war. They fell into such disrepair that French naval forces easily captured and destroyed their facilities in 1779 raids.[88]

Other factors contributed to the steep decline in the British slave trade to the British Caribbean islands during the Revolutionary War. One was a credit crunch that started in the Windward Islands in 1772 and arrived in Jamaica in 1775. According to British slave trade historian Nicholas Radburn, the surge in Jamaica's slave imports between 1772 and 1775 was spurred by easy credit availability. In particular, slave ship captains often received bills of exchange as consideration for selling their captives. These bills of exchange were a promise to pay by the trading house that issued them in the Caribbean. Banks in Britain often guaranteed them, so the bills of exchange could almost circulate as money, with little discount. But in 1775, Jamaican planters in particular began experiencing difficulties obtaining credit to purchase African captives. Slave trading houses in Jamaica that purchased African captives from slave ship captains began lengthening the terms of repayment of their bills of exchange, and in Britain bankers began to refuse making guarantees of repayment.[89] A Liverpool slave ship captain wrote in September 1777, "'tis not ye American War, 'tis not the state of ye trade on ye Coast of Africa, but merely the low ebb of West India Credit that occasions a temporary stagnation of ye [slave] trade."[90]

However, Radburn makes it clear that the "onset of the American War exacerbated" the credit crunch. In particular, Radburn focused on American privateers, starting in July 1776, "operating in the Caribbean, capturing sugar ships carrying remittances back to England, driving up the cost of freight and insurance, and imperiling the over-stretched Guinea factors' standing with their metropolitan guarantees."[91]

The following numbers indicate that the depredations of American privateers had more of an impact on the British slave trade to Jamaica than did the credit crunch. In Jamaica, the number of newly arrived African captives retained on the island increased from 13,870 in 1775 (the year of the credit crunch) to 15,016 in 1776. Then the number fell by two-thirds, to 5,049, in 1777, and next, to 4,419 in 1778, the two years the American privateers had their greatest impact on the slave trade.[92]

Thus, the American Revolution caused a significant, even if temporary, reduction in the number of Africans taken from their homelands and sold as enslaved people in the British Caribbean and North America. This was a good development for Africans residing in Africa. Tens of thousands avoided being captured and sold into slavery to coastal traders, held in prison-like conditions until they could be sold to a slave ship captain, stuffed into crowded, hot, and fetid lower holds of slave ships, forcibly transported across the Atlantic Ocean, and, if they survived each of these travails, sold into a lifetime of slavery on a Caribbean island. The role of American privateers in this positive development was substantial.

Alexander Falconbridge, serving as a British slave ship surgeon in 1785, thought the decline of the slave trade in Africa caused by the Revolutionary War had resulted in only a single British ship arriving in the prior three years at the previously important slave trading port at Bonny (now in Nigeria). Falconbridge wrote that the decline had the beneficial effect of restoring "peace and confidence" among the local Africans and "a suspension of kidnapping." A slave trader at Bonny complained to Falconbridge that he and other slave traders had resorted to "work for our maintenance" by "dig[ging] the ground and planting yams."[93]

Still, it must be kept in mind that the American privateersmen who disrupted the British slave trade did not intend to do so out of any humanitarian impulse. They did intend to harm an important aspect of British trade. But the reduction in the number of Africans forced onto British slave ships was an unintended consequence of the privateersmen's depredations against British shipping and their hunger for profits. Moreover, Babcock and the others who captured British slave ships with enslaved Africans on board in effect themselves became slave traders, seeking to sell their human cargo at the highest price possible.

The focus of this book is the role of American privateers attacking British slave trade interests from August 1776 to August 1778. Two important points must be noted. First, the time period was before the French navy (and later the Spanish navy) entered the war on the American side starting in mid-1778. Second, the role of American privateers limiting the African slave trade was temporary.

As to the first point, once France joined the war on the side of the Americans in mid-1778, and Spain became allied with France the next year, they became major causes of the continued decline in the British African slave trade. France and Spain both possessed powerful navies. They battled with the Royal Navy for supremacy around the world, including in Africa and the Caribbean. Still, American privateers continued to capture British slave ships until the end of the war, even if at a slower pace than from 1776 to 1778. The last slaver was captured by the privateer *Porus*, out of Salem,

Massachusetts, which took "a prize ship from Africa, with upwards of 200 slaves on board," reportedly just before Congress announced a cessation of hostilities "either by sea or by land" on April 11, 1783.[94]

Appendix D indicates that British slave ships delivered to the British Caribbean only about 6,900 African captives for each of 1779 and 1780, even fewer than were shipped in each of 1777 and 1778. The captives delivered increased somewhat to 11,364 in 1781 and 15,522 in 1782. These relatively low numbers (compared to the prewar years) reflect the presence of the French and Spanish fleets, in addition to the American privateers, and the increasing numbers in 1781 and 1782 also demonstrate that by 1781 and 1782, the Royal Navy was having some success against all of its enemies.

The French and British navies disrupted each other's slave trading operations by attacking enemy slave trading posts in Africa. In early 1779, a French naval squadron of two frigates and three corvettes, with 430 marines on board, surprised and overwhelmed British slave trading posts in Upper Guinea. The island and fort at Saint-Louis easily fell due to unique circumstances. In July 1778, a devastating yellow fever epidemic swept the island. In early 1779, Governor Clark died in office, and the demoralized remnants of the British garrison got drunk and began shooting at the habitants from the walls of their fort. The habitants and their enslaved people rose up and killed most of the British soldiers. Three days later, on January 30, 1779, the French naval squadron arrived and seized the fort and island without firing a shot.[95]

A smaller French force sailed up the Gambia River and easily razed James Fort on February 11. A French ship sailed farther up the Gambia and seized all the British slave trading factories and posts not yet destroyed by Africans. Chevalier de Pontevèz-Guin, departing Gorée with two frigates and a corvette, on March 8 occupied the Isles de Los, including Miles Barber's slave trading facilities, which Captain Babcock and his *Marlborough* crew had already sacked a year earlier. Sailing farther south, on March 11, Pontevèz-Guin destroyed a major British slave trading post that included a fort on Bance Island. A Royal Navy expeditionary force gained some revenge by capturing Gorée in June 1779. At the time of its surrender, Gorée was under the command of Charles-Joseph-Bonaventure Boucher, whom Babcock had dealt with in February 1778.[96]

Under the peace terms agreed to in 1783, France kept Saint-Louis and Gorée, while Britain was allowed to return to James Fort. The effort to establish a British colony at Senegambia, however, ended.[97]

Across the Atlantic, after the French navy became active in August 1778, the French seized many of the formerly British-controlled islands in the Caribbean. French military forces seized from Britain in 1778 the island of Dominica and in 1779 the islands of Grenada and St. Vincent, while St. Lucia was captured from the French by Britain. In 1781, Britain suffered the loss of Tobago to the French. In 1782 more French successes occurred, with St. Kitts, Monserrat, and Nevis capitulating. Only Admiral Sir George Rodney's victory over Admiral François-Joseph Paul, comte de Grasse's French fleet at the Battle of the Saints on April 12, 1782, fought between Martinique and Guadeloupe, saved Britain's remaining sugar colonies of Jamaica, Barbados, and Antigua.[98]

The continued captures by American privateers, the ravages of war caused by France's and Spain's navies battling with the Royal Navy for dominance in the Caribbean, drought in Antigua and Barbados, and several incredibly devastating hurricanes brought misery to Caribbean island residents, particularly to enslaved people, who were the last priority for scarce food. The enslaved people who were already working on British Caribbean islands were the first victims of the war brought to the shores of the Caribbean islands. Many faced starvation and, with a poor diet and malnutrition, the risk of contracting deadly diseases. According to one estimate, some fifteen thousand enslaved people died of starvation or disease because of malnutrition during the Revolutionary War in the British Caribbean islands.[99] Eventually, by mid-1777, the Royal Navy had improved its system of convoys of fleets of transports carrying food to the Caribbean.

As indicated above, various causes converged to lead to the mass starvation. Still, while the actions of American privateers (unintentionally) helped save perhaps sixty-thousand or more Africans from being forced across the Atlantic, those privateers also contributed to the misery of the Africans already in the Caribbean.

It should be emphasized that the sharp decline in the British slave trade during the Revolutionary War was temporary. With the successes of the Royal Navy, British privateers and Loyalist privateers against the French navy and American privateers, by 1781 British slave merchants began to re-enter the slave trade, albeit slowly.

After war's end in 1783, many British slave ship captains and traders returned to the West African coast. One of them was Miles Barber, whose slave trading post at Isle de Kassa was sacked and burned by the crew of the *Marlborough* in February 1778. Barber reconstructed his slave trading buildings on Isle de Kassa. Indeed, he made them even more impressive, adding more warehouses and shops, and a dock that slave ships could conveniently use. Barber also expanded his operations to include eleven floating and other small slave trading posts at Cape Mount, Cape Mesurado, Bassa, and other locations on the mainland coast.[100]

Still, as noted above, the war had a profound impact on the British slave trade, which did not return to its pre-Revolutionary War numbers until 1791.

The war had an even more profound effect on American participation in the slave trade. During or shortly after the war, each state (except Georgia) banned imports of African captives. In 1794, Congress passed its first legislation intended to ban American participation in the slave trade with other countries. But the US Constitution, which took effect in 1789, prevented Congress from interfering with the right of states to import African captives before 1808, a provision that South Carolina delegates insisted on. South Carolina shocked the country by permitting imports of African captives from 1803 to 1807.[101]

Rhode Island continued its participation in the slave trade. By the 1790s, the dominant port in North America for sending out slave ships had shifted from Newport up Narragansett Bay to the small port of Bristol. From 1787 to 1807, Bristol's D'Wolf family financed at least ninety-six slave trading voyages, many of them illegal under Rhode Island and US law, bringing more than ten thousand African captives to the Americas, mostly to Cuba and other Spanish-controlled islands.[102] Interestingly, Bristol had a Black community named Gorée. In Providence, merchant Cyprian Sterry had his ship captains purchase African captives at Gorée and the Isles de Los and disembark them at Savannah, Georgia, in one voyage in 1794, three in 1796, and one more in 1797.[103]

Officially, participation in the African slave trade did not end for Britain until 1807 and for the United States until a year later. The end of US participation in the African slave trade can be traced to the abolitionist and anti-slave trade sentiment stirred by the American Revolution, particularly in the Northern states.

Appendix A

Officers and Crew of the *Marlborough*

There is no complete list of the *Marlborough*'s officers and sailors, nor of others associated with its voyage to Africa. The following partial list is gleaned from the ship's log and other contemporary sources.

A. OFFICERS AND COMMON SAILORS NAMED IN THE SHIP'S LOG[1]

1. OFFICERS

George Waite Babcock, captain

James Eldred, first lieutenant

Francis Bradfield, second lieutenant and prize master of the *Fancy*

Nathaniel Brown, third lieutenant

John Linscom Boss, captain's clerk

Christopher Brown, captain of marines (died of disease on the return voyage)

J. Peters, Master

Mr. Cleveland, probably a master or mate

N. Daggett, could be first mate

John Finn, boatswain

Doctor (not named)

Ichabod Holloway, prize master (of the *Betsey* and later the *Sally*)

John Bissell, prize master (of the *Fort Rose* and later the *Kitty*)

S. Kelley, prize master (of the *Betsey*)

2. COMMON SAILORS

Samuel Babcock (Captain Babcock's brother; died of smallpox on voyage to Africa)

Mr. Smith (cared for Samuel Babcock)

Thomas Carpenter (cared for Samuel Babcock)

Thomas Brown (cared for Samuel Babcock)

David Wilcox (died of smallpox on voyage to Africa)

John Larkin (survived smallpox on voyage to Africa)

Jedediah Collins (died of smallpox on voyage to Africa)

Stephen Congden (probably Congdon; gunner's boy; died of smallpox on voyage to Africa)

John Davis (died of smallpox on voyage to Africa; originally from England)

Thomas Evans (died of unknown disease on return voyage; a boy, he enlisted at the Isles de Los)

John M. Entese (sp?) (American prisoner who was on board Spanish ship freed by Captain Babcock and who later signed the *Marlborough*'s articles)
Ship's carpenter (not named)

B. OFFICERS AND COMMON SAILORS OF THE *Fancy*, MENTIONED IN GEORGE W. BABCOCK'S ORDERS TO FRANCIS BRADFIELD, MARCH 7, 1778[2]

The following officers and sailors of the *Marlborough* were ordered to sail on the prize *Fancy*

1. OFFICERS
Francis Bradfield, commander
George Smith, first mate
John Neal, second mate

2. COMMON SAILORS
Alexander McDougal
Mayhew Allen
Oliver Clark
Comfort Bucklin
John McEntire
Richard Allen
John Butler
Thomas Carpenter
Benjamin Hammond
Lawrence Peterson, boy
John Adley, boy
John Williams, boy
Elisha Tew (his name was crossed out; this likely meant he was not included in the *Fancy*'s crew, but remained part of the *Marlborough*'s original crew)
M___ Case (his name was also crossed out, but is mostly legible)

C. DOCTOR NAMED IN GEORGE W. BABCOCK'S AGREEMENT WITH HIM, MARCH 9, 1778[3]
Dr. John Anderson, doctor on board the *Fancy*

D. A PRIZE MASTER AND EIGHT COMMON SAILORS OF THE *Marlborough* DERIVED FROM VARIOUS OTHER SOURCES
William Wallace, prize master (of *John*)[4]
David Bissell, common sailor (of Exeter and North Kingstown, Rhode Island)[5]
Silas Daggett, common sailor (of Tisbury, Martha's Vineyard, Massachusetts)[6]
Cornelius Marchant, common sailor (of Edgartown, Martha's Vineyard, Massachusetts)[7]

William Wever[8]
Thomas Buckley[9]
Samuel Babcock Jr.[10] (also named above)
John Shearman[11]
Samuel Allen (of South Kingstown, Rhode Island, possibly)[12]

E. OTHERS NAMED IN THE SHIP'S LOG
At Gorée:
    Alexandre-Davis-Armény de Paradis, governor of French-controlled Gorée
    Charles-Joseph-Bonaventure Boucher, lieutenant governor of French-controlled Gorée
    An unidentified owner of a French merchant vessel (the snow in Boss's drawing)
    Richard Roberts, master of the *Fort Rose* and a slave trader
At the Isles de Los, including at Isle de Kassa:
    King Tom, a local African leader
    Captain William Moore, commander of the *Sally*, slave trader, and pilot for the *Marlborough*
    Thomas Hereford and Stephen Hammond, slave traders originally from Rhode Island
    Solomon Prevoit, captain of the French slaver *Seine*
    Peter Brancker, commander of the *Pearl*
    Paul Cross, pilot on board the ship from the Isles de Los and slave trader
After the Isles de Los:
    Joseph Fisher, commander of the *Kitty* and slave trader
    Robin Gray, a local African leader
    Captain William Allanson, commander of the *Fancy*
    Mr. Richards and Captain Ireland Grace and his girls (on board captured sloops)
On Voyage to North America:
    Unnamed African girl who fell overboard and was saved
    Unnamed African woman who died of disease

F. OTHERS NAMED IN SHIP'S LOG ON THE *Marlborough*'S SECOND VOYAGE
These men might also have sailed on the *Marlborough*'s first voyage:
    Josiah Arnold, prize master[13]
The following men were listed as injured in an engagement with a Royal Navy sloop of war: Thomas Stanton, the cook (killed); Jesse Thomson (killed); Robert Wheaton (wounded); S. Steward (wounded); John Larkin (wounded, named above); and Matt Almy (wounded).[14]

Appendix B

British Slave Ships Captured by American Privateers with No Enslaved Africans On Board, August 1776 to August 1778

The voyage number, if available, is from the Trans-Atlantic Slave Trade Database (TSTD), www.slavevoyages.org. Those without numbers are newly discovered by the author's research.

1. *Lancashire*. Captain Jones; out of Liverpool; TSTD no. 92726; captured on August 2, 1776, after delivering some 328 enslaved Africans to Jamaica by the *Enterprize* out of Baltimore; carried to Chincoteague Island, Maryland.

A Maryland privateer captured the first British slave ship returning from the Caribbean after it had dropped off its African captives. The privateer was the schooner *Enterprize,* carrying ten guns and with a crew of sixty men, and was owned by John Crocket and others of Baltimore. See A List of Commissions of Letters of Marque and Reprisal Granted by the Council of Safety for the State of Maryland, March 1777, in Crawford et al., eds., *Naval Documents*, 8:139. About August 2, 1776, the *Enterprize* out of Baltimore and commanded by James Campbell captured a "Guineaman" (as slave ships were called) carrying fourteen or fifteen hogsheads of sugar and rum, as well as $600 in cash, and sent it into Chincoteague Island off the Eastern Shore of Maryland. The slave ship had joined a convoy of 120 British commercial ships sailing from Jamaica but became separated after the convoy was attacked by numerous American privateers. The captured slaver was the eighty-ton *Lancashire*, commanded by John Jones and owned by the prominent slave merchant Yates family out of Liverpool. It carried four cannon and a crew of sixteen. *Pennsylvania Journal,* Aug. 14, 1776; Intelligence from Antigua, Aug. 24, 1776, *Pennsylvania Journal,* Oct. 9, 1776, in Crawford et al., eds., *Naval Documents,* 6:297; Extract of a Letter from Bristol, Sept. 22, 1776, *Public Advertiser* (London) in ibid., 608; Capt. James Campbell to John Hancock, Sept. 8, 1776, in ibid., 749; Extract of a Letter from Providence, Aug. 13, 1776, in *New York Gazette,* Aug. 19, 1776, and *Maryland Journal*, Aug. 28, 1776; Desmarais, *Revolutionary War at Sea*, 1:206 (collecting US newspaper sources); Extract of a Letter from Liverpool, Oct. 2, in *Lloyd's Evening Post*, Oct. 7, 1776. The *Lancashire* had been reported as trading on the African coast in August 1776 and taken on its homeward journey from Jamaica. See TSTD, www.slavevoyages.org/voyage/search (voyage no. 92726). Some American newspapers reported the capture but were not aware of the name of the captured vessel or the American privateer that made the capture, but they were aware it was a Maryland privateer, a "Guinea" ship from Jamaica, and that a sizable amount of cash had been siezed on board. These sources, relying on an August 10, 1776, letter written by a Philadelphian, stated that when taken, the vessel carried just seven hogsheads of sugar and eight or nine hogsheads of rum but had on board $7,000 in cash. Extract of a Letter from Philadelphia, Aug. 10, 1776, in *New York Gazette*, Aug. 19, 1776, and *Maryland Journal*, Aug. 28, 1776; Desmarais, *Revolutionary War at Sea*, 1:203 (collecting US newspaper sources). This was likely the *Lancashire*, seized by the *Enterprize*. The author believes this was the first letter reporting the capture, but at the time the letter writer did not know the applicable details, which were revealed in later reports.

2. *Isaac*. Captain Ashburn; out of Liverpool; TSTD no. 92720; captured in mid-August 1776 after delivering about 328 enslaved Africans to Tortola by the *Warren* out of Bedford, Massachusetts; carried to Marblehead, Massachusetts.

"On Saturday advice came from Liverpool that two of their homeward bound vessels which sailed without convoy are taken by an American privateer, viz. the *Isaac*, Craig, from Tortola, and the *Lancaster* [*Lancashire*], Jones, from Jamaica, both laden with sugar and rum. The captains were put aboard a French vessel." Extract of a Letter from Liverpool, Oct. 2, in *Lloyd's Evening Post*, Oct. 7, 1776; *Daily Advertiser* (London), Oct. 8, 1776; *London Chronicle*, Oct. 8, 1776. Sometime in early or mid-August, Captain John Phillips, commanding the six-gun Massachusetts privateer sloop *Warren*, took Captain Ashburn's 350-ton slave ship *Isaac* on its return trip to Liverpool. Ashburn had purchased most of his estimated 359 enslaved captives at the Isles de Los, an island off the African coast that is now part of Guinea that would be targeted by George Waite Babcock and his privateer the *Marlborough* in February 1778. The *Isaac* had disembarked its surviving African captives at the British Caribbean island of Tortola. On its return voyage, it carried more than five hundred hogsheads of sugar, forty-two puncheons of rum, some old copper and turtle. The prize originally arrived at Bedford, Massachusetts, on August 18, 1776. Captain Phillips then sent the prize into Marblehead, Massachusetts, but upon entering the harbor there, the former slaver and its prize crew were chased by the Royal Navy frigate HMS *Milford*. The British warship fired some twenty cannon shots at the *Isaac* but was eventually driven away by land-based artillery from forts in Marblehead Harbor. The prize was then subjected to admiralty court procedures at Salem. See Dr. David Cobb to Robert Treat Paine, Aug. 19, 1776, in Crawford et al., eds., *Naval Documents*, 6:233; Masters Log of HMS *Milford*, Aug. 24, 1776, in ibid., 298; W. Knox to H. Knox, Aug. 25, 1776, in ibid., 298-99; Petition of Thomas Cragg to the Massachusetts Council, Sept. 4, 1776, in ibid., 675; Libels Filed in Massachusetts Admiralty Court, about Aug. 29, 1776, in ibid., 348; *New England Chronicle*, Aug. 29, 1776, in ibid., 347; *Continental Journal* (Boston), Aug. 29, 1776; *Lloyd's List*, Dec. 27, 1776; *London Chronicle*, Oct. 8, 1776. See TSTD, www.slavevoyages.org/voyage/search (voyage no. 92720).

3. *Africa*. Captain Baker; out of Bristol; TSTD no. 17886; captured on August, 22, 1776, while sailing to Africa by the *Rover* out of Salem, Massachusetts; blew up at sea during the engagement.

The 140-ton slaver *Africa*, commanded by Captain John Baker, on its way from Bristol to Africa, was intercepted off the coast of Portugal by the Massachusetts privateer sloop *Rover*, carrying eight carriage guns plus around 10 swivel guns. Baker put up a fight, but his ship exploded, killing all but three men of his crew of twenty-eight. Copy of a Letter from Capt. T. P. Braithwaite, Sept. 20, 1776, *London Chronicle*, Sept. 24, 1776, in Crawford et al., eds., *Naval Documents*, 6:607; Letter from Capt. Moore, Sept. 26, 1776, in ibid., 613; Memorandum of the Activities of the Massachusetts Privateer Rover, British Admiralty Records, Sept. 30, 1776, in ibid., 620; David Richardson, ed., *Bristol, Africa and the Eighteenth-Century Slave Trade to America, The Final Years, 1770–1807*, vol. 4, *Bristol Record Society's Publications*, vol. 47 (Bristol, UK: Bristol Record Society, 1996), 70; TSTD, www.slavevoyages.org/voyage/search (voyage no. 17886). For the *Rover*, see Crawford et al., eds., *Naval Documents*, 6:298n3; 5:870-71, 1034-35. For more on this episode, see Walter E. Minchinton, "The Voyage of the Snow 'Africa,'" *Mariner's Mirror* 37 (1951): 187-96.

4. *Swallow*. Captain Griffiths; out of London; TSTD no. 17884; captured in September 1776, after delivering some 195 enslaved Africans to Tobago by the *Warren* out of Gloucester, Massachusetts; carried to Cape Anne, Massachusetts.

In early September, Captain William Coas, commanding the eight-gun Massachusetts privateer schooner *Warren*, took the seventy-ton slaver *Swallow*, which was returning to London on the third leg of its journey after having sailed from the coast of Africa to the island of Tobago where it had dropped off its cargo of African captives. The *Swallow* mounted six valuable brass cannon and ten swivel guns on its deck, but its captain, Benjamin Griffiths, did not resist. Elephant ivory and gold dust were also found on board. What also made this capture remarkable was that it occurred near the coast of England. Coas sent the prize into Cape Anne, Massachusetts. *Independent Chronicle*, Sept. 19, 1776, in Crawford et al., eds., *Naval Documents*, 6:899; *Boston Gazette*, Sept. 23, 1776, in ibid., 952; Libels Filed Against Various Prizes in the Massachusetts Admiralty Court, Sept. 26, 1776, in ibid., 1002; *Essex Journal* (Newburyport, MA), Sept. 20, 1776; Desmarais, *Revolutionary War at Sea*, 1:233-34 (collecting US newspaper sources); Richardson, ed., *Bristol*, 4:69. On September 13, 1775, the *Swallow* received permission from the Board of Trade in London to carry gunpowder and arms to trade on the Windward Coast in Africa. Ledward, ed., *Journals of the Board of Trade*, 13:117. Two months later, on November 13, 1775, it departed from Bristol, England. It disembarked about 195 captive Africans at the British Caribbean island of Tobago, probably in July or August 1776. The *Swallow's* voyage is covered at TSTD, www.slavevoyages.org/voyage/ search (voyage no. 17884). This *Warren* was not the same as the *Warren* in entry no. 2, above.

5. *William*. Captain Bond; out of Liverpool; TSTD no. 92314; captured in September 1776, after delivering about 328 enslaved Africans to Jamaica by the *Chance* out of Pennsylvania; carried to Philadelphia.

In early-to-mid-September 1776, the 250-ton slaver *William*, out of Liverpool and commanded by John Bond, was captured by the American six-gun privateer schooner *Chance* commanded by James Armitage. *Pennsylvania Journal*, Oct. 2, 1776, in Crawford et al., eds., *Naval Documents*, 6:1107; Libel Filed in Pennsylvania Libel Court Against the Prize Ship *William*, in *Pennsylvania Evening Post*, Oct. 1, 1776, in ibid., 1092-93; Letter from Portsmouth, Jan. 12, 1777, *Public Advertiser* (London), Jan. 15, 1777, in ibid., 8:520. The *William* had purchased more than three hundred enslaved people at the Isles de Los and had dropped off the survivors at Jamaica, probably in August. The Isles de Los would be visited by George W. Babcock and his crew on the *Marlborough's* voyage to West Africa. The *William* had departed Jamaica on September 1, 1776. See TSTD, www.slavevoyages.org/voyage/search (voyage no. 92314); *Lloyd's List*, Oct. 18, 1776.

6. *Sally*. Captain Jackson; out of Liverpool; TSTD no. 92442; captured September 22, 1776, after delivering some 328 enslaved Africans to Jamaica by the *Defence* out of New London, Connecticut; carried to New London.

On September 22, 1776, Captain Seth Harding, commanding the privateer *Defence* out of New London, Connecticut, captured a slave ship on its return trip to Liverpool, England, the 140-ton *Sally*. Owned by William James, Liverpool's most prolific slave merchant, and commanded by William Jackson, the *Sally* had earlier dropped off about three hundred African captives at Jamaica on June 22, 1776. Harding sent his prize to his home port of New London. See A List of Prizes Taken, Brought in, and Condemned in the County of New London in the State of Connecticut, in Crawford et al., eds., *Naval Documents*, 6:1101; *Connecticut Gazette*, Oct. 4, 11, 1776, in ibid., 1127, 1217; *Connecticut Courant* (Hartford), Oct. 14, 1776; Desmarais, *Revolutionary War at Sea*, 1:257 (collecting US newspaper sources); TSTD, www.slavevoyages.org/ voyage/search (voyage no. 92442).

7. *Britannia*. Captain Hughes; out of Liverpool; TSTD no. 92518; captured in October 1776 after delivering an unknown number of enslaved Africans to Jamaica by the *Congress* and *Chance* out of Pennsylvania; retaken by HMS *Orpheus*; recaptured by the *Joseph* out of Providence; carried to Bedford, Massachusetts.

As with regular prizes, sometimes seized British slave ships were recaptured by a Royal Navy warship, only to be taken again. In early September 1776, the small American privateers *Chance* and *Congress* captured the seventy-ton *Britannia*, which had a large amount of money on board. On November 1, 1776, the British frigate HMS *Orpheus* recaptured the *Britannia*. A British midshipman, given command of the *Britannia*, was ordered to sail it to New York. But later in November, Captain Thomas West on his Providence, Rhode Island, privateer sloop *Joseph* retook the *Britannia*. The midshipman was sent to Providence to join the vessel's former captain, Benjamin F. Hughes. The *Britannia* was brought to Bedford, Massachusetts, and condemned in the maritime court at Plymouth, Massachusetts, on January 17, 1777. See Journal of HMS *Orpheus*, Nov. 1, 1776, in Crawford et al., eds., *Naval Documents*, 7:12, 7:12n2; Extract of a Letter from Capt. B. F. Hughes, dated Providence, Dec. 5, 1776, *London Chronicle*, Feb. 20, 1777, in ibid., 375; Libel Filed Against the *Britannia* in Massachusetts Maritime Court, *Boston Gazette*, Jan. 13, 1777, in ibid., 943; Desmarais, *Revolutionary War at Sea*, 1:301, 353 (collecting US newspaper sources). TSTD states the slaver was from Liverpool, its captain was Benjamin Francis Hughes, and it dropped off some 195 enslaved people at Dominica. TSTD, www.slavevoyages.org/ voyage/search (voyage no. 92518). See also *Lloyd's List*, April 6, 1776 (the *Britannia*'s arrival in Africa from Liverpool).

Captain Hughes precipitated a tawdry transatlantic dispute on a prior voyage in 1775 commanding the *Britannia*. At Annamaboe, where Hughes purchased most of his captives, he also hired as a free sailor for his trip to Jamaica a man named Amissa. But at Jamaica, Hughes sold Amissa to a local planter who enslaved him. On his 1776 voyage commanding the *Britannia*, Hughes told Amissa's parents that their son had died in the Middle Passage, but as a result of a transatlantic network of information, Amissa's family learned that he was enslaved in Jamaica. After Amissa's family and the town of Annamaboe complained to Britain's Company of Merchants Trading in Africa, the company agreed to commission a captain of another slave ship intending to call on Jamaica to redeem him. After nearly three years of enslavement, Amissa was located and freed. He then traveled to England, where he successfully sued Captain Hughes, obtaining a judgment of £300 in damages. By July 1779, Amissa was reunited with his family at Annamaboe. See Randy J. Sparks, "The Peopling of an African Slave Port: Annamaboe and the Atlantic World," *Almanack* 24, no. ed00719 (2020), 25-26; TSTD, voyage no. 92491 (1775 voyage).

8. *King George*. Captain Williams; out of Bristol; TSTD no. 17876; captured on October 22, 1776, after delivering about 328 enslaved Africans to Jamaica by the *General Montgomery* out of Baltimore; carried to Baltimore.

On October 22, 1776, Captain James Montgomery, commanding the Maryland privateer brig *General Montgomery*, captured "a fine, large, well-built Guineaman" on its voyage from Jamaica to Bristol, England. The prize was the one-hundred-ton *King George* out of Bristol, commanded by Edmund Williams. It had earlier dropped off about 328 African captives at Jamaica before commencing its return voyage. Its captured cargo included gold dust and ivory from Africa, and sugar and rum from Jamaica. After Captain Montgomery sent the prize into Baltimore, it (and another captured British slaver, the *Sam*) was purchased by the Pennsylvania state navy for use as fire ships in the Delaware River. Minutes of the Pennsylvania Navy Board, Feb. 28, and March 1, 1777, in Crawford et al., eds., *Naval Documents*, 7:1321 (orders) and 8:9 (the *King George* purchased by state); *Maryland Journal*, Oct. 27, 1776; *Pennsylvania Gazette*, Nov. 17, 1776; *Pennsylvania Packet*, Dec. 18, 1776; *Cornwall Chronicle* (Montego Bay, Jamaica), March 8, 1777, Supplement ("sent into Philadelphia the 21st of November last"); Richardson, ed., *Bristol*, 4:65; *Lloyd's List*, Dec. 27, 1776; see Seizures by the Continental Navy Not Included in Chart Above at the end of appendix B for a discussion of the capture of the *Sam* by the Continental navy sloop *Independence*; TSTD, www.slavevoyages.org/voyage/search (voyage no. 17876). The *King George* was an old slaver owned by John Anderson of Bristol, having been captured as a prize from the French during the Seven Years' War and thereafter completing six African voyages from 1765 to 1775. TSTD, www.slavevoyages.org/voyage/search (voyages nos. 17594, 17674, 17704, 17758, 17838, 17787).

9. *Swallow*. Captain Moffat; out of London; captured at sea while sailing to Africa in November 1776, possibly on the 9th, with no enslaved Africans aboard by the *Snow-Bird* out of Providence, Rhode Island; carried to Providence.

In July 1775, the sloop *Swallow*, from forty to sixty tons, owned by James Mather of London, sailed from London to the island at Saint-Louis off the Coast of Senegambia, where it purchased an estimated 119 captives. Sometime in the first three quarters of 1776, the *Swallow* sailed to the region of what is now the southern United States to an area then called Mississippi and sold the captives there, presumably to Spanish buyers. This voyage is listed in TSTD, www.slavevoyages.org/voyage/search (voyage no. 78194). The *Swallow* then loaded a cargo of lumber, pitch, and tar, and set out either for London or Senegal. On this voyage, the *Swallow* was captured by the Rhode Island privateer sloop *Snow-Bird*, commanded by Israel Ambrose, and brought to Providence, where the ship and cargo were libeled on November 28, 1776, and sold in December pursuant to admiralty court procedures. "List of All the Vessels and Cargoes," in Crawford et al., eds., *Naval Documents*, 7:647-48 (capture no. 50); *Providence Gazette*, Nov. 30, 1776; Desmarais, *Revolutionary War at Sea*, 1:311 (collecting US newspaper sources). Five of the sailors on the *Swallow* were free black mariners. Rhode Island authorities treated them as ordinary white enemy prisoners and exchanged them for American prisoners held by the British in Newport on February 1, 1777. List of Prisoners Sent to Newport for Exchange, Feb. 1, 1777, in Crawford et al., eds., *Naval Documents*, 7:1079-80. Rhode Island documents stated that the *Swallow* was on its way back to Senegal; if that was true, it may have been to supply a British slave fort or factory, such as at the Isles de Los. However, based on its cargo, it seems more likely it was headed back to London.

10. *Rio Pongo*. Captains Roberts, Cherry; out of Liverpool; TSTD no. 92435; captured on November 11 or 12, 1776, after delivering about 141 enslaved Africans to Jamaica by the *Eagle* out of Massachusetts; delivered to Providence, Rhode Island.
   Captain Barzilla Smith's Massachusetts privateer schooner *Eagle* took the British slaver *Rio Pongo* on its return voyage from Jamaica to Liverpool, in November 1776. The *Rio Pongo* carried thirty-three tons of ivory and twelve tons of camwood, and Smith sent the prize to Providence, where the ship and cargo was tried on December 21 and sold under admiralty court procedures. "List of All the Vessels and Cargoes," in Crawford et al., eds., *Naval Documents*, 7:647-48 (capture no. 51); *Providence Gazette*, Dec. 7, 1776, Jan. 11, 1777; Desmarais, *Revolutionary War at Sea*, 1:311 (collecting US newspaper sources). On June 10, 1776, the *Rio Pongo* was at Cape Mount, with fifty African captives. *Lloyd's List*, April 19, 1776. See also TSTD, www.slavevoyages.org/voyage/search (voyage no. 92435). This listing provides that the *Rio Pongo*'s owner was Samuel Sandys, a slave merchant from Liverpool, but in the condemnation proceedings in Providence, the jury determined that the slave ship was owned by "Miles Barber and Company, merchants, of Liverpool." Admiralty Court Minute Books, 1776–1783, vol. 2, RI State Archives, 68. Sandys and Barber often invested in slave voyages together. The TSTD listing also states that the captains of the ship were John Roberts and a man with the last name of Cherry; the Providence admiralty court records indicate the captain was Walter Cherry. "List of All the Vessels and Cargoes," in Crawford et al., eds., *Naval Documents*, 7:647. Roberts may have died during the voyage.

11. *Mary*. Captain Jones; out of Liverpool; TSTD no. 91817; captured November 21, 1776, after delivering an estimated 328 enslaved Africans to Barbados and St. Kitts by the *American Revenue* out of New London, Connecticut; carried to Bedford, Massachusetts.
   The privateer sloop *American Revenue*, commanded by Samuel Champlin and owned by New London merchant Nathaniel Shaw, carrying twelve guns

and manned by a crew of one hundred, followed a convoy of ships bound for England. On November 21, 1776, the privateer's crew captured "the Guinea ship called the *Mary* commanded by William Jones." Sailing from Liverpool, the *Mary* had earlier dropped off some 328 enslaved Africans on the islands of Barbados and St. Kitts and was caught on its return trip to Liverpool. The ship's owners in Liverpool were Samuel Sandys, James Kendall, and Andrew White. Jones, with his vessel mounting six guns, put up a brief fight before surrendering. Captain Champlin ordered a prize crew to sail the *Mary* into Bedford, Massachusetts. See S. Champlin to N. Shaw, March 9, 1776, in Crawford et al., eds. *Naval Documents*, 8:68, 68nn1, 2; Desmarais, *Revolutionary War at Sea*, 2:336-37 (collecting US newspaper sources); TSTD, www.slavevoyages.org/voyage/search (voyage no. 91817); *Lloyd's List*, March 25, 1777.

12. *Mercury*. Captain Griffiths; out of London; TSTD no. 78231; captured in December 1776 after delivering some 198 enslaved Africans to St. Kitts by the *Harlequin* out of Salem, Massachusetts; carried to Salem.

Some sources indicated that the *Mercury* was captured after departing Africa. See *Lloyd's List*, May 27, 1777 ("The *Mercury*, Griffiths, from Africa to the West Indies, is taken"); *St. James's Chronicle* (London) ("The *Mercury*, Griffiths, from Africa to St. Kitt's, is taken by the Americans"). Other sources indicate that the slaver was seized on its way from St. Kitts to Africa. See *General Evening Post* (London), May 29, 1777 ("The *Mercury*, Griffiths, from St. Kitts to Africa, is taken and carried into Salem by an American privateer of 14 guns"); *London Chronicle*, May 29, 1777 (same). The slaver *Mercury*, with Griffiths in command, sailed from Deal in England in May 1776. *Morning Post* (London), May 24, 1776. It appears the *Mercury* was captured by the Salem, Massachusetts, privateer schooner *Harlequin* with no enslaved people on board on its way back to London, since American sources reported that the vessel was brought into Salem and was carrying rum and sugar. *Independent Chronicle*, Jan. 9, 1777, in Crawford et al., eds., *Naval Documents*, 7:906 ("In behalf of the officers and company and owners of the armed schooner called the *Harlequin* . . . against the snow *Mercury* of about 100 tons burthen, Eaglesfield Griffith late master"); *Independent Chronicle*, Dec. 13, 1776, in ibid, 8:473 ("Captain Tucker, in a privateer from Salem, has taken a prize snow, laden with rum, sugar, etc."); *Boston Gazette*, Dec. 16, 1776, in ibid., 8:493 (same). John Tucker commanded the *Harlequin*. Ibid., 494n1. The capture of the *Mercury* is reported in TSTD, www.slavevoyages.org/voyage/search (voyage no. 78231). It provides that the ship's owner was prominent London slave merchant Richard Oswald. (For more on Oswald, see appendic C, note 1.) This vessel should not be confused with another vessel named *Mercury* that was captured around the same time; this other *Mercury*, commanded by William Seaton, was a commercial vessel that sailed between London and St. Kitts. See *Daily Advertiser* (London), May 3, 1777; *Public Advertiser*, Dec. 9, 1776 (*Mercury*, Seaton, in convoy of commercial vessels from London bound for St. Kitts).

13. **Unknown.** An unidentified vessel was captured on December 6, 1776, after delivering about 80 enslaved Africans to an unknown location by the *American Revenue* out of New London, Connecticut; delivered to Chatham, Massachusetts. On December 6, Samuel Champlin (see no. 11, above) captured another slaver, a "light Guineaman," on its return journey to England. Mounting six carriage guns, the unidentified slaver put up some resistance, but it eventually surrendered to the *American Revenue*. Champlin sent the prize to Chatham, Massachusetts. *Connecticut Gazette*, Dec. 20, 1776, in Crawford et al., eds., *Naval Documents*, 7:528.

14. **One of "Two Guineamen."**
15. **Second of "Two Guineamen."**
On December 12, 1776, an unidentified American privateer sailed into Martinique with "two Guineamen, a ship and a brig" in tow. Governor Thomas Shirley to Vice Admiral James Young, Dec. 16, 1776, in ibid., 10:747. It is not known whether the captured vessels had captives on board. Given that no enslaved people were mentioned as being on board, the author assumes none were.

16. *Penelope.* Captain Booth; out of Liverpool; TSTD no. 92725; captured in March 1777 on a voyage to Africa by the *Freedom* out of Massachusetts; carried to Boston. The *London Chronicle*, in its April 19, 1777, edition, informed readers that the *Penelope*, bound for Africa and commanded by Captain William Booth, was seized by the *Freedom*. The *Freedom*, a Massachusetts state navy brigantine under the command of Captain John Clouston, had been sailing between Africa and Europe. In a seven-week voyage it took eleven other prizes, sending seven of them, including the *Penelope*, to Boston, before it was itself captured by a British warship in late April. The 130-ton *Penelope*, from London, carried, in addition to other cargo intended to trade for African captives, gunpowder and arms that the American armies desperately needed. See *London Chronicle*, April 19, 1777, in Crawford et al., eds., *Naval Documents*, 8:781, 781n1; Captain J. Jervis to P. Stephens, April 29, 1777, in ibid., 8:800; *Boston Gazette*, June 2, 1777, in ibid., 9:5, 5n1; *Independent Chronicle* (Boston), June 19, 1777; *St. James's Chronicle* (London), April 19, 1777; *London Evening Post*, July 29, 1777 (quoting United States newspapers on the safe arrival of the *Freedom's* prize); Desmarais, *Revolutionary War at Sea*, 2:77 (collecting US newspaper sources); *Lloyd's List*, April 22, 1777. For other details, see Libels Filed Against Five British Prizes in the Massachusetts Admiralty Court for the Middle District, *Independent Chron-*

icle, June 5, 1777, in Crawford et al., eds., *Naval Documents*, 9:21. Massachusetts and the *Freedom*'s crew each received more than £3,575 from the sale of *Penelope*. Crawford et al., eds., *Naval Documents*, 9:5n1. The *Penelope*'s voyage is covered in TSTD, www.slavevoyages.org/voyage/search (voyage no. 92725). William Booth was likely the same Captain Booth who in September 1777, while commanding the *Betsey*, was captured by an American privateer with enslaved Africans on board. See appendix C, voyage no. 19.

17. *Hero*. Captain Woodville; out of Liverpool; TSTD no. 92454; captured in late April 1777 after delivering some 328 enslaved Africans to Tobago by an unknown privateer.

The slave ship *Hero* was captured by an unidentified privateer, probably American, sometime in April 1777. The *Hero* had sailed out of Liverpool under Captain William Woodville on October 7, 1776. After forcing on board captive Africans, it dropped off about 328 survivors at the island of Tobago, presumably in the second half of April 1777. See TSTD, www.slavevoyages.org/ voyage/search (voyage no. 92454). See also *Gazetteer and New Daily Advertiser* (London), June 28, 1777 ("The Hero, Capt. Woodville, from Africa, with 270 slaves on board, is safe arrived at Tobago"); *Lloyd's List*, June 20, 1777. For more on Captain Woodville and his map of the Isles de Los, see main text in chapter 7 accompanying notes 15-17.

18. **Unknown**. An uidentified vessel was captured on a voyage to Africa in August or September 1777 by the *Washington* out of Boston; carried to Boston.

The brigantine *Washington* out of Boston brought in an unnamed Guineaman bound for Africa carrying sixty hogsheads of rum, likely to be traded for captive Africans. The schooner was captured in late August or early September 1777. *Continental Journal* (Boston), Sept. 25, 1777; Desmarais, *Revolutionary War at Sea*, 2:256 (collecting US newspaper sources).

19. **Unknown**. An unidentified vessel was captured in May 1777 by the *Sturdy Beggar* out of Baltimore; carried to Martinique.

The June 13, 1777, edition of *North Carolina Gazette* reported, "The *Sturdy Beggar* privateer, belonging to Baltimore," had returned from "a very successful cruise, having taken four Guineamen and many other valuable prizes." *South-Carolina and American General Gazette*, July 3, 1777 (citing as its source the June 13, 1777, edition of the *North Carolina Gazette*), in Crawford et al., eds., *Naval Documents*, 9:108. The names of all of the four slavers are not known. One of them was the *St. George*, with about 450 enslaved people on board. (For more information on the *St. George*'s capture and about the *Sturdy Beggar*, see appendix C, no. 7.) This entry covers one of the three unidentified "Guineamen." The following seized vessel may have been one of the three slavers. A letter in late March 1777, said, "*Sturdy*

Beggar had some hard fighting from Martinico. . . . On the 7th Feby engaged a ship mounting 14 guns from Bristol and took her after five hours resistance value £8,000 sterling. She is not yet arrived but hope soon will." George Woolsey to John Pringle, March 24, 1777, in Crawford et al., eds., *Naval Documents*, 8:192-93.

20. *Fly*. Captain Bray; out of London; captured in December 1777 on a voyage to Africa by the *Oliver Cromwell* out of Salem, Massachusetts; carried to Salem.
"The *Fly*, Bray, from London to Senegal, is taken by a privateer of 16 six-pounders, within a few leagues of Tenerife." *Daily Advertiser* (London), Dec. 31, 1777; *Morning Chronicle* (London), Dec. 31, 1777; *Lloyd's List*, Dec. 30, 1777; J. Almon, ed., *Remembrancer, or Impartial Repository of Public Events* (London: 1775-1784) [1777], 5:514. The channel off the island of Tenerife was a typical route for a British slave ship bound for Africa, and one that the *Marlborough* would take as well. The seventy-ton *Fly* was captured by the Salem, Massachusetts, privateer brigantine *Oliver Cromwell*, commanded by William Cole, with a crew of 130 and mounting sixteen carriage guns. The prize and its cargo were sold after admiralty court proceedings in Boston on January 16, 1777. Libels Filed in the Massachusetts Maritime Court of the Middle District, *Independent Chronicle*, Jan. 1, 1778, in Crawford et al., eds., *Naval Documents*, 11:11, 12n4. It is possible the *Fly* was a trading vessel and not a slaver, although the vast majority of ships clearing for Africa were slave-trading vessels.

21. *Betsey*. Captured on February 20, 1778, off Africa by the *Marlborough* out of Providence, Rhode Island.
See discussion of the capture of the slaver *Betsey* by the *Marlborough* in main text in chapter 7 accompanying note 28; for its fate, see main text in chapter 9 accompanying notes 2-3. The author believes the *Betsey* was likely a slaver because of the tobacco and other goods found on board that were typically used for trading for African captives, because the schooner was captured near the slave trading post at Isle de Kassa, and because the vast majority of British ships sent to Africa were slave ships. However, it is possible the *Betsey* was a "produce" vessel, that is, interested only in trading for nonhuman African goods such as ivory and gum.

22. *Kitty*. Captain Fisher; out of Liverpool; TSTD no. 91909; captured off Africa on March 5, 1778, by the *Marlborough* out of Providence, Rhode Island.
See discussion of the capture of the slaver *Kitty* by the *Marlborough* in main text in chapter 8 accompanying notes 3-5; for its fate, see main text in chapter 9 accompanying notes 10-13.

23. *Hannah.* Captains Dalziel, Anderson; out of Jamaica; captured in May 1778 on a voyage to Africa by the *Sprightly*; possibly carried to Boston.

Archibald Dalziel (later spelled Dalzell), a well-educated Scotsman, had financed and personally completed a slave voyage from London to Jamaica, ending in 1777. See *Morning Chronicle* (London), March 6, 1777 ("*Hannah,* Dalziel, from Africa, are arrived at Kingston"); TSTD, www.slavevoyages. org/voyage/search (voyage no. 75602). In a letter dated January 14, 1778, Dalziel wrote his sister, "I have been two months at Jamaica . . . fitting out the old vessel [*Hannah*] once more for a voyage to Africa, not choosing to go home in the winter in a crazy ship." Archibald Dalziel to Betsy (his sister), Kingston, Jamaica, Jan. 14, 1778, in Archibald Dalzell Papers, Centre for Research Collections, Edinburgh University Library, Edinburgh. In another letter, Dalziel explained what happened next: "She was accordingly armed and loaded with a cargo of rum for the Gold Coast. I sailed with the Jamaica convoy last May and kept company through the Gulf but ten days after leaving the frigate I fell in with a Yankee privateer to which I was obliged to strike after an hour's engagement. This put the finishing stroke to my affairs. I came home by way of Holland and found myself in insolvent circumstances." Archibald Dalziel to Gerard Portman, London, January 26, 1779, Records of the Royal African Companies, Detached Papers, T70/1538, British National Archives. The following appeared in the *Morning Chronicle* (London), July 22, 1778: "The *Hannah,* Dalziel, from Montego Bay, in Jamaica, to Africa, for slaves, was taken by an American privateer of 14 guns in longitude 50." However, the next day, the following was reported in the *St. James Chronicle* (London), July 23, 1778, based on an Extract from another letter from Portsmouth, July 22: "The *Porcupine* [Captain Finch] likewise retook the *Hannah,* Dalziel, from Jamaica to the Coast of Guinea, with 260 puncheons of rum, which had been taken by the *Sprightly* American privateer." A relative, in a letter, stated that the American privateer ordered the prize *Hannah* to Boston, indicating *Sprightly* could have been a Boston privateer. See Elizabeth Lindsay, to George Lindsay, Aug. 27, 1778, in Archibald Dalzell Papers, Centre for Research Collections, Edinburgh University Library. However, no record of the *Sprightly* could be found. The seizure of the *Hannah* pushed Dalziel into bankruptcy. *Daily Advertiser* (London), Sept. 9, 1778; *Gazetteer and New Daily Advertiser*, Sept. 9, 1778; *Lloyd's Evening Post*, Sept. 9, 1778.

24. *John and Jane.* Captain Adams; out of Liverpool; TSTD no. 92430; captured on July 3, 1778, after delivering an estimated 93 enslaved Africans to Tobago by an unidentified American privateer.

John Adams was the *John and Jane*'s captain and owner. The vessel was just twenty tons. This voyage and the capture are covered in TSTD, www.slave voyages.org/voyage/search (voyage no. 92430).

25. *Swift.* Captain Brighouse; out of Liverpool; TSTD no. 92728; captured in August 1778 after delivering some 180 enslaved Africans to Jamaica by the *General Arnold* out of Boston; possibly carried to Boston.

> The *Swift*, an eighty-ton slaver, was built in Rhode Island in 1764. William Davenport of Liverpool was one of its owners. The *Swift* landed about 180 African captives at Jamaica on June 30, 1778. It was captured after departing Jamaica on August 1, 1778. TSTD, www.slavevoyages.org/voyage/search (voyage no. 92728). The following is in Williams, *History of Liverpool Privateers*, 254: "The barque *Swift*, Captain W. Brighouse, belonging to Messrs. W. Davenport & Co., having lost sight of the Jamaica fleet and convoy, off the west-end of Cuba, proceeded on her passage alone, and was captured by the *General Arnold* privateer, 20 guns and 85 men, Captain James M'Gee [Magee] of Boston." See also See *Lloyd's List*, Jan. 29, 1779.

26. *Unity.* Captain Heblethwaite; out of Liverpool; TSTD no. 92570; captured in August 1778 after delivering about 328 enslaved Africans to Jamaica by an unidentified American privateer.

> Captain John Heblethwaite, commanding a crew of forty men and the one-hundred-ton *Unity*, sailed from Liverpool on December 16, 1777. The ship disembarked an estimated 328 enslaved people in July 1778. The Liverpool owners included John Dobson and Thomas Hodgson. This voyage and the capture are covered in TSTD, www.slavevoyages.org/voyage/search (voyage no. 92570). See also *Lloyd's List*, Jan. 29, April 27, 1779.

BRITISH SLAVE SHIPS PLUNDERED BY AMERICAN PRIVATEERS BUT NOT TAKEN

At least two British slavers in the applicable time period are known to have been stopped by American privateers and plundered but were not seized and sold as prizes. The slave ship *Union*, when sailing from St. Kitts to Liverpool on September 7, 1776, was halted by the Providence privateer *Sally*, which removed 611 elephant tusks, two tons of pepper, cannon, small arms, and gunpowder, as well as an enslaved boy, but did not keep the slave ship. The *Sally* was partially owned by John Brown. The *Union* was subsequently captured a second time by the *Cabot*, a Continental navy fourteen-gun brig, but the *Union* was saved when a large British warship chased the *Cabot* away.[1]

The slave ship *Cornwall*, commanded by James Bruce, sailing from Jamaica to Bristol, was pummeled by a storm, leaving it with three broken masts and seven feet of water in its holds. On January 23, 1777, the *Cornwall*, using makeshift jury masts and limping along near Barbados, was easily overtaken by the Massachusetts privateer *Boston*, which for four days stripped everything of value from the vessel and crew, including elephant tusks. Probably because the *Cornwall* was no longer seaworthy, it was not kept as a prize.[2]

SEIZURES BY THE CONTINENTAL NAVY

Seizures by Continental navy ships are not included in the above chart. The slave ship *Thomas,* on its voyage from Barbados to Bristol, was captured by the Continental navy brig *Andrea Doria,* commanded by Captain Isaiah Robinson, on December 12, 1776. The *Thomas* was recaptured by the British frigate *Perseus* off of Cape May, New Jersey, on January 12, 1777.[3]

The *Sam,* carrying four guns, on November 25, 1776, was siezed by the Continental navy sloop *Independence,* which carried ten guns and forty-five men and was commanded by John Young. The *Sam* was taken five days after departing Barbados for Liverpool. The vessel had on board $20,000 in silver coins, two-and-a-half tons of ivory, and one hundred bars of iron. At an auction of the ship at the London Coffee House in Philadelphia, the *Sam,* as well as the former slave ship *King George* (no. 8 above) were purchased by the Pennsylvania state navy for use as fire ships on the Delaware River.[4] The *Sam,* captained by Samuel Richardson and owned by slave merchant William Davenport of Liverpool, had carried 208 enslaved people to Barbados, where they were sold on October 18, 1776 (122 adult males, 35 male children, 25 adult females, and 26 female children, at a price for most captives ranging from £30 to £35). The sales records also show that 170 of the captives were sold in a single transaction. Given this fact and that $20,000 worth of silver coin was found on the *Sam,* the 170 captives were most likely sold to a Spanish buyer and shipped from Barbados to a Spanish-controlled island. Captain Richardson must have been released within about a month after the capture, because in late December 1776, he sailed from Dominica to Antigua to meet with Admiral James Young of the Royal Navy to inform him of the taking of his vessel.[5]

SEIZURES OF PRODUCE VESSELS

While most British ships doing business in Africa were slave ships, a few were "produce vessels," that is, ships whose captains intended to trade with Africans for products native to Africa but not for enslaved people. American privateers captured some of them too.

A London newspaper reported that the American privateer *Alligator,* "of 16 guns," but of which little is else is known, captured two ships near the Madeira Islands and "an English ship from the coast of Guinea" in late December 1777.[6] If the captured vessel was sailing from Africa for England, it was likely a produce vessel.

The following two British ships may have been produce vessels: "Two ships from the Coast of Guinea . . . were lately taken by the *Deane* provincial privateer, and brought into this harbor [Lisbon, Portugal], where the crews were set at liberty, and on application being made to the [British] Admiralty, the prizes were seized, and, it is said, will be restored to the owners. This affair has greatly dissatisfied the friends of America, who talk loudly of the injustice of the transaction."[7]

In March 1778, George Waite Babcock's *Marlborough* captured the *Pearl* on the coast of West Africa. Commanded by Peter Brancker and hailing from Liverpool, the *Pearl* when seized was fully loaded with mostly elephant ivory and other African trade goods in its holds, indicating that it was a produce vessel about to depart for Liverpool.[8]

On August 9, 1778, an unidentified prize ship arrived at Boston Harbor. It had been captured by the Connecticut privateer brig *Favourite*, commanded by Captain John Lamb. One Boston newspaper, the *Continental Journal*, stated that the prize had been "bound from the coast of Africa for England, laden with elephant's teeth, dye wood, etc. She mounts 16 carriage guns and is said to be a fine vessel." Another Boston newspaper, the *Independent Chronicle*, stated that the prize had been from the British Caribbean and was bound to Africa "laden with logwood, etc." However, it is doubtful that a ship sailing to Africa to trade with local merchants would be trading wood. Accordingly, I believe the first newspaper's description was accurate. Captain Lamb's privateer brigantine *Favourite* was taken in mid-June 1778, so its capture of the ship bound for Africa must have occurred prior to then. The *Favourite* was commissioned in Massachusetts on May 27, 1778.[9]

The above list of 26 vessels does not include captured ships that were formerly used in slave trading voyages. For example, the *True Blue* was captured in June 1776 and taken into Providence for admiralty procedures. This ship, registered in Lancaster, England, had been used for a slave trading voyage out of Liverpool that was completed in June 1774. When captured, the *True Blue* was carrying goods from Jamaica to Lancaster, but this time it was not on a slave trading voyage.[10]

Appendix C

British Slave Ships Captured by American Privateers with Enslaved
Africans On Board, August 1776 to August 1778

The voyage number, if available, is from the Trans-Atlantic Slave Trade Database
(TSTD), www.slavevoyages.org. Those without numbers are newly discovered by
the author's research.

1. *Bacchus*. Captain Forsyth; out of Liverpool; TSTD no. 91993; captured in January
1777, possibly bound for Dominica with 220 enslaved Africans on board, by an
unidentified American privateer; carried to St. Lucia.

In early January 1777, the *Bacchus*, commanded by Captain Forsythe, out
of Liverpool, after departing Africa with 220 enslaved people on board, was
captured by an unidentified privateer in the Middle Passage and carried into
French-controlled St. Lucia. London newspapers reported the capture of
the *Bacchus*, Captain Forsyth, of Liverpool, in the Middle Passage. *London
Chronicle*, March 20 to 22, 1777, in Crawford et al., eds., *Naval Documents*,
8:699; *Daily Advertiser* (London), March 21, 1777; *St James's Chronicle*
(London), March 20, 1777; *Morning Chronicle* (London), March 21, 1777;
Public Advertiser (London), March 21, 1777; *Lloyd's List*, March 21, 1777.
The newspaper squibs did not say if enslaved people were on board or how
many were on board, but this can be inferred since the vessel was captured
in the Middle Passage. However, another version of the capture that appeared in a London newspaper was that the *Bacchus* had been captured sailing not in the Middle Passage but while sailing from Barbados to Jamaica.
General Evening Post (London), March 21, 1777. Even if this was true, the
vessel would still have been carrying its captives in order to sell them in Jamaica. The following report contains the most authoritative details: "we
have intelligence here of a Guineaman belonging to Mr. [William] Earle
of Liverpool with 220 slaves being taken by a small American schooner and
carried into St Lucia where the slaves are selling." William Bartlett,
Grenada, to Alexander Bartlett, London, Jan. 11, 1777, Exchequer, King's
Remembrancer, Exhibits, E140/2/5, British National Archives. The captured slaver must have been the *Bacchus*, as one of its owners was William
Earle of Liverpool and the dates are in the correct range. This was probably
the same *Bacchus* sailing from Liverpool that in 1774 had delivered some
two hundred enslaved people to Charleston, South Carolina. TSTD,
www.slavevoyages.org/voyage/search (voyage no. 91992). Thus, the report
that the *Bacchus* was carrying about two hundred enslaved people in 1777

is in line with the 1774 voyage. TSTD covers *Bacchus*'s 1776–1777 voyage, commanded by John Forsyth and purchasing captives on the West African coast at Cape Mount. Ibid. (voyage no. 91993).

The following sworn statement by the master of the British sloop *Nancy* describes how the *Bacchus*'s African captives were disposed of at St. Lucia. In this description, the slave ship that was captured was not named, but it must have been the *Bacchus* based on the dates provided and the St. Lucia location. On January 5, 1777, the *Nancy*, bound from British-controlled St. Vincent's for St. Lucia, was taken by an American privateer schooner commanded by one Welch two miles off St. Lucia. The prize was brought to a bay at St. Lucia and anchored next to a "Guineaman" the same Americans had also recently taken (this ship must have been the *Bacchus*). The next morning the Americans removed all the cargo and other items of value from the two prizes and loaded them onto two American schooners and a sloop. The privateersmen also promised to burn the *Bacchus* and the *Nancy* "and take the Negroes" on board their vessels "if a person could not be found to ransom or buy them." A local British merchant purchased the African captives. The slave ship *Bacchus* was then set on fire and allowed to drift, while burning, toward the St. Lucia shoreline. See Deposition of James Erving, Master of the Sloop *Nancy*, May 6, 1777, Secretaries of State, State Papers Foreign, France, Lord Stormont, SP78/302, f.417, British National Archives. Rather than take this approach to disposing of captured Africans, American privateer captains in the near future would be permitted to sell them to French buyers at Martinique and Guadeloupe.

2. Unknown.
3. Unknown. Two unknown vessels were captured in January 1777, destination unknown, carrying a total of 140 enslaved Africans between the two vessels, by the *Boston* out of Boston; carried to North Carolina.

In either January or early February, the armed sloop *Boston*, commanded by Captain William Brown and sailing from Boston, captured two slave ships carrying a total of 140 enslaved people. A Boston newspaper reported that one of the captured vessels was sent into North Carolina where "many of the poor slaves perished soon after their arrival." *Independent Chronicle* (Boston), Feb. 20 and March 5, 1777, in Crawford et al., eds., *Naval Documents*, 8:37; Desmarais, *Revolutionary War at Sea*, 2:15 (collecting US newspaper sources). Captain Brown likely captured the two slave ships in the Caribbean and, believing there was no prospect of selling them there, sailed more than 1,800 miles to North Carolina. The additional sailing time likely explains the poor condition of the enslaved people when they arrived at the unnamed North Carolina port. The *Boston* was armed with twenty-two guns, and had a crew of 210 men. Crawford, et al., eds., *Naval Documents* 6:922n2.

4. *Apollo*. Captain Smith; out of London; TSTD no. 75092; captured on February 10, 1777, bound for Barbados with 292 enslaved Africans on board, by the *Fanny* out of Connecticut and another unidentified American privateer; carried to Martinique.

On February 10, 1777, an unidentified American privateer captured the slave ship *Apollo* of London and bound for Africa. This was reported in several newspapers in London, although it would turn out later that the captured vessel was not bound for Africa. *London Evening Post*, May 1, 1777; *General Evening Post* (London), May 1, 1777; *Daily Advertiser* (London), April 30, 1777. A later notice indicated that the prize, commanded by Andrew Smith, was seized in February "with her cargo of slaves on board" and sent to Martinique, apparently the first slaver of many ultimately delivered to that French colonial island by American privateers. *Morning Post* (London), May 3, 1777; *Lloyd's List*, May 2, 1777. A Jamaican newspaper wrote that "Capt. Smith, of the snow *Apollo*, belonging to Messrs. Camden and Calvert of London, with 292 slaves on board, for Barbados, taken within sight of her port, by a brig and a schooner." *Cornwall Chronicle* (Montego Bay, Jamaica), March 15, 1777. Subsequent reports indicated that the American privateer brig was the *Fanny*, owned by Connecticut investors and commanded by Captain Whittlesey of Connecticut but fitted out in Providence. The *Apollo* had departed the Gold Coast in Africa on December 5, 1776, headed to Barbados. Captain Smith and his officers said in a sworn statement that "on Monday the tenth of the present month of February being then about four leagues to the eastward of the said island of Barbados, they were taken by two American privateers, one of which was a brig mounting fourteen double fortified four pounders & three pounders thereabouts, commanded by one Whittlesea. The other was an armed schooner of ten four pounders and about fifty or sixty men." Andrew Smith, George Muckle, Thomas Potter, and Henry Wright deposition to George William Gordon, Feb. 20, 1777, Secretaries of State, State Papers Foreign, France, Lord Stormont, SP78/302, f.229, British National Archives. See also Andrew Smith to Anthony Calvert, London, in ibid., f.225. The name of the privateer's captain, Whittlesey, and the privateer's description, provide key clues. A British report of March 10, 1777, indicated that among the privateers operating out of Martinique and St. Lucia was a brig, name unknown, mounting fourteen guns and carrying one hundred men, commanded by a Whittlesey. Henry Haffey, St. Vincent's, to Gill Slater, London, dated St. Lucia, March 10, 1777, Secretaries of State, State Papers Foreign, France, Lord Stormont, SP78/302, f.334, British National Archives. Separately, it was reported that the American privateer brig *Fanny*, owned by Connecticut investors and commanded by Captain Whittlesey of Connecticut but fitted out in Providence, in February or March 1777, captured a Guineaman on its way to the Caribbean, with 297 enslaved people on board. Captain Azariah Whittlesey was reported to have sent his prize to Martinique, where the vessel was condemned, and all the captives were sold. See *Independent Chronicle* (Boston), April 10, 1777; *Providence Gazette*, April 12, 1777, in Crawford et al., eds., *Naval Documents*, 8:308-09, 326; Desmarais, *Revolutionary War at Sea*, 2:69 (collecting US newspaper sources). The voyage of the 110-ton *Apollo*, sailing out of London and commanded by Andrew Smith, is covered in TSTD, www.slavevoyages.org/voyage/search (voyage no. 75092). The *Apollo* was likely the unidentified vessel described in the following squib: "Letters from Barbados, dated the 15th of February, mention that a large Guineaman was taken in sight of a number of people off that island, by an American privateer, who carried her into Martinico, and there sold the slaves before the captain's face, who applied to the Governor [the French governor of Martinique], but he told him he could give him no redress." *Daily Advertiser* (London), May 3, 1777; *General Evening Post* (London), May 3, 1777; *London Evening Post*, May 3, 1777. Captain Peleg Clark of Newport had seen the *Apollo*, which had just arrived from London, at Cape Coast Road back in July 1776. P. Clarke to J. Fletcher, July 6, 1776, in Donnan, ed., *Documents of the Slave Trade*, 3:319-20.

5. *Industry*. Captain Nuttal; out of Liverpool; TSTD no. 92596; captured in February 1777, bound for Jamaica with 195 enslaved Africans on board, by an unidentified American privateer, reportedly from Boston; possiby carried to Guadeloupe. "The *Industry*, ___ [*sic*], from Africa to the West Indies, is taken by the Rebels." *Lloyd's List*, April 29, 1777; *Public Advertiser* (London), April 30, 1777. A Liverpool newspaper stated that the *Industry* had been taken by a Boston privateer en route from Liverpool and Africa to America. *Williamson's Liverpool Advertiser*, May 2, 1777. The following squib appeared in London newspapers: "We have just received advice of a Guineaman, three vessels from Newfoundland, and a store ship, being taken and carried into Martinico, and a Guineaman carried into Guadeloupe." Extract of a letter from Dominica, Feb. 17, in *London Chronicle*, May 20, 1777, in Crawford et al., eds., *Naval Documents*, 7:1225; *Daily Advertiser* (London), May 20, 1777; *Gazetteer and New Daily Advertiser* (London), May 20, 1777. The word of a slave ship "carried into Martinico" could be the *Apollo* (no. 4 above), while the "Guineaman carried into Guadeloupe" could be the *Industry*. TSTD, www.slavevoyages.org/voyage/search (voyage no. 92596), provides that the *Industry*, owned by Samuel Sandys of Liverpool and commanded by John (or Jonathan) Nuttal, began its voyage from Liverpool on November 5, 1774, that it picked up its cargo of some 210 enslaved people at the Isles de Los, and that the vessel with about 195 surviving captives was taken prior to arriving at its destination of Jamaica. It is possible this voyage was a prior one and that TSTD did not cover the second one that ended in the capture. The Schofield Archive indicates that the *Industry* was captured by an American privateer, but was subsequently recaptured at Ja-

maica and renamed the *Yg Edward*. The vessel arrived at Liverpool November 11, 1777. Files on the *Industry* (slave voyage no. 92596), Schofield Archive, Wilberforce Institute, University of Hull.

6. *Endeavour*. Captain Dwyer; out of Liverpool; TSTD no. 24810; captured on March 4, 1777, destination unknown, with 42 enslaved Africans on board, by the *Rutledge* out of Charleston, South Carolina; carried to Martinique.

On March 4, 1777, the *Rutledge* privateer, sailing out of Charleston, South Carolina, and commanded by Jacob Mulligan, captured the brigantine *Endeavour* off Barbados carrying "42 slaves, a large quantity of elephant teeth, etc." Mulligan courageously captured his prize, which mounted ten guns, "almost under the guns of a fort at Barbados, and in sight of several vessels at anchor," including reportedly a Royal Navy warship that gave chase but lost the privateer and the *Endeavour* with its prize crew. Following his narrow escape, Mulligan sold the captives at Martinique. *South-Carolina and American General Gazette*, April 3, 1777, and *Gazette of the State of South-Carolina*, April 9, 1777, in Crawford et al., eds., *Naval Documents*, 8:268, 308. See also *Virginia Gazette*, June 20, 1777 (reporting that while the *Endeavour* was bound to Barbados, the capture occurred in sight of Carlisle Bay at Antigua); *Maryland Journal*, June 10, 1777; *Liverpool General Advertiser*, May 23, 1777; Desmarais, *Revolutionary War at Sea*, 2:92 (collecting US newspaper sources). The *Endeavour's* captain, Thomas Dwyer, had commenced his long voyage in Liverpool around May 1776. The *Endeavour's* capture is reported in TSTD, www.slave voyages.org/voyage/search (voyage no. 24810). Another letter claimed that the American privateer was the *Rattlesnake*, which found on board the *Endeavour* "40 slaves, between nine and ten tons of ivory, and a considerable quantity of returned goods." Extract of a Letter from Barbados, March 25, 1777, in *London Chronicle*, May 27, 1777, in Crawford et al., eds., *Naval Documents*, 8:202. However, the letter writer apparently misidentified the American privateer; it was *Rutledge*. An Englishman wrote in a letter, "Two slave ships were carried" into Martinique "about the beginning of March; one Enfanton purchased both cargoes from the pirates and, sold them afterwards all over the island." News from St. Christopher, April 16, *Pennsylvania Journal*, May 28, 1777, in ibid., 8:354. The *Endeavour* could have been one of the two ships; the slaver *Mary* captured by the French colonial privateer *Puissance* could have been the other one. See "Other Captures: French Privateers," below.

7. *St. George*. Captain Moore; out of London; TSTD no. 77186; captured on March 25, 1777, bound for Grenada with 458 enslaved Africans on board, by the *Sturdy Beggar* out of Baltimore; carried to Martinique.

A letter from Grenada, dated March 28, 1777, said, "The 25th instant, the *St. George*, Moore, with 400 slaves, was taken by an American privateer a little to the windward of Grenada. She was from the Gold Coast . . . she had touched at Barbados, and applied for convoy to this island, but could not procure it." Extract of a Letter from Grenada, March 28, in *London Chronicle*, May 29, 1777. According to a British letter writer from Grenada in mid-April, an American brig mounting fourteen guns captured the *St. George*, Captain Moore in command, bound for Grenada, carrying "450 Negroes, some thousand weight of gold dust, and a great many elephant's teeth, the whole cargo being computed to be worth £20,000 sterling." Extract of a Letter from Grenada, April 18, 1777, in Crawford et al., eds., *Naval Documents*, 8:372. The capture was also noted in London newspapers, with the squib, "The *St. George*, from Africa to the West Indies, with 450 slaves, is taken by an American privateer, of 16 guns, and a number of swivels." See, for example, *St. James's Chronicle* (London), May 27, 1777; *Daily Advertiser* (London), May 27, 1777; *Gazetteer and New Daily Advertiser* (London), May 27, 1777. The *Sturdy Beggar*, a 135-ton privateer brig from Baltimore, carrying fourteen cannon and ten swivels and a crew of about one hundred, commanded by John McKeel, made the impressive capture. According to an advertisement the ship's captain had published to attract more sailors, the *Sturdy Beggar* "is allowed to be the handsomest vessel ever built in America, is completely furnished with all kinds of warlike stores, ammunition, etc., and is remarkable for fast sailing, having never chased a vessel but she soon came up with." Advertisement, *North-Carolina Gazette*, Aug. 8, 1777, in Crawford et al., eds., *Naval Documents*, 9:706. See also A List of Commissions of Letters of Marque and Reprisal Granted by the Council of Safety for the State of Maryland, March 1777, in ibid., 8:139.

Word of this remarkable capture was apparently slow in arriving at some places, as a slew of articles about the *Sturdy Beggar*'s capture of the *St. George* ran in American and Caribbean newspapers in May and June. A Charleston, South Carolina, newspaper wrote, "*Sturdy Beggar*, privateer, Capt. McKeel, of Baltimore, in Maryland" had in tow a prize, "*St. George*, late of London, Moore her late master, having 400 slaves on board." See *Gazette of the State of South-Carolina*, May 12, 1777, in Crawford et al., eds., *Naval Documents*, 8:957. The *Pennsylvania Journal*, May 14, 1777, edition reported that the American privateer *Sturdy Beggar* had captured an unnamed vessel, which had on board, besides African captives, twenty-seven tons of ivory and £7,000 worth of gold dust, and was taken into Martinique. Ibid., 8:965-66. The prize was likely the *St. George*. The *Maryland Journal*, June 10, 1777, edition reported four hundred enslaved people were captured by the *Sturdy Beggar*. See also Desmarais, *Revolutionary War at Sea*, 2:4, 62, 112 (collecting US newspaper sources). A Jamaican source stated that the *Sturdy Beggar* took "a very large ship from Africa and carried her into Port Dauphine [in Martinique], where they sold the cargo." *Cornwall Chronicle* (Montego Bay, Jamaica), May 10, 1777.

This *St. George* was likely the same one that Newport slave captain Peleg Clarke had spotted off Cape Coast Road in July 1776. After collecting some five hundred captives at Cape Coast Road, Annamaboe, and the Gold Coast, the 250-ton ship owned by London investors finally departed the African coast in mid-January 1777, bound for Grenada, almost one year after it had departed London. During the Middle Passage, its commander, William Moore, apparently lost about fifty captives before his ship was seized. The *St. George* had been built in Philadelphia, in 1773, before it was sent to the London slavers who had financed the construction. P. Clarke to J. Fletcher, July 6, 1776, in Donnan, ed., *Documents of the Slave Trade,* 3:320; TSTD, www.slavevoyages.org/voyage/search (voyage no. 77186). For the *St. George* likely departing Cape Coast Castle in mid-January, see William Moore (captain of the *St. George*) to Richard Miles (governor of Cape Coast Castle), Jan. 9, 1777, Records of the Royal African Companies, T70-1534, British National Archives. For the capture by the *Sturdy Beggar* of a slave ship with no enslaved people on board, see appendix B, no. 19. William Moore was likely the same man who commanded a small trading vessel captured by the *Marlborough* in Africa in March 1778. See "Captures of Small Slave Trading Vessels on the African Coast by the *Marlborough*," below.

8. **Unknown**. An unidentified slaver, destination unknown with 511 enslaved Africans on board, was captured in April 1777 by the *Rattlesnake* out of Pennsylvania; carried to an unknown location.

The privateer *Rattlesnake*, commanded by David McCulloch, sometimes sailed with another Pennsylvania privateer, the fourteen-gun schooner *American Security*, captained by John Ord Jr. and jointly owned by Robert Morris, the important delegate from the Continental Congress, and William Bingham, the US emissary to Martinique. The *Pennsylvania Journal* published an April 5 letter from St. Eustatius (a Dutch possession in the Caribbean) stating that "the privateer *Rattlesnake*, in company with Capt. Ord and others, have taken and sent into that place two ships from Cork [in Ireland], and six or seven sail from the same port into Martinico; also some ships from Africa with slaves." In another letter, this one from April 25, Nicholas Way wrote, "The privateer *Rattlesnake* has taken several prizes, among others a Guinea ship with 500 slaves. This *Rattlesnake* is such a noted runner that she is said to be a terror to the English Islands," that is, the British-controlled Caribbean islands. *Pennsylvania Journal*, April 23, 1777; Nicholas Way to Owen Biddle, April 25, 1777, in Crawford et al., eds., *Naval Documents*, 8:430. Another source said "the vessel from Guinea had 511 slaves by our accounts." Extract of a Letter from St. Eustatia, May 8, *Pennsylvania Journal*, June 17, 1777, in Crawford et al., eds., *Naval Documents*, 8:936. The captured slave ship has not been identified. This entry represents one of the "ships from Africa with slaves" mentioned in the April 5 letter.

The *Rattlesnake* schooner was said to mount eighteen 9-pound guns, all brass, and carry a crew of 150 men. Extract of a Letter from a Gentleman at St. Lucia, to a Merchant in this Town [London], March 10, 1777, in ibid., 8:81; Extract of a Letter from Capt. Cook . . . , Nov. 1, 1777, in ibid., 10:373; Desmarais, *Revolutionary War at Sea*, 2:81 (collecting US newspaper sources). A Jamaican source described *Rattlesnake* as being "as large a schooner as ever was built in America." *Cornwall Chronicle* (Montego Bay, Jamaica), May 3, 1777.

9. *Hawke.* Captain Mill; out of London; TSTD no. 75621; captured in April 1777, bound for Grenada with 454 enslaved Africans on board, by the *Rattlesnake*, out of Pennsylvania; carried to Martinique.

Sometime, likely in April 1777, an unidentified American privateer captured perhaps the richest cargo from any Guineaman taken in 1777. The victim was the 260-ton *Hawke*, with an astonishing 454 captives and "a large quantity of ivory and gold dust" on board. *Lloyd's List*, June 24, 1777. A report in London newspapers stated, "The *Hawke*, Mill, from Africa to Grenada, with 454 slaves, is taken by the *Rattlesnake* privateer, and carried into Martinique." See, for example, *London Chronicle*, June 24, 1777; *Public Advertiser* (London), June 25, 1777; *London Evening Post*, June 26, 1777. See also Almon, ed., *Remembrancer* [1777], 5:108. This entry represents one of the "ships from Africa with slaves" mentioned in the April 5 letter cited in the previous entry.

Captain Peleg Clark of Newport had seen the *Hawke*, which had sailed from London, at Cape Coast Road in July 1776. P. Clarke to J. Fletcher, July 6, 1776, in Donnan, ed., *Documents of the Slave Trade*, 3:319-20. The *Hawke's* capture is reported in TSTD, www.slavevoyages.org/voyage/search (voyage no. 75621). It reports that Captain Mill, having departed Africa on January 22, 1777, after embarking about five hundred African captives, had some forty-six of the captives die in the Middle Passage before the *Hawke* was captured prior to disembarking its enslaved people. There was a duplicate listing for the *Hawke's* voyage. See TSTD, www.slavevoyages.org/voyage/search (voyage no. 78220). This listing indicates that the *Hawke* was owned by John Shoolbred of London. Shoolbred would testify before Parliament regarding the impact of American privateers on the British slave trade in February 1778. See main text in chapter 11 accompanying notes 20-24. The listing also indicates the ship's captains were George Clieland and Mill. It appears these two listings should be combined into one. This *Hawke* may have been the first slave ship to have copper sheathing installed on the bottom of its hull to prevent damage by shipworms. Rawley and Behrendt, *Transatlantic Slave Trade*, 220.

David Mill, from August 1770 to January 1777 the governor of the key British slave trading fort at Cape Coast Castle (now part of Ghana), worked for sixteen years in the slave trade on the African coast for various British slave trading interests. He had "all of his property" he had accumulated in that time on the slave ship *Hawke* when it was seized by an American privateer on its way from Africa to Antigua in April 1777. After the prize was taken to the French-controlled island of Martinique, Mill desperately tried to reacquire his property by offering to pay a steep ransom for it, but he failed. Report of Arthur Piggott, July 3, 1777, in Crawford et al., eds., *Naval Documents*, 9:459; Sparks, *Where the Negroes Are Masters*, 254; Donnan, ed., *Documents of the Slave Trade*, 3:228n5. Captain Hercules Mill was the brother of David Mill. "Minutes of Enquiry into Administration of the West Indian Trade," Feb. 14, 1777, in Ledward, ed., *Journals of the Board of Trade*, 14:309; St. Clair, *Door of No Return*, 88. A British officer wrote from Cape Coast Road on December 15, 1776, "The *Hawk*, Mill (lying here) has got very few goods. Gov'r Mill intends going off in her [the *Hawke*], from Whydah [modern-day Ouidah in Benin], the beginning of the year." J. Bell to J. Fletcher, Dec. 15, 1776, in Donnan, ed., *Documents of the Slave Trade*, 3:323.

10. *Gascoyne*. Captain Thoborn; out of London; TSTD no. 77085; captured in April 1777, destination unknown, but taken near Barbados, with 345 enslaved Africans on board, by the ***Rattlesnake*** and ***American Security***, out of Pennsylvania; carried to Martinique.

Robert Morris, reading of the accounts of his privateer from Philadelphia as he served as a delegate to the Continental Congress, wrote to William Bingham, Congress's agent at Martinique, "I have lately had the pleasure to hear that Ord in company with the *Rattlesnake* had taken and sent into Martinique nine sail of transport ships [and] two Guineamen, and two sails of transports into St. Eustatius. If this be true, and it seems well authenticated, we shall make a fine hand of it." Quoted in Alberts, *Golden Voyage*, 51, 485n (citing R. Morris to W. Bingham, April 25, 1777, William Bingham Papers, Manuscript Reading Room, Library of Congress, which the author did not find in this file). The report was true, except the slavers were brought into Martinique. The two armed British slave ships, the 160-ton *Gascoyne* and the 250-ton *Fox*, both sailing out of London, when captured had a total of 498 Africans on board as well as ivory tusks. Alberts, *Golden Voyage*, 51, 485n; P. Clarke to J. Fletcher, July 6, 1776, in Donnan, ed., *Documents of the Slave Trade*, 3:320. The captures of *Gascoyne* and *Fox* are covered in TSTD, www.slavevoyages.org/voyage/search (voyages nos. 77085, 75595). See also *Lloyd's List*, Aug. 5, 1777 ("*Gascoyne*, Captain Thoburn, from Africa, is captured and taken to Martinique"); *London Evening Post*, Aug. 7, 1777 (same); *General Evening Post* (London), Sept. 30, 1777 ("The *Fox*, Capt. [James] Farley, from Africa, for the West Indies [is] taken by an American privateer of 22 guns and 120 men, and carried into Martinico");

London Chronicle, Sept. 30, 1777 (same); *Daily Advertiser* (London), Oct. 1, 1777 (same, except no mention of the American privateer's guns and crew). See also main text in chapter 3 accompanying notes 23-27.

11. *Fox.* Captain Farley; out of London; TSTD no. 75595; captured in April 1777, bound for Grenada with 150 enslaved Africans on board, by the *Rattlesnake* and *American Security* out of Pennsylvania; carried to Martinique.

See discussion and sources under the previous entry. In addition, *Fox* had on board property belonging to the British governor of Cape Coast Castle in Africa, Richard Miles. See R. Miles to Capt. William Chapman, James Fort, Feb. 19, 1778, Records of the Royal African Companies, T70/1479/2, British National Archives. Miles wrote, "it was lucky I did not engage the storeship [*Fox*] for you, as she has been since taken by the Americans with 150 slaves besides my property on board." Ibid.

12. *St. George.* Captain Patton; out of London; TSTD no. 24797; captured between April 27 and May 2, 1777, destination unknown, carrying 200 enslaved Africans, by the *Oliver Cromwell* out of Pennsylvania; carried to St. Lucia.

A merchant from St. Vincent reported that in the week from April 27 to May 2, 1777, "the American frigate *Oliver Cromwell,* took three prizes last week, one a Guineaman with 300 slaves [whom] they are now discharging at St. Lucia." Extract of a Letter from St. Vincent's to a Merchant in Liverpool, dated May 5, in *St. James's Chronicle* (London), June 24, 1777, and *Daily Advertiser* (London), June 24, 1777. See also *London Chronicle,* June 24, 1777, in Crawford et al., eds., *Naval Documents,* 8:917. (A similar item of "intelligence" is copied in John Dobson, Liverpool, to Lord George Germain, London, June 20, 1777, Secretaries of State, State Papers Foreign, France, Lord Stormont, SP78/302, f.419, British National Archives; it stated the captured vessel had "500 slaves" on board, but that is likely a mistake in the transcription.)

The American privateer that made the capture was the impressive twenty-two-gun brigantine *Oliver Cromwell* sailing out of Philadelphia and commanded by Harman Courter with a crew of 150 men. The *Pennsylvania Journal,* in its May 14, 1777, edition, said "the *Oliver Cromwell* of this port has taken several prizes," including "the brig *St. George,* from Africa, with 190 slaves," which safely arrived at Martinique. This squib appears to be fairly accurate. See also TSTD, www.slavevoyages.org/voyage/search (voyage no. 24797), which reports that Captain Patton had 236 captives on board. The following letter from the Campbell firm in Grenada to the Campbell firm in London is the most authoritative account: "We are sorry to inform you that our brig that we sent last year to the [African coast] was taken about a month ago near Barbados by an American privateer with 200 slaves on board, and the vessel and cargo carried to Martinique and disposed of in that Island." Fortunately for the Campbells, the brig's cargo and out-fitting were insured for £5,000 and the firm was only a one-third owner in the venture. James Campbell & Co, Grenada, to Alexander Campbell & Co, London, Apr 28, 1777, Exchequer, King's Remembrancer, Exhibits, E140/2/5, British National Archives. See also Deposition of Richard Webb, April 25, 1777, CO 101/20, f.186, in ibid. The method adopted by Captain Courter of the *Oliver Cromwell* in selling the captives at Martinique was described as follows: "The *Oliver Cromwell* privateer brig took a Guinea-man, with upwards of 400 slaves and sold them at Martinico for 8 to 12 Joes per head. Their method of selling them was this: they took the negroes on shore in a small craft, to prevent any disputes of their being sold on shore, and whoever wanted to purchase [went] to the privateersmen and bought." *Cornwall Chronicle* (Montego Bay, Jamaica), May 3, 1777.

13. **Unknown**. An unidentified vessel bound for Dominica with 318 enslaved Africans on board, captured in late May 1777 by the *American Security* and *Fly* out of Pennsylvania and Martinique; carried to Martinique.

In late May 1777, one of Robert Morris's and William Bingham's privateers, the Pennsylvania schooner *American Security*, commanded by Captain John Ord Jr. and carrying fourteen guns, and the privateer sloop *Fly*, commanded by Captain Thomas Palmer and also carrying fourteen guns, seized "a large Guineaman, with 318 slaves on board, bound for Dominica" and sent the prize to nearby Martinique where it arrived on June 1. Ord, as Morris had previously directed, likely had the African captives on the captured vessel sold at the French-controlled island. *South Carolina Gazette*, June 26, 30, 1777, in Crawford et al., eds., *Naval Documents*, 9:180, 195. The *Fly* was fitted out in Martinique and likely had a commission from the Continental Congress; Thomas Palmer hailed from New England. Ibid., 11:740n.

14. *Lady Mary*. Captured in May or June 1777, bound for Honduras with an es-timated 100 enslaved Africans on board, by an unidentified American privateer; carried to Hispaniola.

Probably in May or June 1777, an American privateer sailed to the Mos-quito Coast off of Central America, where it captured the slaver *Lady Mary*, commanded by Captain Gray, reportedly on its way from the coast of Africa. The unidentified privateer took its prize to a Spanish port in Hispaniola (currently the Dominican Republic). *London Chronicle*, Aug. 21, 1777, in Crawford et al., eds., *Naval Documents*, 9:591; *Westminster Gazette* (London), Aug. 14, 1777; *London Evening Post*, Aug. 21, 1777. The *Lady Mary* could have been transporting enslaved people from one British colony to another (the intercolonial slave trade) and not participating in the transat-lantic slave trade. See Other Captures—Intercolonial Slave Trade at the end of this appendix.

15. *Rose*. Captain Lewis; out of London; TSTD no. 91928; captured in July 1777, bound for Jamaica with an estimated 200 enslaved Africans on board, by an unidentified American privateer; carried to Martinique.

    The "Guineaman" *Rose* was overtaken by an American privateer and engaged in a fierce gun battle with it, until a cask of gunpowder accidentally exploded on the slaver, killing one and wounding two. In the confusion of the aftermath of the explosion, privateersmen boarded the *Rose* and captured it, and then sailed it into Martinique. In his detailed letter, a Captain Lewis said the privateer had only one American sailor on board, with the rest being French, Spanish, and Dutch, but that it did have a Continental Congress commission. Lewis wrote that a few days before his ship's capture, it had not lost a single African captive and that a storm had damaged the mainmast. Extract of a letter from Captain Lewis, of the *Rose* Guineaman, dated Martinico, Aug. 5, in *London Evening Post*, Oct. 23, 1777. See also *Stamford Mercury*, Oct. 30, 1777.

    TSTD, www.slavevoyages.org/voyage/search (voyage no. 91928) reports a voyage by the one-hundred-ton *Rose* out of Liverpool, sailing from Africa to Grenada, with John Houghton in command and carrying ten cannon. It reports that the estimated 328 African captives on board were disembarked safely at Grenada and another port and that no capture occurred. This is likely a different *Rose* as TSTD states this voyage ended back in Liverpool on June 6, 1777, it had a different commander, and the vessel was apparently used on future voyages (indicating this was not the one that was captured). Ibid. (voyage no. 92433 in 1778 and voyage no. 92434 in 1779).

    The identity of Captain Lewis is not known. A Thomas Lewis commanded several slave voyages from Bristol from 1770 to 1776. Ibid. (voyages nos. 17692, 17768, 17794, 17845, 17864, 17881).

16. **Unknown**. An unidentified vessel bound for Jamaica with 400 enslaved Africans on board was captured in mid-August 1777 by an unidentified American privateer; carried to Martinique.

    "A propos we have just received advice of a Guineaman from Bonny, bound here, with 400 slaves, being taken by an American frigate, and carried into Martinico, where her cargo was immediately sold." Extract of a letter from Port Royal, in Jamaica, dated Aug. 20, in *St. James's Chronicle* (London), Sept. 30, 1777, and *Adams Weekly Current* (Chester, England), Oct. 7, 1777. "Bonny" is now part of Nigeria.

17. *Sisters*. Captain Graham; out of Liverpool; TSTD no. 91871; captured about September 1777, possibly bound for Jamaica or Grenada with 163 enlsaved Africans on board, by an unidentified American privateer; carried to Martinique.

    Probably in about September 1777, the *Sisters*, a Liverpool slaver commanded by Captain William Graham and owned by William James and George Evans of Liverpool, was taken on its passage from Africa to the

Caribbean and carried into Martinique with 163 enslaved people on board. The seventy-ton vessel mounted eight cannon, but they were not enough to ward off the unknown American privateer that captured it. See *London Chronicle*, Nov. 11, 1777 ("The *Sisters*, Captain Graham, from Africa, bound for America, is taken by the Rebels"); *Daily Advertiser* (London), Nov. 12, 1777 (same); *General Evening Post* (London), Nov. 13, 1777 (same); *London Evening Post*, Nov. 17, 1777 ("The *Sisters*, Graham, from Africa for the West Indies, is taken by an American privateer, and carried into Martinico, with 163 slaves"); *Morning Chronicle* (London), Nov. 18, 1777 (same); *Gazetteer and New Daily Advertiser* (London), Nov. 19, 1777 (same, except added that the privateer had twenty-two guns). This newspaper squib may refer to the capture of the *Sisters*, given the time frame: "A Guineaman, with slaves on board, is taken off Jamaica, and carried into St. Pierre, in Martinico." *St. James's Chronicle* (London), Nov 13, 1777; *London Chronicle*, Nov. 15, 1777. If so, the *Sisters* on this trip had been heading to Jamaica before its capture. The capture of the *Sisters* is in TSTD, www.slavevoyages.org/voyage/search (voyage no. 91871). The *Sisters* on a previous voyage had dropped off approximately 267 African captives on the island of Grenada in 1776. Ibid. (voyage no. 91870).

Captain Graham frequently commanded slave ships for William James, one of Liverpool's most substantial slave merchants. In 1771, American slave trader Paul Cross (discussed in main text in chapter 7 accompanying notes 35-38 and in chapter 8 accompanying notes 32-33, 49) sold African captives he purchased on the Upper Guinea Coast to Graham, then commanding the *Sally*, which was owned by James. See Accounts of Slaves Purchased, 1771–1772, Paul Cross Papers, South Caroliniana Library, University of South Carolina.

18. *Clifton*. Captain Collins. Captured in the fall of 1777 near Antigua with 300 enslaved Africans on board by an unidentified American privateer; carried to an unrecorded location.

"The *Clifton*, Collins, from Africa to the West Indies, is taken near Antigua, with 300 slaves on board, and sent into Salem." *St. James Chronicle* (London), Nov. 27, 1777; *Daily Advertiser* (London), Nov. 28, 1777; *Morning Post* (London), Nov. 28, 1777. It is unlikely the *Clifton* was sent to Salem, Massachusetts, with enslaved people on board. Instead, it is likely that the captives were sold at a French-controlled island; after that, the *Clifton* may have been sold at the same island, or brought to Salem. The reference to Salem in the newspaper squib is an indication that the American privateer may have hailed from Salem. Captain Collins's identity is not known.

19. *Betsey*. Captain Booth. Captured in the fall of 1777, likely September, while en route to the West Indies with 170 enslaved Africans on board, by an unidentified American privateer; carried to Guadeloupe.

"The *Betsey*, Booth, Africa to the West Indies, with 170 slaves, is taken by an American privateer and carried into Guadeloupe." *St. James's Chronicle* (London), Nov. 20, 1777; *Daily Advertiser* (London), Nov. 21, 1777; *Manchester Mercury and Harrop's General Advertiser* (England), Nov. 25, 1777. This Captain Booth was likely William Booth, who commanded the slave ship *Penelope* when it was captured around March 1777 on its voyage to Africa by a Massachusetts brigantine. See appendix B, no. 16.

20. **Black Prince**. Captains Cooke, Wallace; out of London; TSTD no. 78244; captured October 4, 1777, while en route to Dominica with 219 enslaved Africans on board, by the *St. Peter* out of Massachusetts; carried to Fort Royal, Martinique.
On October 4, 1777, an eighteen-gun American privateer with a crew of 130 sailors, the *St. Peter*, under the command of Captain Samuel Chase, captured "a Guineaman with 219 Negroes" and sent the prize to Fort Royal, the administrative capital of Martinique. *Connecticut Gazette*, Nov. 14, 1777, in Crawford et al., eds., *Naval Documents*, 10:197n1; Desmarais, *Revolutionary War at Sea*, 2:257 (collecting US newspaper sources); TSTD, www.slavevoyages.org/voyage/search (voyage no. 78244). See also *Lloyd's List*, Dec. 30, 1777 ("The *Black Prince*, Cook, late Wallace, from Senegal to the West Indies, with 215 slaves, is taken by the *St. Peter* privateer, and carried into Martinico"); *Daily Advertiser* (London), Dec. 30, 1777. The captured slave ship, which had sailed from the Senegal coast headed for Dominica under Captain John Cook, was the 130-ton brig *Black Prince*, owned by a London merchant. The privateer *St. Peter* was owned in part by the Hutchinson brothers from Massachusetts, Godfrey and William, who operated out of Fort Royal in Martinique, investing in Massachusetts privateers. Governor T. Shirley to Marquis de Bouillé, Oct. 17, 1777, in Crawford et al., eds., *Naval Documents,* 10:197; Extract of a Letter from Capt. Cook ..., Nov. 1, 1777, in ibid., 373; editor's note, ibid., 231n1 (the Hutchinson brothers were merchants who invested in Massachusetts privateers). There is some evidence that the *St. Peter* was commissioned in Maryland. An Account of the American Privateers and Armed Vessels Taken by the King's Ships under Admiral Young at Barbados and the Leeward Islands, 25 November 1775 to July 1778 (ADM 1/310), in Jamieson, "American Privateers in the Leeward Islands, 1776–1778," 27, table 2.
The *Black Prince*'s capture is reported in TSTD, www.slavevoyages.org/ voyage/search (voyage no. 78244), which says the slave ship's captives were embarked from St.-Louis in Senegal. The thirty-six-gun frigate HMS *Pallas* was ordered to convoy the *Black Prince* and other ships bound from London to the Senegal River in Africa on February 17, 1777. Lords Commissioners of the Admiralty to Captain Richard Cotton, Feb. 17, 1777, in Crawford et al., eds., *Naval Documents*, 8:592-93. In 1775, the *Black Prince* had dropped off some 224 enslaved people at St. Vincent. TSTD,

www.slavevoyages.org/voyage/search (voyage no. 75168). See the next entry for other likely references to the *Black Prince*.

21. *Derby*. Captain Rimmer; out of Liverpool; TSTD no. 92582; captured in October 1777, while en route to Dominica with 259 enslaved Africans on board, by the *St. Peter* and *Fly* out of Massachusetts or Maryland and Martinique; carried to Martinique.

The Hutchinson brothers experienced difficulties with a large British armed slave ship, the *Derby*, commanded by Captain James Rimmer, owned by Liverpool merchants, including John and Thomas Yates, and sailing out of Liverpool. On August 8, 1777, the *Derby* left the mouth of the Bonny River, in present-day Nigeria, headed for Dominica, carrying 349 African captives. Deadly disease broke out in the Middle Passage, killing some ninety captives and ten white sailors, leaving alive 259 enslaved people and a smaller crew. On October 7, to the west of Barbados, the slave ship was attacked by the *Fly*, a privateer sloop mounting twelve 4-pounders and with ninety-five sailors on board, under the command of New Englander Thomas Palmer and fitted out of Martinique (see entry 13, above). Palmer's decision was a bold one, as he faced the 146-ton and much larger *Derby*, which had been constructed in Liverpool relatively recently, in 1774. In fact, the *Derby*, mounting fourteen cannon, possessed more firepower than the *Fly*. Rimmer's disadvantage was in the number of men he could bring to bear in the fight. The illness that had ravaged the captives on his ship also had reduced the number of his crew from thirty-two to twenty fit for duty to defend the ship. Still, Rimmer and his healthy sailors fought back, driving away the smaller but pesky *Fly* three times. Palmer then decided to keep his *Fly* away from the *Derby* but to stay near it to wait to see if any American reinforcements appeared. On October 9, a reinforcement did arrive in the form of Captain Samuel Chase's *St. Peter*, carrying eighteen 6-pounders and with a crew of 130 men. Determining that both privateers could not be defeated, Captain Rimmer surrendered the *Derby*, which was carried into Martinique, where its human cargo of 259 enslaved people was quickly sold. The American officers of the *St. Peter*, impressed by the *Derby*'s defense, bought the vessel intending to fit it out as a new privateer. See Extract of a Letter from a Mate of the Derby, to his Brother in Liverpool, Dated Dominica, Oct. 28, 1777, *London Packet*, Jan. 21, 1777, in Crawford et al., eds., *Naval Documents*, 10:337; Governor T. Shirley to Marquis de Bouillé, Oct. 17, 1777, in ibid., 197. TSTD, www.slavevoyages.org/voyage/search (voyage no. 92582) covers the *Derby*'s voyage and capture.

In capturing the *Derby*, the *St. Peter* and *Fly* had removed one of the more active ships employed in the British slave trade. Owned by prominent slave merchants John and Thomas Yates, as well as other Liverpool merchants, it had completed African voyages in 1775 and 1776, dropping off some 287 enslaved people at Antigua in 1775 and more than 300 at Jamaica in 1776. During the 1775 Middle Passage, the ship's captain, Samuel Lang, lost some 65 captives of 352 originally embarked in Africa, and four of thirty-five crewmen. See TSTD, www.slavevoyages.org/voyage/search (voyages nos. 92524, 92523). There is a report that the *Derby* was recaptured by a British warship, apparently in about May. "The *Derby*, Rimmer, from Africa for America, that was taken and carried into Martinico, is since retaken and carried into Dominica." *Daily Advertiser* (London), July 7, 1778; *General Evening Post* (London), July 7, 1778; *London Chronicle*, July 7, 1778. Any recapture would have been well after the enslaved people had been sold at Martinique. No slave ship under the name *Derby* operated in this time frame following its recapture.

The *Derby* was the ship that sparked the Liverpool riots by sailors in late August and early September 1775. See main text in chapter 11 accompanying note 5. The *Derby* received permission to carry ammunition and arms to Africa and trade with Africans on September 12, 1775. Ledward, ed., *Journals of the Board of Trade*, 13:92.

22. **Unknown**. An unidentified vessel was captured in October 1777 at sea with an estimated 300 enslaved Africans on board by the *Lydia* out of New Bern, North Carolina; carried to Guadeloupe.

In mid-October 1777, the sloop *Lydia*, mounting twelve carriage guns and with a crew of fifty sailors, operating out of New Bern, North Carolina, captured, according to the November 28, 1777, edition of the *North Carolina Gazette* "a large ship with slaves and other valuable articles from the Coast of Africa." The *Lydia's* captain, Benjamin Appleton, carried the prize vessel into the French island of Guadeloupe and began selling the enslaved people and dry goods, "said to be worth between £20,000 and £30,000." Ibid., in Crawford et al., eds., *Naval Documents*, 10:628. The identity of the seized slave ship is unknown. The *Lydia* itself was captured by HMS *Daphne* on its voyage from Guadeloupe to North Carolina. Journal of HMS *Daphne*, Oct. 20, 1777, in ibid., 230.

23. *Fair Lady*. Captain Taylor; captured in the last quarter of 1777 while en route to Jamaica with 270 enslaved Africans on board by an unidentified American privateer; carried to an unknown location and then to Boston.

"The *Fair Lady*, Taylor, from the Gold Coast to Jamaica, with 270 slaves on board, is taken by a large American privateer and sent into Boston." *St. James's Chronicle* (London), Dec. 23, 1777; *Morning Chronicle* (London), Dec. 24, 1777 (200 enslaved people on board). It is not likely that the African captives were brought to Boston. There is no record of it.

24. *Two Brothers*. Captain Mason; captured in the last quarter of 1777 at sea with an estimated 250 enslaved Africans on board by an unidentified American privateer; carried to Martinique.

"The *Two Brothers*, Mason, from the coast of Guinea, is taken and carried into Martinico." *New Jersey Gazette*, Dec. 17, 1777. It is presumed the *Two Brothers* had African captives on board, since the vessel was brought into Martinique, but that is not known for certain. Captain Mason's background is not known, but a Benjamin Mason commanded the slaver *Mermaid*, which left London for Gambia on October 2, 1777. See TSTD, www.slave voyages.org/voyage/search (voyage no. 78275); *Lloyd's List*, Nov. 28, Dec. 2, 1777. There is no further record of the *Mermaid*.

25. *Whim*. Captain French; out of Liverpool; TSTD no. 91749; captured on December 20, 1777, en route to Barbados with 198 enslaved Africans on board, by the *Fairfield* out of Providence, Rhode Island; carried to Martinique.

On December 20, 1777, the American privateer brigantine *Fairfield*, mounting twelve or fourteen guns and commanded by James Hovey, captured the *Whim*, a seventy-ton snow out of Liverpool. The *Whim*, owned by slave merchants Thomas and Clayton Case of Liverpool and commanded by Dominick French also of Liverpool, had departed that port for the coast of Africa on January 1, 1777. After purchasing some 214 African captives at the Banana Islands (off the coast of Sierra Leone), it had departed for Barbados on November 17 before being captured. Hovey brought the *Whim* into Carbet Bay in Martinique and sold the approximately two hundred enslaved people who had survived the Middle Passage at "very low prices" on December 26. *Fairfield* was commissioned in Providence. Deposition of Dominick French, John Spruitt and Hopkin Lewellin, Jan. 7, 1778, in Crawford et al., eds., *Naval Documents*, 11:61-62, 63n1. TSTD, www.slave voyages.org/voyage/search (voyage no. 91749), covers the voyage and capture. The London newspapers reported the capture in March, although they sometimes mislabeled the vessel the *Wynn*: "The *Wynn*, French, of Liverpool, from Africa to the West Indies, is taken by an American privateer, and carried into Martinico." *General Advertiser and Morning Intelligencer*, March 13, 1778; see also *London Evening Post*, March 12, 1778 (*Wynn*); *St. James's Chronicle* (London), March 12, 1778 (*Whim*); *Morning Chronicle* (London), March 13, 1778 (*Whim*). In taking the *Whim*, Hovey removed another active slave trading ship. From 1772 to 1776, it had completed three African voyages, each time disembarking about two hundred captives to a British Caribbean island. TSTD, www.slavevoyages.org/voyage/search (voyages nos. 91746, 91747, 91748).

26. *John and Richard.* Captain Gould; TSTD no. 26331; captured late 1777 en route to Jamaica with 180 enslaved Africans on board by an unidentified American privateer; carried to Martinique.

"The *John and Richard,* Gould, from the Coast of Africa to Jamaica, with 180 slaves on board, is taken by an American privateer of 14 guns and carried into Martinico." *St. James Chronicle* (London), Feb. 24, 1778; *London Evening Post,* Feb. 26, 1778 (same). See also *General Evening Post* (London), Feb. 24, 1778; Almon, ed., *Remembrancer* [1778], 6:39 ("with 180 slaves" reference mistakenly placed in line above the *John and Richard*). TSTD, www.slavevoyages.org/voyage/search (voyage no. 26331), reports the capture. Given that news typically took about two months to cross the Atlantic Ocean to London, the following reference in the February 17, 1778, edition of London's *Gazetteer and New Daily Advertiser* to two unnamed "Guineamen" being taken was likely to the *Whim* and the *John and Richard*: "Yesterday advice was received that two ships from Africa, full of slaves, were taken by the Americans, but neither of their names were mentioned." In the following London newspaper item, the first reference was likely to the *Jane* driving off the *Fly* (see "American Privateers that Failed to Defeat British Slave Ships," below) and the second reference was likely to the *Whim* or the *John and Richard*: "A Guineaman of this place beat off an American privateer of 14 guns; and a Guineaman is taken, but their names are not mentioned." See Extract of a letter from Liverpool, Feb. 13, *Morning Chronicle* (London), Feb. 17, 1778.

27. *Sally.* Captain Roberts; captured in early 1778 en route to Jamaica with 400 enslaved Africans on board by the *Independent* out of Boston; carried to an unkown location and thence to Boston.

"The *Sally,* Roberts, from Africa to Jamaica, with 400 slaves on board, is taken by the *Independent* privateer of 14 guns and carried into Boston." *St. James's Chronicle* (London), March 5, 1778. See also Almon, ed., *Remembrancer* [1778], 6:40. The privateer could have been the *Independence,* commissioned on December 31, 1777, in Boston and under the command of Peter Pollard of Boston. See American War of Independence—At Sea, https://www.awiatsea.com/Privateers/I/Independence%20Massachusetts%20Sloop%20[Pollard%20Brown].html. The American privateer could also have been the *Cumberland* as explained in the following entry.

28. *Matty and Betty.* Captain Hewan; out of Liverpool; TSTD no. 92591; captured early 1778 at sea with 324 enslaved Africans on board by the *Cumberland* out of Boston; carried to Martinique.

"The *Matty and Betty,* Hawan, from Africa to the West Indies, is taken and carried into Martinico." *London Chronicle,* March 24, 1778; *Public Advertiser* (London), March 24, 1778; *St. James's Chronicle* (London), March 24, 1778.

The capture of the slave ship *Matty and Betty* is covered in TSTD, www.slavevoyages.org/voyage/search (voyage no. 92591). The listing provides that the vessel was owned by Thomas Ratcliffe of Liverpool and that on April 6, 1778, it sailed from that port under the command of Captain John Hewan. The listing further provides that the slaver had about 328 African captives on board at the time of its capture. It also says the capture was made by the French. However, the person who prepared this particular listing may not have known that American privateers commonly sailed their prizes into French-controlled Martinique.

The American privateer *Cumberland*, out of Boston, had a successful encounter with a British vessel from Africa. Weighing 296 tons, mounting twenty 6-pounder carriage guns, four 3-pounder carriage guns, and fifteen swivel guns, commanded by James Collins, and with a crew of 150 seamen, the impressive *Cumberland* was strong enough to take on a large Guineaman. It did, apparently in late January 1778, capturing a slave ship (unidentified) with about three hundred to four hundred captives on board, and taking the vessel into Martinique, where the enslaved people were probably sold. One American who learned of the capture gushed to one of the privateer's owners, "This privateer will make you a fortune." William Hoskins (from Boston) to Col. Jeremiah Wadsworth, Feb. 7, 1778, quoted in Crawford et al., eds., *Naval Documents,* 11:301. For information on the *Cumberland,* see ibid., n3; Allen, *Massachusetts Privateers,* 106. The author believes the *Cumberland* captured the *Matty and Betty* and/or the *Sally,* given the time frames and mentions of Martinique. The author is not treating the *Cumberland*'s taking of the unidentified slave ship as a separate capture.

29. *Susanna.* Captain Loft; captured on February 1, 1778 en route to Jamaica with 450 enslaved Africans on board by the *Resolution*; carried to Martinique.

"The *Susanna,* Capt. Loft, from Africa to Jamaica, with 450 slaves on board, was taken the 1st of February, by the *Resolution* privateer, and carried into Martinique." *General Advertiser and Morning Intelligencer* (London), March 27, 1778; *London Evening Post,* March 28, 1778. There is no record for a privateer named *Resolution* capable of seizing a large slave ship in this period; therefore, it is not known what privateer captured the *Susanna.*

30. *Betsy.* Captain Crost; captured in early 1778 en route to Barbados with 260 enslaved Africans on board by the *Experiment* out of Charleston, South Carolina; carried to Guadeloupe.

"The *Betsy,* Crost, from Africa to Barbados, with 260 slaves on board, is taken and carried into Guadeloupe by the *Experiment* privateer of 16 guns." *St. James's Chronicle* (London), April 2, 1778; *London Evening Post,* April 4, 1778. The *Experiment* was a South Carolina privateer commanded by Captain Francis Morgan that in June 1777 was reported to carry twelve guns and forty men. See Deposition of William Bray Concerning the Sloop *Chester,* in Crawford et al., eds., *Naval Documents,* 10:950. The *Experiment* sometimes sailed with the *Fair American,* another South Carolina privateer, this one commanded by Francis Morgan's brother, Charles Morgan. Ibid.

31. *Defiance.* Captain Woodward; TSTD no. 26332; captured in early 1778 at sea with 300 enslaved Africans on board by the *Experiment* out of Charleston, South Carolina; carried to Martinique.

"The *Defiance,* Woodward, from Africa, with 300 slaves on board, is taken by the *Experiment* privateer, of 18 guns, and carried into Martinique." *St. James's Chronicle* (London), April 7, 1778; *Daily Advertiser* (London), April 7, 1778; *London Chronicle,* April 7, 1778. TSTD, www.slavevoyages.org/voyage/search (voyage no. 26332), covers the capture, citing the *Daily Advertiser* (London), April 7, 1778, for support. (For more on the *Experiment* see prior entry.)

32. *London.* Captain Welsh. Captured in early 1778 en route to Jamaica with 300 enslaved Africans on board by an unidentified American privateer; carried to Guadeloupe.

"The *London,* Welsh, from Africa to Jamaica, with 300 slaves, is taken and carried into Guadeloupe." *St. James's Chronicle* (London), April 7, 1778; *General Advertiser and Morning Intelligencer* (London), April 8, 1778.

33. *Railton.* Captain Welsh. Captured in early 1778 en route to the West Indies with 200 enslaved Africans on board by an unidentified (assumed to be American) privateer; carried to Martinique.

"The *Railton,* Welsh, from Africa, with 200 slaves for the West Indies, is taken and carried into Martinico." *St. James's Chronicle* (London), April 11, 1778; *Daily Advertiser* (London), April 13, 1778; *Morning Chronicle* (London), April 13, 1778; *London Chronicle,* April 14, 1778.

34. *Fancy.* Captain Allanson; out of Liverpool; TSTD no. 92483; captured March 6, 1778, with 310 enslaved Africans on board by *Marlborough,* out of Providence, Rhode Island; ordered to South Carolina or French-controlled island.

For the *Fancy's* capture, see main text in chapter 8 accompanying notes 10-18. For its fate, see main text in chapter 9 accompanying notes 14-33. TSTD, www.slavevoyages.org/voyage/search (voyage no. 92483), covers the capture.

35. *Polly.* Captain Westcoate. Captured about March 1778 en route to Jamaica with 200 enslaved Africans on board by an unidentified American privateer; carried to Guadeloupe.

"The *Polly,* Westcoate, from Africa to Jamaica, with 200 slaves, is taken by an American privateer and carried into Guadeloupe." *St. James's Chronicle*

(London), May 9, 1778; *Gazetteer and New Daily Advertiser* (London), May 11, 1778; *Public Advertiser* (London), May 11, 1778. The thirty-six-gun frigate HMS *Pallas* was ordered to convoy *Polly* and other ships bound from London to the Senegal River in Africa on February 17, 1777. Lords Commissioners of the Admiralty to Captain Richard Cotton, Feb. 17, 1777, in Crawford et al., eds., *Naval Documents,* 8:592-93.

36. *Nancy.* Captain Edwards; captured about March 1778 en route to Jamaica with an estimated 300 enslaved Africans on board by the *Element;* carried to Martinique.

"The *Nancy,* Edwards, from Africa to Jamaica, full of slaves, is taken by the *Element* privateer, of 10 guns, and carried into Martinique." *General Evening Post* (London), May 12, 1778. Because the report said the slave ship was "full of slaves," three hundred enslaved people are estimated as being on board. No information was found about the privateer *Element.* It was likely issued a Continental Congress commission by the American counsel out of Martinique.

37. *Diana.* Captain Colley; out of Liverpool; TSTD no. 92593; captured about March 1778 en route to Tobago with 378 enslaved Africans on board by the *General Moultrie* and *Fair American* out of Charleston, South Carolina; carried to Curaçao.

The slave ship *Diana,* commanded by Captain James Eckley Colley, from Liverpool, bound from Africa for the Caribbean, was captured thirty leagues windward of Tobago, by the American privateer *General Moultrie,* commanded by Captain Phillip Sullivan, carrying eighteen guns and manned by two hundred, and the brig *Fair American,* commanded by Captain Charles Morgan, with fourteen guns and ninety men. The prize was carried to Dutch-controlled Curaçao, "where her cargo, consisting of 278 slaves, 30 tons camwood, and about 3 tons of ivory, was sold; the slaves at ten 'Joes' per head." Williams, *History of the Liverpool Privateers,* 245-46. TSTD, www.slavevoyages.org/voyage/search (voyage no. 92593), provides that the *Diana* departed Liverpool on August 8, 1777, with sixteen guns under Colley, purchased African captives at the Isles de Los, departed there on January 30, 1778, and was captured after leaving Africa, with the surviving 378 (as opposed to 278) of the captives landed at Curaçao on March 12, 1778. The *Fair American,* a South Carolina privateer brigantine commanded by Morgan, carrying fourteen guns, and the *General Moultrie* privateer ship commanded by Sullivan, carrying eighteen guns, were part of the South Carolina state navy. See Crawford et al., eds., *Naval Documents,* 11:114n2, 3; 361n3; 838nn7, 9. A contemporary deposition indicates that in June 1777, the *Fair American* carried twenty guns and had a crew of fifty men. See Deposition of William Bray Concerning the Sloop *Chester,* in Crawford et al., eds.,

Naval Documents, 10:950. A British source stated that the *Diana* was brought into Spanish-controlled Hispaniola. *Public Advertiser* (London), July 7, 1778. Other British sources say it was carried into Martinique. *Daily Advertiser* (London), July 7, 1778; *General Evening Post* (London), July 7, 1778; *London Chronicle*, July 7, 1778. This was James Eckley Colley's last slave trading voyage; from 1769 to 1778 he was the ship captain for eight voyages that carried captives from the Upper Guinea to the Caribbean.

38. *Sukey*. Captain Mitchell. Captured in the spring of 1778 while en route to the West Indies with 160 enslaved Africans on board by an unidentified American privateer; carried to Martinique.

"The *Sukey*, Capt. Mitchell, from Africa to the West Indies, with 160 slaves on board, is taken by the Americans and carried into Martinico." *Daily Advertiser* (London), June 4, 1778; *St. James's Chronicle* (London), June 4, 1778; *General Advertiser and Morning Intelligencer* (London), June 4, 1778.

39. *St. Augusta*. Captain Nicholson. Captured on May 1, 1778, near Antigua with 270 enslaved Africans on board by an unidentified American privateer; carried to Martinique.

"The *St. Augusta*, Nicholson, from African to the West Indies, with 270 slaves, was taken the 1st of May, near Antigua, by an American privateer, of 18 guns, and taken into Martinico." Extract of a Letter from Portsmouth, Aug. 10, in *Northampton Mercury* (England), Aug. 17, 1778. See also similar squib, without mentioning the letter written from Portsmouth, England, in *General Evening Post* (London), Aug. 13, 1778.

40. *Dispatch* or *Despatch*. Captain Ward. Captured in the spring of 1778 while en route to the West Indies with 300 enslaved Africans on board by an unidentified American privateer; carried to Guadeloupe.

"The *Despatch*, Ward, from Africa to the West Indies, with 300 slaves, is taken by an American privateer, and carried into Guadeloupe." *St. James's Chronicle* (London), July 11, 1778; *General Advertiser and Morning; Intelligencer* (London), July 13, 1778; *Public Advertiser* (London), July 13, 1778; *London Chronicle*, July 14, 1778. Another British source had a different spelling of the name of the ship (*Dispatch*, probably the correct spelling) and an account of fewer enslaved people on board (one hundred). *Lloyd's Evening Post*, July 13, 1778, in Crawford et al., eds., *Naval Documents*, 13:1041.

41. *Valiant*. Captain Briggs; out of Liverpool; no. TSTD 92595; captured at sea in the summer of 1778 with an estimated 300 enslaved Africans on board by an unidentified American privateer; carried to an unknown location.

The *Valiant*, owned by Liverpool slave merchants Samuel Parker, John Yates, Thomas Yates, and Thomas Spencer Dunn, was built and registered in Liverpool. It weighed 150 tons and mounted sixteen guns. Commanded by William Briggs, it had a large crew of fifty men. Its voyage began on May 19, 1777. TSTD, www.slavevoyages.org/voyage/search (voyage no. 92595). The TSTD entry indicates the *Valiant* was captured by privateers before its captives were embarked. I estimated, given that the capture occurred in summer 1778, it is likely the *Valiant* had three hundred captives on board when seized, based on a review of how many captives other 150-ton ships carried from 1770 to 1783. It is not clear when the capture occurred. Based on when the voyage began, I estimate it was sometime from May to August 1778.

An estimated total of 10,786 enslaved Africans were taken in these forty-one captures.

OTHER CAPTURES: FRENCH COLONIAL PRIVATEERS

At least two captures were made by French colonial privateers from August 1776 to August 1778. Sometimes an American privateer that had received a Continental Congress commission from William Bingham in Martinique had primarily a French colonial crew; but each of those privateers typically had an American captain and American investors, in addition to the Continental Congress commission. In a few instances, a purely French privateer made the capture. This was apparently the case in at least two instances in 1777, with African captives on board the seized vessel.

On February 1, 1777, the London sloop *Amelia*, commanded by John Tyrie, with either 68 or 204 Africans on board (sources differ) and bound for St. Kitts, was captured by the *Tyger*, a French colonial privateer.[1] In early March 1777, the Liverpool slave ship *Mary*, with ninety Africans on board and bound for Grenada, was seized by the *Puissance*, a French colonial privateer operating from Martinique.[2]

Because these two vessels were captured by purely French privateers, they are not included in the above chart. However, they are mentioned because they likely never would have occurred but for the many captures of British slave ships by American privateers. (It should be noted that a British crewman claimed that the French crew carried ashore at Hispaniola two free Senegalese seamen captured on board the *Amelia*.[3] Presumably, the Senegalese men were sold as enslaved people.)

Paschall Bonavitta, a Corsican by birth but a resident of Martinique, owned and commanded a small privateer schooner based in Spanish-controlled Trinidad. The privateer vessel apparently had a Continental commission and a single American who purported to be its commander. On September 20, 1777, Bonavitta sailed his schooner to the British-controlled island of Tobago and landed on its shores a small party of men who seized and carried off thirty-seven enslaved people, whom he disposed of at Trinidad.[4]

From a British list of ten privateers operating out of Martinique in March 1777, seven were identified as American privateers and three (including *Puissance*) were each said to be owned by "a House in Martinico."[5]

OTHER CAPTURES: INTERCOLONIAL SLAVE TRADE

There was an active intercolonial slave trade among British Caribbean and North American colonies. An important part of the British slave trade was that buyers from British slave ship captains in, say, Jamaica could resell some of the captives at a profit at, say, South Carolina, Georgia, or Spanish-controlled New Orleans.[6] American privateers made at least three captures of intercolonial slave trading ships.

A letter written in Grenada on March 30, 1777, said:

> The pirates out of Martinico are very numerous and daring, at which we are not a little alarmed. About 20 days ago, they took a sloop belonging to this island, close along the shore of Tobago, where she was going with 60 new negroes, belonging to planters there, all which, together with the sloop and sailor negroes, were publicly sold at Martinico. The negroes that were bought out of the yards here at £39 and £40 sterling each, were there sold at from £20 to £25 sterling each. The owner of the sloop went over to the Governor at Martinico, but could not get the least satisfaction or relief.[7]

The letter writer indicates that the "new" captives were bought directly from an auction yard in Grenada, where a British slave ship captain would first sell his human cargo. The captured sloop was the *Swallow*, commanded by a Captain Hindman. British observers complained that the privateer that captured his vessel, even though it flew "American colors," was "manned entirely by Frenchmen and other foreigners," except for the captain, who hailed from Tobago.[8]

Apparently in early September 1777, Captain Lemuel Palmer, sailing in the privateer *Nancy* out of Wilmington, North Carolina, captured a British slave ship with about one hundred enslaved people on board. Palmer conducted this valuable prize into Savannah, Georgia, where the captives were presumably sold. The slaver was a snow called the *Invermay* and was caught sailing from Jamaica to British-held Pensacola, Florida, "with rum and slaves said to be worth £35,000."[9] Palmer was the second American privateer captain to bring a captured British slave ship with enslaved people on board into a United States port. See captures no. 2 and no. 3 above for the first privateer captain to do that.

The schooner *Dispatch*, commanded by James McCraight, sailed from Kingston, Jamaica, with a cargo that included more than fifty "prime negroes" owned by David Ross & Company, an English mercantile firm. After landing at Pensacola, Florida, then under British control, McCraight carried on toward Spanish-controlled New Orleans. Just outside the Mississippi River, his schooner, including its remaining forty-eight enslaved people, was taken by the privateer schooner *Reprisal*, commanded by Joseph Calvert. This privateer had been paid for and fitted out by Oliver Pollock, who in 1777 had been appointed by the Continental Congress as the commercial agent of the United States at New Orleans. As with William Bingham at Martinique, it appears Pollock invested his own personal funds in the privateering venture and not money belonging to the Continental Congress. Pollock proceeded to begin to sell some of the enslaved captives locally. Meanwhile, Robert Ross petitioned the governor of Spanish Louisiana, Don Bernardo de Gálvez, for the return of the African captives, the other cargo, and his schooner. Because the vessel had been taken in Spanish-controlled territory, Gálvez later ordered it to be restored to Ross. The fate of the enslaved people, however, is unknown. They had likely all been sold by Pollock before Gálvez rendered his decision.[10]

CAPTURES OF SMALL SLAVE TRADING VESSELS ON THE AFRICAN COAST BY THE
Marlborough
The *Marlborough* seized small vessels that were used to transport African captives up large rivers and along the West African Coast, including to British slave trading posts, but were not used in the transatlantic slave trade. They included two schooners: the *Sally*, commanded by William Moore, and the *Fort Rose*, commanded by Richard Roberts. Captain Babcock seized three African captives held on board each vessel. The *Marlborough* also captured a schooner, a sloop, and a number of shallops, taking from them a total of twenty-five African captives.[11]

AMERICAN PRIVATEERS THAT FAILED TO DEFEAT BRITISH SLAVE SHIPS
On a number of occasions, American privateers failed to force well-armed British slave ships to surrender, even after fierce engagements. Even though the American privateers in these instances did not capture the slave ships, the fighting would have given slave merchants back in England pause about investing in another slave voyage.

For example, according to an Englishman from the British-controlled Caribbean island of St. Vincent, writing on April 20, 1777, "About 20 days ago the Ship *Brook* [*Brooks*], Capt. Noble, belonging to Liverpool, from Africa with slaves, was met by an American privateer, of ten guns, who engaged her about an hour, till Capt. Noble luckily shot away the privateer's masts, and would have brought her in, had not another privateer came to engage him, which Captain Noble thought it safer to leave than run the risk of another."[12]

In a separate instance, London newspapers reported in May 1777, "The *Two Brothers*, Fisher, and the *Constantia*, Capt. Rolie, from Africa, are both safe arrived at [Grenada with a total of] 600 slaves on board, after beating off two American privateers, after an engagement of six hours."[13]

By December 1777, British slavers seemed to have been better armed. Based on the following account and others, the slave ship *Jane* inflicted a severe drubbing on the American privateer *Fly*, which, under Captain Thomas Palmer, had previously participated in the captures of two slave ships (see no. 14 and no. 22 above). The following item from the January 10, 1778, edition of the *Jamaica Gazette* likely has the most accurate description of the engagement (other than the names employed):

The ship *Jean* [the *Jane*], Capt. Spyers [Syers], who arrived here from the coast of Guinea, on Tuesday last, the beginning of December, fell in with an American privateer, to the windward of Barbados, with whom he was closely engaged for upwards of four hours, when the privateer thought proper to shear off, being greatly damaged in her hull and rigging; the *Jean* [the *Jane*] lost seven men in the action.

A gentleman just arrived from Martinico informs us that the above privateer, named the *Fly*, Captain Mansfield, of 14 carriage guns and 190 men, put into St. Pierre [in Martinique], the 6th of December, to refit. She had 12 men killed, and 18 wounded. Capt. Mansfield's right arm was shot off, the first lieutenant received a musket ball through his shoulder, and two swivel balls through his arm, [and] the second lieutenant was blown up by a powder flask, which the boatswain was preparing to throw on board the *Jean* [the *Jane*].[14]

In February 1778, an officer on the 140-ton British snow *Adventure* wrote:

We arrived [at Tobago] with a valuable cargo of slaves, which has turned out to great advantage [because of high sales prices]. The Americans have taken almost every ship from Africa for some time; we have, however, escaped them, but not without having a smart engagement; for upon making the island of Tobago, a large sloop full of men, with 12 guns, attacked, and endeavored to board us, but as briskly we returned the same. We were hard at it from one in the afternoon till nine at night, and beat them off five times, our white men in number only 17; I imagine the privateer had 100. Our slaves likewise fought valiantly. The captain was wounded in his hip, the second mate was shot in the arm, the chief mate and four men were blown up with powder, and much burnt, but are all likely to do well. We had nine slaves greatly burnt, some of whom died of their wounds. By a vessel from Martinique to this island, we hear the privateer [arrived at] that place, with some men killed, and many wounded.[15]

The report of African captives helping to defend against the privateer was unusual, but not unprecedented. The enslaved defenders would not have understood why their ship was being attacked.

Appendix D

African Captives Carried by British and US Slave Ships to the British Caribbean, 1752–1792

YEAR	ON BRITISH SHIPS	ON US SHIPS	TOTAL
1752	21,076	1,822	22,898
1753	20,924	1,748	22,672
1754	23,000	1,238	24,283
1755	25,823	2,339	28,162
1756	20,098	1,238	21,336
1757	16,435	2,561	18,996
1758	19,953	1,811	21,764
1759	19,466	1,520	20,986
1760	27,793	1,710	29,503
1761	28,965	3,074	32,039
1762	22,530	2,880	25,410
1763	23,727	3,473	27,200
1764	34,399	4,238	38,637
1765	30,566	3,739	34,305
1766	34,399	2,488	37,172
1767	28,028	2,862	30,890
1768	27,656	2,211	29,867
1769	30,406	2,850	33,256
1770	33,649	3,369	37,018
1771	35,007	3,307	38,314
1772	35,904	4,003	39,097
1773	31,040	4,835	35,875
1774	38,892	5,714	44,606
1775	36,875	2,540	39,415
1776	33,478	510	33,988
1777	19,983	0	19,983
1778	9,321	140	9,461
1779	6,985	0	6,985
1780	6,817	0	6,817
1781	11,364	0	11,364
1782	15,522	270	15,792
1783	20,302	939	21,241

YEAR	ON BRITISH SHIPS	ON US SHIPS	TOTAL
1784	36,758	931	37,689
1785	28,682	2,388	31,070
1786	25,783	1,585	27,368
1787	26,337	2,083	28,420
1788	32,335	835	33,170
1789	25,813	2,141	27,954
1790	24,569	2,648	27,217
1791	36,939	2,537	39,476
1792	39,939	5,252	45,191
TOTALS	1,066,278	89,874	1,156,152

Sources: The Trans-Atlantic Slave Trade Database, www.slavevoyages.org/voyage/assessment/estimates (using search terms "Flag" and "Only Embarked," taking into account only British Flag and US Flag vessels bound for the British Caribbean). The formula does not include British and American slave ships carrying African captives to what would become the United States or to Caribbean islands controlled by other European countries. Done April 10, 2021. From 1752 to 1775, "US Ships" means ships departing from the thirteen North American mainland colonies that became the United States in 1776.

Appendix E

Liverpool Slave Trading Merchants Bankrupted, 1772–1783, and Their Slave Ships Captured by American Privateers, 1776–1778

Year=year of bankruptcy; Slave ship with=Slave ship captured with enslaved Africans aboard; Slave ship without=Slave ship captured without enslaved Africans aboard

MERCHANT	YEAR	SLAVE SHIP WITH	DATE OF CAPTURE	SLAVE SHIP WITHOUT	DATE OF CAPTURE
Crosbie, John	1772				
Crosbie, William	1772				
Barber, Miles	1772				
Woodville, William	1775				
Fletcher, Thomas	1775				
Barber, Miles*	1777			*Rio Pongo*	Nov. 1776
Sandys, Samuel	1777			*Rio Pongo*	Nov. 1776
				Mary	Nov. 1776
		Industry	Feb? 1777		
Kendall, John	1777			*Rio Pongo*	Nov. 1776
				Mary	Nov. 1776
White, Andrew	1777			*Rio Pongo*	Nov. 1776
				Mary	Nov. 1776
Wetherhead, Christopher	1777				
Yates, John	1777			*Lancashire*	Aug. 1776
		Rose	July 1777		
		Derby	Oct. 1777		
Yates, Thomas	1777	*Derby*	Oct. 1777	*Lancashire*	Aug. 1776
Dunn, Thomas Spencer	1777	*Derby*	Oct. 1777		
Parker, Samuel Hilton	1777	*Derby*	Oct. 1777		
Case, Thomas	1778	*Whim*	Dec. 1777		
		Fancy	Mar. 1778		
Dobson, John	1778	*Diana*	Mar. 1778		
Gildart, James	1778				
Grimshaw, Robert	1780				
Brown, Charles	1781				
Roberts, John	1783				
Roberts, James	1783				

* Barber's entry reflects his investment for the period 1773–1777, after he made a recovery from his first bankruptcy. See Elder, *Slave Trade of Lancaster*, 148-50; Hancock, *Citizens of the World*, 199n72.

Sources: For the captured vessels, see appendix B and appendix C, as applicable. For the list of bankrupted merchants, see *Bailey's List of Bankruptcies, Dividends, and Certificates from the Year 1772 to 1793, with the Names and Residence of the Different Solicitors Under Each,* 2 vols. (London: T. Wilkins, 1794). The author thanks Nicholas Radburn for identifying the bankrupt Liverpool slave merchants.

Notes

CHAPTER ONE: JOHN BROWN, GREAT BRITAIN, AND THE AFRICAN SLAVE TRADE

1. Diary entry, Dec. 25, 1777, in Frederick Mackenzie, *Diary of Frederick Mackenzie, Giving a Daily Narrative of his Military Service as an Officer of the Regiment of Royal Welch Fusiliers During the Years 1775–1781 in Massachusetts, Rhode Island and New York*, 2 vols. (Cambridge, MA: Harvard University Press, 1930; repr., New York: New York Times and Arno Press, 1968), 1:226-27.

2. Log of HM *Kingsfisher*, Dec. 25, 1777, in Michael J. Crawford, William B. Clark, William J. Morgan, et al., eds. *Naval Documents of the American Revolution*, 13 vols. (Washington, DC: Government Printing Office, 1964–2019), 10:805; journal entry, Dec. 24, 1777, in John Linscom Boss, Journal of the Ship *Marlborough*, in ibid., 805n1. For a more detailed discussion of the breakout, see main text in chapter 5 accompanying notes 29-35.

3. James A. Rawley with Stephen D. Behrendt, *The Transatlantic Slave Trade: A History*, rev. ed. (Lincoln: University of Nebraska Press, 2005), 291. Smaller ports included Lancaster, Whitehaven, Preston, and Glasgow. In 1760, thirteen percent of British ships clearing for Africa went from the smaller ports. Ibid., 208. From 1757 to 1776, eighty-six vessels cleared from Lancaster to Africa, and forty-six cleared from Whitehaven. Melinda Elder, *The Slave Trade and the Economic Development of 18th-Century Lancaster* (Edinburgh: Edinburgh University Press, 1992), 170.

4. David Eltis and David Richardson, *Atlas of the Transatlantic Slave Trade* (New Haven and London: Yale University Press, 2010), 26.

5. Ibid., 23. See also The Trans-Atlantic Slave Trade Database (hereinafter TSTD), www.slavevoyages.org/assessment/estimates (using search terms "Flag" and "Only embarked").

6. Rawley and Behrendt, *Transatlantic Slave Trade*, chs. 7-11.

7. Julie Flavell, *When London Was Capital of America* (New Haven: Yale University Press, 2010), 169-70; Andrew Jackson O'Shaughnessy, *An Empire Divided: The American Revolution and the British Caribbean* (Philadelphia: University of Pennsylvania Press, 2000), 73.

8. James A. Rawley, *London, Metropolis of the Slave Trade* (Columbia: University of Missouri Press, 2003), 2, 9.

9. O'Shaughnessy, *Empire Divided*, 11.

10. Ray Porter, *English Society in the 18th Century* (London and New York: Penguin, 1982), 37.

11. A British Merchant [Malachy Postlethwayt], *The African Trade, The Great Pillar and Support of the British Plantation Trade in America* (London: privately printed, 1745), 6. Postlethwayt worked for the Royal Africa Company from 1743 to 1746. He may have borrowed in part from the English writer Daniel Defoe. Defoe wrote in 1713, "The case is as plain as cause and consequence: Mark the climax. No African trade, no negroes; no negroes no sugars, ginger, indigo, etc. . . . ; no sugars etc. . . no islands; no islands no continent; no continent no trade." Peter Earle, *The World of Defoe* (London: Atheneum, 1977), 131.

12. At another Barbados plantation, from 1767 to 1785, there were 142 births and 210 deaths. O'Shaughnessy, *Empire Divided*, 11.

13. Lowell Joseph Ragatz, *The Fall of the British Planter Class in the British Caribbean, 1763–1833* (New York and London: Century, 1928), 34-35.

14. Ibid., 35, 35n9. Ragatz later wrote that only after the prohibition of the British slave trade in 1807 did West Indian planters focus on replenishing their slave stock by natural births rather than by purchasing new African captives, "hence more attention was given the condition of pregnant females and to a reduction of the shocking infant mortality rate" that had previously existed. Ibid., 278.

15. Ibid., 34-35, 87. Trevor Burnard writes about Jamaica, "death rates in the first three years of 'seasoning' were always high, with perhaps 15-20 percent of the new Africans arriving on the island dying during this initial period of adjustment to plantation labor." Trevor Burnard, *Jamaica in the Age of Revolution* (Philadelphia: University of Pennsylvania Press, 2020), 92-93, citing John R. Ward and Jessica Bird Ward, *British West Indian Slavery, 1750–1834: The Process of Amelioration* (Oxford: Clarendon Press, 1988), 124-29. Nicholas Radburn studied twenty-five African captives brought onto one Jamaica plantation from slave ships in 1754 and 1755, and found that three had died of disease within six months, which amounted to a death rate of twelve percent. In addition, he found that one woman drowned herself, another man died of disease within six years of his arrival, and that all but four had been confined to the plantation hospital within one year of their arrival. He further found that all but six bore scars from whipping, four were branded on their cheeks, and one man was disfigured. See Radburn, "'[M]anaged at First as if They Were Beasts': The Seasoning of Enslaved Africans in Eighteenth-Century Jamaica," *Journal of Global Slavery* 6 (2021): 27-28.

16. Ward and Ward, *British West Indian Slavery*, 45, 65.

17. Billy G. Smith, *Ship of Death: A Voyage that Changed the Atlantic World* (New Haven CT: Yale University Press, 2013), 44-45. In 1779, Dalrymple would serve as a lieutenant in the Royal Navy stationed at Gorée, a slave trading post that the British seized from the French that year. Ibid.; testimony of Hugh Dalrymple, 1788 or 1789, in *Report of the Lords of the Committee of Council . . . concerning the present state of the trade to africa*, part 1 (London: 1789). John Brown's *Marlborough* would visit Gorée in February 1778 when it was still held by the French.

18. Letter from Captain John Samuel Smith to the Reverend Mr. Hill, Jan. 20, 1786, in John Samuel Smith testimony, 1788 or 1789, in *Report of the Lords*, part 3.

19. Eltis and Richardson, *Atlas of the Transatlantic Slave Trade*, 201; TSTD, www.slavevoyages.org/assessment/estimates (using search terms "Specific Disembarkation Regions" and "Only Disembarked").

20. Adam Hochschild, *Bury the Chains: Prophets and Rebels in the Fight to Free an Empire's Slaves* (Boston: Houghton Mifflin, 2005), 67. Philip D. Curtin was the first to make the connection that fewer than five percent of all Africans forced into the Atlantic slave trade arrived in North America, yet by 1950, about one-third of all people of African descent in

the Western Hemisphere lived in the United States. Philip D. Curtin, *The Atlantic Slave Trade: A Census* (Madison: University of Wisconsin Press, 1969), 91-92, 177-78.

21. Hochschild, *Bury the Chains,* 67.

22. O'Shaughnessy, *Empire Divided,* 76 (quoting Malachy Postlethwayt).

23. Burnard, *Jamaica in the Age of Revolution,* 206.

24. See appendix D.

25. The leading online source of information on African slave trading voyages concludes that North American ships carried 2.4 percent of all African captives. TSTD, www.slavevoyages.org/assessment/estimates (using search terms "Flag" and "Only Embarked"). See also Stephen D. Behrendt, "The Transatlantic Slave Trade," in *The Oxford Handbook of Slavery in the Americas,* eds. Robert L. Paquette and Mark M. Smith, 251-74 (Oxford: Oxford University Press, 2010), 263, table 11.1, which shows the same 2.4 percent figure.

26. TSTD, www.slavevoyages.org/assessment/estimates (using search terms "Flag" and "Only Embarked").

27. Eltis and Richardson, *Atlas of the Transatlantic Slave Trade,* 17, 19. The leading online source of information on African slave trading voyages concludes that 3.6 percent of all African captives disembarked in the New World were carried to North America. TSTD, www.slavevoyages.org/assessment/estimates (using search terms "Broad Disembarkation Regions" and "Only Disembarked"). See also Behrendt, "The Transatlantic Slave Trade," 263, table 11.1 (3.7 percent). However, intercolonial slave trading increased the number of enslaved people brought to the mainland North American colonies. For example, from 1700 to 1770, about 3,200 enslaved people were shipped from the Caribbean to each of New York, Pennsylvania/New Jersey, and New England. Gregory E. O'Malley, *Final Passages: The Intercolonial Slave Trade of British North America, 1619–1807* (Chapel Hill: University of North Carolina Press, 2014), 202, table 12.

28. Rawley and Behrendt, *Transatlantic Slave Trade,* 145, table 7.3.

29. Stephen Hopkins, "Remonstrance of the Colony of Rhode Island to the Lords Commissioners of Trade and Plantations, Jan. 1764," in John R. Bartlett, ed., *Records of the Colony of Rhode Island and Providence Plantations,* vol. 6, 378-83 (Providence, RI: A. C. Greene & Bros., 1861), 380.

30. Jay Coughtry, *The Notorious Triangle: Rhode Island and the African Slave Trade, 1700–1807* (Philadelphia: Temple University Press, 1981), 21.

31. Sean M. Kelley, *The Voyage of the Slave Ship* Hare*: A Journey into Captivity from Sierra Leone to South Carolina* (Chapel Hill: University of North Carolina Press, 2016), 30. Coughtry, in an earlier study, concludes that thirty-five percent of Rhode Island's rum was exported to Africa. *Notorious Triangle,* 16.

32. Coughtry, *Notorious Triangle,* 7, 16, 85-86; Randy J. Sparks, *Where the Negroes Are Masters: An African Port in the Era of the Slave Trade* (Cambridge, MA: Harvard University Press, 2014), 164.

33. Rachel Chernos Lin writes about how many ordinary Rhode Islanders, and not just elite merchants, invested in Rhode Island slave trade voyages, in *The Rhode Island Slave-Traders: Butchers, Bakers and Candlestick-Makers, Slavery & Abolition* 23, no. 3 (2002): 21-38. Lin does not make it clear, however, if that situation existed in colonial times.

34. See, for example, "A Wedge Grows," in Slavery in the Revolution, https://amrevnc.com/slavery-american-revolution/ ("Newport, Rhode Island, still famous for its rich residents, was largely built on the slave trade"); "The Underground Railroad in American History," 12, in *Underground Railroad Resources in the U.S. Theme Study,* PDF (Washington, DC: US Department of the Interior, National Park Service, 1995), 12 ("Newport, Rhode Island's prosperity was tied to slave trade shipping"); "Local Rally Expresses Opposition to Racism,"

Newport Daily News, Aug. 13, 2017, https://www.newportri.com/lifestyle/2017/08/13/local-rally-express-opposition-to/1275815 (at a rally in Newport against racism after the march by white supremacists at Charlottesville, Virginia, a Newport resident "pointed to Newport's ugly history in the slave trade, which built immense wealth").

35. See Sarah Deutsch, "The Elusive Guineamen: Newport Slavers, 1735–1774," *New England Quarterly* 55, no. 2 (June 1982): 229-53. Virginia Platt concludes that "the triangular trade . . . was not a major factor in the commerce of colonial New England." Virginia Beaver Platt, "'And Don't Forget the Guinea Voyage': The Slave Trade of Aaron Lopez of Newport," *William and Mary Quarterly* 32, 3rd ser. (1975): 618.

36. Hopkins, "Remonstrance," in Bartlett, ed., *Records of Rhode Island*, 6:379-80. Hopkins cited as his source Newport's custom house books. In 1774, Newport custom house books showed that 539 vessels departed Newport, with 204 of those departing for the Caribbean in the carrying trade. A total of twenty-five voyages were made to Africa. Coughtry, *Notorious Triangle*, 15, 260-61 (chart "Rhode Island Slaving Voyages, 1709–1807"). By comparison, the voyages departing Newport had increased substantially by 1763 from fifteen years earlier. From March 25, 1748, to March 25, 1749, a total of 160 vessels cleared out of Newport. William Douglass, *A Summary, Historical and Political, of the . . . British Settlements in North-America*, vol. 2 (Boston: Daniel Fowle, 1751), 2:90. In this same period, there were only two African slave voyages. Coughtry, *Notorious Triangle*, "Rhode Island Slaving Voyages, 1709–1807," 245.

37. Hopkins, "Remonstrance," in Bartlett, ed., *Records of Rhode Island*, 6:380.

38. Elaine Foreman Crane, *A Dependent People: Newport, Rhode Island in the Revolutionary Era* (New York: Fordham University Press, 1985), 17.

39. A recent study confirms that on average, Newport sent about eighteen voyages per year to Africa from 1762 to 1774. See Alexander Boyd Hawes, *Off Soundings: Aspects of Maritime History of Rhode Island* (Chevy Chase, MD: Posterity Press, 1985), 110, and 269, appendix, table I. Historian Jay Coughtry, for the same period, arrives at an average of nineteen voyages per year, with the average from 1770 to 1774 increasing to twenty-one voyages per year. The high was twenty-eight in 1772. "Rhode Island Slaving Voyages, 1709–1807," in Coughtry, *Notorious Triangle*, 251-61.

40. Coughtry, *Notorious Triangle*, 77.

41. Ibid., 90-100; Rawley and Behrendt, *Transatlantic Slave Trade*, 317. On British ships, insurance could cost six to eight percent in peacetime, and it typically did not cover natural deaths or insurrections. Rawley and Behrendt, *Transatlantic Slave Trade*, 223.

42. Coughtry, *Notorious Triangle*, 56.

43. Ibid., 73.

44. P. Clarke to J. Fletcher, April 21, 1775, in Elizabeth Donnan, ed., *Documents Illustrative of the History of the Slave Trade to America*, 4 vols. (Washington, DC: Carnegie Institution, 1930-35), 3:309.

45. Coughtry, *Notorious Triangle*, 154-55; Rawley and Behrendt, *Transatlantic Slave Trade*, 246. "Of 1,080 persons sent to Africa by the Company of Merchants Trading to Africa from 1751 to 1788, 653 died; 333 of these perished in the first year, with a somewhat higher mortality for military than civilian employees." Rawley and Behrendt, *Transatlantic Slave Trade*, 245.

46. Deutsch, "The Elusive Guineamen," 253.

47. Roger Anstey, *The Atlantic Slave Trade and Abolition* (London: Humanities Press, 1975), 46; see also Rawley and Behrendt, *Transatlantic Slave Trade*, 227-28.

48. Nicholas Radburn, "William Davenport, the Slave Trade, and Merchant Enterprise in Eighteenth-Century Liverpool" (master's thesis, Victoria University of Wellington, 2009),

appendix B, 188-222. Davenport experienced his lowest profits during the years of the American Revolution. Ibid. David Richardson made the first close study of Davenport's voyages, and based on examining seventy-four of his voyages, he arrived at a profit margin of 10.5 percent. David Richardson, "Profits in the Liverpool Slave Trade: the Accounts of William Davenport, 1757–1784," in Roger Anstey and Paul Hair, eds., *Liverpool, the African Slave Trade, and Abolition: Essays to Illustrate Current Knowledge and Research*, 60-90 (Liverpool: Historical Society of Lancashire and Cheshire, 1976), 76, appendix, 82-87. He arrived initially at an average profit margin of 15.7 percent but then made adjustments for duration and remittance to arrive at 10.5 percent. Ibid., 73-74. Liverpool slave merchant John Tarleton, who was active in the slave trade before and after the American Revolution, once testified that "Ten per cent ought to be the net profit in the African trade." Ibid., 75. David Hancock, examining thirty-four African slave voyages invested in by the London owners of the Bance Island slave trading post from 1748 to 1784, arrived at an average profit margin of just six percent. David Hancock, *Citizens of the World: London Merchants and the Integration of the British Atlantic Community, 1735-1785* (Cambridge: Cambridge University Press, 1995), appendix 4, 419-24. Hancock found that gains and losses fluctuated from a 222 percent profit on one voyage to a 94 percent loss on another voyage. Slave trade historian Herbert Klein surveyed the research on the topic in 1990 and found that the average profit rate for French and English slave traders in the eighteenth century was ten percent, which he described as "a good profit rate at the time but not out of the range of other contemporary investments." Herbert S. Klein, "Economic Aspects of the Eighteenth-Century Atlantic Slave Trade," in *The Rise of Merchant Empires, Long-Distance Trade in the Early Modern World, 1350–1750*, ed. James D. Tracy, 287-310 (Cambridge: Cambridge University Press, 1990), 299. For some criticisms of Richardson's and Anstey's conclusions, and arguments that the profit percentage was from fourteen to seventeen percent, see ibid., 424n36; Joseph E. Inikori, "Market Structure and the Profits of the British African Trade in the Late Eighteenth Century," in *Journal of Economic History* 41 (Dec. 1981): 745-46. For more on some exaggerated claims of the profitability of the African slave trade, see Rawley and Behrendt, *Transatlantic Slave Trade*, 224-28.

49. Marcus Rediker, *The Slave Ship: A Human History* (New York: Viking, 2007), 50. In 1775, Adam Smith called a ten percent profit for British merchants "a good, moderate, reasonable profit; terms which I apprehend mean no more than a common and usual profit." Adam Smith, *An Inquiry into the Nature and Causes of the Wealth of Nations* (London, 1776), 200. While Nicholas Radburn found that Davenport had an average profit margin of 10.9 percent, he also concluded that Davenport had a 9.6 percent average profit margin on his other investments, which accounted for about one-third of his total investments. Radburn, "William Davenport," master's thesis, 106, table14: William Davenport's Business Investments and Profits, 1757–1797.

50. See discussion in note 39 above. Slave trade historian Sean E. Kelley concludes, "The West Indian and other traders were responsible for more clearances and probably generated more profits, but slave trading was integral to [Rhode Island's] local economy." Kelley, *Voyage of the Slave Ship* Hare, 22. I am close to Kelley's position, but would not go as far as he does. Kelley adds, "nor do we have reliable statistics on earnings from the carrying trade, which surely outstripped the slave trade and export trades by a wide margin, perhaps amounting to as much as 62 percent of all payments." Ibid. For more on the controversy regarding the importance of the African slave trade to Newport and Rhode Island, see ibid., 22 and 222n19. Historian Elaine Forman Crane argues that "Although it must be acknowledged that the greater part of Newport's trade was intercolonial, the triangular trade represented a crucial element in [Newport's] economy." *Dependent People*, 16. For her argument, see 16-23.

51. I start with Hopkins's numbers: 184 foreign clearances (18 of which were to Africa and 166 were not) and 352 clearances in the North American coastal trade. I increase the number of African voyages to 20, assuming there was a slight undercount. Under this approach, the total number of weighted clearances would be 764 (352 clearances in the North American coastal trade plus 332 weighted clearances in the Caribbean carrying and other foreign trade [166 multiplied by a factor of two] and 80 weighted clearances for Africa [20 multiplied by a factor of four]). Of the weighted 764 number, 80 is 10.5 percent (80 divided by 764).

52. Using a source never before considered in this context, I make a rough estimate of the percentage of Newport merchants' annual revenues from the slave trade. British Customs Office papers in London reveal the value of Rhode Island exports shipped each year to foreign destinations from 1768 to 1772. On average each year during this period, Rhode Island shipped £73,255 of goods to foreign destinations, £11,331 of which were shipped to Africa, which is 15.5 percent of the total value of foreign exports. See Lynne Withey, *Urban Growth in Colonial Rhode Island, Newport and Providence in the Eighteenth Century* (Albany: State University Press of New York, 1984), 121, table B-3, Value of Rhode Island Exports, 1768–72. The numbers are not broken down by departures from specific ports. Given that at this time Newport by far dominated the slave trade in Rhode Island, I assumed ninety percent of the goods shipped to Africa were by Newport vessels. I further assumed that two-thirds of the non-African foreign voyages were by Newport ships. From these numbers, I roughly estimate that seventeen percent of the foreign goods shipped by Newport vessels were transported to Africa. From here, I take into account several factors that merit adjustments to the seventeen percent estimate. First, a downward adjustment must be made because the seventeen percent figure does not take into account the North American mainland coastal trade, which then accounted for almost two-thirds of all departures of vessels from Newport. (In addition to Hopkins's 1763 numbers, see table B-2, Percentage of Rhode Island Shipping to Major Destinations, All Rhode Island, 1720–39 and 1763–74, in ibid.) On the other hand, the values of the goods shipped by each vessel in the coastal trade were much less than on foreign voyages. I assume the figure was on average one-quarter of the value of an African voyage. This results in the percentage of the value of all goods shipped by Newport merchants to Africa to be about 10.8 percent. Second, as an upward adjustment, the profits earned in the African slave trade were likely somewhat better than those earned in the Caribbean carrying trade and other foreign trade, and much better than in the North American coastal trade. I estimate that this factor increases Newport revenues by 1.2 percent. All told, I estimate (which admittedly is a rough estimate) that this works out to about twelve percent of annual shipping revenues from Newport merchants being attributable to the African slave trade from 1768 to 1772.

From 1768 to 1772, American-distilled rum shipped by Rhode Island merchants to Africa had the second-highest value of any commodity shipped overseas. Almost all the rum was shipped to Africa. Here are the top values of commodities (in British pounds) shipped by Rhode Island merchants to foreign destinations from 1768 to 1772:

Spermaceti Candles:	£66,327
American Rum:	£55,125
Bread/Flour:	£48,326
Fish:	£43,719
Livestock:	£38,138
Whale Oil:	£32,875
Lumber:	£28,026

Source: Table B-4, Value of Commodities Shipped from Rhode Island to Various Locations, 1768–72, in Withey, *Urban Growth*, 122 (from British Customs Office records).

53. Hopkins, "Remonstrance," in Bartlett, ed., *Records of Rhode Island*," 6:380. Most of the other remittances came from the carrying trade with the Caribbean and trading for goods such as rice in South Carolina. Withey, *Urban Growth*, 38, 94. One Newport merchant wrote in 1760 that the Newport slave trade "has been carried on from this place with great success" and "is still the only sure way of making remittances" to British merchants. Quoted in Crane, *Dependent People*, 16.

54. Coughtry, *Notorious Triangle*, 31, 33. Jay Coughtry has written the most detailed work on Rhode Island's role in the slave trade; it is an outstanding book whose conclusions have stood the test of time and should be republished for more people to be able to read it.

55. James B. Hedges, *The Browns of Providence Plantations: The Colonial Years* (Providence, RI: Brown University Press, 1952), 71.

56. Ibid., 71-72.

57. Coughtry, *Notorious Triangle*, 146. This number is based on all Rhode Island slave voyages from 1752 to 1807. Mortality rates likely were higher in colonial times than from 1784 to 1807. Coughtry also found that "80 percent of Rhode Island slavers sustained losses of fifteen percent or less." Ibid. Another estimate, reviewing only Rhode Island colonial voyages, shows that the mortality rate was 15.1 percent. TSTD, www.slavevoyages.org/voyage/databasesearchid=KOYTsmYJ (go to summary statistics tab). Using a similar approach and looking only at British ships sailing from 1750 to 1775, the mortality rate was 17.3%. Ibid., www.slavevoyages.org/voyage/databasesearchId=fHmLN8OX.

58. Coughtry, *Notorious Triangle*, 118-20, 128-29.

59. Nicholas Brown & Company to A. Whipple, G. Hopkins and N. Power, Dec. 22, 1765, quoted in Darold D. Wax, "The Browns of Providence and the Slaving Voyage of the Brig *Sally*, 1764–765," *American Neptune* 32 (1972): 179. The summary of the *Sally*'s voyage in the main text is based primarily on Center for Digital Scholarship, Brown University Library, "Voyage of the Slave Ship Sally, 1764–1765," http://cds.library.brown.edu/projects/sally/. This website, in which James Campbell was the lead author, has links to images of many of the original documents from the John Carter Brown Library at Brown University and the Rhode Island Historical Society. The summary also relies on Hedges, *Browns: The Colonial Years*, 72-81, and Wax, "Browns of Providence," 171-79. For Providence's role, and that of the Brown family in particular, in slave trading, see Charles Rappleye, *Sons of Providence: The Brown Brothers, the Slave Trade, and the American Revolution* (New York: Simon & Schuster, 2006), 53-74, and "Slavery, the Slave Trade, and Brown University," 7-23, in *Slavery and Justice Report: Report of the Brown University Steering Committee on Slavery and Justice*, 2006), http://www.brown.edu/Research/Slavery_Justice/documents/SlaveryAndJustice.pdf.

60. Hedges, *Browns: The Colonial Years*, 81; Coughtry, *Notorious Triangle*, 257.

61. Mack Thompson, *Moses Brown: Reluctant Reformer* (Chapel Hill: University of North Carolina Press, 1962), 83. The deed of manumission was recorded November 13, 1773. Ibid., 83n20 (citing Probate Court Records, Probate Wills, Book 6, 73, City Hall, Providence).

62. Thompson, *Moses Brown*, 84.

63. Hochschild, *Bury the Chains*, 3-4. Even then it took Britain twenty years to end its participation in the slave trade.

64. For more on this topic, see Christian McBurney, "The American Revolution Sees the First Efforts to Limit the African Slave Trade," in *Journal of the American Revolution, Annual Volume 2021*, ed. Don N. Hagist, 153-87 (Yardley, PA: Westholme, 2021).

65. W. E. B. DuBois, *The Suppression of the African Slave Trade to the United States of America, 1638–1870* (New York: Longmans, Green, 1896), 41.

66. James Otis, "The Rights of the British Colonies Asserted and Proved," in *The American Revolution, Writings from the Pamphlet Debate 1764–1776*, ed. Gordon Wood, vol. 1, 43-119 (New York: Library of America, 2015), 69-70.

67. Quoted in William R. Staples, *Annals of Providence: From Its First Settlement to the Organization of the City* (Providence, RI: privately printed, 1843), 235-36.

68. Resolution, June 1774 session, in Bartlett, ed., *Records of Rhode Island* 7:251-52; Thompson, *Moses Brown*, 97.

69. Stephen Fried, *Rush: Revolution, Madness and the Visionary Doctor Who Became a Founding Father* (New York: Crown, 2018), 94.

70. Ibid., 96.

71. Fairfax County Resolves, July 18, 1774, in Peter Force, ed., *American Archives*, 4th ser., vol. 1 (Washington, DC: M. St. Clair and Peter Force, 1853), 600.

72. David Ammerman, *In the Common Cause: American Response to the Coercive Acts of 1774* (Charlottesville: University Press of Virginia, 1974), 86, also 86n44 ("The Fairfax Resolutions were also sent to other towns. There is, for example, a copy of them in the Boston Comm. of Corr. Papers.").

73. Rawley and Behrendt, *Transatlantic Slave Trade*, 275.

74. An Account of All the Rateable Estate Belonging to John Brown, this 10th Day of January 1778, in John Brown Papers, MSS 312, ser. 1, box 1, folder 2, Rhode Island Historical Society (hereinafter "RI Hist. Soc."), Providence. The first two enslaved men were likely the same Black people listed as living in Brown's household in a Rhode Island 1774 census. John R. Bartlett, ed., *Census of the Inhabitants of the Colony of Rhode Island and Providence Plantations Taken by the Order of the General Assembly, in the Year 1774* (Providence, RI: Knowles, Anthony, 1858), 38. In 1782, four Black people were recorded as living in Brown's household. John Mack Holbrook, ed., *Rhode Island 1782 Census* (Oxford, MA: Holbrook Research Institute, 1979), 19. They were likely all enslaved.

75. Resolution, Sept. 27, 1774, in Worthington C. Ford, ed., *The Journals of the Continental Congress*, 34 vols. (Washington, DC: Library of Congress, 1905–37), 1:43; Oliver Perry Chitwood, *Richard Henry Lee: Statesman of the Revolution* (Morgantown: West Virginia Library, 1967), 68.

76. H. Laurens to J. Laurens, Aug. 14, 1776, in David R. Chesnutt, C. James Taylor, Peggy J. Clark, Philip M. Hamer, and George C. Rogers, eds., *The Papers of Henry Laurens*, 16 vols. (Columbia: University of South Carolina Press, 1968-2002), 11:224.

77. Continental Association, Oct. 20, 1774, in Ford, ed., *Journals of the Continental Congress*, 1:77.

78. Ibid., 80-81.

79. H. Laurens to S. Bull, Jan. 10, 1776, in Crawford et al., eds., *Naval Documents*, 3:730.

80. Entries into the Port of Baltimore, March 13, 1775, to March 1776, in ibid., appendix B, 1367.

81. S. Ward to J. Dickinson, Dec. 14, 1774, in Paul H. Smith, ed., *Letters of Delegates to Congress, 1774–1789*, 26 vols. (Washington, DC: Library of Congress, 1976–2000), 1:269. Samuel Ward had residing in his household five Black people in 1774, all or most of whom at that time were likely enslaved. See Bartlett, ed., *Census of Rhode Island 1774*, 32.

82. TSTD, www.slavevoyages.org/voyage/search (search voyages beginning in 1774). The Newport ships were owned (and captained) by a Wanton (Captain Benjamin Remington); unknown (Captain James Duncan); Christopher and George Champlin (Captain Robert Champlin); William and Joseph Wanton (Captain Abraham Auld); and unknown (Captain William Gardner). The Bristol ship that departed on November 28 was owned by Simeon Potter and captained by Mark Anthony D'Wolf. Ibid.

83. Committee of Correspondence of Newport, Rhode Island, to Committee of Correspondence of Philadelphia, Jan. 5, 1775, in Force, ed., *American Archives*, 4th ser., 1:1098-99.
84. S. Hopkins to Dr. Erskine, Dec. 28, 1774, quoted in Arthur Zilversmith, *The First Emancipation: The Abolition of Slavery in the North* (Chicago: University of Chicago Press, 1967), 107.
85. C. and G. Champlin to Threlfal and Anderson, Jan. 17, 1775, in Donnan, ed., *Documents of the Slave Trade*, 3:301.
86. Robert Champlin undertook two voyages in 1775 and 1776. TSTD, voyages nos. 24784, 36510. See also *Lloyd's List*, Nov. 23, 1776; P. Clarke to J. Fletcher, Oct. 21, 1776, in Donnan, ed., *Documents of the Slave Trade*, 3:321n2.
87. Memorial of Samuel Whitemarsh, et al., to the General Assembly, Sept. 19, 1775, in Crawford et al., eds., *Naval Documents*, 2:156-57.
88. P. Clarke to J. Fletcher, Dec. 1, 1776, in Donnan, ed., *Documents of the Slave Trade*, 3:322. See also Newport Custom House Records, *Newport Mercury*, July 3, 1775 (Stanton, commanding the brig *Minerva*, cleared for departure from Newport to the Caribbean).
89. Resolution, April 6, 1776, in Ford, ed., *Journals of the Continental Congress*, 4:257-58.
90. Ibid., 259.

CHAPTER TWO: JOHN BROWN INVESTS IN PRIVATEERS

1. Withey, *Urban Growth*, 33-45. Nicholas, Moses, John, and Joseph ranked first, second, third, and eighth, respectively, in assessed wealth in Providence in 1775. Ibid., 44-45.
2. Ibid., 40; Hedges, *Browns: The Colonial Years*, 86-154.
3. One source claims that before Brown built his mansion on Power Street in 1787, he lived at 37 South Main Street in Providence, and that the home was later torn down for the construction of the Mechanics Bank building. L. Francis Herreshoff, *Capt. Nat Herreshoff: The Wizard of Bristol; The Life and Achievements of Nathanael Greene Herreshoff* (Dobbs Ferry, NY: Sheridan House, 1953), 34.
4. Letter by an anonymous author, *Providence Gazette*, Jan. 9, 1773.
5. For the most accurate description of the events surrounding the seizure and burning of the *Gaspee*, see Stephen Park, *The Burning of His Majesty's Schooner Gaspee* (Yardley, PA: Westholme, 2016), 15-18. Park's book also has the most accurate description of the aftermath of the event, including the failed investigation and associated trials.
6. J. Brown to N. Cooke, June 12, 1775, in Crawford et al., eds., *Naval Documents*, 1:665. Brown wrote to Governor Nicholas Cooke, "As I fared so badly by means of undertaking to purchase the flour for the [Rhode Island] government, I choose you should keep my name concealed from the House."
7. Diary entries, April 26–27, 1775, in Franklin B. Dexter, ed., *Literary Diary of Ezra Stiles, D.D., L.L.D.*, 2 vols. (New York: Charles Slocum, 1901), 2:40-41; *Providence Gazette*, April 29, 1775; *Newport Mercury*, May 1, 1775.
8. Hedges, *Browns: The Colonial Years*, 211-13; *Providence Gazette*, May 6, 1775.
9. Hedges, *Browns: The Colonial Years*, 214.
10. G. Washington to N. Cooke, Aug. 4, 1775, in Dorothy Twohig, Philander D. Chase, Theodore J. Crackel, W. W. Abbot, and Edward G. Lengel, eds., *The Papers of George Washington, Revolutionary War Series*, 24 vols. (Charlottesville: University of Virginia Press, 1985–2016), 1:222.
11. Hedges, *Browns: The Colonial Years*, 219.
12. J. Brown to G. Washington, Nov. 3, 1775, in Twohig et al., eds., *Washington Papers*, 2:293-94. Brown's brig, the *Sally*, returned from Surinam with forty-five casks of gunpowder,

sixty pounds of bullets, twenty small arms, and twenty pairs of pistols. See Manifest of Military Stores Brought in the Brig *Sally*, Jan. 19, 1776, in Crawford et al., eds., *Naval Documents*, 3:859.

13. S. Moylan to J. Brown, Nov. 8, 1775, in Twohig et al., eds., *Washington Papers*, 2:294n3; Bartlett, ed., *Records of Rhode Island*, 7:386.

14. Quoted in Hedges, *Browns: The Colonial Years*, 219.

15. J. Brown to G. Washington, Nov. 3, 1775, in Twohig et al., eds., *Washington Papers*, 2:294.

16. William M. Fowler Jr., *Rebels under Sail: The American Navy during the Revolution* (New York: Charles Scribner's Sons, 1976), 209. The other two sites were in Salisbury, Connecticut, and Abington, Massachusetts. Ibid.

17. See Contract Between Hope Furnace and John Langdon for Cannon for the Continental Frigate *Raleigh*, Sept. 6, 1776, in Crawford et al., eds., *Naval Documents*, 6:722; Hedges, *Browns: The Colonial Years*, 269-79; Fowler, *Rebels under Sail*, 209-11. The Brown brothers were accused of overcharging for the cannon to be supplied to the *Raleigh*. J. Langdon to J. Bartlett, Sept. 14, 1776, in Crawford et al., eds., *Naval Documents*, 6:815-16; Fowler, *Rebels under Sail*, 211-14. In March 1776, Hope Furnace offered the following prices: swivels, £6 per pair; 4-pounders, £36 per pair; 6-pounders, £56 per pair; 9-pounders, £84 per pair; and 12-pounders, £110 per pair. Thomas Durfee to Nicholas Brown, March 15, 1776, B20 F.13, Miscellaneous Letters1775–1782, Brown Family Business Records, John Carter Brown Library, Brown University, Providence, RI.

18. Hedges, *Browns: The Colonial Years*, 225-26; J. and N. Brown to J. Hewes, Jan. 20, 1776, Contract Between Nicholas and John Brown and the Secret Committee in Congress, Jan. 26, 1776, and Contract Between Nicholas and John Brown and the Secret Committee in Congress, Feb. 6, 1776, in Crawford et al., eds., *Naval Documents*, 3:878, 879-80, 1153-54.

19. Michael J. Crawford, ed., *The Autobiography of a Yankee Mariner: Christopher Prince and the American Revolution* (Washington, DC: Brassey's, 2002), 139-40; Kylie A. Hulbert, *The Untold War at Sea: America's Revolutionary Privateers* (Athens: University of Georgia Press, 2022), 33-34. Michael Crawford details typical admiralty court procedures: Before trial, the privateer was to publish a "libel" against the ship and cargo in the newspapers. Legal ownership of the ship and cargo would not transfer until the court ruled on whether the "prize" was indeed enemy property and legally captured. For this reason, the privateer's crew was not supposed to "break a bulk," that is, open up or remove captured cargo, before trial. If the court found for the captors, it would condemn the ship and cargo and order it sold by the sheriff. Michael J. Crawford, "The Privateering Debate in Revolutionary America," *Northern Mariner/le marin du nord* 21, no. 3 (July 2011), 220.

20. Massachusetts Act, Nov. 1, 1775, in Crawford et al., eds., *Naval Documents*, 2:834-39.

21. Hulbert, *Untold War at Sea*, 15-18.

22. Resolution, March 18, 1776, in Bartlett, ed., *Records of Rhode Island*, 7:482-86; *Providence Gazette*, Jan. 27, 1776.

23. J. Adams to J. Warren, Nov. 7, 1775, in Crawford et al., eds., *Naval Documents*, 2:897.

24. R. Morris to S. Deane, June 5, 1776, in ibid., 5:384.

25. Resolution, March 23, 1776, in Ford, ed., *Journals of the Continental Congress*, 4:229-33; Hulbert, *Untold War at Sea*, 103-06.

26. Crawford, ed., *Autobiography of a Yankee Mariner*, 210. This point was also emphasized in Robert H. Patton, *Patriot Pirates: The Privateer War for Freedom and Fortune in the American Revolution* (New York: Pantheon Books, 2008), xx-xxi, and Michael Thomin, "The 'P' Is for Profit: Revolutionary War Privateers and the Slave Trade," *Journal of the American Revolution*, Dec. 2, 2016, https://allthingsliberty.com/2016/12/p-profit-revolutionary-war-privateers-slave-trade/.

27. See Christian M. McBurney, *Kidnapping the Enemy: The Special Operations to Capture Major Generals Charles Lee & Richard Prescott* (Yardley, PA: Westholme, 2014), 119, 126.

28. Wilkins Updike, *History of the Episcopal Church in Narragansett* (New York: Henry M. Onderdonk, 1847), 134.

29. See, for example., W. Vernon to J. Adams, Dec. 17, 1778, in Rhode Island Historical Society, ed., *Papers of William Vernon and the Navy Board, 1776–1794* (Providence, RI: Snow & Farnham, 1901), 59-60; Crawford, "Privateering Debate," 225n24; Hulbert, *Untold War at Sea*, 151-52.

30. E. Hopkins to Continental Marine Committee, Sept. 22, 1776, in Crawford et al., eds., *Naval Documents*, 6:949; J. P. Jones to R. Morris, Oct. 17, 1776, in ibid., 1303; see also Hulbert, *Untold War at Sea*, 149-51, 159-61.

31. David Syrett, *Shipping and the American War, 1775–1783: A Study of British Transport Organization* (London: Anthlone Press, 1970), 63, 131, 139, 216.

32. Crawford, "Privateering Debate," 222-23, 226.

33. Mark M. Boatner, *Encyclopedia of the American Revolution* (New York: D. McKay, 1974), 897. Boatner estimated that between 1775 and 1783, American privateers captured about six hundred British vessels. Boatner's estimate of the number of ships seized is too low. British observers counted more than seven hundred seized by the end of 1777 alone. See main text in this chapter accompanying note 36, below. Michael Scott Casey later counted 3,176 British vessels taken between 1775 and 1782, of which 893 were retaken by Royal Navy warships or British or Loyalist privateers. Michael Scott Casey, "Rebel Privateers— The Winners of American Independence" (master's thesis, US Army Command and General Staff College, 1990), 65.

34. American Commissioners in France to the Secret Committee of the Continental Congress, Feb. 6, 1777, in Crawford et al., eds., *Naval Documents*, 8:571.

35. Testimony of Alderman Woolridge, Feb. 6, 1778, Proceedings in the Lords Respecting the Commercial Losses Occasioned by the American War, in ibid., 11:967.

36. Ibid.; testimony of William Creighton, Feb. 6, 1778, in ibid., 969; Andrew Jackson O'Shaughnessy, *The Men Who Lost America: British Leadership, the American Revolution, and the Fate of the Empire* (New Haven, CT: Yale University Press, 2013), 332. See also Crawford, "Privateering Debate," 219-34.

37. See Maritime Papers, Bonds, Masters of Vessels, vol. 2 (Jan.–July 1776) and vol. 3 (Aug. 1776–Dec. 1778), and Maritime Papers, Letters of Marque, Petitions and Instructions, 1776–1780, Rhode Island State Archives, Providence (hereinafter "RI State Archives"). The first source (Maritime Papers, Bonds, Masters of Vessels) contains applications for commissions, and the second source (Maritime Papers, Letters of Marque, Petitions and Instructions) contains the actual commissions. From reviewing both sources, the author arrived at the same number of fifty-nine commissions applied for and received. Some privateers received more than one commission. The author did not count cargo vessels that did not obtain a letter of marque. The first privateer commission the author found in the above sources was dated May 6, 1776. Interestingly, prizes began arriving at Providence in April 1776. Prizes were brought into Providence in April by the Rhode Island privateers *Montgomery*, *Diamond*, *Independence*, *Yankee Ranger*, *York*, and *General Schuyler*. See "List of All the Vessels and Cargoes etc. Brought into the Port of Providence and Libelled, Tried and Condemned in the Maritime Court AD 1776," in Crawford et al., eds., *Naval Documents*, 7:642. It appears that either these vessels did not bother to obtain privateering commissions or they obtained them from Massachusetts. Continental ships and state row galleys also brought prizes into Providence during this time.

38. Diary Entry, Oct. 12, 1776, in Dexter, ed., *Stiles Diary* 2:77. By October 22, 1776, a letter writer from Providence reported that thirty-two prizes had been brought into the port since the Rhode Island legislature had authorized privateers in March that year. Extract of a Letter from Providence, Oct. 22, 1776, quoted in Force, ed., *American Archives*, 5th ser., 2:1194.

39. E. Hopkins to W. Ellery, Nov. 7, 1776, in Crawford et al., eds., *Naval Documents*, 7:84.

40. Edwin M. Stone, *Life and Recollections of John Howland, Late President of the Rhode Island Historical Society* (Providence, RI: G. H. Whitney, 1857), 82. Abigail Adams wrote to her husband, John, in September 1776 from her home in Braintree, Massachusetts, "the Rage for privateering is as great here as anywhere and I believe the success has been as great." A. Adams to J. Adams, Sept. 7, 1776, in Crawford et al., eds., *Naval Documents*, 6:731.

41. List of All the Vessels and Cargoes, in Crawford et al., eds., *Naval Documents*, 7:642-47 (captures nos. 4 through 13 list their sales prices). While this list has fifty-one items, four of them are not vessels (captures nos. 18, 19, 20, and 45). In testimony before the House of Lords, Alderman Woolridge estimated that the "average value of a ship and cargo, trading to Jamaica, was £8,000 on her outward" voyage from Britain to Jamaica, and "£10,000 on her homeward voyage." In addition, Woolridge testified that "the average value of a ship and cargo, trading to the other West India islands, was £6,060 outward, and £8,000 homeward." Testimony of Alderman Woolridge, Feb. 6, 1778, Proceedings in the Lords Respecting the Commercial Losses Occasioned by the American War, in ibid., 11:967. These values are somewhat consistent with the auction prizes at Providence.

42. Manuscript of song for the *Montgomery*, undated, quoted in ibid., 6:117n2 (in the collections of the Rhode Island Historical Society). The original 1694 ballad, written for Henry Every's pirate ship the *Fancy*, is set forth in "A Copy of Verses Composed by Captain Henry Every, Lately Gone to Sea to seek his Fortune," 1694, in C. H. Firth, ed., *Naval Songs and Ballads* (London: Navy Records Society, 1908), 131.

43. "List of All Vessels and Cargoes," in Crawford et al., eds., *Naval Documents*, 7:642-47 (nos. 21, 22, 23, 24).

44. See list of commissioned vessels from August 1, 1776, to December 13, 1777, in Maritime Papers, Bonds, Masters of Vessels, Aug. 1776–Dec. 1778, vol. 3, RI State Archives, nos. 3 and 10 (sloop *Polly*), 14 and 66 (sloop *Hawke*), 16 and 65 (sloop *Sally*), 17 and 105 (sloop *Diamond*), 41 (sloop *Industry*), 42 and 69 (sloop *Favourite*), 52 (sloop *Charming Sally*), 57 and 91 (sloop *Retaliation*), 70 (ship *Blaze-Castle*), and 71 and 94 (ship *Oliver Cromwell*). Several went on more than one privateering voyage in this period. A few voyages were solely to carry cargo. Ibid., nos. 83 (sloop *Polly*) and 85 (schooner *Sally*). This list in the Maritime Papers does not necessarily record every vessel in which Brown had an ownership interest, since some information was incomplete and others said the main owner and simply added, "and others," without naming them. For a list of twenty-four vessels owned by John Brown, nine of which were privateers, see Vessels Owned by John Brown, March 13, 1777, John Brown Papers, MSS 312, series 1, box 1, folder 2, RI Hist. Soc.

45. Application for Commission for Rhode Island Privateer Sloop *Diamond*, July 6, 1776, in Crawford et al., eds., *Naval Documents*, 5:945 (signed by John Brown); Commission, July 6, 1776, in Maritime Papers, Bonds, Masters of Vessels, vol. 2, Jan.–June 1776, no. 125, RI State Archives. The owners of the *Diamond* were John Brown, William Chace, and Lemuell Wyatt. Owners of the Rhode Island Privateer Sloop *Diamond* to Captain Thomas Stacy, Aug. 21, 1776, in Crawford et al., eds., *Naval Documents*, 6:253.

46. J. Brown to W. Chace, July 11, 1776, in Crawford et al., eds., *Naval Documents*, 5:1026-27. Interestingly, Nicholas Brown issued Captain Chace separate orders. See N. Brown to W. Chace, July 9, 1776, B529 V-D5, Vessels Diamond, Brown Family Business Records, John Carter Brown Library.

47. Quoted in Hedges, *Browns: The Colonial Years*, 282.
48. See Interrogatories of George W. Babcock regarding the Prize Star and Garter, Aug. 12, 1776, in Admiralty Papers, 1776, vol. 9, no. 83, RI State Archives; Norman Desmarais, *The Guide to the American Revolutionary War at Sea, 1775–1783*, PDF, 7 vols. (Lincoln, RI: Revolutionary Imprints, 2016), 1:194, 198, 200 (collecting US newspaper sources).
49. Interrogatories of Thomas Stacy regarding the Prize Jane, Aug. 7, 1776, in Crawford et al., eds., *Naval Documents*, 6:93-94.
50. "List of All the Vessels and Cargoes," in Crawford et al., eds., *Naval Documents*, 7:642-43 (captures nos. 8, 10, and 11).
51. See Desmarais, *Revolutionary War at Sea*, 1:258 and 263 (collecting original US sources).
52. Ibid., 279 (collecting original US sources); *Providence Gazette,* Nov. 16, 1776. The officer Stacy assigned to sail the prize to Providence accidentally grounded it in Narragansett Bay, but it was refloated at high tide, and brought to Providence. Ibid.
53. Desmarais, *Revolutionary War at Sea*, 1:290, 319 (collecting US newspaper sources); *Providence Gazette*, Nov. 2, 1776. See also Owners of the Rhode Island Privateer Sloop Diamond to Captain Thomas Stacy, Aug. 21, 1776, in Crawford et al., eds., *Naval Documents*, 6:252-53 (containing Stacy's orders).
54. "List of All the Vessels and Cargoes," in Crawford et al., *Naval Documents*, 7:642, 644 (captures nos.8, 10, 11, 16, 21, 23, 28, 29, 31, 37, 40, and 41).
55. Ibid., 644 (captures no. 30 and 32); *Providence Gazette*, Nov. 2, 1776 (advertising for sale at "Mr. John Brown's Wharf" the *Peggy* and its cargo consisting of rum, sugar, and other goods on November 7); J. Brown to N. Cooke, Sept. 14, 1776, in Maritime Papers, Letters of Marque, Petitions and Instructions, 1776–1780, no. 28, RI State Archives.
56. Vessels Owned by John Brown, March 13, 1777, John Brown Papers, MSS 312, series 1, box 1, folder 2, RI Hist. Soc.
57. Testimony of Alderman Woolridge, Feb. 6, 1778, Proceedings in the Lords Respecting the Commercial Losses Occasioned by the American War, in Crawford et al., eds., *Naval Documents*, 11:967, 971n4; Duke of Richmond speech, Feb. 11, 1778, in ibid., 994.
58. An Account of All the Rateable Estate Belonging to John Brown, this 10th Day of January 1778, in John Brown Papers, MSS 312, ser. 1, box 1, folder 2, RI Hist. Soc.
59. Ibid.
60. Ibid. These were the sloop *Polly* (one hundred percent owned by Brown, total value £2,625), the sloop *Favourite* (one hundred percent owned by Brown, total value £2,400); the sloop *Retaliation* (seven-eighths owned by Brown, total value £2,625); the sloop *Division* [*Desirous?*] (one-half owned by Brown, total value £3,000), and the brig *Industry* (three-sixteenths owned by Brown, total value £5,600).

CHAPTER THREE: JOHN BROWN DECIDES TO SEND A PRIVATEER TO AFRICA

1. David Syrett, *The Royal Navy in European Waters during the American Revolutionary War* (Columbia: University of South Carolina Press, 1998), 1-6.
2. William P. Sheffield, *An Address Delivered by William P. Sheffield, Before the Rhode Island Historical Society, in Providence, February 7, A. D. 1882, with Notes* (Newport, RI: Sanborn, 1883), 55-56n9. Several other Rhode Island slavers were taken by French privateers in the Caribbean. Ibid.
3. See Julian S. Corbett, *England in the Seven Years War*, 2 vols., 2nd ed. (London: Longmans, Green, 1918), 1:353-54, 362.
4. See entry for the *Lancashire* (no. 1) listing in appendix B.
5. See entry for the *Africa* (no. 3) listing in ibid.

6. See entry for the *Rio Pongo* (no. 10) listing in ibid.

7. See entry for the *Britannia* (no. 7) listing in ibid.

8. See British Slave Ships Plundered by American Privateers but Not Taken after the chart in appendix B. For the owners of the sloop *Sally*, see list of commissioned vessels in Maritime Papers, Bonds, Masters of Vessels, vol. 3, 1776–1780, RI State Archives (no. 16).

9. Journal of the Continental Navy Brig *Andrea Doria*, April 5, 1776, in Crawford et al., eds., *Naval Documents*, 4:669; "List of All the Vessels and Cargoes," in ibid., 7:642 (capture no. 19, "7 Negro Men").

10. *Providence Gazette*, Sept. 14, 1776.

11. List of Prisoners Taken in the H.M. Bomb Brig *Bolton*, in Crawford et al., eds., *Naval Documents*, 4:669-70.

12. E. Hopkins to W. Ellery, Nov. 7, 1776, in ibid., 7:84.

13. See entry for the *Swallow* (no. 9) listing in appendix B. Three enslaved boys, each of whom was a servant to a white passenger seized by the Providence privateer *Montgomery* in three separate captures in 1776, were treated the same as the white prisoners. British Prisoners Granted Permission to Depart for Great Britain, undated [about November 1776], in Crawford et al., eds., *Naval Documents*, 7:162-66.

14. Testimony of John Shoolbred, Feb. 6, 1778, Proceedings in the Lords Respecting the Commercial Losses Occasioned by the American War, in Crawford et al., eds., *Naval Documents,* 11:971.

15. See Charles Rappleye, *Robert Morris, Financier of the American Revolution* (New York: Simon & Schuster, 2010), 104-05; O'Shaughnessy, *Empire Divided*, 155; Robert C. Alberts, *The Golden Voyage: The Life and Times of William Bingham, 1752–1804* (Boston: Houghton Mifflin, 1969), 20-24.

16. Syrett, *Royal Navy*, 9; *Daily Advertiser* (London), Jan. 25, 1777.

17. See entry for the *Bacchus* (no. 1) listing in appendix C.

18. See entries for two unidentified British slave ships (nos. 2 and 3) captured by the *Boston* in appendix C.

19. For longer voyages to Jamaica or North America having perilous consequences for the health of the African captives, see Nicholas Radburn, "Keeping 'the Wheel in Motion': Trans-Atlantic Credit Terms, Slave Prices, and the Geography of Slavery in the British Americas, 1755–1807," *Journal of Economic History* 75, no. 3 (2015): 669-70.

20. See entry for unidentified British slave ship (no. 4) captured by the *Fanny* in appendix C.

21. See entry for the *St. George* (no. 7) in appendix C.

22. R. Morris to W. Bingham, Dec. 4, 1776, quoted in Crawford et al., eds., *Naval Documents*, 7:368-69.

23. Extract of a Letter from a Gentleman at St. Lucia, to a Merchant in this Town [London], March 10, 1777, in ibid., 8:81; Extract of a Letter from Capt. Cook . . ., Nov. 1, 1777, in ibid., 10:373; Desmarais, *Revolutionary War at Sea*, 2:81 (collecting US newspaper sources).

24. Nicholas Way to Owen Biddle, April 25, 1777, in Crawford et al., eds., *Naval Documents*, 8:430. For more on the two captures, see entries for no. 8 and no. 9 in appendix C.

25. Quoted in Alberts, *Golden Voyage*, 51 (citing R. Morris to W. Bingham, April 25, 1777, William Bingham Papers, Manuscript Reading Room, Library of Congress, Washington, DC, which the author did not locate in this file).

26. Ibid.; see entries for the *Gascoyne* (no. 10) and *Fox* (no 11) in appendix C.

27. See Alberts, *Golden Voyage*, 485n51. The *Golden Voyage* book cites a document called "Adventures of Ships Owned by William Bingham, 1777–1779," in the Library of Philadelphia. The document was located, but not the entries for the *Gascoyne* and *Fox*.

28. Charles R. Foy, "Eighteenth Century 'Prize Negroes': From Britain to America," *Slavery & Abolition* 31, no. 3 (Sept. 2010): 381.

29. Ibid., 385.

30. Extract from *Grenada Gazette*, in *Public Advertiser* (London), Sept. 19, 1777.

31. See, e.g., Gardner W. Allen, *A Naval History of the American Revolution* (Boston: Houghton Mifflin, 1913), 45-46; Sydney G. Morse, "State or Continental Privateers?," *American Historical Review* 52, no. 1 (Oct. 1946): 68-73.

32. *Daily Advertiser* (London), June 7, 1777; *Morning Post* (London), June 7, 1777. For other instances of armed British slave ships beating back privateers, see "American Privateers Fail to Defeat British Slave Ships" in appendix C.

33. TSTD, www.slavevoyages.org/voyage/search (voyage no. 36327).

34. King George III to Lord Sandwich, Aug. 25, 1775, in Crawford et al., eds., *Naval Documents*, 2:687.

35. British Admiralty Orders, Sept. 18, 1775, in ibid., 721-22.

36. British Admiralty Orders, Nov. 11, 1775, and Jan. 20, 1776, in ibid., 3:364, 518. The *Pallas* and *Weazle* had patrolled the Atlantic Coast of Africa, looking out for American ships seeking to purchase gunpowder, from January to April 1775. Peter Erik Flynn, "H.M.S. *Pallas*: Historical Reconstruction of an 18th-Century Royal Navy Frigate" (master's thesis, Texas A&M University, 2006), 125.

37. Keith P. Herzog, "Naval Operations in West Africa and the Disruption of the Slave Trade during the American Revolution," *American Neptune* 55, no. 1 (1995), 46n1.

38. *General Evening Post* (London), June 20-22, 1776; *Morning Post* (London), June 22, 1776; *Lloyd's Evening Post* (London), June 21-24, 1776; *London Evening Post*, Oct. 3-5, 1776; *Daily Advertiser* (London), Oct. 7, 1776.

39. Herzog, "Naval Operations," 42.

40. An Account of American Ships and Vessels Taken as Prizes of War, by His Majesty's Ships and Vessels under the Command of Vice-Admiral Young at Barbados, and the Leeward Islands, Between the 1st and 27th of July 1776, in Crawford et al., eds., *Naval Documents*, 5:1254.

41. TSTD, www.slavevoyages.org/voyage/search (voyage no. 36327, commanded by Robert Elliot). The vessel completed its two-year voyage on November 6, 1767.

42. Extract of a Letter from Captain Jacob Dunnell, dated St. Pierre's, Martinico, July 17, 1776, *New England Chronicle*, Sept. 12, 1776, in Crawford et al., eds., *Naval Documents*, 5:1120.

43. Ibid.

44. British Admiralty Orders, Nov. 11, 1775, in Crawford et al., eds., *Naval Documents*, 3:365. See also British Admiralty Orders to Captain John Stott of the *Weazle*, Feb. 11, 1777, in Crawford et al., eds., *Naval Documents*, 8:579-80.

45. Extract of a Letter from Captain Jacob Dunnell, in ibid., 5:1120.

46. *London Chronicle*, April 16-18, 1776, in ibid., 4:1054.

47. Extract of a Letter from Captain Jacob Dunnell, in ibid., 5:1120.

48. W. Cornwallis to P. Stephens, Jan. 30, 1776, in ibid., 544.

49. Journal of the HMS *Pallas*, Jan. 28, 1776, in ibid., 3:540 and 540n3.

50. Ibid. See also Flynn, "H.M.S. *Pallas*," master's thesis, 126-37 (arguing that Cornwallis exceeded his authority by acquiring the *St. John*).

51. Extract of a Letter from Captain Jacob Dunnell, in Crawford et al., eds., *Naval Documents*, 5:1120-21.

52. *Boston Gazette*, Sept. 16, 1776, in ibid., 6:852. The report indicated that the *Hester's* cargo consisted of "ivory, wax, dry goods and wood," which, if true, indicates the vessel may not have been a slaver but was instead trading for African products.

53. British Admiralty Orders to Captain John Stott of the *Weazle*, Feb. 11, 1777, in Crawford et al., eds., *Naval Documents*, 8:578-80.
54. *Lloyd's List* (London), March 4, 1777; Flynn, "H.M.S. *Pallas*," master's thesis, 128 (citing ship's logs).
55. J. P. Jones to R. Morris, Oct. 17, 1776, in Crawford et al., eds., *Naval Documents*, 6:1303-04.
56. J. P. Jones to R. Morris, Jan. 12, 1777, in ibid., 7:938.
57. Evan Thomas, *John Paul Jones: Sailor, Hero, Father of the American Navy* (New York: Simon & Schuster, 2003), 21-22. The main text associated with this entry is the first in print to discuss the details of the slave voyages that Jones likely took. I gleaned the information on them from TSTD, www.slavevoyages.org/voyage/search (voyage nos. 24613, 25379). The *King George* was owned by Whitehaven merchant John Selkirk, while the *Two Friends* was owned by Philadelphia Quaker merchant Henry Drinker. The *King George* also undertook a slave voyage starting from Whitehaven in 1763–1764. Ibid. (voyage no. 24587). This ship named *King George* should not be confused with others by the same name, including one from Bristol that sailed on several slave voyages before it was captured by an American privateer in 1776. See appendix B, no. 8. I assume Jones enlisted on the *King George* from his hometown and not the one from Bristol.
58. R. Morris to J. P. Jones, Feb. 5, 1777, in Crawford et al., eds., *Naval Documents*, 7:1109-11.
59. L. Wickes to the American Commissioners in France, March 5, 1777, in ibid., 8:641-42.
60. Fowler, *Rebels under Sail,* 120-24.
61. P. Henry to R. H. Lee, May 28, 1778, in Crawford et al., eds., *Naval Documents,* 12:475. The French officer was Captain Denis-Nicholas Cottineau de Kerloguen of the French armed ship *Ferdinand.* See ibid., 476n2.
62. Report on Operations in Which Our Naval Forces Could be Employed Against England, Jan. 1778, in ibid., 11:960.
63. See Christian M. McBurney, *The Rhode Island Campaign: The First French and American Operation in the Revolutionary War* (Yardley, PA: Westholme, 2011), chs. 4-7.
64. See Alan G. Jamieson, "American Privateers in the Leeward Islands, 1776–1778," *American Neptune* 43, no. 1 (1983): 27-29. For the *St. Peter*'s captures of the slave ships, see appendix C, nos. 20 and 21.

CHAPTER FOUR: GEORGE WAITE BABCOCK IS SELECTED AS COMMANDER

1. See, e.g., Journal of the Committee Appointed to Build Two Continental Frigates in Rhode Island, Jan. 8–9, 12, 19, and Feb. 5, 12, 1776, in Crawford et al., eds., *Naval Documents*, 3:677-678, 691, 751, 859, 1133, 1228.
2. See Journal of the Committee Appointed to Build Two Continental Frigates in Rhode Island, Jan. 10, 19, 25, and Feb. 19, 1776, in ibid., 3:715, 858, 972, 1228, and 4:8; John F. Millar, *Early American Ships* (Williamsburg, VA: Thirteen Colonies Press, 1986), 166-67, 205-06.
3. List of Prizes Taken by Vice Admiral James Young's Leeward Island Squadron from May 1 to June 12, 1777, in Crawford et al., eds., *Naval Documents*, 9:104 (Sloop *Beaver* captured the *Oliver Cromwell* privateer, Herman Courter, 24 guns and 150 men); Survey of the *Beaver's Prize* (formerly the captured privateer *Oliver Cromwell* sailing from Pennsylvania), Aug. 19, 1777, in Crawford et al., eds., *Naval Documents*, 9:768-69 (*Oliver Cromwell* was 265 tons).
4. See appendix C, no. 12.
5. Journal of HM Sloop *Beaver*, May 19, 1777, in Crawford et al., eds., *Naval Documents*, 8:999. The *Oliver Cromwell* had thirteen men killed and twenty wounded in the engage-

ment, while the *Beaver* had only three wounded. Ibid. Due to manning prize ships, the *Oliver Cromwell* had a crew of 125 at the time of the engagement. Captain James Jones to Vice Admiral James Young, May 25, 1777, in ibid., 1029. At the time of this letter, Jones said fifteen enemy sailors had died. Ibid.

6. Survey of the *Beaver's Prize* (formerly the captured privateer *Oliver Cromwell* sailing from Pennsylvania), Aug. 19, 1777, in Crawford et al., eds., *Naval Documents*, 9:768-69; Millar, *Early American Ships*, 149-51. The Royal Navy survey experts concluded that the ship should carry one hundred men and fourteen cannon. The survey did not include the length of the ship. John Millar estimated it based on the other information provided. Millar believes the *Oliver Cromwell* was built in Providence in 1774, based on the design of the ship. Millar, *Early American Ships*, 150.

7. Ibid., 151.

8. David Baugh, "Elements of Naval Power in the Eighteenth Century," in *Maritime History: The Eighteenth Century and the Classic Age of Sail*, ed. John B. Hattendorf, vol. 2, 119-35 (Malabar, FL: Krieger, 1997), 123.

9. This estimate is based on two examples where the mix of ship's guns are known. The privateer *Blaze-Castle*, which departed Providence in December 1777, was captured in June 1778 carrying eighteen 6-pounders and four howitzers. Crawford et al., eds., *Naval Documents*, 13:80n1. The privateer *Oliver Cromwell* based in Providence, in a November 1776 voyage, carried sixteen 6-pounders and four 3-pounders, as well as twelve swivel guns mounted on the top railing of the deck. Application for a privateer commission for the *Oliver Cromwell*, Nov. 25, 1776, in Maritime Papers, Letters of Marque, 1776-1778, no. 55, RI State Archives.

10. James N. Arnold, ed., *Vital Records of Rhode Island, 1636–1850*, 21 vols. (Providence, RI: Narragansett Historical Publishing, 1891–1912), 5:39, 226; Stephen Babcock, *Babcock Genealogy* (New York: Eaton & Mains, 1903), 142.

11. Births, Marriages, Deaths, 1744–1883, vol. 2, 227, Exeter Town Clerk's Office, Exeter, RI; Arnold, ed., *Vital Records*, 5:39.

12. Arnold, ed., *Vital Records*, 5:6; Babcock, *Babcock Genealogy*, 142.

13. Births, Marriages, Deaths, 1744–1883, vol. 2, 27, Exeter Town Clerk's Office; Arnold, ed., *Vital Records*, 5:6, 14. Simeon Fowler must have moved to South Kingstown shortly after his daughter's marriage. See Bartlett, ed., *Census of Rhode Island 1774*, 87.

14. Bartlett, ed., *Census of Rhode Island 1774*, 76. A minor was reported living with them too. There is no record of their having had a child together. The minor was probably Samuel Babcock, George's younger brother. See main text in chapter 4 accompanying note 57.

15. Births, Marriages, Deaths, 1744–1883, vol. 2, 27 in chapter 4; Arnold, ed., *Vital Records*, 5:7, 5 (Hopkinton).

16. *Massachusetts Soldiers and Sailors in the War of the American Revolution*, 17 vols. (Boston: Commonwealth of Massachusetts, 1896–1908), 1:393 (description of Babcock in 1781 as commander of the privateer *Venus*).

17. See main text in chapter 10 accompanying notes 38-39 (*Hope*), 41 (*Nancy*), 51 (*Elephant*), 54-58 (*Tartar*), 76 (*Brothers*).

18. For more on the *Diamond*'s initial voyage, see main text in chapter 2 accompanying notes 48-50.

19. Interrogatories of George W. Babcock regarding the Prize *Star and Garter*, Aug. 12, 1776, in Admiralty Papers, 1776, vol. 9, no. 83, RI State Archives; orders from W. Chace to G. W. Babcock, July 25, 1776, in ibid., no. 84; court ruling, undated, in ibid, no. 94.

20. Same sources as in prior note; Desmarais, *Revolutionary War at Sea*, 1:294 (collecting US newspaper sources); George T. Hewes Declaration, Oct. 16, 1832, in George T. Hewes,

Rhode Island, Revolutionary War Pension Application, National Archives, Washington, DC (Hewes sailed on the *Diamond* with Babcock).

21. Interrogatory of George W. Babcock regarding the Prize *Mary and Joseph*, Oct. 26, 1776, in Admiralty Papers, 1776, vol. 9, no. 138, RI State Archives.

22. Distribution of Dead Shares in Prizes Taken by the Rhode Island Privateer Sloop *Diamond*, Aug. 22, 1776, in Crawford et al., eds., *Naval Documents*, 6:263-64.

23. Commission, Nov. 20, 1776, in Maritime Records, Bonds, Masters of Vessels, vol. 3, Aug. 1776–Dec. 1778, no. 69, RI State Archives.

24. See McBurney, *Kidnapping the Enemy*, 105, 122, 131.

25. Bartlett, ed., *Records of Rhode Island*, 8:174; J. Garzia to N. Cooke, March 15, 1777, Letters to the Governor, vol. 9, RI State Archives; J. Varnum to N. Cooke, March 17, 1777, in ibid; N. Cooke to Sheriff of King's County, March 26, 1777, General Assembly Papers, Rev. War Suspected Persons Record Book, 1775–1783, folio 63, RI State Archives.

26. Compare *Newport Gazette*, April 20, 1777 (party of forty people) with T. Clarke to N. Cooke, March 27, 1777, Letters to the Governor, vol. 10, RI State Archives (the party consisted of Babcock and four others).

27. In his report to Governor Cooke, Major Clarke names John Slocum as one of the party that apprehended the Slocum brothers. T. Clarke to N. Cooke, March 27, 1777, Letters to the Governor, vol. 10, RI State Archives.

28. The most detailed descriptions of this incident are in the *Newport Gazette*, April 20, 1777; Ebenezer Slocum Revolutionary War Loyalist Claim, British Public Records Office, AO 45 12, microfilm, David Library Collections, American Philosophical Society, Philadelphia; T. Clarke to N. Cooke, March 27, 1777, Letters to the Governor, vol. 10, RI State Archives. See also *Providence Gazette*, March 29, 1777 (the date of the incident); Bartlett, ed., *Records of Rhode Island*, 8:192 (King's County Sheriff Beriah Brown compensated for his services "to convey Ebenezer and Charles Slocum to Major Clarke, by order of this Assembly").

29. T. Clarke to N. Cooke, March 27, 1777, Letters to the Governor, vol. 10, RI State Archives.

30. *Newport Gazette*, April 20, 1777.

31. Bartlett, ed., *Records of Rhode Island*, 8:196-97. See also Petition of George Waite Babcock and Thirty-Four Others, April 17, 1777, Petitions to the General Assembly (Rhode Island), vol. 16, no. 106, RI State Archives, Providence, RI.

32. Joseph J. Smith, ed., *Civil and Military List of Rhode Island*, 2 vols. (Providence, RI: Preston and Rounds, 1900), 1:348; David Sherman Baker Jr., *An Historical Sketch of North Kingstown* (Providence, RI: F. A. Johnson, 1876), 18, 20.

33. For more on the British plot to use counterfeit money as a weapon against the Patriots, see Christian McBurney, *Spies in Revolutionary Rhode Island* (Charleston, SC: History Press, 2014), 27.

34. Diary entries, Feb. 10, 12, 27, and March 4, 1777, Hugh Percy Diary, Hugh Percy Papers, British Manuscript Project, reel Aln 27, Microform Reading Room, Library of Congress, Washington, DC.

35. Diary entries, April 11–12, 1777, in ibid.

36. *Newport Gazette*, May 15, 29, 1777.

37. See McBurney, *Spies in Revolutionary Rhode Island*, 29.

38. Wanton Casey Recollection, in J. R. Cole, *History of Washington and Kent Counties, Rhode Island* (New York: Preston, 1889), 127.

39. See McBurney, *Spies in Revolutionary Rhode Island*, 30-31.

40. John A. McManemin, *Captains of the Privateers during the Revolutionary War* (Spring Lake, NJ: Ho-Kus Publishing, 1985), 103.

41. Arnold, ed., *Vital Records,* 5:44 (James Eldred born May 12, 1749, of William and Abigail).

42. See, e.g, Smith, ed., *Civil and Military List,* 1:73, 162, 171, 179.

43. Bartlett, ed., *Census of Rhode Island 1774,* 78. James Eldred married Lucy Reynolds in 1761. Stephen F. Tillman, *Christopher Reynolds and His Descendants* (Chevy Chase, MD: privately printed, 1959), 239.

44. Newport Customs House Records, Inward and Outward Entries, in *Newport Mercury,* June 17, and October 21, 1771.

45. Journal of the Committee Appointed to Build Two Continental Frigates in Rhode Island, May 27, 1776, in Crawford et al., eds., *Naval Documents,* 5:269; Appointments of Officers Made by the Committee Appointed to Build Two Continental Frigates in Rhode Island, Sept. 2, 1776, in ibid., 6:651. Eldred is listed as residing in South Kingstown at the time. Eldred probably decided to move out of Updike's Newtown and into the interior out of fear of being abducted by Loyalists or British seamen operating in ships off the coast.

46. Smith, *Civil and Military List,* 1:368, 379, 380.

47. Bartlett, ed., *Census of Rhode Island 1774,* 76; Mildred M. Chamberlain, ed., *The Rhode Island 1777 Military Census* (Baltimore: Genealogical Publishing, 1985), 60. Aaron Lopez, the Jewish immigrant who became colonial Newport's most successful merchant, hired Bradfield to command a small sloop that sailed from Rhode Island to Jamaica in 1767. See Aaron Lopez to Henry Crueger Jr., Feb. 5, 1767, Isaac Pereira Mendes to Aaron Lopez, April 10, 1767, and Abraham Lopez to Aaron Lopez, April 14, 1767, in *Commerce of Rhode Island, 1726–1774,* in *Massachusetts Historical Society Collections,* 7th ser., vol. 9 (1914):185, 196, 197-98. Incomplete Newport Custom House records published from 1771 to 1775 reveal that Bradfield commanded at least five voyages to the Caribbean and the Carolinas. Newport Custom House Records, Inward and Outbound Entries, in *Newport Mercury,* Sept. 2, 1771; May 15, 1773; Sept. 18, 1773; Oct. 2, 1773; and June 12, 1775. See also *Newport Mercury,* Jan. 10, 1774 (ship captain reports meeting Captain Francis Bradfield, commanding the sloop *Freelove,* four days out of Newport bound for North Carolina).

48. Bartlett, ed., *Records of Rhode Island,* 7:412; Owners of the Rhode Island Privateer Sloop *General Greene* to Governor Nicholas Cooke, July 3, 1776, in Crawford et al., eds., *Naval Documents,* 5:890-91.

49. Bartlett, ed., *Census of Rhode Island 1774,* 142; Chamberlain, ed., *Rhode Island 1777 Military Census,* 131.

50. Bartlett, ed., *Census of Rhode Island 1774,* 76; Chamberlain, ed., *Rhode Island 1777 Military Census,* 60; Smith, ed., *Civil and Military List,* 1:348. Christopher Brown married Penelope Holley of Newport on January 19, 1769. Arnold, ed., *Vital Records,* 7:349.

51. See Beriah Brown Papers, MSS 109, box 4, notes by Rhode Island Historical Society and Severely Damaged Manuscript file, RI Hist. Soc., Providence.

52. A list of the crew of the Providence privateer *Independence,* made in September 1776, included three prize masters. This privateer had a crew of sixty men and boys and weighed about fifty tons. Charles W. Farnham, "Crew List of the Privateer *Independence,* 1776," *Rhode Island History* 26, no. 4 (Oct. 1967): 127.

53. In the 1774 census of Rhode Island, Joseph headed the only household of Holloways in Exeter. Bartlett, ed., *Census of Rhode Island 1774,* 165. In the 1782 census, Ichabod Holloway and Joseph Holloway each headed a household in Exeter, as did two other Holloways. Holbrook, ed., *Rhode Island 1782 Census,* 64.

54. *Newport Mercury,* Jan. 2, 1775. See also *Newport Mercury,* Aug. 7, 1775 (Captain Samuel Holloway died without a will and was insolvent).

55. David Bissell Declaration, Feb. 15, 1840, in John Bissell Jr., Rhode Island, Revolutionary War Pension Application, National Archives; Job Sherman Declaration, Dec. 13, 1839, in ibid.; Smith, *Civil and Military List*, 1:352; *Providence Gazette*, Aug. 9, 1777.

56. Bartlett, ed., *Census of Rhode Island 1774*, 84 (listing as heads of households in South Kingstown with several other males in each household, Philip Boss, Peter Boss, and William Boss). Several other Boss families resided in Richmond. Ibid., 198. John Linscom Boss may have lived in Richmond in 1777, as he later married his second cousin from Richmond, Sarah Boss, on February 21, 1779. William G. Boss, *Inquiry Concerning the Boss Family and the Name Boss* (Chicago: Ben Franklin Co., 1902), 52. See also journal entry, May 6, 1778, in John Linscom Boss, Journal of a Voyage in the Good Ship Marlborough George Wt. Babcock Commander Bound on a Five Month Cruise Against the Enemies of the United States of America from Rhode Island, Dec. 23, 1777–June 12, 1778, microfilm, Morristown National Historical Park, Morristown, NJ (hereinafter Journal of the *Marlborough*) (Boss turned age twenty-one).

57. Town Council Minutes, May 28, 1776, Town Council and Probate Records, vol. 4, 1756–1786, 1, Exeter Town Clerk's Office, Exeter, RI.

58. Farnham, "Crew List," 127-28. Three names of common sailors included men with first names that were common for Rhode Island enslaved or formerly enslaved men: Pero Waterman, Cezar Bliss (cook), and Prime Powers. There were likely several other Black men in the crew whose first names were common for both Black and white men.

59. See W. Jeffrey Bolster, *Black Jacks: African American Seamen in the Age of Sail* (Cambridge, MA: Harvard University Press, 1997), 153.

60. See articles of agreement for the cruise of the *Independence*, in Farnham, "Crew List," 126.

61. Articles of Agreement for the Armed Sloop Called the *Revenge*, June 27, 1778, HFM 198, Mystic Seaport Collections.

62. Remarks of Our Gunner on Charlestown, in S.C., in Timothy Boardman, *Log-Book of Timothy Boardman; Kept on Board the Privateer Oliver Cromwell, During a Cruise from New London CT., to Charleston, S.C., and Return in 1778; also a Biographical Sketch of the Author by the Rev. Samuel W. Boardman, D.D.* (Albany, NY: Joel Munsell's Sons, 1885), 73.

CHAPTER FIVE: THE *Marlborough* BREAKS OUT

1. Resolution, April 2, 1776, Ford, ed., *Journals of the Continental Congress*, 4:247-48.

2. Ibid., 251-52; Hulbert, *Untold War at Sea*, 22.

3. Letter of Marque for the *Marlborough*, Dec. 13, 1777, Maritime Papers, Bonds, Masters of Vessels, Aug. 1776–Dec. 1778, vol. 3, no. 107, RI State Archives. This letter did not provide the *Marlborough*'s tonnage. Another one stated that it weighed 250 tons. See Crawford et al., eds., *Naval Documents*, 10:805n1. The letter, once at Morristown National Historical Park, has been lost.

4. *Independent Chronicle* (Boston), June 18, 1778.

5. An Account of All the Rateable Estate Belonging to John Brown, this 10th Day of January 1778, in John Brown Papers, MSS 312, ser. 1, box 1, folder 2, RI Hist. Soc.

6. Ibid. Brown owned three-sixteenths of the privateer *Blaze-Castle* and assigned it a total value, including its twenty-two cannon and stores, of £13,500, making it one of the most valuable privateers that sailed from Providence during the war. Ibid. Brown did not place a value on the *Oliver Cromwell*.

7. See McBurney, *Kidnapping the Enemy*, 122, 131.

8. Diary entries, June 4 and 5, 1777, Mackenzie, 1:135, 136.

9. Thomas Stacy Interrogatories, Aug. 7, 1776, in Crawford et al., eds., *Naval Documents*, 6:93-94 (merchant ship *Jane* captured); A List of Rebel Ships & Privateers at Providence,

Dec. 11, 1776, in ibid., 7:447 (privateer *Jane* carries twenty guns); application for a privateer commission for the *Oliver Cromwell*, Nov. 25, 1776, in Maritime Papers, Letters of Marque, 1776–1778, no. 55, RI State Archives (types of cannon).

10. An Account of All the Rateable Estate Belonging to John Brown, this 10th Day of January 1778, in John Brown Papers, MSS 312, ser. 1, box 1, folder 2, RI Hist. Soc.

11. Letter of Marque and Reprisal for the *Oliver Cromwell*, Aug. 4, 1777, Maritime Papers, Bonds, Masters of Vessels, Aug. 1776–Dec. 1778, vol. 3, no. 94, RI State Archives; J. Russell to his wife, Aug. 28, 1777, quoted in Crawford et al., eds., *Naval Documents*, 9:825n2.

12. Diary entry, Aug. 27, 1777, Mackenzie, *Diary*, 1:170; *Providence Gazette*, Aug. 30, 1777; Log of HM *Kingsfisher*, Aug. 27, 1777, in Peter E. Jones, "Grant Us Commission to Make Reprisals upon Any Enemies Shiping," *Rhode Island History* 34, no. 4 (Nov. 1975): 105n1.

13. Diary entry, Aug. 27, 1777, Journal of Lieutenant-Colonel Christopher French, Manuscript Reading Room, Library of Congress, Washington, DC.

14. Journal of the Regiment von Huyn, Aug. 26, 1777, Lidgerwood Collection, microfilm, Morristown National Historical Park, Morristown, NJ.

15. J. Russell to his wife, Aug. 28, 1777, quoted in Crawford et al., eds., *Naval Documents*, 9:825n2.

16. An Account of All the Rateable Estate Belonging to John Brown, this 10th Day of January 1778, in John Brown Papers, MSS 312, ser. 1, box 1, folder 2, RI Hist. Soc.

17. Syrett, *Royal Navy*, 70.

18. Ibid., 57-60, 68-72.

19. N. Cooke to H. Cooke, Dec. 1, 1777, in Jones, "Revolutionary Correspondence," *Proceedings of the American Antiquarian Society* (Oct. 1926): 36:349-50. See also diary entry, Dec. 14, 1777, Mackenzie, *Diary*, 1:216. In his letter, Governor Cooke specifically named the ship *Thomas*, commanded by Captain James Munro, and small vessels from Providence, Warren, Pawtuxet, and East Greenwich, all slipping out on the night of November 29, and the privateer *Montgomery*, commanded by Captain Phineas Potter, John Brown's privateer sloop *Diamond*, captained by Thomas Stacy, and an unidentified brig escaping the night of November 30. The brig was the eighteen-gun privateer *Minerva*. See Register of Vessels (Rhode Island), 1776–1778, no. 68, RI State Archives (brig *Minerva* registered on November 18, 1777). The ship *Thomas* was registered on November 7. Ibid., no. 60. A total of seventeen vessels registered in Rhode Island in November and December, and apparently all of them escaped the British blockade. Ibid., 60-76. This register, for unknown reasons, did not include all ships departing Providence or other Rhode Island ports, such as the *Marlborough*.

20. Diary entry, Dec. 14, 1777, in Mackenzie, *Diary*, 1:223.

21. Official British maritime document, Aug. 16, 1774, Admiralty Papers, vol. 9, 1776, no. 195, RI State Archives; *Independent Chronicle* (Boston), Sept. 26, 1776.

22. Council of War Records (Rhode Island), vol. 2, March 3, 1777, RI State Archives. See also Letter of Marque for *Blaze-Castle*, Nov. 7, 1777, Bonds, Masters of Vessels, Aug. 1776–Dec. 1778, vol. 3, no. 106, RI State Archives (number of guns and size of crew); advertisement in *Connecticut Gazette*, Dec. 26, 1777 (number of guns); Crawford et al., eds., *Naval Documents*, 13:80n1 (eighteen 6-pounders found on board when captured); An Account of All the Rateable Estate Belonging to John Brown, this 10th Day of January 1778, in John Brown Papers, MSS 312, ser. 1, box 1, folder 2, RI Hist. Soc. (Brown's ownership).

23. Diary entry, Nov. 30, 1777, in Mackenzie, *Diary*, 1:216.

24. Advertisement in *Connecticut Gazette*, Dec. 26, 1777; *Independent Chronicle* (Boston), June 18, 1778 (arrival in Boston of two prizes taken by the *Blaze-Castle*); *Providence Gazette*, June 27, 1778; Journal of HM *Unicorn*, June 11, 1778, in Crawford et al., eds., *Naval Documents*, 13:80. The *Providence Gazette* reported that because Captain James Munroe's crew

had been reduced by the need to man the five prizes in order to sail them back to safe ports, when the HMS *Unicorn* squared off against the *Blaze-Castle*, the undermanned American ship struck its colors without firing a shot. When captured, the *Blaze-Castle* reportedly had a crew of fifty-six men. Crawford et al., eds., *Naval Documents*, 13:80n1.

25. Log of HMS *Amazon*, Nov. 27–28, 1777, in Crawford et al., eds., *Naval Documents*, 10:622; diary entry, Nov. 27, 1777, Journal of Lieutenant-Colonel Christopher French, Manuscript Reading Room, Library of Congress; List of Vessels Seized, Destroyed or Retaken by the American Squadron Between October 25, 1777 Through September 28, 1778, Admiral Howe Correspondence, British Public Records, ADM 1/488, transcript, Library of Congress, Washington, DC; Maritime Papers, Outward and Inward Entries, 1776–87, Outward Entry for the *Phoenix*, Nov. 8, 1777, RI State Archives.

26. Log of HMS *Amazon*, Dec. 10, 1777, in Crawford et al., eds., *Naval Documents*, 10:699; *Providence Gazette*, Dec. 13, 1777; List of Vessels Seized, Admiral Howe Correspondence, British Public Records, ADM 1/488, transcript, Library of Congress.

27. Maritime Papers, Outward and Inward Entries, 1776–87, RI State Archives (seventy-nine vessels registered from Dec. 18, 1776, through July 29, 1778); Bonds, Masters of Vessels, Aug. 1776–Dec. 1778, vol. 3, RI State Archives (an additional four privateers received letters of marque during same period, not including whaleboat privateers and other small armed vessels mostly operating in Narragansett Bay).

28. Maritime Papers, Outward and Inward Entries, 1776–87, RI State Archives.

29. See McBurney, *Rhode Island Campaign*, appendix B, 233.

30. For the number of guns carried by the *Kingsfisher* and *Alarm*, and the sizes of their crews, see Ibid.

31. Log of HMS *Kingsfisher*, Dec. 25, 1777, in Crawford et al., eds., *Naval Documents*, 10:805.

32. Ibid.; journal entry, Dec. 24, 1777, in Boss, Journal of the *Marlborough*.

33. Log of HMS *Kingsfisher*, Dec. 25, 1777, in Crawford et al., eds., *Naval Documents*, 10:805.

34. Diary entries, Dec. 25 and 26, 1777, in Mackenzie, *Diary* 1:226, 227.

35. Ibid., 227; *Newport Gazette*, Jan. 1, 1778; diary entries, Dec. 26 and 29, 1777, Journal of Lieutenant-Colonel Christopher French, Manuscript Reading Room, Library of Congress; List of Vessels Seized, Admiral Howe Correspondence, British Public Records, ADM 1/488, transcript, Library of Congress; Maritime Papers, Outward and Inward Entries, 1776-87, Outward Entry for the *Peggy and Betsy*, Dec. 5, 1777, RI State Archives. Mackenzie said that on December 25, Admiral Peter Parker applied for a detachment of Hessians to burn the *Peggy and Betsy*, but that there were no boats available; that the next day a British galley was driven away by two American artillery pieces; and that finally, on December 27, a party was sent to the brig and successfully torched it. Diary entries, Dec. 25–27, 1777, in Mackenzie, *Diary*, 1:226-27. The *Newport Gazette* reported that a noncommissioned officer from Lieutenant Colonel Innes's Royal Artillery company performed the task. *Newport Gazette*, Jan. 8, 1778. The HMS *Flora* on December 29 sent a "long boat and pinnace with the Lieutenant in order to set [the 'rebel brig'] on fire." Log of HMS *Flora*, Dec. 29, 1777, in Crawford et al., eds, *Naval Documents*, 10:823. The *Kingsfisher* and *Alarm* were both scuttled and set on fire by their crews to avoid capture by a French fleet in early August 1778. See McBurney, *Rhode Island Campaign*, 86.

36. Journal entries, Dec. 25–26, 1777, in Boss, Journal of the *Marlborough*.

37. Journal entries, Dec. 29–Jan. 2, 1777, ibid.

38. Journal entries, Jan. 1–2, 1778, ibid.

39. Jay Coughtry states that the ratio of crew to tonnage on a Rhode Island slave ship was about one to thirteen, which would have given the 250-ton *Marlborough* a slave voyage crew

of about nineteen. Coughtry, *Notorious Triangle,* 19. A British slave ship the size of the *Marlborough* would have had a larger crew, about twenty-eight to thirty-two officers and sailors.
40. Marcus Rediker, *Between the Devil and the Deep Blue Sea: Merchant Seamen, Pirates and the Anglo-American Maritime World* (Cambridge: Cambridge University Press, 1987), 159.
41. Journal entries, Dec. 31, 1777, and Jan. 1–2, 1778, in Boss, Journal of the *Marlborough.*

CHAPTER SIX: THE *Marlborough* ARRIVES IN AFRICA
1. Kelley, *Voyage of the Slave Ship* Hare, 53.
2. Paul E. Lovejoy, "Forgotten Colony in Africa: The British Province of Senegambia (1765–83)," in *Slavery, Abolition and the Transition to Colonialism in Sierra Leone,* eds. Paul E. Lovejoy and Suzanne Schwarz, 109-141 (Trenton, NJ: Africa World Press, 2014), 109.
3. Ibid., 115, table 6.1 (using TSTD, www.slavevoyages.org).
4. Alexander Falconbridge, *An Account of the Slave Trade on the Coast of Africa,* 2nd ed. (London: James Phillips,1788), 48. According to Falconbridge, who served as a physician on several British slave voyages, this event occurred in 1786, and the vessel was owned by Miles Barber and Co. of Liverpool. More will be heard from Miles Barber in the next chapter.
5. Journal entries, Jan. 13–14, 1778, in Boss, Journal of the *Marlborough.*
6. Journal entry, Jan. 23, 1778, in ibid. The ship's log was kept from noon one day to noon the next day; Samuel Babcock died after midnight on January 24.
7. Elizabeth A. Fenn, *Pox Americana: The Great Smallpox Epidemic of 1775–1782* (New York: Hill and Wang, 2001), 32–33.
8. Town Council minutes, Dec. 10, 1777, Town Council and Probate Records, vol. 4, 1756–1786, 38, Exeter Town Clerk's Office, Exeter, RI.
9. Journal entries, Jan. 20 and 29, 1778, in Boss, Journal of the *Marlborough.* Wilcox died on January 29. The American privateer *Defence,* shortly after sailing out of New London, Connecticut, in early 1778, had five sailors break out with smallpox, at least one of whom died of the disease. Journal entries, April 7 and 9, 1778, in Boardman, *Log-Book of Timothy Boardman,* 51. See also Hulbert, *Untold War at Sea,* 56-58.
10. Journal entries, Jan. 26–27, 1778, in Boss, Journal of the *Marlborough.*
11. Journal entries, Feb. 1, 5, and 11, 1778, in ibid. Collins died on February 1 and Congdon on February 2.
12. Journal entry, Jan. 19, 1778, in ibid.
13. Kelley, *Voyage of the Slave Ship* Hare, 56.
14. Journal entry, Jan. 16, 1778, in Boss, Journal of the *Marlborough.*
15. Journal entry, Jan. 26, 1778, in ibid.
16. Journal entries, Jan. 25–29, 1778, in ibid.
17. Stephen R. Berry, *A Path in the Mighty Waters: Shipboard Life & Atlantic Crossings to the New World* (New Haven, CT: Yale University Press, 2015), 143.
18. Journal entry, April 14, 1778, in Boardman, *Log-Book of Timothy Boardman,* 51.
19. Berry, *Path in the Mighty Waters,* 144.
20. Journal entry, Jan. 31, 1778, Journal of the *Marlborough,* in Crawford et al., eds., *Naval Documents,* appendix C, 12:817, 828n6-7.
21. Journal entries, Feb. 3–5, 1778, in Boss, Journal of the *Marlborough.*
22. See Corbett, *England in the Seven Years' War,* 2:336-37; Jonathan R. Dull, *The French Navy and the Seven Years' War* (Lincoln: University of Nebraska Press, 2005), 116.
23. See James Searing, *West African Slavery and Atlantic Commerce* (Cambridge: Cambridge University Press, 1993), 115-16. The population was 3,018 in 1779. In July 1778, a severe epidemic of yellow fever significantly reduced the island's population. Ibid., 97, 227n86.

24. *Public Advertiser* (London), Aug. 3, 1776; *General Evening Post* (London), Aug. 20–22, 1776; *Daily Advertiser* (London), Sept. 30, 1776, and Oct. 19, 1776.

25. Searing, *West Africa Slavery and Atlantic Commerce*, 152.

26. David Eltis, Paul E. Lovejoy, and David Richardson, "Slave-Trading Ports: Towards an Atlantic-Wide Perspective," in *Ports of the Slave Trade (Bights of Benin and Biafra)*, eds. Robin Law and Silke Strickrodt, 12-34 (Stirling, UK: Centre of Commonwealth Studies, University of Stirling, 1999), 8-19, table 1. The periods covered in table 1 were 1670–1690, 1713–1740, 1748–1775, 1783–1793, and 1815–1830. The top five places in Upper Guinea in order of shipping the most African captives were James Fort, Saint-Louis, Sierra Leone, Cape Mount, and the Isles de Los.

27. Hugh Thomas, *The Slave Trade: The Story of the Atlantic Slave Trade: 1440–1870* (New York: Touchstone, 1997), 333.

28. Journal entry, Feb. 6, 1778, in Boss, Journal of the *Marlborough*.

29. Jules Machat, *Documents sur les Establissement Francais de L'Afrique Occidentale au xviii* siècle (Paris: privately printed, 1906), 120.

30. Journal entries, Feb. 7–9, 1778, in Boss, Journal of the *Marlborough*.

31. Journal entry, Feb. 9, 1778, in ibid.

32. See A. J. Marsh, "The Taking of Gorée, 1758," *Mariner's Mirror* 51 (May 1965): 117–30; Dull, *French Navy*, 116.

33. Searing, *West Africa Slavery and Atlantic Commerce*, 197.

34. Ibid., 226n60. See also Eltis, Lovejoy, and Richardson, "Slave-Trading Ports," 18-19, table I (Gorée shipped the eighth-most African captives from Upper Guinea, at just 2.9 percent of the total; its "role in the slave trade has sometimes been exaggerated").

35. Thomas, *Slave Trade*, 337; Sparks, *Where the Negroes Are Masters*, 252.

36. Journal entry, Feb. 9, 1778, Journal of the *Marlborough*, in Crawford et al., eds., *Naval Documents*, appendix C, 12:818. For the Continental navy frigate *Raleigh* and ship *Alfred* visiting Gorée in early February 1778, see Muster Book of Continental Navy Frigate *Raleigh*, Feb. 2, 1778, entries, in ibid., appendix A, 807 (several sailors from the prize sloop *Granville* enlisted on February 2); *London Chronicle*, May 21–23, 1778, in ibid., 739, 739n1.

37. Eltis, Lovejoy, and Richardson, "Slave-Trading Ports," 18-19, table I.

38. Captain Heatley Testimony, 1788 or 1789, in *Report of the Lords*, Part 1.

39. See Machat, *Documents sur les establishments français de l'Afrique Occidentale*, 121-24. The French reported in early 1779, probably with some exaggeration, that James Fort had fifty cannon. Ibid.

40. See McBurney, *Rhode Island Campaign*, 70-73.

41. John Blondfield to American Commissioners in France, May 8, 1778, in Crawford et al., eds., *Naval Documents*, 12:680. The governor was Alexandre-Davis-Arméry de Paradis, governor of Senegal from 1777–78. See ibid., 680n6; Machat, *Documents sur les Establisse-ment Francais de L'Afrique Occidentale*, 120-24.

42. American Commissioners in France to Captain T. Thompson, Nov. 25, 1777, in Crawford et al., eds., *Naval Documents*, 10:1026.

43. Committee for Foreign Affairs to the American Commissioners in France, Dec. 2, 1777, in ibid., 651.

44. See Muster Book of the Continental Navy Frigate *Raleigh*, Feb. 2, 1778, entries, in ibid., appendix A, 798-99, 807; *London Chronicle*, May 21–23, 1778.

45. Captain T. Pringle to Vice Admiral J. Young, March 18, 1778, in Crawford et al., eds., *Naval Documents*, 11:708; ibid., 9:46n2, 3; Fowler, *Rebels Under Sail*, 134; "*Raleigh* I (Frigate), 1776–1778," Naval History and Heritage Command, https://www.history.navy.mil/research/histories/ship-histories/danfs/r/raleigh-i.html.

46. See *Lloyd's Evening Post*, Feb. 20–23, 1778, in Crawford et al., eds., *Naval Documents*, 11:1035; *Daily Advertiser* (London), Feb. 23, 1778; *London Evening Post*, Feb. 21–24, 1778. See also Desmarais, *Revolutionary War at Sea*, 2:300 (collecting US newspaper sources).

47. Journal entries, Feb. 9–16, 1778, in Boss, Journal of the *Marlborough*.

48. Searing, *West Africa Slavery and Atlantic Commerce*, 95.

49. Journal entry, Feb. 17, 1778, Journal of the *Marlborough*, in Crawford et al., eds., *Naval Documents*, appendix C, 12:818-19.

50. See Journal entry, Feb. 23, 1778, in ibid., 821.

51. This legal point was reiterated in a maritime case involving Captain Babcock. On August 19, 1781, the *General Mifflin*, under Babcock's command, seized a prize, the small brig *Brunette*, with a Dutch captain bound for Ireland. In subsequent admiralty proceedings in Massachusetts, the jury determined that the vessel was owned by Dutchmen, and so the vessel was not a valid prize, but that the valuable wine and other cargo found on board was British property intended for Ireland, and so such cargo was properly seized. See depositions and other records in George Waite Babcock v. The Brigantine *Brunette*, 1781, Massachusetts, Maritime Court for the Middle District, filed Feb. 23, 1780, in Revolutionary War Prize Cases: Records of the Court of Appeal in Case of Capture, 1776–1787, M162, RG267, National Archives, Washington, DC. The jury's verdict was affirmed on appeal in Philadelphia on August 4, 1781. Ibid. The *Brunette* case is summarized in detail in Hulbert, *Untold War at Sea*, 127-34.

52. The estimate of the date is based on a letter Captain Moore wrote to Richard Miles, the governor of Cape Coast Castle, dated January 9, 1777. William Moore (captain of the *St. George*) to Richard Miles, Jan. 9, 1777, Records of the Royal African Companies, Richard Miles Letter Book, 1776–1777, T70-1534, British National Archives, Kew Gardens, England.

53. See appendix C, no. 7.

54. *Jamaica Gazette*, May 9, 1778, in Crawford et al., eds., *Naval Documents*, 12:318.

55. Journal entry, Feb. 18, 1778, Journal of the *Marlborough*, in ibid., 821.

56. Ibid. As with other journal entries when the *Marlborough* was at sea, this one went from noon (on February 18) to noon (on February 19).

57. See Accounts of Trade on the African Coast, 1774–1775, in Donnan, ed., *Documents of the Slave Trade*, 3:281.

58. Journal entry, Feb. 25, 1778, Journal of the *Marlborough*, in Crawford et al., eds., *Naval Documents*, appendix C, 12:822.

59. Journal entry, Feb. 18, 1778, Journal of the *Marlborough*, in ibid., 821.

CHAPTER SEVEN: THE ATTACK ON THE ISLES DE LOS

1. Journal entry, Feb. 19, 1778, in ibid., 819-20.

2. Silvester Meinrad Xavier Golberry, *Travels in Africa [. . .]*, 2 vols., 2nd ed. (London: Jones and Bumford, 1808), 1:167.

3. Bruce L. Mouser, "Iles de Los as Bulking Center in the Slave Trade, 1750–1800," in *Revue Française d'Histoire d'Outre-mer*, tome 83, n313, 4e trimestre (1996), 79.

4. Sparks, *Where the Negroes Are Masters*, 253.

5. For what may be the best description of how a slave fort or factory worked, see the description of the slave trading fort at Bance Island, in Hancock, *Citizens of the World*, 172-220, particularly 192-95 and 198-203. Bance Island had perhaps the largest British slave trading post in Upper Guinea. Prior to the outbreak of the American Revolutionary War, the British fort at Bance Island employed 35 whites and 142 grumettas. By 1778, as a con-

sequence of the war, only 17 whites were employed at the post (the number of grumettas was not stated). Ibid., 193 and 214.

6. Les États de L'Enterprise Barber, undated (around 1784), in annex to Yvan Debbasch, "L'Espace du Sierra Leone et La Politique Francaise de Traite a La Fin de L'Ancien Regime," in *De la Traite àL'Esclavage: du V au XVIII Siècles. Actes du Colloque International sur la traite des Noirs, Nantes 1985*, ed. Serge Daget, vol. 1, 205-12 (Nantes, France: Centre de Recherche sur L'Histoire du Monde Atlantique, 1988), 209; Joseph Hawkins, *A History of a Voyage to the Coast of Africa and travels into the interior of that country: containing particular descriptions of the climate and inhabitants, and interesting particulars concerning the slave trade*, 2nd ed. (Troy, NY: Luther Pratt, 1797), 81-82.

7. Mouser, "Iles de Los," 84n16 (citing a 1779 source).

8. Eltis, Lovejoy, and Richardson, "Slave-Trading Ports," 18, table 1.

9. *Lloyd's List*, Sept. 23, 1777 (*Charlotte*), April 19, 1776 (*Sally*).

10. See appendix B, nos. 2 and 5.

11. See appendix C, no. 37.

12. Les États de L'Enterprise Barber, undated (around 1784), in annex to Yvan Debbasch, "L'Espace du Sierra Leone et La Politique Francaise de Traite," 211 While the French report stated that Barber had initially entered into an agreement with King Tom in 1754, this seems unlikely, since Miles Barber at that time was just twenty-one and was not known to have started trading in slaves yet. Barber was in a better position to invest in African slave voyages after he acquired, at age twenty-five, a moderate inheritance from his deceased father. See Elder, *Slave Trade of Lancaster*, 149. For more on Barber, see ibid., 147-50. It seems more likely that Barber, working through his white agents and ship captains, entered into an agreement with King Tom at a later time, perhaps around 1763, after the end of the Seven Years' War. The first slave ship Barber financed that used the Isles de Los as the principal place of purchasing African captives departed England in August 1763. See TSTD, www.slavevoyages.org/voyage/search (voyage no. 91108). Barber financed his first slave voyage, when he was one of five co-investors, in 1758. Ibid. (voyage no. 17434). See also Jonathan Huddleston, *And the Children's Teeth Are Set on Edge, Adam Hodgson & the Razing of Caton Chapel* (self-published, PDF, 2nd. ed., 2011), 122.

13. See Mouser, "Iles de Los," 88. See also Hancock, *Citizens of the World*, 202 ("The kings and their chiefs set rents for which Bance Islanders paid for permission to trade" enslaved captives).

14. Journal entry, Dec. 11, 1773, Henry Smeathman's Journal, Book 1, MS D.26, no. 3, University of Uppsala Library, Uppsala, Sweden,

15. In 1775 and 1776, Woodville had commanded his first slave voyage, working for Miles Barber, Samuel Sandys, and James Kendall of Liverpool. On this voyage, Woodville had stopped at the Isles de Los, where Miles Barber had his factory. See TSTD, www.slavevoyages.org/voyage/search (voyage no. 91911). Woodville commanded another voyage to Africa, leaving Britain in late 1776 and departing Africa in 1777. See ibid. (voyage no. 92454). He likely visited the Isles de Los on this voyage too, based on the title of the map, *The Volcanic Islands Named Ilhas Dos Idolos and by the English and French Sailors Isles de Loss, Surveyed by Mr. Wm. Woodville 1777*. Woodville and his slave ship the *Hero* were captured on the return voyage to Britain, probably by an American privateer sometime in April 1777. See appendix B, no. 17. Woodville is also listed in 1775 as a bankrupt Liverpool slave merchant, which may have spurred him to engage in commanding slave ships. See appendix E.

16. *Volcanic Islands Named Ilhas Dos Idolos*, cited in previous note. The map was first published in *The African Pilot*, a collection of maps of the African coast, in 1794, and in *Woodfall's Register*, June 11, 1789. An 1804 edition of the *African Pilot* is held by the Library of

Congress in its Geography and Reading Room. See *The African Pilot, Being a Collection of New and Accurate Charts, on a Large Scale, of the Coasts, Islands, and Harbors of Africa* (London: Robert Laurie and James Whittle, 1804), in G2446, .P5L37, 1804.

17. Journal entry, Dec. 10, 1773, Henry Smeathman's Journal, Book 1, MS D.26, envelope 2, no. 3, University of Uppsala Library.
18. Golberry, *Travels in Africa*, 169-70.
19. Hancock, *Citizens of the World*, 193. The owners of Bance Island, in a 1752 letter to the Board of Trade, wrote that Bance Island had "dwelling houses, warehouses, slave houses, shops, magazines & other conveniences sufficient for all the trade that can be carried on at that settlement." Ibid., 190n45. In a 1749 report for the British fort at Cape Coast Castle in what is now Ghana, fourteen occupations performed by Africans were listed. William St. Clair, *The Door of No Return: The History of Cape Coast Castle and the Atlantic Slave Trade* (New York: BlueBridge, 2007), 134-35.
20. Kenneth Morgan, "Liverpool Ascendant: British Merchants and the Slave Trade on the Upper Guinea Coast, 1701–1808," in *Slavery, Abolition and the Transition to Colonialism in Sierra Leone*, eds. Paul E. Lovejoy and Suzanne Schwarz, 29-50 (Trenton, NJ: Africa World Press, 2014), 40; Rawley and Brehrendt, *Transatlantic Slave Trade*, 235.
21. Les États de L'Enterprise Barber, undated (probably around 1784), in annex to Yvan Debbasch, "L'Espace du Sierra Leone et La Politique Francaise de Traite," 209-12. This French intelligence report has been used as a primary source for a published work only in Mouser, "Iles de Los," 86. The above summary of this report is the most detailed in print. The author of this report could have been Golberry.
22. Hancock, *Citizens of the World*, 189.
23. Morgan, "Liverpool Ascendant," 42-43, table 2.2 (using TSTD, www.slavevoyages.org).
24. Journal entry, Feb. 19, 1778, Journal of the *Marlborough*, in Crawford et al., eds., *Naval Documents*, appendix C, 12:820.
25. Boss's log does not clarify if the *Marlborough* sailed to the east side of Isle de Kassa (facing mainland Africa) or the west side (facing Crawford Island). It is assumed that the *Marlborough* sailed to the east side to an area labeled "the Port" on William Woodville's map of Isle de Kassa. The author of the most authoritative article on the Isles de Los writes that "Ocean-worthy vessels often anchored" on the west side of the island, while long boats working on the African coast used the east side of the island. Mouser, "Iles de Los," 87. Woodville's map shows that Isle de Kassa is very narrow at the place where Barber kept his factory.
26. Journal entry, Feb. 20, 1778, Journal of the *Marlborough*, in Crawford et al., eds., *Naval Documents*, appendix C, 12:820.
27. Journal entries, Feb. 20 and 28, 1778, in ibid., 820, 823.
28. Journal entry, Feb. 20, 1778, in ibid., 820.
29. See, for example, Lords Commissioners to Captain William Cornwallis of the *Pallas*, Nov. 11, 1775, in ibid., 3:365; Lord Commissioners to Captain J. Stott of the *Minerva*, Feb. 11, 1777, in ibid., 8:580.
30. Journal entry, Feb. 20, 1778, Journal of the *Marlborough*, in ibid., appendix C, 12:820.
31. Ibid.
32. Journal entry, Feb. 20, 1778, in ibid., 820.
33. Journal entry, Feb. 21, 1778, in ibid., 821.
34. Ibid. In the journal entry, the names of the two men are spelled "T. Hereford and Stephen Harmond." For Hereford's joint ventures with Liverpool merchants, see Morgan, "Liverpool Ascendant," 42-43, table 2.2 (using TSTD, www.slavevoyages.org). An unidentified New England merchant captain sold more than 1,100 gallons of rum, as well as tobacco and gunpowder, to Hereford at the Isles de Los in January and February 1775, which

296 | *Notes to Pages 117–121*

Hereford must have used to purchase African captives for the 1775 voyage. The same merchant sold more than 500 gallons of rum to Stephen Hammond in March 1775, some at the Rio Pongo River and the rest at the Isles de Los. See Accounts of Trade on the African Coast, 1774–1775, in Donnan, ed., *Documents of the Slave Trade*, 3:281, 283. The same merchant purchased seventeen African captives from the Isles de Los from January to March 1775 on six different days. Ibid., 282.

35. See the correspondence in the Paul Cross Papers, South Caroliniana Library, University of South Carolina, Columbia, including John Cross to Paul Cross, Dec. 4, 1783, in which Paul's brother John encourages Paul to come stay at Beaufort, South Carolina, where John had leased a house. The University of South Carolina's South Caroliniana Library, which holds the Paul Cross Papers, states that Paul Cross resided in Charleston at some point in the early 1770s. See description of manuscript, not dated, circa 1770s, Memorandum Book, ibid.

36. Journal entry, March 13, 1778, Journal of the *Marlborough*, in Crawford et al., eds., *Naval Documents*, appendix C, 12:827. Boss did not mention Paul Cross until after the *Marlborough* had departed the Isles de Los, but Boss mentioned that Cross came aboard the American privateer as a pilot at the Isles de Los. Journal entry, March 11, 1778, ibid., 826. Cross is sometimes described as an Englishman, but Boss's journal indicates he was an American.

37. Kelley, *Voyage of the Slave Ship* Hare, 79.

38. See, for example, Stephen Hammond to Paul Cross, not dated but from the 1770s, in Paul Cross Papers, South Caroliniana Library, University of South Carolina; P. Hughes to Paul Cross, April 16, 1780, in ibid. (mentioning that Thomas Hereford was dead).

39. Journal Entry, Feb. 21, 1778, Journal of the *Marlborough*, in Crawford et al., eds., *Naval Documents*, appendix C, 12:821.

40. Ibid.

41. Sparks, *Where the Negroes Are Masters*, 42.

42. Ibid., chs. 1-2, 4-6.

43. Journal entry, Feb. 22, 1778, Journal of the *Marlborough*, in Crawford et al., eds., *Naval Documents*, appendix C, 12:821. From February 22–24, when the New Englanders were on land, Boss kept his journal using regular time, from midnight to midnight.

44. Journal entry, Feb. 23, 1778, in ibid.

45. Journal entry, Feb. 24, 1778, in ibid.

46. Ibid., 821-22.

47. Journal entries, Feb. 24–25, 1778, in ibid., 822.

48. Journal entry, Feb. 25, 1778, in ibid. In his February 25 entry, Boss reverted back to keeping time from noon to noon.

49. The *Pearl* was owned by William Gregson, Joseph Bridge, and Robert Gutside of Liverpool. See TSTD, www.slavevoyages.org/voyage/search (voyage no. 92451). Because the *Pearl* was not known ever to have been used in a slave trading voyage, it is not included in the chart in appendix B, but it is included in appendix B at the end under Seizures of Produce Vessels Not Included in the above Chart. The *Pearl* did complete a slave trading voyage in 1774, under a Captain Poultney, but there are no details of this voyage that would tie it to Brancker's vessel. TSTD, www.slavevoyages.org/voyage/search (voyage no. 24747).

50. See Muster Roll for the Brigantine Pearl, in Registry of Shipping and Seamen: Agreements and Crew Lists, Series I, Port of Registry: Liverpool, BT98/37, 139, British National Archives.

51. *Gazetteer and New Daily Advertiser* (London), Jan. 24, 1778; *London Chronicle*, Jan. 22–24, 1778.

52. See main text in chapter 6 accompanying note 46 and "Seizures of Produce Vessels" in appendix C.

53. See Muster Roll for the Brigantine Pearl, in Registry of Shipping and Seamen: Agreements and Crew Lists, Series I, Port of Registry: Liverpool, BT98/37, 139, British National Archives.

54. See TSTD, www.slavevoyages.org/voyage/search (voyages nos. 92465, 80251, 81852, 81026, 82813, 8099, 81000). See also *London Courant*, May 11, 1780; *Morning Chronicle* (London), May 13, 1780; *Public Advertiser* (London), Feb. 17, 1782, and Oct. 2, 1783.

55. See Donnan, ed., *Documents of the Slave Trade*, 2:644, 655, 655n4.

56. Journal entry, Feb. 25, 1778, in Crawford et al., eds., *Naval Documents*, appendix C, 12:822.

57. Journal entries, Feb. 25–27, 1778, in ibid.

58. Journal entries, Feb. 26–27, 1778, in ibid., 822-23.

59. Silas Daggett Declaration, Oct. 24, 1818, Silas Daggett, Massachusetts, Revolutionary War Pension Application, National Archives.

60. See Jan Parmentier, "The Sweets of Commerce: The Hennesys of Ostend and Their Network in the Eighteenth Century," in *Irish and Scottish Mercantile Networks in Europe and Overseas in the Seventeenth and Eighteenth Centuries*, eds. David Dickson, Jan Parmentier, and Jane Ohlmeyer, 67-92 (Gent, Belgium: Academia Press, 2007), 83; Thomas M. Truxes, *Irish-American Trade, 1660–1783* (Cambridge: Cambridge University Press, 1988), 45, 87, 185.

61. See Truxes, *Irish-American Trade*, 60.

62. Quoted from the *Jamaica Gazette* (Kingston, Jamaica), May 9, 1778, in Crawford et al., eds., *Naval Documents*, 12:318. The *Jamaica Gazette* mistakenly referred to the company as "Andrew, French," but it was actually named after partner Andrew French. See Parmentier, "The Sweets of Commerce," in *Irish and Scottish Mercantile Networks*, 83; Truxes, *Irish-American Trade*, 47, 87 185.

63. Barber traded with James Kendall, Andrew White, and Samuel Sandys of Liverpool. Kendall, White, and Sandys, without Barber, also sent slave ships to the Isles de Los. See Morgan, "Liverpool Ascendant," 42-43, table 2.2 (using TSTD, www.slavevoyages.org).

64. See appendix E, which lists Miles Barber, James Kendall, Andrew White, and Samuel Sandys as bankrupts. Miles Barber, "late of Liverpool" and Lancaster, along with his partners James Kendall and Andrew White (who partnered with Barber to sell enslaved people from the Isles de Los) were to appear as bankrupts at Guildhall, London, on three dates in October and November 1777. See *London Chronicle*, Oct. 4–7, 1777; *Daily Advertiser* (London), Oct. 6, 1777; and *Gazetteer and New Daily Advertiser* (London), Oct. 6, 1777.

65. See Machat, *Documents sur les establishments français de l'Afrique Occidentale*, 124, 128n2.

66. Thomas, *Slave Trade*, 341.

67. Benjamin Armstrong, *Small Boats and Daring Men: Maritime Raiding, Irregular Warfare, and the Early American Navy* (Norman: University of Oklahoma Press, 2019), 17-32. For another take on Jones's raid, see Christian McBurney, *Abductions in the American Revolution: Attempts to Kidnap George Washington, Benedict Arnold and Other Military and Civilian Leaders* (Jefferson, NC: McFarland, 2016), 69-71.

68. Journal entry, Feb. 27, 1778, Journal of the *Marlborough*, in Crawford et al., eds., *Naval Documents*, appendix C, 12:823.

69. Journal entry, Feb. 27, 1778, in ibid., 823.

70. Journal entry, Feb. 28, 1778, in ibid.

71. Journal entry, Feb. 27, 1778, in ibid.

72. Journal entries, Feb. 27–28, in ibid.

73. Journal entry, Feb. 28, 1778, in ibid.

CHAPTER EIGHT: THE CAPTURE OF THE *Fancy* "ALL SLAVED"

1. Ship's Log of the *Dolphin, Rising Sun, Fame,* and *William,* June 17, 1795, MSS 828, box 12, folder 2, RI Hist. Soc.; Journal of the Sloop *Mary,* 1795–1796, in Donnan, ed., *History of the Slave Trade,* 3:360-75. See also Kelley, *Voyage of the Slave Ship* Hare, 54-107 (Newport slave ship the *Hare* stopped at numerous places to make private purchases, including from Sierra Leone to the Isles de Los, to Bance Island, and past Cape Mount).

2. Journal entry, March 5, 1778, Journal of the *Marlborough,* in Crawford et al., eds., *Naval Documents,* appendix C, 12:824.

3. Journal entry, March 6, 1778, in ibid. Boss wrote that the *Kitty* mounted "14 carriage guns." Ibid. A British description of the vessel stated the *Kitty* weighed 160 tons and carried "ten 4-pounders." Ibid., 830n65 (citing *Lloyd's Register of Shipping, 1777–1778*). Later, Boss stated four "cohorns and swivel guns" were transferred from the *Kitty* to the *Marlborough.* Journal entry, March 8, 1778, Journal of the *Marlborough,* in Crawford et al., eds., *Naval Documents,* appendix C, 12:825. Thus, in describing the *Kitty* as mounting fourteen carriage guns, Boss may have inadvertently included the four cohorns and swivel guns.

4. Journal entry, March 6, 1778, Journal of the *Marlborough,* in Crawford et al., eds., *Naval Documents,* appendix C, 12:824. The *Kitty*'s voyage is reported in the TSTD. The *Kitty*'s owners were Christopher Butler, Francis Ingram, John Kaye, and Richard Chadwick of Liverpool. The commander of the *Kitty* was reported in the TSTD as Joseph Fisher, while Boss, in his journal, wrote John Fisher. TSTD, www.slavevoyages.org/voyage/search (voyage no. 91909). Because Joseph Fisher commanded several slave trading voyages, I am using Joseph as his first name. See, for example, ibid. (voyages nos. 91780, 91531, 80821).

5. I arrive at this conclusion for several reasons. First, TSTD, www.slavevoyages.org/voyage/search (voyage no. 91909), indicates that the *Kitty* had a crew of twenty-five, the number of men Babcock captured (not including Captain Fisher). A slaver that was a brig typically had a crew of about twenty, and Fisher probably wanted a few more to help handle the ten cannon on his ship. In addition, the fact that Boss did not mention unfree Africans on board the *Kitty* indicates that none of the prisoners were enslaved. Boss typically mentioned how many African captives were captured, since they were treated as property and could be sold for the benefit of him and rest of the *Marlborough*'s crew.

6. See TSTD, www.slavevoyages.org/voyage/search (voyages nos. 91907, 91908).

7. Journal entry, March 6, 1778, Journal of the *Marlborough,* in Crawford et al., eds., *Naval Documents,* appendix C, 12:824.

8. Nathaniel Cutting Journal and Letterbooks, 1786–98, January 7–9, 1790, Massachusetts Historical Society, Boston.

9. Journal entry, March 6, 1778, Journal of the *Marlborough,* in Crawford et al., eds., *Naval Documents,* appendix C, 12:824.

10. TSTD, www.slavevoyages.org/voyage/search (voyage no. 92483).

11. See TSTD, www.slavevoyages.org/voyage/search (voyages nos. 91996, 91997, 91998 [Allanson captain]). There is some evidence that the vessel could have been known as *Fanny.* A vessel was registered as *Fanny* on June 16, 1773. It was issued a letter of marque on May 1, 1777, as *Fanny,* but was described in official privateer records, dated May 15, 1777, as the *Fancy.* See the file on the *Fancy* (voyage no. 92483) in the Schofield Archive, Wilberforce Institute, University of Hull, Hull, UK. See also Letters of Marque: Declarations Against America, 1777–1783, HCA26/60-70, ADM7/317-318, folio 132, microfilm, Archives and Special Collections, Harriet Irving Library, University of New Brunswick, Fredericton, New Brunswick, Canada.

12. TSTD, www.slavevoyages.org/voyage/search (voyage no. 92483).

13. See Letters of Marque: Declarations Against America, 1777–1783, Harriet Irving Library, University of New Brunswick (letter of marque granted, dated May 15, 1777, to the *Fancy*, 167 tons, of the port of Liverpool, William Allanson commander); editor's note, in Crawford et al., eds., *Naval Documents*, appendix C, 12:830n70 (citing *Lloyd's Register of Shipping, 1777–1778*); journal entry, March 6, 1778, in ibid., 12:824.

14. Journal entry, March 6, 1778, Journal of the *Marlborough*, in Crawford et al., eds., *Naval Documents*, appendix C, 12:824.

15. Gomer Williams, *History of the Liverpool Privateers and Letters of Marque with an Account of the Liverpool Slave Trade* (London: W. Heinemann, 1897), 207.

16. TSTD, www.slavevoyages.org/voyage/search (voyage no.92483), states the *Fancy* was 120 tons. The letter of marque that was granted for the *Fancy* said the ship was 167 tons. See Letters of Marque: Declarations Against America, 1777–1783, Harriet Irving Library, University of New Brunswick. *Lloyd's Register of Shipping, 1777–1778* (London: Lloyd's Register Foundation, Heritage & Education Centre, 1778) indicated the *Fancy* was a two-hundred-ton ship.

17. Richard Miles to Company of Merchants Trading to Africa, Cape Coast Castle, April 4, 1778, Records of the African Companies, Inward Letter Books, T70/32, British National Archives ("James Lees, 2nd Mate [of either the *Fancy* or the *Kitty*] will give you the particulars"). The crew size of the *Fancy* was originally thirty-two (TSTD, www.slavevoyages.org/voyage/search [voyage no. 92483]), but only twenty-five crewmen were on board when the *Fancy* was captured. Lees and a few other crewmen were likely on shore engaged in purchasing provisions or more captives.

18. Journal entry, March 7, Journal of the *Marlborough*, in Crawford et al., eds., *Naval Documents*, appendix C, 12:824-25.

19. Ibid., 825. For the amount of rice, see Orders, from George W. Babcock to Francis Bradfield, Captain of the Fancy, March 7, 1778, Gail and Stephen Rudin Slavery Collection, no. 4681, box 16, folder 43, Division of Rare and Manuscript Collections, Cornell University Library, Ithaca, NY.

20. Journal entry, Dec. 10, 1773, Henry Smeathman's Journal, Book 1, MS D.26, envelope 2, no. 3, University of Uppsala Library.

21. Deirdre Coleman, "Henry Smeathman and the Natural Economy of Slavery," in *Slavery and the Cultures of Abolition: Essays Marking the Bicentennial of the British Abolition Act of 1807*, eds. Carey Brycchan and Peter J. Kitson, 130–49 (Cambridge: D. S. Brewer, 2007), 135.

22. Rediker, *Slave Ship*, 81.

23. Kelley, *Voyage of the Slave Ship* Hare, 185.

24. Rawley and Behrendt, *Transatlantic Slave Trade*, 233-34. See also Dr. Andrew Spaarman Testimony, 1788 or 1789, in *Report of the Lords*, Part 1; Hugh Dalrymple Testimony, 1788 or 1789, in ibid.; James Penny Testimony, 1788 or 1789, in ibid.; Major General Rooke Testimony, 1788 or 1789, in ibid. ("there had been two battles fought on the [mainland] during his stay" for the purpose of obtaining slaves, "and was told it was not an uncommon practice"). British Lieutenant Hugh Dalrymple testified to the following: "Another mode by which people of the country are sometimes made slaves is by wandering tribes of Moors who inhabit the north side of the Niger, and cross into Guinea, and make slaves what they can, whom they sell to Europeans. These generally consist of women and children, whom they steal out of the villages while the men are at work in the fields." Ibid.

25. The following summary is based on Venture Smith's narrative, originally published in 1798 in New London. I relied on an edition published in 1835. See Venture Smith, *A Narrative of the Life and Adventures of Venture, a Native of Africa: But Resident above Sixty Years*

in the United States of America, Related by Himself (New London, CT: privately printed, 1835).

26. The details of this voyage are in "Rhode Island Slave Trading Voyages, 1709–1807," in Coughtry, *Notorious Triangle*, 25, and TSTD, www.slavevoyages.org/voyage/search (voyage no. 36067).

27. Journal entries, March 7 and 14, 1778, Journal of the *Marlborough*, in Crawford et al., eds., *Naval Documents*, appendix C, 12:825, 828. On March 14, Boss stated that the *Marlborough* carried twenty-seven enslaved people, but before then Babcock had sent several of them to the *Fancy*.

28. Journal entries, March 7–8, 1778, in ibid., 825.

29. Journal entry, March 8, 1778, in ibid.

30. Ibid.

31. Journal entries, March 8-9, in ibid.

32. See Sparks, *Where the Negroes Are Masters*, 255; Kelley, *Voyage of the Slave Ship* Hare, 75-76.

33. Accounts of Slaves Purchased, 1771–1772, Paul Cross Papers, South Caroliniana Library, University of South Carolina; Sean Kelley, "The Dirty Business of Panyarring and Palaver: Slave Trading on the Upper Guinea Coast in the Eighteenth Century," in *Slavery, Abolition and the Transition to Colonialism in Sierra Leone*, eds. Paul E. Lovejoy and Suzanne Schwarz, 90-107 (Trenton, NJ: Africa World Press, 2014), 40 (citing the Paul Cross Papers).

34. When the two-hundred-ton *Apollo* was taken by an American privateer with 296 African captives on board, a physician was listed as a crew member. Protest of Andrew Smith and Others, Antigua, Feb. 20, 1777, Secretaries of State, State Papers Foreign, France, Lord Stormont, SP78/302, f.229, British National Archives.

35. Certificate to Dr. John Anderson for three prime slaves from George W. Babcock, March 9, 1778, box 1, folder 22, Ralph Carpenter Collection, Redwood Library and Athenaeum, Newport, RI.

36. Journal entries, March 9–10, 1778, Journal of the *Marlborough*, in Crawford et al., eds., *Naval Documents*, appendix C, 12:825. Boss never gives Dr. Anderson's name in the ship's logs. Anderson's name is only found in the March 9 agreement cited in the previous note.

37. Journal entry, March 10, 1778, in ibid.

38. Ibid.

39. Journal entry, March 11, 1778, in ibid.

40. D. H. Lamb, "Volume and Tonnage of the Liverpool Slave Trade 1772–1807," in *Liverpool, the African Slave Trade, and the Abolition: Essays to Illustrate Current Knowledge and Research*, eds. Roger Anstey and Paul Hair, 91-112 (Liverpool: Historic Society of Lancashire and Cheshire, 1976), 103.

41. Berry, *Path in the Mighty Waters*, 21-22.

42. Journal entry, March 11, 1778, Journal of the *Marlborough*, in Crawford et al., eds., *Naval Documents*, appendix C, 12:826.

43. Ibid.

44. Ibid.

45. Journal entry, March 12, 1778, in ibid., 827.

46. TSTD, www.slavevoyages.org/voyage/search (voyage nos. 91666, 91815, 91947, 92528); Huddleston, *And the Children's Teeth are Set on Edge*, 168, 185-86.

47. Journal entry, March 12, 1778, Journal of the *Marlborough*, in Crawford et al., eds., *Naval Documents*, appendix C, 12:827.

48. Journal entry, March 12, 1778, in ibid. Babcock also left behind the sloop's small boat. Ibid.

49. Quoted in Kelley, *Voyage of the Slave Ship* Hare, 80 (citing Paul Cross Papers).

50. Journal entry, March 13, 1778, Journal of the *Marlborough*, in Crawford et al., eds., *Naval Documents*, appendix C, 12: 827-28.

51. See, for example, Sparks, *Where the Negroes Are Masters*, ch. 2.

52. Journal entry, March 14, 1778, Journal of the *Marlborough*, in Crawford et al., eds., *Naval Documents*, appendix C, 12:828.

53. Ibid.

CHAPTER NINE: THE FATES OF THE *Fancy, Pearl, Kitty,* AND *Betsey,* AND THEIR CAPTIVE AFRICANS

1. Eltis and Richardson, *Atlas of the Transatlantic Slave Trade*, 160.

2. Donald G. Shomette, *Privateers of the Revolution: War on the New Jersey Coast, 1775–1783* (Atglen, PA: Schiffer, 2016), 78-79. Loyalist privateers began illegally operating out of Antigua and other British-controlled Caribbean islands in 1777. One British privateer, also named *Marlborough*, arrived at British-controlled Newport in 1779. Ibid.

3. This report was repeated in the *London Chronicle,* Aug. 6, 1778, in Crawford et al., eds., *Naval Documents*, 12:318, and in the *London Evening Post*, Aug. 6, 1778.

4. See also *Daily Advertiser* (London), Aug. 18, 1778 ("Liverpool, Aug. 14. The *Pearl*, Brancker, belonging to this Port, who was taken upon the Coast of Africa, is retaken and carried into Jamaica"); *St. James's Chronicle* (London), Aug. 18, 1778 (repeating report).

5. *General Evening Post* (London), Sept. 19, 1778; Muster Roll for the Brigantine *Pearl*, in Registry of Shipping and Seamen: Agreements and Crew Lists, Series I, Port of Registry: Liverpool, BT98/37, 139, British National Archives (Brancker arrived back at Liverpool on Sept. 15, 1778).

6. *Providence Gazette*, Aug. 22, 1778. The information was received from "a letter from Egg Harbor" and described Holloway as "Capt. Ichabod Holloway." Ibid. See also *Maryland Journal*, Sept. 22, 1778 (repeating report).

7. Memorial from John Henderson and Ichabod Holloway to Continental Congress, Feb. 25, 1779, Continental Congress Papers, m247, r54, i42, v3, f.375, National Archives, Washington, DC. It might have been the case that the admiralty court suspected that the claimants were actually Loyalists. Henderson's and Holloway's memorial was read at a session of the Continental Congress on January 9 and 21, and February 25, 1779. See Ford, ed., *Journals of the Continental Congress*, 13:44, 96, 251.

8. Holbrook, ed., *Rhode Island 1782 Census*, 64.

9. Public Announcement, Jan. 25, 1787, in *Newport Mercury*, March 5, 1787.

10. *London Evening Post,* July 21, 1778; *St. James's Chronicle* (London), July 21, 1778.

11. *London Evening Post,* Aug. 20, 1778; *Morning Chronicle* (London), Aug. 20, 1778; *Public Advertiser* (London), Aug. 20, 1778; *St. James's Chronicle* (London), Aug. 20, 1778.

12. A John Bissell was listed as residing in North Kingstown in 1774. Bartlett, ed., *Census of Rhode Island 1774*, 75. This was probably the prize captain's father. In a 1777 military census, a John Bissell, aged sixty or older, and a John Bissell Jr., aged between sixteen and fifty, were recorded as residing in North Kingstown. Both Bissells were also listed as residing in North Kingstown in 1782, with the father living by himself, and the son in a household of four white people. Holbrook, ed., *Rhode Island 1782 Census*, 14.

13. John Bissell, Jr., Rhode Island, Revolutionary War Pension Application, National Archives; David Bissell Declaration, Oct. 4, 1833, in David Bissell, Rhode Island, Revolutionary War Pension Application, ibid. John Bissell's pension application includes the following: "John Bissell, Junior, while residing in Exeter," was called 'Junior' because his Uncle

John lived there." David Bissell's declaration also stated that he sailed on the *Marlborough*'s second voyage in September 1778 and later on the *General Mifflin* in 1779.

14. Journal entry, March 11, 1778, Journal of the *Marlborough*, in Crawford et al., eds., *Naval Documents*, appendix C, 12:826.

15. Orders, from George W. Babcock to Francis Bradfield, Captain of the *Fancy*, March 7, 1778, Gail and Stephen Rudin Slavery Collection, no. 4681, box 16, folder 43, Division of Rare and Manuscript Collections, Cornell University Library. An image of the orders was initially obtained by the author from the website of Bonham's auction house of New York City. The orders were sold in 2007 as Lot 15291. The author thanks Tim Tezer of Bonham's for pointing out where the online version could be downloaded on Bonham's website and for identifying the current holder of the orders.

16. Ibid.

17. Resolution, April 6, 1776, in Ford, ed., *Journals of the Continental Congress*, 4:259.

18. Edward Hay to Lord George Germain, Feb. 4, 1778, in Crawford et al., eds., *Naval Documents*, 11:285; Journal of HMS *Seaford*, Jan. 18, 1778, in ibid., 157.

19. Kelley, *Voyage of the Slave Ship* Hare, 182; Radburn, "Keeping 'the Wheel in Motion,'" 660-80.

20. Orders, from George W. Babcock to Francis Bradfield, Captain of the *Fancy*, March 7, 1778, Gail and Stephen Rudin Slavery Collection, no. 4681, box 16, folder 43, Division of Rare and Manuscript Collections, Cornell University Library.

21. Journal entry, March 11, 1778, Journal of the *Marlborough*, in Crawford et al., eds., *Naval Documents*, appendix C, 12:826.

22. Orders, from George W. Babcock to Francis Bradfield, Captain of the *Fancy*, March 7, 1778.

23. South Carolina Pre-Federal Admiralty Records on microfilm, M1180, National Archives, Atlanta, do not contain records from the American Revolutionary War.

24. *Lloyd's List*, May 25, 1779; E. Arnot Robertson, *The Spanish Town Papers, Some Sidelights on the American War of Independence* (New York: Macmillan, 1959), 131-32; TSTD, www.slavevoyages.org/voyage/search (voyage no. 31637). Robertson, who reviewed documents captured from the French slaver, wrote that 683 captives were on board.

25. TSTD, www.slavevoyages.org/voyage/search (search Allanson's name under captain's name).

26. Certificate to Dr. John Anderson for three prime slaves from George W. Babcock, March 9, 1778, box 1, folder 22, Ralph Carpenter Collection, Redwood Library and Athenaeum.

27. See Bartlett, ed., *Census of Rhode Island 1774*, 76; Chamberlain, ed., *Rhode Island 1777 Military Census*, 60.

28. Holbrook, ed., *Rhode Island 1782 Census*, 16. In the *Rhode Island Republican* edition of August 28, 1802, the following death notice appeared: "At North Kingstown, the 15th instant, Mrs. Sarah Bradfield, widow of the late Captain Francis Bradfield, in the 79th year of her age."

29. Log of HMS *Portland*, May 5–7, 1778, in British Admiralty Records, Captains' Logs, ADM 51/107, Part 6, British National Archives. See also Crawford et al., eds., *Naval Documents*, 12:294 (quoting part of the ship's log entry). The editors of *Naval Documents of the American Revolution* wrote, "*Suprize* was an Antiguan privateer schooner commanded by James Morres; nothing more is known about *Fansey* [*Fancy*] or the prize." Ibid., 294-95n1.

30. Herbert S. Klein, "Economic Aspects of the Eighteenth-Century Atlantic Slave Trade," 305-06. Klein added, "If such a mortality rate had occurred among young adult peasants in eighteenth-century France, it would be considered an epidemic rate." Ibid., 306. See also

Rediker, *Slave Ship*, 274 (the mortality rate on healthy voyages ranged from five to seven percent).

31. Journal entry, March 7, 1778, in Journal of the *Marlborough*, Crawford et al., eds., *Naval Documents*, appendix C, 12:825.

32. See testimony of John Anderson, 1788 or 1789, in *Report of the Lords*, Part 2. This John Anderson was not the one who was a doctor on the *Marlborough*.

33. See TSTD, www.slavevoyages.org/voyage/search (voyages nos. 91996, 91997, 91998).

34. This summary is based on Olaudah Equiano's narrative, *An Interesting Narrative of the Life of Olaudah Equiano, or Gustavus Vassa, the African*, originally published in 1788 in London and reprinted many times. I relied on *The Interesting Narrative of the Life of Olaudah Equiano, Written by Himself*, ed. Robert J. Allison (Boston and New York: Bedford/St. Martin's, 1995). For an excellent and detailed summary of Equiano's narrative, see Rediker, *Slave Ship*, 108-31. For doubts on Equiano's story of his time in Africa and its continuing usefulness for scholars, see O'Malley, *Final Passages*, 32-34. I independently arrived at the same conclusion as Martin Rediker did that Equiano's narrative is valuable even if he did not personally experience enslavement in Africa and the Middle Passage, in part because he would have spoken with many Africans who had survived being taken captive and endured the Middle Passage. See Rediker, *Slave Ship*, 109.

35. Berry, *Path in the Mighty Waters*, 109.

CHAPTER 10: THE FATES OF THE *Marlborough*, ITS AFRICAN CAPTIVES, AND GEORGE WAITE BABCOCK

1. Kelley, *Voyage of the Slave Ship* Hare, 53-55.

2. Journal entries, May 11, 17, 20, 1778, in Boss, Journal of the *Marlborough*. Brown died at six p.m. on March 20.

3. See Rhode Island Historical Cemetery Commission, Cemetery Database, www.rihistoriccemeteries.org/searchgravesnameonly.aspx (search for Brown, Christopher, 1778). The cemetery is on Scrabbletown Road in North Kingstown. Ibid.

4. Journal entry, June 3, 1778, in Boss, Journal of the *Marlborough*.

5. Journal entries, April 4, 21–24, and May 5, 8, 1778, in ibid.

6. Journal entry, May 11, 1778, in ibid. For William Wallace as prize master, see appendix D.

7. Journal entry, May 12, 1778, in Boss, Journal of the *Marlborough*.

8. See E. Cornell to Gov. W. Greene, June 19, 1778, with List of 36 Prisoners from the *Marlborough* attached, in Admiralty Court Records, 1776–1783, vol. 2, RI State Archives.

9. Journal entry, May 14, 1778, in Boss, Journal of the *Marlborough*.

10. Journal entries, May 24-27, 1778, in ibid. See also Crawford, et al., eds., *Naval Documents*, 12:453 (identifying location as Spry Harbour).

11. Journal entry, May 30, 1778, in Boss, Journal of the *Marlborough*.

12. Journal entry, June 1, 1778, in ibid.

13. Journal entry, April 3, 1778, in ibid.

14. Journal entry, May 28, 1778, in ibid.

15. Journal entry, June 3, 1778, in ibid.

16. Journal entries, June 6–8, 1778, in ibid.

17. Journal entries, June 1–10, 1778, in Log of HMS *Unicorn*, British Admiralty Records, Captain's Logs, ADM 51/1017, Part 6, British National Archives; Extract of a Letter from Yorktown, June 13, 1778, in *Providence Gazette*, June 27, 1778.

18. Journal entries, June 9–10, 1778, in Boss, Journal of the *Marlborough*.

19. Journal entry, June 12, 1778, in ibid.

20. Births, Marriages, Deaths, 1744–1883, vol. 2, 27, Exeter Town Clerk's Office, Exeter, RI; Arnold, ed., *Vital Records*, 5:19; Babcock, *Babcock Genealogy*, 142.

21. See *Massachusetts Spy* (Worcester), June 21, 1778; *Connecticut Journal* (New Haven), June 24, 1778; *Maryland Gazette* (Baltimore), June 30, 1778; Desmarais, *Revolutionary War at Sea*, 3:92, 239 (collecting US newspaper sources).

22. See, for example, *London Evening Post*, July 9, 1778 (*Pearl* and *Fancy*); *General Advertiser and Morning Intelligencer* (London), July 9, 1778 (same); *Public Advertiser* (London), July 9, 1778 (same); *Liverpool Advertiser and Mercantile Chronicle*, July 10, 1778 (same); *London Evening Post*, July 28, 1778 (*Kitty*); *St. James's Chronicle* (London), July 28, 1778 (*Kitty*); *Liverpool Advertiser and Mercantile Chronicle*, July 24, 1778 (*Kitty*).

23. *St. James's Chronicle* (London), July 21, 1778; *Public Advertiser* (London), July 21, 1778; *London Evening Post*, July 21, 1778; *General Advertiser and Morning Intelligencer* (London), July 21, 1778.

24. See Resolution, June 9, 1778, in Council of War Records (Rhode Island), vol. 3, 87, RI State Archives; Christian McBurney, "British Treatment of Prisoners during the Occupation of Newport, 1776–1779," *Newport History* 79, no. 263 (Fall 2010): 1-41.

25. Resolution, June 10, 1778, in Council of War Records (Rhode Island), vol. 3, 88, RI State Archives; Council of War Order for Payment, June 10, 1778, Military Papers of the Revolutionary War, microfilm reel no. 12, RI State Archives (Babcock reimbursed his costs of transporting the prisoners by the state of Rhode Island); E. Cornell to Gov. W. Greene, June 19, 1778, with List of 36 Prisoners from the *Marlborough* attached, in Admiralty Court Records, 1776–1783, vol. 2, RI State Archives. One prisoner was too sick to move so he remained at Barnstable. The prisoners were escorted by Lieutenant Andrew Stanton, of Charleston, Rhode Island, and seven of his men, from the Rhode Island 2nd State Regiment. List of Expense by Andrew Stanton, June 19, 1778, attached to General Cornell's letter, RI State Archives.

26. See McBurney, "British Treatment of Prisoners," 18.

27. For William Wallace and John Brown traveling to Boston, see note at bottom of List of Expense by Andrew Stanton, June 19, 1778, attached to E. Cornell to Gov. W. Greene, June 19, 1778, with List of 36 Prisoners from the *Marlborough* attached, in Admiralty Court Records, 1776–1783, vol. 2, RI State Archives.

28. Resolution, Massachusetts General Court, Sept. 16, 1776, quoted in Donnan, ed., *Documents of the Slave Trade*, 3:78n3 (citing Massachusetts Archives 215, 95-96).

29. Resolution, Sept. 13, 1776, in ibid., 78.

30. Petition of Cuba, a Negro Woman, to the Massachusetts Council, Nov. 21, 1777, in Crawford et al., eds., *Naval Documents*, 10:556-57. Had Chapman followed through on his threat to sell Cuba in Jamaica, he would have violated Congress's ban on Americans conducting business with a British-controlled island.

31. Council Orders, Dec. 3, 1777, in ibid., 557 (citing Massachusetts Archives, vol. 168 [Council Papers]).

32. Resolution, June 1774 session, in Bartlett, ed., *Records of Rhode Island*, 7:251-52.

33. *Providence Gazette*, Sept. 14, 1776.

34. See E. Hopkins to W. Ellery, Nov. 8, 1776, in Crawford et al., eds., *Naval Documents*, 7:84; E. Hopkins to E. Hinman, Nov. 8, 1776, in ibid., 85; see main text in chapter 3 accompanying notes 9-12.

35. See main text in chapter 1 accompanying notes 63-73; McBurney, "American Revolution Sees First Efforts," 153-87.

36. Land Records, vol. 9, 402, East Greenwich Town Clerk's Office, East Greenwich, RI; Bruce MacGunnigle, "Strolling in Historic East Greenwich: The Silas Jones House, 1515

South Rd," in *East Greenwich Pendulum*, Aug. 25, 2018, https://www.ricentral.com/east _greenwich_pendulum/news/local_news/strolling-in-historic-east-greenwich-the-silas-jones-house-1515-south-rd/article_6e5d35fe-a6dd-11e8-a6c8-fbde4b1a7799.html.

37. McManemin, *Captains of the Privateers*, 104.

38. Journal entry, Sept. 20, 1778, in John Linscom Boss, Journal of an Intended Cruise in the Good Ship Marlborough George Wt. Babcock Commander (By God's Permission) Against the Enemies of the United States of America Kept by John Linscom Boss from the Port of Boston, Sept. 13–Dec. 20, 1778, microfilm, Morristown National Historical Park, Morristown, NJ (hereinafter Boss, Journal of a Cruise in the Ship *Marlborough*). The men killed were cook Thomas Stanton and sailor Jesse Thomson. The wounded men were Robert Wheaton, S. Steward, John Larkin, Matt Almy, and Chichester Cheyne. Ibid. The fifteen-year-old Cheyne, who claimed he was a Loyalist, had been a prisoner seized from the prize *John* and, according to him, was forced to enlist on the *Marlborough*'s second voyage. See Nicholas Bell-Romero, "A Series of Unfortunate Events: Chichester Cheyne's Revolutionary War," in the *Journal of the American Revolution*, https://allthingsliberty.com/2016/01/a-series-of-unfortunate-events-chichester-cheynes-revolutionary-war-1778-1783/. Cheyne was later a member of a prize crew on the prize *Elephant*. That ship was subsequently captured by a Scottish privateer and taken to Scotland. Cheyne eventually gained his freedom. Ibid.

39. Excerpt from the *Halifax Gazette*, Sept. 29, 1778, reprinted in the *Massachusetts Spy* (Worcester), Nov. 5, 1778, and the *Boston Gazette*, Jan. 18, 1779.

40. Journal entry, Nov. 4, 1778, in Boss, Journal of a Cruise in the Ship *Marlborough*. One of the prize's prisoners died shortly before the privateer returned to Boston. Journal entry, Dec. 18, 1778, in ibid. The *Marlborough* captured an unidentified brig from Cork in Ireland and bound for St. Kitts. Babcock had his second lieutenant and ten of his sailors sail the prize. Journal entry, Nov. 9, 1778, in ibid. However, there is no record of it returning to the United States, so the prize and its crew may have been captured.

41. Journal entry, Nov. 12, 1778, in ibid. For the most complete description of the battle and capture, see Declaration of Alexander Southerland, and various others, all dated Feb. 15, 1779, to An Appeal from Judgment of Court of Admiralty of the State of Massachusetts Bay, *Geo. Wait Babcock v. Ship* Nancy, Lodged May 19, 1779, Referred to the Committee on Appeals of the Continental Congress, in Revolutionary War Prize Cases-Captured Vessels, Massachusetts, 1779, case no. 47, M162, RG267, National Archives. This source also indicates that the investor group for the *Marlborough* for this voyage included merchant James Godfrey of Taunton and trader Peter Guyer of Boston.

42. Extract of a letter from Capt. James Payne, of the *Lord Claire*, dated Boston, Dec. 22, in *London Chronicle*, Feb. 23, 1779. See also *Gazetteer and New Daily Advertiser* (London), Jan. 30, 1779.

43. Journal entries, Dec. 5–20, 1778, in Boss, Journal of a Cruise in the Ship *Marlborough*; *Independent Ledger* (Boston), Dec. 21, 1778; *Independent Chronicle* (Boston), Dec. 24, 1778; Notice of Libels, *Boston Gazette*, Jan. 18, 1779 (libeling the *Lord Clarke* [should be *Lord Claire*] and merchandise of the *Nautilus*); *Lloyd's List*, London, Jan. 29, Feb. 16, 1779; *Providence Gazette*, Dec. 26, 1778 (the *Marlborough*'s return to Providence).

44. *Providence Gazette*, Jan. 16, 23, 30, Feb. 25, 1779.

45. Committee on Appeals Decree, Aug. 9, 1779, in Smith, ed., *Letters of Delegates*, 13:338, 338n1. See also Resolution, May 12, 1779, in Ford, ed., *Journals of the Continental Congress*, 14:579 ("appeal from the judgment of the court of Admiralty for the State of Massachusetts Bay, on the libel *George Waite Babcock v. Ship* Nancy, was lodged with the Secretary and referred to the Committee on Appeals"); appeal documents cited in note 41 above. With his

earnings from enemy captures, Rathbun purchased a tavern in the village of Little Rest (now Kingston) in South Kingstown in July 1780 and filled it with fine mahogany furniture. Christian M. McBurney, *A History of Kingston, R.I., 1700–1900, Heart of Rural South County* (Kingston, RI: Pettaquamscutt Historical Society, 2004), 30, 67-68, 330. Sadly, on a subsequent cruise on a privateer, Rathbun and his crew were captured off the coast of England and he died shortly thereafter in Mill Prison in Plymouth, England, in July 1782. See Eric Sterner, "Captain John Peck Rathbun: As Audacious as John Paul Jones," *Journal of the American Revolution*, Sept. 6, 2016, https://allthingsliberty.com/2016/09/captain-john-peck-rathbun-audacious-john-paul-jones/.

46. Agency Agreement between George Waite Babcock, Beriah Brown and Peter Guyer (of Boston), March 31, 1779, Beriah Brown Papers, MSS 109, box 4, folder 8, RI Hist. Soc.

47. See John Linscom Boss, Journal of an Intended Cruise in the Good Ship General Mifflin George Wt. Babcock Commander (By God's Permission against the Enemies of the United States of America), Kept by John Linscom Boss, April 8–July 9, 1779, microfilm, Morristown National Historical Park, Morristown, NJ (hereinafter Boss, Journal of the *General Mifflin*). For more on the discovery of this journal, see the acknowledgments to this book.

48. Journal entry, May 1, 1779, in ibid.

49. G. W. Babcock to B. Brown, May 2, 1779, in James N. Arnold, ed., "Selections from Sheriff Brown Papers," *Narragansett Historical Register,* vol. 2 (1883–84), 194, and Beriah Brown Papers, MSS 109, box 4, folder 8, RI Hist. Soc.; Journal entry, May 2, 1779, in Boss, Journal of the *General Mifflin.*

50. Journal entry, May 2, 1779, in Boss, Journal of the *General Mifflin.*

51. Journal entries, May 9–10, 1779, in ibid. See also *Evening Post* (London), June 28, 1779 (giving name of commander as "Lieut. Long"); *Lloyd's List*, June 29, 1779 (same).

52. Journal entry, May 13, 1779, in Boss, Journal of the *General Mifflin.* Samuel Phillips, serving as a lieutenant on the *General Mifflin* on this voyage, wrote the following in about 1805, although he must have misremembered the enemy ship's name as the *Prosper* rather than its real name, *Elephant*: "cruising upon the Banks of Newfoundland, we fell in with the transport ship *Prosper*, mounting 18 guns, 100 troops and 30 seamen, and after an engagement of three quarters of an hour close on board, and killing the captain and 16 men, she struck [her flag] to us." Updike, *History of the Episcopal Church*, 121-22. Boss's journal states that a prize crew of only four men sailed the *Elephant* toward Boston, but that seems too small. Journal entry, May 13, 1779, in Boss, Journal of the *General Mifflin.* British sources state it was fourteen men. *Lloyd's List*, June 29, 1779; *Lloyd's Evening Post*, June 28, 1779.

53. *Lloyd's Evening Post* (London), June 28, 1779; *St. James's Chronicle* (London), June 17, 1779; Extract of a Letter from Portsmouth, July 7, in *London Evening Post*, July 8, 1779; *Lloyd's List*, June 15, 1779.

54. Journal entries, May 16–17, 1779, in Boss, Journal of the *General Mifflin.*

55. Journal entry, May 17, 1779, in ibid. For his May 21 entry, Boss wrote, "At 9 a.m. departed this life John Babcock, after laying ill 5 days of his wounds in his forehead. He was a worthy lad." Ibid. The next day, "the body of John Babcock" was committed "to the watery deep." Ibid.

56. J. Williams to B. Franklin, July 13, 1779, in William B. Willcox, Barbara B. Oberg, and Claude A. Lopez, eds., *The Papers of Benjamin Franklin*, vols. 26-30 (New Haven, CT: Yale University Press, 1987–93), 30:103-04; J. Williams to B. Franklin, July 22, 1779, in ibid., 127-28. See also *Lloyd's List*, June 15, 1779 (the engagement lasted "nine glasses" [probably meaning four-and-a-half hours], and the *Tartar's* captain, Greatrix, was killed); *Independent Chronicle* (Boston), Aug. 5, 1779 (the *Tartar* had its captain and twenty-two hands killed,

besides some wounded; the *General Mifflin* had two men killed) (this information likely was provided by Nathaniel Brown or another officer returning to Boston on the *Tartar*); *Independent Ledger*, Oct. 25, 1779; *Boston Gazette*, Oct. 25, 1779; Samuel Phillips recollections in Updike, *History of the Episcopal Church*, 122 (the engagement lasted two-and-a-half hours; the *Tartar* suffered 23 dead; the *Tartar* had 26 guns, 14 swivel guns, and 162 men, while the *General Mifflin* had 130 men on board, plus 80 prisoners to guard); recollections of Jonathan Mix, in William Phipps Blake, *A brief account of the life and patriotic services of Jonathan Mix of New Haven [. . .]* (New Haven, CT: Tuttle Morehouse and Taylor, 1886), 29–30 (the engagement lasted three glasses [probably meaning three hours]; the *Tartar* lost thirty-four dead and the *General Mifflin* lost five dead, three mortally wounded, and twenty-four slightly wounded).

The *Tartar*'s lieutenant stated that he fought on for two more hours after Captain Osborne Greatrix was killed but was obliged to strike only because his vessel had four feet of water in the hold. The lieutenant concluded that his ship suffered twenty-five dead, including the captain of marines, and "many wounded." Extract of a Letter from Cork, June 6, in *Reading Mercury and Oxford Gazette* (England), July 5, 1779. See also Extract of a Letter from Portsmouth, July 7, in *London Evening Post*, July 8, 1779, and *Northampton Mercury* (England), July 12, 1779.

57. Extract of a Letter from Portsmouth, July 7, in *London Evening Post*, July 8, 1779, and *Northampton Mercury* (England), July 12, 1779 (*Mifflin* sent 220 prisoners to Galway, "and this morning they were all impressed into His Majesty's Service" at Portsmouth); Extract of a Letter from Cork, June 6, in *Reading Mercury and Oxford Gazette*, July 5, 1779, and *London Courant and Westminster Chronicle*, Jan. 19, 1780 (printing letter agreement, dated May 19, 1779, regarding sending prisoners on the *Betsey*, signed by Babcock and the captains of the prize vessels); *Lloyd's List*, June 15, 1779 (the *Betsey*, commanded by its former master, arrived at Galway with the prisoners on board). See also Samuel Phillips recollections, in Updike, *History of the Episcopal Church*, 122 (*General Mifflin* had eighty prisoners on board before the engagement commenced).

58. B. Franklin to J. D. Schweighauser, July 25, 1779, in Willcox et al., eds., *Franklin Papers*, 30:138.

59. A List of Officers and Men's Names & Stations & Shares on Board the Ship *Tartar*, undated, in Beriah Brown Papers, MSS 109, box 4, folder 8, RI Hist. Soc. Boss does not mention Samuel Phillips in his ship's log for the *General Mifflin*, but Phillips is on this list with the rank of first lieutenant on board the *Tartar*.

60. Journal entries, May 23–24, 1779, in Boss, Journal of the *General Mifflin*.

61. Desmarais, *Revolutionary War at Sea*, 4:250 (collecting US newspaper sources).

62. *Independent Ledger* (Boston), July 31, 1780. According to a North Kingstown historian, it was James Eldred, not Nathaniel Brown, who commanded the *Tartar* on its return journey. David Sherman Baker recollections, in Baker, *Historical Sketch*, 20. The North Kingstown historian stated in 1879 that Eldred "sailed triumphantly into the harbor of Boston." Ibid. But the contemporary documents establish that Lieutenant Eldred stayed with Babcock on the *General Mifflin* and that Lieutenant Brown commanded the *Tartar* on its return voyage to Boston. Samuel Phillips also recalled after the engagement with the *Tartar*, "We arrived at Boston with her and a number of prizes." Samuel Phillips recollections, in Updike, *History of the Episcopal Church*, 122. The *Tartar* was refitted and later taken out as a privateer, with Phillips serving as first lieutenant. The Boston privateer took several prizes out of Montego Bay in Jamaica before running aground and having to be abandoned at Martinique. Ibid.

63. Journal entries, July 6–9, 1779, in Boss, Journal of the *General Mifflin*. On July 9, Boss wrote, "we are refitting as fast as possible." At this point, the copy of Boss's journal ends. Boss probably continued with the log on the voyage back to Boston, but it is not part of this microfilm copy.

64. *New Lloyd's List*, Dec. 24, 1779 ("The *Elizabeth*, Folger, from the southern whale-fishery was taken by the latter-end of Sept. last by the *General Mifflin* privateer"); *Public Ledger* (London), Dec. 24, 1779 (same, except noting that the *Elizabeth* was bound for London); *Boston Gazette*, Oct. 25, 1779 (on return voyage from France, the *General Mifflin* took prizes and retook another); John Ash Declaration, Oct. 15, 1832, John Ash, Rhode Island, Revolutionary War Pension Application, National Archives (on voyage back to Boston "we took a vessel laden with sperm oil" and off the Banks of Newfoundland "captured a vessel laden with sugar and salt, which we brought into Boston"); Granville W. Hough, List of Vessels, 1775–1783, American War of Independence—At Sea, www.awiatsea.com/Hough/Hough%20List%20V.html (British brig *Varnet* claimed as the *General Mifflin*'s prize in August 1779). The following claims for pay by crewmen appear to be for this voyage: "Received Feb. 12, 1780, of Beriah Brown, Jun., £250 for and in full of my share in the brig *Elizabeth* and snow *Susannah*, prizes captured by Capt. George Waite Babcock; Edward Smith, his mark," in Arnold, ed., "Selections from Sheriff Brown Papers," 195; Edward Smith receipt for £130 paid by Beriah Brown for all his rights in the prize brig *Beliat*, taken from the enemy by the privateer *General Mifflin*, commanded by George Waite Babcock, Feb. 12, 1780, in ibid.; Clark Hopkins receipt for $510, dated Feb. 9, 1780, for "the late cruise in the Mifflin," in ibid. On August 19, the *General Mifflin* seized a prize, the small brig *Brunette*, with a Dutch captain bound for Ireland. In subsequent admiralty proceedings in Massachusetts, the jury determined that the vessel was owned by Dutchmen and so was not a valid prize, but that the valuable wine and other cargo found on board were British property intended for Ireland and so such cargo was properly seized. See depositions and other records in *George Waite Babcock v. The Brigantine Brunette*, 1781, Massachusetts, Maritime Court for the Middle District, filed Feb. 23, 1780, in Revolutionary War Prize Cases: Records of the Court of Appeal in Case of Capture, 1776–1787, M162, RG267, National Archives. The jury's verdict was affirmed on appeal in Philadelphia on August 4, 1781. Ibid. The *Brunetta* case is summarized in Hulbert, *Untold War at Sea*, 127-34. See also *Lloyd's Evening Post*, Sept. 13, 1779 ("The *Brunetta*, Grablin, from Oporto to Dublin, was taken the 12th ulto, by the *General Mifflin* privateer, and sent for Boston"); *New Lloyd's List*, Sept. 10, 1779 (same).

65. Journal entry, Sept. 7, 1779, in Journal of Seaman Jonathan Carpenter, excerpted in McManemin, *Captains of the Privateers*, 105; *Boston Gazette*, Oct. 25, 1779 (encounter occurred on Oct. 7); Desmarais, *Revolutionary War at Sea*, 4:250 (collecting US newspaper sources); Squier Darby Declaration, Oct. 29, 1832, Squier Darby, Massachusetts, Revolutionary War Pension Application, National Archives; John Ash Declaration, Oct. 15, 1832, John Ash, Rhode Island, ibid.; recollections of Jonathan Mix, in Blake, *Brief account of the life*, 30. Jonathan Carpenter had been captured on the privateer *Reprisal* by a British frigate, imprisoned in England, exchanged on July 22, 1779, and set at liberty in France. He then enlisted on the *General Mifflin* for its cruise from France to Boston. Jonathan Carpenter, Massachusetts, Revolutionary War Pension Application, National Archives.

66. Babcock, *Babcock Genealogy*, 79-80.

67. Declaration of George Fowler, Aug. 30, 1832, in George Fowler, Rhode Island, Revolutionary War Pension Application, National Archives. See also John Ash Declaration, Oct. 15, 1832, John Ash, Rhode Island, ibid. (the engagement with the "British Letter of Marque lasted nearly two hours in which our vessel was very much injured and we lost a number of men; she ran from us").

68. *Boston Gazette,* Oct. 25, 1779.

69. The *Elephant* storeship, with a small American prize crew of about fourteen sailors, was retaken by a Scottish privateer and brought into Greenock, Scotland. *Lloyd's List,* June 29, 1779; *Lloyd's Evening Post,* June 28, 1779; Chichester Cheyne Petition, A.O. 13/97/237-239, British National Archives, quoted in Bell-Romero, "Series of Unfortunate Events." (Cheyne was a member of the prize crew on board the *Elephant* when it was recaptured). The August 5, 1779, edition of Boston's *Independent Chronicle* also reported, "The *Mifflin* had also taken 4 other prizes, one of which we hear is since retaken and carried into Newport." Thus, Babcock and his crew may have lost a second prize to an enemy vessel, just as it was about to reach safety in a New England port. The *Independent Chronicle*'s report was repeated in the Providence newspaper *American Journal and General Advertiser,* Aug. 5, 1779.

70. *American Journal and General Advertiser,* May 24, 1780; G. W. Babcock to B. Brown, May 10, 1780, in Arnold, ed., "Selections from Sheriff Brown Papers," 194. A London newspaper mentioned the capture but likely got the name of the prize wrong. *Public Ledger* (London), Dec. 24, 1780 ("Ship *Holden,* 20 guns, and 75 men, from Jamaica to New York, 500 puncheons of rum, and 50 hogsheads of sugar, is taken 1st May, by the *Mifflin,* Capt. Babcock").

71. G. W. Babcock to B. Brown, May 10, 1780, in Arnold, ed., "Selections from Sheriff Brown Papers," 194.

72. See *Independent Ledger* (Boston), July 31, 1780; Desmarais, *Revolutionary War at Sea,* 5:60, 62, 63, 81, 88, 117 (collecting US newspaper sources); *New Lloyd's List* (London), Sept. 29, 1780 ("*Le Robuste,* Deblois, from Savannah to Antigua, is taken by the *General Mifflin* privateer, and arrived at Boston").

73. Desmarais, *Revolutionary War at Sea,* 5:131, 155 (collecting US newspaper sources).

74. Several of the sailors on board the *General Mifflin* hailed from Exeter and North Kingstown, Rhode Island, as indicated in agreements on their receiving advances on their wages. See agreements on advances between sailors and George Waite Babcock, March 29, 1779 (two) and March 31, 1779 (three), July 12, 1779 (one), Sept. 21, 1779 (two), in Arnold, ed., "Selections from Sheriff Brown Papers," 193-99; agreements on advances between sailors and George Waite Babcock, March 29-31, 1779, Beriah Brown Papers, MSS 109, box 4, folder 8 (four), RI Hist. Soc. Surviving receipts for payments of the shares of the prizes also indicate that four others hailed from Exeter. See Arnold, ed., "Selections from the Sheriff Brown Papers," 193-99 (1883–84) and Receipts of Payments for Service on General Mifflin, by four Exeter men, March 1780, in Beriah Brown Papers, MSS 109, box 4, folder 8, RI Hist. Soc. At least five North Kingstown, South Kingstown, and Exeter, Rhode Island, men who filed applications for Revolutionary War pensions, stated that they served on the *General Mifflin.* See Declaration of George Fowler, Aug. 30, 1832, in George Fowler, Rhode Island, Revolutionary War Pension Application, National Archives; Declaration of Gideon Bentley, Sept. 24, 1832, in Gideon Bentley, Rhode Island, ibid.; Declaration of John Austin, Sept. 30, 1832, John Austin, Rhode Island, ibid. (three months in spring 1779); Declaration of John Ash, Oct. 15, 1832, John Ash, Rhode Island, ibid.; David Bissell Declaration, Oct. 4, 1833, David Bissell, Rhode Island, ibid.

75. Gardner Weld Allen, *Massachusetts Privateers of the Revolution* (Boston: Massachusetts Historical Society, 1927), 149 (commission for the *General Mifflin* dated Aug. 7, 1780, and privateer allowed to proceed to sea on Sept. 11, 1780).

76. Capt. Anthony Gilchrist to his Ship's Owners in Newcastle, Dec. 1, 1780, in *London Chronicle,* March 1, 1781.

77. Ibid. See also *Providence Gazette,* Jan. 10, 24, 1781; *American Journal and General Advertiser* (Providence), Jan. 13, 1781; Captain Thompson of the *Hyaena* to P. Stephens, Jan.

13, 1781, excerpted in *Norfolk Chronicle, or the Norwich Gazette* (England), March 31, 1781; Desmarais, *Revolutionary War at Sea*, 5:181-82, 191 (collecting US newspaper sources).

78. "Raleigh I (Frigate), 1776–1778," Naval History and Heritage Command, https://www.history.navy.mil/research/histories/ship-histories/danfs/r/raleigh-i.html.

79. James Tennant Declaration, Aug. 7, 1832, in James Tennant, Rhode Island, Revolutionary War Pension Application, National Archives.

80. John Niles, *The Life of Oliver Hazard Perry* (Hartford, CT: R. Storrs, 1820), 16-17.

81. *Providence Gazette*, Jan. 24, 1781.

82. Charles H. Lincoln, ed., *Naval Records of the American Revolution, 1775–1788. Prepared from the Originals in the Library of Congress* (Washington, DC: Government Printing Office, 1906), 238 (*Betty*) and 326 (*Happy Return*); McManemin, *Captains of the Privateers*, 107. Holloway had previously commanded the *Betsey* on a privateer voyage from Providence to the Caribbean, returning to Providence in July 1780. *Providence Gazette*, July 29, 1780. James Eldred died at North Kingstown on April 3, 1818, at seventy-eight. *Rhode Island Republican*, April 22, 1818.

83. Holbrook, ed., *Rhode Island 1782 Census*, 8; Lincoln, ed., *Naval Records*, 326.

84. Captain's log, HMS *Danae*, July 16, 1781, quoted in McManemin, *Captains of the Privateers*, 107; *American Vessels Captured by the British during the Revolution and War of 1812, Records of the Vice-Admiralty Court at Halifax, Nova Scotia* (Salem, MA: Essex Institute, 1911), 89; *Stamford Mercury* (England), Oct. 25, 1781; Lincoln, ed., *Naval Records*, 486. For Babcock's letter, see George Waite Babcock to Unknown [probably Nicholas Brown], May 13, 1781, B675 F.3, Vessels, Miscellaneous Letters April 26, 1776–Nov. 23, 1781, Brown Family Business Records, John Carter Brown Library. The Providence investors owned the following shares: John Brown, one-fourth; Nicholas Brown, one-eighth; Joseph Brown, one-sixteenth; Nicholas Power, one-sixteenth. See letter from them to unknown Massachusetts authorities, Aug. 10, 1781, in ibid.

85. *Independent Chronicle* (Boston), Aug. 16, 1781; *Providence Gazette*, Aug. 18, 1781; Massachusetts Privateer Ship *Venus*, commander George Wait Babcock, American War of Independence—At Sea, https://awiatsea.com/Privateers/V/Venus%20Massachusetts%20Ship%20%5bBabcock%5d.pdf. One sailor from Rehoboth, Massachusetts, Jonathan Allyn, reported that while many of his fellow sailors from the *Venus* were exchanged shortly after their incarcerations on prison ships at Halifax, he was "kept prisoner between five or six months, as near as I can recollect when I was released by a cartel and was landed at Portsmouth, New Hampshire." Jonathan Allyn Pension Application, Massachusetts, Revolutionary War Pension Application, National Archives. Joseph Moors of Groton, Massachusetts, another sailor who served on the *Venus* and was captured, recalled that he was confined at Halifax "in a prison ship for some time and then made his escape in a dark and rainy night." Joseph Moors Declaration, Oct. 13, 1832, in Joseph Moors, Massachusetts, Revolutionary War Pension Application, National Archives.

86. Holbrook, ed., *Rhode Island 1782 Census*, 8.

87. Land Records, vol. 9, 484, East Greenwich Town Clerk's Office; MacGunnigle, "Strolling in Historic East Greenwich"; Allen, *Massachusetts Privateers*, 175 (the *Hero* registered with Massachusetts authorities on September 10, 1781, but it apparently did not sail at that time); Lincoln, ed., *Naval Records*, 335 (the *Hero* was registered with Massachusetts authorities on May 28, 1782).

88. *Boston Gazette*, July 15, 1782; An Account from a Passenger, July 5, 1782, in *New Hampshire Gazette* (Portsmouth), July 31, 1782; McManemin, *Captains of the Privateers*, 107-08; Allen, *Massachusetts Privateers*, 175; "Sack of Lunenburg, 'An Elegantly Situated Town,'"

American War of Independence—At Sea, https://www.awiatsea.com/incidents/1782-07-01%20Sack%20of%20Lunenburg.htmlT000068B.

89. *Boston Gazette,* July 15, 1782.

90. See *Boston Gazette,* July 15, 1782; An Account from a Passenger, July 5, 1782, in *New Hampshire Gazette* (Portsmouth), July 31, 1782; McManemin, *Captains of the Privateers,* 107-08; Allen, *Massachusetts Privateers,* 175; *Boston Gazette,* Aug. 5, 1782 (notice of auction for merchandise seized and ships taken); *New Hampshire Gazette,* July 15, 1782 (estimate of £8,000 of property carried off); Desmarais, *Revolutionary War at Sea,* 7:133 (collecting US newspaper sources). For the London newspapers, see, for example, *London Chronicle,* Sept. 21–24, 1782; *London Evening Post,* Sept. 24, 1782; *Morning Post,* Sept. 24, 1782. In Boston on August 9 and August 20, 1782, Babcock signed as one of the bonders for two small Massachusetts privateers. Lincoln, ed., *Naval Records,* 479, 483. One of the privateers was again the *Hero* and the other was named the *Tryall.* Babcock is not listed as commander of either vessel. One of the witnesses to the signatures for the *Hero* was Samuel Phillips, very likely the man from North Kingstown.

91. See Boss v. Babcock, Inferior Court of Common Pleas, Newport, Record Book I 1/2, May Term, 1783 (judgment entered June 20, 1783), 456-57, Rhode Island Judicial Archives, Supreme Court Judicial Records Center, Pawtucket, RI. Interestingly, the dispute was decided by an arbitration panel of Newport merchants Francis Malbone, John Malbone, and George Champlin. The three "referees" submitted their written report to the court, which the court adopted. Boss was described as a "trader" residing in Newport, while George Waite Babcock was described as a "mariner" residing in Boston.

92. Deed of Property, June 29, 1784, by the Estate of George Waite Babcock, in *Inhabitants and Estates of the Town of Boston, 1630–1800 and The Crooked and Narrow Streets of Boston, 1630–1822,* New England Historic Genealogical Society, https://www.americanancestors.org/DB530/i/14226/2007/260079292, reference code 3694. The use of the term "Estate" hints that Babcock may have died, but it is not necessarily so.

93. Deed, Aug. [illegible], 1784, Land Evidence Records, vol. 14b, 85-86, North Kingstown Town Clerk's Office, Wickford, RI.

94. Some writers state that while serving as treasurer of the town of South Kingstown, George Waite Babcock was jailed seven times from 1782 to 1787, on account of the town failing to pay its proper taxes to the state's coffers. For the jailing, see McBurney, *History of Kingston, R.I.,* 69, 86. But this was a different George Babcock, one without a middle name and from a different line of the Babcock family. See Babcock, *Babcock Genealogy,* 47-48 (parents George and Elizabeth Babcock have a son George born in South Kingstown in 1747); Richard Anson Wheeler, *History of the Town of Stonington, County of New London, Connecticut, from Its First Settlement in 1649 to 1900* (New London, CT: Press of the Day, 1900), 218 (see also 213, no. 50, and 215, no. 99); Bartlett, ed., *Census of Rhode Island 1774,* 76 (George W. Babcock residing in North Kingstown) and 84 (George Babcock residing in South Kingstown); Holbrook, ed., *Rhode Island 1782 Census,* 8 (George of South Kingstown and George W. of East Greenwich listed next to each other). George Babcock of South Kingstown died on December 3, 1807, at seventy-two. *Providence Gazette,* Jan. 3, 1807. See also court judgment obtained by Thomas Carpenter against "George Babcock of said South Kingstown Esq. Town Treasurer of said Town," April 23, 1775, in Beriah Brown Papers, MSS 109, box 6, folder 9, RI Hist. Soc.

In addition, Babcock family genealogists sometimes report George W. Babcock dying peacefully in Hopewell, New York, in 1816, but the evidence indicates this was another man. For one thing, the George Babcock who died at Hopewell, in Ontario County, New York, on March 16, 1816, did not have the middle name "Waite" or "Wait." In addition, he was born on July 27, 1749, in Stonington, Connecticut, and hailed from there, not Rhode Island. He married Susanna Sheldon of Ostego County, New York, and the couple must have decided to move there because of her roots in that county. See Babcock, *Babcock Genealogy*, 51-54.

95. Boss, *Boss Family*, 52.

96. Holbrook, ed., *Rhode Island 1782 Census*, 15 (John Boss resides in Newport with his wife and two young children).

97. Boss, *Boss Family*, 53.

98. Ibid., 66. For Boss's official short biography as a member of Congress, see "Boss, John Linscom, Jr.," Biographical Dictionary of Congressmen, http://bioguide.congress.gov/scripts/biodisplay.pl?index=B000650.

99. The prize ship was probably the brig "laden with wine" that arrived at Boston on June 13, 1778, after being captured by the Rhode Island privateer *Blaze-Castle*. *Boston Gazette*, June 15, 1778; J. Brown to G. Washington, July 9, 1778, in Twohig et al., eds., *Washington Papers*, 16:42, 42-43n1. Washington thanked Brown in a note on July 28, but added that the wine had not yet arrived. G. Washington to J. Brown, July 28, 1778, in ibid., 190.

100. Rhode Island Privateer Ship *General Washington*, American War of Independence—At Sea, https://www.awiatsea.com/Privateers/G/General%20Washington%20Rhode%20Island%20Ship%20[Munro%20Talbot].pdf.

101. Rappleye, *Sons of Providence*, 239-40, 304-12.

102. Quoted in *United States Chronicle* (Providence), March 26, 1789. John Brown wrote under the pseudonym "A Citizen," but everyone in Providence knew it was him. Thompson, *Moses Brown*, 196-97.

103. Rappleye, *Sons of Providence*, 226-31, 239-40, 304-12, 317-18; Coughtry, *Notorious Triangle*, 214-15; Jay Coughtry, Guide to the Microfilm edition, in Papers of the American Slave Trade, Series A: Selections from the Rhode Island Historical Society, ed. Jay Coughtry, Part 1: Brown Family Collections (microfilm project, University Publications of America, 1998), 3.

104. Hedges, *Browns: Colonial Years*, 284-85; James B. Hedges, *The Browns of Providence Plantations: The Nineteenth Century* (Providence, RI: Brown University Press, 1968), 16-20, 22-33; Millar, *Early American Ships*, 106.

105. Hedges, *Browns: Nineteenth Century*, 71-72; Millar, *Early American Ships*, 106.

106. Quoted in Coughtry, Guide to the Microfilm edition, in Papers of the American Slave Trade, 3.

107. Ibid.

CHAPTER ELEVEN: AMERICAN PRIVATEERS REDUCE BRITAIN'S AFRICAN SLAVE TRADE

1. See Radburn, "Keeping 'the Wheel in Motion,'" 675-76; Selwyn H. H. Carrington, *The British West Indies during the American Revolution* (Dordrecht, Holland: Foris, 1988), 66; Thomin, "'P' Is for Profit" (online source). See also Herzog, "Naval Operations," 42-48 (focusing on Royal Navy ships disrupting a few American slave traders in Africa).

2. Richard Miles, Cape Coast Castle, to Company of Merchants Trading to Africa, London, April 4, 1778, Records of the Royal African Companies, T70/32, British National Archives. Miles at the time was not sure that the *Marlborough* had departed on its voyage back across the Atlantic. He bragged that if the *Marlborough* instead sailed south to the major British slave fort at Cape Coast Castle, in what is now Ghana, "I think we may promise her a warm reception, provided she only comes near enough in, having now at this castle a much greater force and better disposed towards the sea [with new cannon installed] than has been usual here." Ibid.

3. For the capture of the *Whim*, see appendix C, no. 25. For Thomas Case's bankruptcy, see appendix E.

4. Dennis Conrad, "A Sea Change," Naval History and Heritage Command, https://www.history.navy.mil/content/history/nhhc/research/library/online-reading-room/title-list-alphabetically/s/conrad.html. Dennis Conrad was one of the editors of volume 12 of the *Naval Documents of the American Revolution*.

5. Extract of a Letter from a Gentleman . . ., Sept. 6, 1775, in *Morning Chronicle* (London), Sept. 11, 1775. Another writer gave the following as the reason for the decline of slave ships departing England: "About forty sail of Guinea ships are now laid up, and all that may arrive will be laid up also, for the embargo upon arms prevents any from sailing." Letter from Liverpool, Sept. 1, 1775, in ibid., Sept. 8, 1775. The reference to an arms embargo was to an order issued by the Privy Council on April 5, 1775, limiting the arms and gunpowder British ships could carry, unless proper permission was obtained. The order was issued out of concern that such military supplies might make their way into the hands of the Americans. On August 26, 1775, the British Admiralty announced that it would strictly enforce the order and impose stiff penalties and forfeitures on violators. *The Annual Register, or a View of the History, Politics, and Literature, For the Year 1775*, 4th ed. (London: J. Dodsley, 1783), 19:44. This order presented a problem for British slave ships, beyond the fact that weapons and gunpowder were two major trading goods that British slavers traded for captives with African merchants. British slave ships also typically carried a stash of guns and gunpowder in case they were needed to ward off pirates or other hostile actors on the African coast and, more importantly, to help defeat an insurrection by the captives on the slave ship. Moreover, gunpowder was now needed to defend against American privateers. Reportedly, a few British slave ships ready to sail to Africa were ordered to return to port and remove their arms and gunpowder "for fear any part of them should find its way to the rebels in America." W. Panton to Governor P. Tonyn, Jan. 18, 1776, in Crawford et al., eds., *Naval Documents*, 3:854. On October 27, 1775, the Privy Council modified its Orders in Council and permitted up to fifty barrels of gunpowder to be shipped in a vessel, thus opening the path for British slave traders to continue their voyages to Africa. Modification by Order in Council of Restrictions Against Shipping of Warlike Stores, Oct. 27, 1775, in ibid., 2:782-83. A good description of the Liverpool riots, with copies of contemporary documents, is in Richard Brooke, *Liverpool as It was During the Last Quarter of the Eighteenth Century, 1775–1800* (Liverpool: J. Mawdsley and Son, 1853), 325-48.

6. Intelligence from London, Sept. 25, 1775, in Crawford et al., eds., *Naval Documents*, 2:733.

7. A Petition of the Merchants and Tradesmen of the Port of Liverpool, undated, submitted to Parliament, in Parliamentary Debates, Jan. 25, 1775, in Force, ed., *American Archives*, 4th ser., 1:1532.

8. Nathaniel Bayley's Remarks in the House of Commons Against the Prohibitory Act, Dec. 1, 1775, in Crawford et al., eds., *Naval Documents*, 3:400-01.

9. See Copy of a Letter from Capt. Braithwaite, Sept. 20, 1776, in ibid., 6:607, 607n1; Extract of a Letter from Bristol, Oct. 23, *London Chronicle*, Oct. 26, 1777, in ibid., 7:710. *Rover*, a privateer from Salem, Massachusetts, also captured four British merchant vessels off the coast of Portugal in August 1776. See Syrett, *Royal Navy*, 6.

10. John Cockburn to David Mill, Nov. 30, 1776, Records of the African Companies, T70/1534, British National Archives.

11. G. Pizzoni to his Government in Venice, Sept. 27, 1776 [from London], in Crawford et al., eds., *Naval Documents*, 4:615. See also *Public Advertiser* (London), August 3, 1776, in ibid., 6:524 ("Insurance on Ships from Jamaica for London was done at 20 percent and from the Leeward Islands at 15 percent").

12. Extract of a letter from London to Mr. [Arthur] Lee, Jan. 14, 1777, in ibid., 8:525; American Commissioners in France to the Secret Committee of the Continental Congress, Feb. 6, 1777, in ibid., 8:571; *London Chronicle,* March 15, 1777, in ibid., 678.

13. Extract of a letter from London to Mr. [Arthur] Lee, Jan. 14, 1777, in ibid., 525. See also Patton, *Patriot Pirates,* 135 (during the Seven Years' War, insurance rates only rose to six percent).

14. John Mill to David Mill, London, Aug. 25, 1776, Records of the African Companies, T70/1534, British National Archives.

15. Proceedings in the Lords Respecting the Commercial Losses Occasioned by the American War, Feb. 11, 1778, in Crawford et al., eds., *Naval Documents,* 11:994. For charts showing insurance rates on voyages between the British Caribbean and England during the Revolutionary War, see Carrington, *British West Indies,* 62-63.

16. Testimony of William Creighton, Feb. 6, 1778, Proceedings in the Lords Respecting the Commercial Losses Occasioned by the American War, in Crawford et al., eds., *Naval Documents,* 11:969-71; Testimony of the Duke of Richmond, Feb. 11, 1778, in ibid., 994.

17. Samuel Martin, Whitehaven, to John Dobson, Liverpool, May 23, 1777, Secretaries of State, State Papers Foreign, France, Lord Stormont, SP78/302, f.335, British National Archives.

18. Extract of a Letter from the Gold Coast, November 16, *London Chronicle,* Jan. 19, 1778, in Crawford et al., eds., *Naval Documents,* 10:998, 998n1.

19. See Richard Miles, Cape Coast Castle, to Captain William Chapman, James Fort, Feb. 19, 1778, Records of the African Companies, Richard Miles Letter Book, T70/1479/2, British National Archives, Kew Gardens, England. For the capture of the *Fox,* see appendix C, no. 11.

20. For the capture of the *Hawke,* see appendix C, no. 10.

21. Testimony of John Shoolbred, Feb. 6, 1778, Proceedings in the Lords Respecting the Commercial Losses Occasioned by the American War, in Crawford et al., eds, *Naval Documents,* 11:971.

22. Ibid.

23. Ibid.

24. Testimony of Duke of Richmond, Feb. 11, 1778, in ibid., 994.

25. Williams, *History of Liverpool,* 183.

26. O'Shaughnessy, *Empire Divided,* 166.

27. Radburn, "Keeping 'the Wheel in Motion,'" 679.

28. See appendix E.

29. Radburn, "Keeping 'the Wheel in Motion,'" 675-76.

30. For more on the various complex economic impacts of the war, see ibid., 660-89.

31. Thomas Clarkson, *An Essay on the Impolicy of the African Slave Trade, In Two Parts,* 2nd ed. (London: J. Phillips, 1788), 29.

32. St. Clair, *Door of No Return,* 115.

33. See appendix B, no. 22 (capture of the *Hannah*); Rawley, *London,* 101-03. Dalziel (later in his life spelled Dalzell) commanded four slave voyages from 1783 to 1790, and he was an investor in three more from 1804 to 1807. TSTD, www.slavevoyages.org/voyage/search (voyages nos. 81323, 81632, 83454, 83725, 80964, 81066, 81866). He served for a time as governor of Cape Coast Castle. St. Clair, *Door of No Return,* 88-89.

34. Report of Arthur Piggott, July 3, 1777, in Crawford et al., eds., *Naval Documents.,* 9:459; Sparks, *Where the Negroes Are Masters,* 254; appendix C, no. 9. See also Benedict Der, "Edmund Burke and Africa, 1772–1792," *Transactions of the Historical Society of Ghana* 11 (1970): 12 (Mill's fortune).

35. See Sparks, *Where the Negroes Are Masters,* 116-19, 279n132; appendix C, nos. 12 (*St. George*) and 11 (*Fox*); Ross & Mill to Richard Miles, Oct. 30, 1777, Records of the Royal

African Companies, T70-1534, British National Archives. Ross & Mill was a prominent London slave trading firm.

36. Radburn, "William Davenport" (master's thesis), 28.

37. See appendix B, no. 25 and "Seizures by the Continental Navy."

38. Clarkson, *Impolicy of the Slave Trade*, 129. One observer of the British slave trade wrote in May 1778 that as a result of the Revolutionary War, "the amounts paid for the negroes in Africa were . . . much smaller than in earlier years." Donnan, ed., *Documents of the Slave Trade*, 2:554n2 (citing John Roberts in "Cursory Observations of the Trade to Africa").

39. See testimony of David Dunn, Feb. 14, 1777, in "Minutes of Enquiry into Administration of the West Indian Trade," in K. H. Ledward, ed., *Journals of the Board of Trade and Plantations*, vols. 13-14 (London: His Majesty's Stationary Office, 1937 and 1938), 14:261 (in October 1775, slave ship captain David Dunn purchased captives in Africa for an average of £23 each and sold them at St. Vincent's and Jamaica at an average of £42 each); testimony of Captain Robert Chalmers, March 21, 1777, in ibid., 311 (in October 1775, Captain Chalmers paid on average £23 for each captive in Africa).

40. Richard Miles, Cape Coast Castle, to John Shoolbred, London, Jan. 15, 1778, Records of the Royal African Companies, Richard Miles Letter Book, 1778, T70/1483, British National Archives, Kew Gardens, England. See also Richard Miles, Cape Coast Castle, to Capt. Thomas King, Liverpool, Jan. 15, 1778, in ibid. (Captain Benjamin Cazneau, commander of the British slave ship *John*, "has bought in one month 540 slaves at almost 12 sterling per head"). Cazneau took the two January 15 letters written by Miles mentioned in this note and the two January 15 letters penned by Miles in the next two notes on his voyage to the Caribbean and back to Liverpool. Ibid.

41. Richard Miles, Cape Coast Castle, to Company of Merchants Trading to Africa, London, Jan. 15, 1778, Records of the Royal African Companies, T70/32, British National Archives.

42. Richard Miles, Cape Coast Castle, to Francis Ingram, Liverpool, Jan. 15, 1778, Records of the Royal African Companies, T70/1483, British National Archives.

43. See Richard Miles, Cape Coast Castle, to Company of Merchants Trading to Africa, London, April 4, 1778, Records of the African Companies, T70/32, British National Archives.

44. See Eltis and Richardson, *Atlas of the Transatlantic Slave Trade*, 3. These numbers were first published in David Eltis, Frank D. Lewis, and David Richardson, "Slave Prices, the African Slave Trade, and Productivity in the Caribbean, 1674–1807," *Economic History Review*, n.s., 58, no. 4 (Nov. 2005): 679, table 2.

45. Taking into account the Caribbean as a whole, Eltis and Richardson arrived at the following prices for the following periods: 1770–1774: £43.01, 1775–1779: £43.07, 1780–1784: £44.44. See Eltis and Richardson, "Prices of African Slaves Newly Arrived in the Americas, 1673–1865: New Evidence on Long-Run Trends and Regional Differentials," in *Slavery in the Development of the Americas*, eds. David Eltis, Frank Lewis, and Kenneth Sokoloff, 181-218 (Cambridge: Cambridge University Press, 2004), 181-218. Most of the sales during these periods were to Jamaica, which had higher prices than in the Leeward Islands and Windward Islands. The captain of the slave ship *Sam* sold 208 enslaved people at Barbados on October 18, 1776, for prices ranging from £30 to £35. See Trading Invoices and Accounts, 1773–1783, Voyages of the Ship "Sam," 1774-1781, Papers of William Davenport & Co., 1745–1797, British Records on the Atlantic World, 1700–1900, microfilm, British Online Archives, http://www.britishonlinearchives.co.uk/9781851171767.php. Another observer stated that a British slave ship sold captives from Africa at Grenada in 1777 for £39 and £40 each. Extract of a Letter from Grenada, dated March 30, 1777, in *General*

Evening Post (London), May 29, 1777, and *London Evening Post*, May 29, 1777. In estimating the losses suffered by British merchants in the African slave trade due to American privateers, John Shoolbred in February 1778 calculated the loss based on an average sales price per captive at £35 each. Testimony of John Shoolbred, Feb. 6, 1778, Proceedings in the Lords Respecting the Commercial Losses Occasioned by the American War, in Crawford et al., eds., *Naval Documents*, 11:971.

46. Eltis, Lewis, and Richardson, "Slave Prices," 679, table 2. The price of sugar in the Caribbean from 1770 to 1774 was £36.18, from 1775 to 1779, £45.36, and from 1780 to1784, £49.10. Ibid.

47. Radburn, "Keeping 'the Wheel in Motion,'" 675-76.

48. Quoted in ibid., 677.

49. Extract of a Letter from Grenada, dated March 30, 1777, in *General Evening Post* (London), May 29, 1777, and *London Evening Post*, May 29, 1777.

50. Samuel Martin to John Dobson, May 23, 1777, Secretaries of State, State Papers Foreign, France, Lord Stormont, SP78/302, f.335, British National Archives.

51. Peter Haffey, St. Vincent's, to Unknown, May 5, 1777, in ibid., f.419 (also quoted in Williams, *History of the Liverpool Privateers*, 200-01). Elizabeth Donnan, the great historian of the Atlantic slave trade, wrote, "The information about the price of slaves during the early years of the Revolution is curiously conflicting." Donnan, ed., *Documents of the Slave Trade*, 2:554n2. She became confused with the low prices of African captives sold in French-controlled Martinique in 1777. She did not realize that this pricing stemmed from an oversupply of captives brought to the small island primarily by American privateers that had taken British slavers with African captives on board before they had reached their destinations in the Caribbean.

52. Thomas Clarkson, *The History of the Rise, Progress and Accomplishment of the Abolition of the African Slave Trade, by the British Parliament*, 2 vols. (London: John W. Parker, 1839), 2:222.

53. *New Cambridge Modern History*, 14 vols. (Cambridge: Cambridge University Press, 1957–1979), 7:570. A historian of Bristol, England, stated that after the outbreak of the American Revolution, the trade was virtually suspended. John Latimer, *The Annals of Bristol in the Eighteenth Century* (Bristol, UK: privately printed, 1893), 416.

54. Clarkson, *Impolicy of the Slave Trade*, 29.

55. Richard Miles, Cape Coast Castle, to John Shoolbred, London, Jan. 15, 1778, Records of the African Companies, T70/1483, British National Archives.

56. Extract of a letter from an Officer on board the Snow *Adventure*, Capt. Muir, at Tobago, dated Feb. 27, 1778, in *Daily Advertiser* (London), May 14, 1778. See also TSTD, www.slavevoyages.org/voyage/search (voyage no. 75016) (the 140-ton *Adventure*, sailing from London to the Gold Coast to Tobago, disembarked from Africa with approximately 370 African captives on board).

57. Gilbert Petrie, Tobago, to Richard Miles, Cape Coast Castle, March 31, 1778, Records of the African Companies, Detached Papers, T70/1538, British National Archives. In another part of this letter, Petrie said he had sold at Barbados twenty captives for the "enormous price of £50 sterling per head."

58. Extract of a letter from an Officer on board the Snow *Adventure*, *Daily Advertiser* (London), May 14, 1778. See also TSTD, www.slavevoyages.org/voyage/search (voyage no. 75016). For more on the *Adventure*'s battle, see American Privateers Fail to Defeat British Slave Ships in appendix C.

59. Nicholas Radburn, "The Long Middle Passage: The Enslavement of Africans and the Trans-Atlantic Slave Trade, 1640–1808" (PhD diss., Johns Hopkins University, 2016), 202.

60. TSTD, www.slavevoyages.org/voyage/search (voyage no. 81852).
61. Radburn, "Long Middle Passage" (PhD diss.), 146. An early example of "tight-packing" occurred with a British slaver that arrived at Jamaica in about March 1777. The British newspapers reported, "The Nancy, Capt. Seaman, from the coast of Africa, is arrived at Kingston in Jamaica, with a cargo of 600 slaves on board, the greatest number ever known to be carried to a market in one ship." *Gazetteer and New Daily Advertiser* (London), May 30, 1777; *General Evening Post* (London), May 31, 1777; *Public Advertiser* (London), May 31, 1777. This voyage is reported in TSTD, www.slavevoyages.org/voyage/database (voyage no. 92549). However, in this report, the *Nancy* is recorded as only embarking about 359 captives and disembarking some 327 captives. On the other hand, the report indicates that the *Nancy* was a Liverpool ship weighing 300 tons, thus likely making it able to carry 600 captives. On the *Nancy*'s prior voyage to Kingston, Jamaica, ending in November 1775, Captain Thomas Seaman had departed Africa with about 350 captives on board. See TSTD, www.slavevoyages.org/voyage/seachdatabase (voyage no. 92550) (from Liverpool). Trevor Burnard, in his history of Jamaica, notes the trend toward cramming slave ships with captives as well. "Before the start of the American Revolution, very few ships carried more than six hundred slaves. . . . But ships carrying enormous numbers of slaves became more frequent after 1778." Bernard, *Jamaica in the Age of Revolution*, 177-78.
62. Quoted in Donnan, ed., *Documents of the Slave Trade*, 2:553n3.
63. American Commissioners in France to the Secret Committee of the Continental Congress, Feb. 6, 1777, in Crawford et al., eds., *Naval Documents*, 8:571.
64. Testimony of Alderman Woolridge, Feb. 6, 1778, in ibid., 11:967; Testimony of William Creighton, Feb. 6, 1778, in ibid., 969; O'Shaughnessy, *Men Who Lost America*, 332. See also Crawford, "Privateering Debate," 219-34.
65. See O'Shaughnessy, *Empire Divided*, 165. Selwyn Carrington estimated that sugar exports from the West Indies declined from approximately 2 million hundredweight in 1775, to 1.7 million in 1776, and to 1.4 million in 1777. See Selwyn H. H. Carrington, *The Sugar Industry and the Abolition of the Slave Trade, 1775–1810* (Gainesville: University Press of Florida, 2002), 57, table 2.12.
66. O'Shaughnessy, *Empire Divided*, 163.
67. Extract of a Letter from Grenada, April 18, 1777, in Crawford et al., eds., *Naval Documents*, 8:372.
68. O'Shaughnessy, *Empire Divided*, 163. For more on American privateers disrupting the food supply in British Caribbean islands, see ibid., 163-64; Ragatz, *Fall of the Planter Class*, 153-54.
69. *Independent Chronicle* (Boston), Dec. 26, 1776. See also O'Shaughnessy, *Empire Divided*, 106.
70. Carrington, *Sugar Industry*, 129.
71. TSTD, www.slavevoyages.org/assessment/estimates (using search terms "Flag" and "Only Embarked," and taking into account only British Flag vessels disembarking enslaved Africans at the British Caribbean).
72. Testimony of John Shoolbred, Feb. 6, 1778, Proceedings in the Lords Respecting the Commercial Losses Occasioned by the American War, in Crawford et al., eds., *Naval Documents*, 11:971.
73. Clarkson, *Impolicy of the Slave Trade*, 129, 131. David Macpherson, in 1805, used the same aggregate numbers for each year. David Macpherson, *Annals of Commerce, Manufactures, Fisheries and Navigation, etc.*, vol. 4 (London: Nichols and Son, 1805), 153. The number of total clearances for Africa from 1780 to 1783 was: 1780, 53; 1781, 77; 1782, 69; 1783, 130. Ibid. The documents Clarkson and Macpherson relied on have apparently been located.

The author of a book on London's role in the slave trade found that the number of British ships clearing for Africa fell from 151 in 1775 to a low of 28 in 1779, and that in 1779, London sent out 17 ships, Liverpool 11, and Bristol none. See Rawley, *London*, 34-35. The annual chart of clearances from Liverpool to Africa is also in Williams, *History of the Liverpool Privateers*, appendix 8, 678. Williams writes, "The majority of these vessels were employed in the slave trade, the rest carrying only wood and teeth. For instance, during the period . . . (1783–93) 43 ships carried wood and teeth, while 878 carried slaves." Ibid.

74. Rawley and Behrendt, *The Transatlantic Slave Trade*, 155, table 8.2. Another historian has the average clearances from English ports to West Africa from 1772–75 as 159 and from 1776–82 as 61. Lamb, "Volume and Tonnage," 92. This historian also estimates that average total tonnage of vessels clearing for Africa from English ports to West Africa fell from 17,083 in the period 1772–75 to 7,759 from 1776–82. Ibid., 94. That resulted in a decline of 64.6 percent.

75. See Elder, *Slave Trade of Lancaster*, 170, 189-91.

76. See Patrick McGrath, *Bristol in the Eighteenth Century* (Newton Abbot, UK: David and Charles, 1972), 173. In 1771, 192 ships cleared for Africa, 107 from Liverpool, 58 from London, 23 from Bristol, and 4 from Lancaster. Ibid. Another historian counts a total of 188 clearances for Africa in 1771, from Liverpool, London, and Bristol, but he did not include other English ports such as Lancaster. Lamb, "Volume and Tonnage," 91.

77. Historian Elizabeth Donnan estimates that in 1771, 195 vessels carried from Africa 47,147 enslaved people, for an average of 242 per ship. See Donnan, ed., *Documents of the Slave Trade*, 2:546n2. In February 1778, in calculating the losses of British slave ships with African captives on board captured by American privateers, Shoolbred assumed that each slave ship carried 257 captives.

78. Carrington, *British West Indies*, 67.

79. Burnard, *Jamaica in the Age of Revolution*, 177.

80. Ibid., 176, 206.

81. See appendix D.

82. British slave trade historian Nicholas Radburn recognized that the British slave trade virtually collapsed during the American Revolutionary War. See Radburn, "Keeping 'the Wheel in Motion,'" 675-76. Selwyn Carrington also made this point. Noting the increase in the transatlantic slave trade during the Seven Years' War, he wrote, "There was therefore no significant loss in the number of slaves retained in the [British Caribbean Islands]. . . ." This was not the case in the American [Revolutionary] War and the number of slaves retained declined markedly." Carrington, *The British West Indies*, 66. See also Richard Pares, *Yankees and Creoles: The Trade between North America and the West Indies before the American Revolution* (London: Longman, 1956), 472-73.

83. See appendix D.

84. See Other Captures—By French Colonial Privateers and Other Captures—Intercolonial Slave Trade, at the end of appendix C.

85. See American Privateers Fail to Defeat British Slave Ships, at the end of appendix C.

86. See Stephen D. Behrendt, David Eltis, and David Richardson, "The Costs of Coercion: African Agency in the Pre-Modern Atlantic World," *Economic History Review* 54, no. 3 (Aug. 2001): 454-76.

87. See Jonathan R. Dull, "Was the Continental Navy a Mistake?," *American Neptune* 45 (1985): 169.

88. See main text of this chapter accompanying notes 94-95.

89. Radburn, "Keeping 'the Wheel in Motion,'" 660-80.

90. Ibid., 680. For more on the impact of the credit crisis on British Caribbean plantations, see O'Shaughnessy, *Empire Divided*, 165-66.

91. Radburn, "Keeping 'the Wheel in Motion,'" 675.

92. Carrington, *British West Indies*, 67.

93. Recollections, in Falconbridge, *An Account of the Slave Trade*, 10.

94. *Boston Gazette*, May 5, 1783. The author thanks Michael Thomin for bringing this capture to his attention. For the cessation of hostilities, see Resolution, April 11, 1783, in Ford, ed., *Journals of the Continental Congress*, 24:239-41.

95. Searing, *West Africa Slavery and Atlantic Commerce*, 115.

96. Machat, *Documents sur les establishments français de l'Afrique Occidentale*, 121-24; Golberry, *Travels*, 197-98; Hancock, *Citizens of the World*, 214. Gorée's governor, Alexandre-Davis-ArMény de Paradis, died in October 1778, resulting in Boucher becoming the island's governor. Machat, *Documents sur les establishments français de l'Afrique Occidentale*, 122n2. Golberry's British translator spelled Chevalier de Pontevèz-Guin's last name as Pontdevéze.

97. See Lovejoy, "Forgotten Colony in Africa," 113.

98. Carrington, *British West Indies*, 98-100; Ragatz, *Fall of the Planter Class*, 155-63. The Great Hurricane of 1780 killed some four thousand enslaved people in Barbados alone. O'Shaughnessy, *Empire Divided*, 194.

99. Nettles, "Founding Fathers," 71. See also O'Shaughnessy, *Empire Divided*, 161 (due to food shortages caused by privateers and a severe drought, one in five of Antigua's thirty-eight thousand enslaved people died between 1778 and 1781).

100. Les États de L'Enterprise Barber, undated (probably around 1784), in annex to Yvan Debbasch, "L'Espace du Sierra Leone et La Politique Francaise de Traite," 209-12. In June 1783, Barber purchased a former French frigate in London from the British Admiralty and renamed it *Count du Norde*. He then sent the frigate off on a slave voyage to Africa. By the time the ship left the African coast on May 30, 1784, its captain had purchased an astounding 705 captives, 27 of whom died even before the vessel departed the coast. When the *Count du Norde* arrived at its destination of Charleston, South Carolina, 105 more of the captives had died during the voyage, many from an outbreak of measles. Radburn, "Long Middle Passage," PhD diss., 202-13.

101. Leonardo Marques, *The United States and the Transatlantic Slave Trade to the Americas, 1776–1867* (New Haven, CT: Yale University Press, 2012), 24-27, 44-52.

102. Ibid., 29. Marques also makes a strong case that the D'Wolf family financed more slave trading voyages after 1808, mostly to Cuba. Ibid., chs. 3 and 4.

103. Rawley and Behrendt, *Transatlantic Slave Trade*, 327.

APPENDIX A: OFFICERS AND CREW OF THE *Marlborough*

1. Boss, Dec. 23, 1777 to May 6, 1778, Journal of the *Marlborough*.

2. Orders, from George W. Babcock to Francis Bradfield, Captain of the Fancy, March 7, 1778, Gail and Stephen Rudin Slavery Collection, no. 4681, box 16, folder 43, Division of Rare and Manuscript Collections, Cornell University Library.

3. Certificate to Dr. John Anderson for three prime slaves from George W. Babcock, March 9, 1778, box 1, folder 22, Ralph Carpenter Collection, Redwood Library and Athenaeum.

4. See E. Cornell to Gov. W. Greene, June 19, 1778, with List of 36 Prisoners from the *Marlborough* attached, in Admiralty Court Records, 1776–1783, vol. 2, RI State Archives. William Wallace is mentioned as "prize master" in a note at the bottom of the list of prisoners.

5. David Bissell Declaration, Oct. 14, 1833, David Bissell, Rhode Island, Revolutionary War Pension Application, National Archives ("In December 1777 . . . [I] signed on a pri-

vateer, called the *Marlborough*, commanded by Captain George W. Babcock, they sailed on a cruise, on the 25th of December 1777, and was absent, about nine months, and returned home in October 1778"). David Bissell was the brother of prize master John Bissell. Ibid.

6. Silas Daggett Declaration, Oct. 19, 1818, Silas Daggett, Massachusetts, Revolutionary War Pension Application, National Archives ("In the fall of 1777 went on board of the ship *Marlborough*, Captain George W. Babcock, Esq., commander, proceeded to coast of Africa, captured a number of English vessels, and destroyed a large factory and fort at the Islands Des Los").

7. Charles Edward Banks, *The History of Martha's Vineyard, Duke's County, Massachusetts*, vol. 1 (Boston: G. H. Dean, 1911), 409.

8. On a list of what appears to be payments of portions of shares from a privateer voyage to sailors on the *Marlborough*'s first voyage, dated March 19, 1779, in Beriah Brown Papers, box 4, folder 8, RI Hist. Soc. Samuel Babcock Jr., who may have been the Babcock who died of smallpox on the *Marlborough*'s first voyage, is also listed in this document, indicating the list may be of sailors from the first voyage.

9. Ibid.

10. Ibid.

11. Receipt for payment to John Shearman for his service "on the late cruise of the ship *Marlborough*," dated Exeter, March 4, 1779, Beriah Brown Papers, box 4, folder 8, RI Hist. Soc. However, it is possible this man could have sailed on the *Marlborough*'s second voyage, but not the first one, which went to Africa.

12. The following notice appeared in the *Providence Gazette*, January 3, 1778, edition: "Deserted from my company, in Col. Elliott's regiment of artillery, Samuel Allen, a matross; he belongs to South Kingstown, and is supposed to have gone in the ship *Marlborough*; he is about 5 feet 6 inches high, talks quick, had on a surtout, and other apparel. . . . Ebenezer Adams, Capt., Tiverton, Dec. 29, 1777."

13. Journal entry, Nov. 12, 1778, in Boss, Journal of a Cruise in the Ship *Marlborough*. The prize vessel (and its prize master Arnold) was captured by a British ship. See Declaration of Alexander Southerland, and various others, all dated Feb. 15, 1779, to An Appeal from Judgment of Court of Admiralty of the State of Massachusetts Bay, *Geo. Wait Babcock v. Ship* Nancy, Lodged May 19, 1779, Referred to the Committee on Appeals of the Continental Congress, in Revolutionary War Prize Cases-Captured Vessels, Massachusetts, 1779, case no. 47, M162, RG267, National Archives.

14. Journal Entry, Sept. 20, 1778, in Boss, Journal of a Cruise in the Ship *Marlborough*. Chichester Cheyne was also wounded in the engagement, but he was definitely not on the *Marlborough*'s first voyage. See Bell-Romero, "Series of Unfortunate Events."

APPENDIX B: BRITISH SLAVE SHIPS CAPTURED BY AMERICAN PRIVATEERS WITH NO ENSLAVED AFRICANS ON BOARD, AUGUST 1776 TO AUGUST 1778

1. The description of the seizure of the slave ship *Union* was from a letter written by the ship's captain, Robert Wilson, after he arrived at Liverpool. Wilson said the initial capture of the *Union* was made by the *Sally*, commanded by James Munro of Providence and carrying ten 6-pounders and a crew of 103 men, on September 7, 1776. Extract of a Letter from Liverpool, Oct. 11, in *London Chronicle*, Oct. 15, 1776, in Crawford et al., eds., *Naval Documents*, 7:685-86. See also *Providence Gazette*, Nov. 9, 16, 1776 (sale of the *Union*'s cargo in Providence advertised, including 611 elephant tusks and "1 Negro Boy"); Desmarais, *Revolutionary War at Sea*, 1:241 (collecting US newspaper sources). The *Sally* was partially owned by John Brown and other members of the Brown family. The *Union*'s voyage is cov-

ered in TSTD, www.slavevoyages.org/voyage/search (voyage no. 92569). It is recorded as hailing from Liverpool and having disembarked an estimated 195 captives at St. Kitts.

2. *Cornwall Chronicle* (Montego Bay, Jamaica), March 8, 1777, Supplement. See also *Lloyd's List*, April 1, 1777; Richardson, ed., *Bristol*, 4:73. The *Cornwall Chronicle* has the most detailed discussion of this incident. It described the American privateer that seized the *Cornwall* as "the *Boston* privateer of 28 carriage guns, with near two hundred men, Captain Brown." The *Boston*, not surprisingly, hailed from Boston and was commanded by Captain William Brown. Brown would later capture two British slave ships from Africa and bring them into North Carolina. See appendix C, nos. 2 and 3. The *Cornwall*'s voyage is covered in TSTD, www.slavevoyages.org/voyage/search (voyage no. 17893).

3. Desmarais, *Revolutionary War at Sea*, 1:363-64 (collecting US newspaper sources). The seventy-two-ton *Thomas*, commanded by Thomas Nicholson, departed from Bristol, England, for Africa, and then, on April 11, 1776, departed Africa for Barbados. The *Thomas* dropped off about 180 enslaved people at Barbados and Jamaica before being captured on its return voyage to Bristol. See Richardson, ed., *Bristol*, 4:69; TSTD, www.slavevoyages.org/voyage/search (voyage no. 17885). The *Thomas*, owned by Thomas Jones of Bristol, had also completed African slave voyages to Jamaica in 1773 and 1775. Ibid. (voyages nos. 17845, 17865).

4. See Extract of a Letter from Barbados, dated November 20, 1776, in *Public Advertiser* (London), Jan. 28, 1777; *Pennsylvania Packet*, Nov. 26, 1776; Libel in Pennsylvania Admiralty Court of Captain John Young Against the Prize Ship *Sam*, in *Pennsylvania Gazette*, Nov. 27, 1776 (ship weighed about 120 tons); *Pennsylvania Evening Post*, Feb. 22, 1777 (auction notice), all in Crawford et al., eds., *Naval Documents*, 7:227-28, 294, 295, 1263. The *Sam* and the *King George* were ordered to be purchased by the state of Pennsylvania as fire ships. Minutes of the Pennsylvania Navy Board, Feb. 28, March 1, 1777, in ibid., 7:1321, 8:9. The letter from Barbados added, "The captain and the boatswain were landed at the port of St. Pierre in Martinico; the doctor, mate, and two servants, and four of the people [sailors], were left on board the *Sam*; all the rest of the hands entered on board the *Independence*." The *Sam*'s capture is reported in TSTD. TSTD, www.slavevoyages.org/voyage/search (voyage no. 91937).

5. See Trading Invoices and Accounts, 1773–1783, Voyages of the Ship "Sam," 1774–1781, Papers of William Davenport & Co., 1745-1797, British Records on the Atlantic World, 1700–1900, microfilm (online source).

6. *General Evening Post* (London), Feb. 21, 1778; *Daily Advertiser* (London), Feb. 23, 1778; *London Evening Post*, Feb. 24, 1778. After capturing more ships, on January 2, 1778, the *Alligator* itself became the victim of a rebellion of all its prisoners. The *Alligator* crew reportedly suffered seven killed, and the prisoners lost five men. See the prior two newspaper citations and *Lloyd's Evening Post*, Feb. 23, 1778, in Crawford et al., eds., *Naval Documents*, 11:1035; *New York Gazette*, June 21, 1778 (quoting London newspapers from February 21, 1778). See also Desmarais, *Revolutionary War at Sea*, 2:300 (collecting US newspaper sources).

7. Extract of a Letter from Lisbon, April 20, 1778, in *New-York Gazette*, Aug. 10, 1778.

8. For the discussion of the capture of the *Pearl* by the *Marlborough*, see main text in chapter 7 accompanying notes 47-49; for its fate, see main text in chapter 9 accompanying notes 3-5.

9. *Continental Journal* (Boston), Aug. 13, 1778; *Independent Chronicle* (Boston), Aug. 13, 1778; *Connecticut Gazette* (New London), June 26, 1778, in Crawford et al., eds., *Naval Documents*, 13:207, 207n1.

10. See British maritime documents found on board the prize *True Blue*, Admiralty Papers, vol. 9, 1776, no. 20, RI State Archives; TSTD, www.slavevoyages.org/voyage/search (voyage no. 91829).

APPENDIX C: BRITISH SLAVE SHIPS CAPTURED BY AMERICAN PRIVATEERS WITH
ENSLAVED AFRICANS ON BOARD, AUGUST 1776 TO AUGUST 1778

1. On February 1, 1777, the French colonial privateer sloop *Tyger* took the *Amelia*, commanded by Captain John McNeill (sometimes spelled McNeal) and registered in London, on its way from Africa to St. Kitts (St. Christopher)—just two miles from its destination. Carrying sixty-eight enslaved people, the *Tyger* brought the *Amelia* into Spanish-controlled Hispaniola, but where the African captives were sold is not known. McNeill, perhaps hoping for a return of the captives he sailed across the Atlantic Ocean, mentioned that each enslaved person had been "branded BI on the left arm, as usual." See Deposition of the Crew of the British Sloop *Amelia*, Sept. 30, 1777, in Crawford et al., eds., *Naval Documents*, 9:986; Capt. John McNeill to Wharton & Douglas, Feb. 14, 1777, in Secretaries of State, State Papers Foreign, France, Lord Stormont, SP78/302, f.232, British National Archives. A fairly reliable British report said that twenty-eight captives with "BI" branded on them (the branding will be discussed below) were sold at St. Eustatius and that the sloop that captured the *Amelia* had been purchased by a St. Eustatius merchant for a French merchant from Guadeloupe. James Warden, St. Croix, to Oswald, Grant & Company, London, Feb. 20, 1777, Secretaries of State, State Papers Foreign, France, Lord Stormont, SP78/302, f.233, British National Archives.

There is uncertainty regarding whether the *Tyger* had a Continental Congress commission. A British sailor claimed that everyone on the *Tyger* was a Frenchman, including its captain, with the last name Davie, except for one American, and that no Continental Congress commission was produced (he was later told by the American that the privateer did have a Continental Congress commission but that it was a forgery.) According to a Royal Navy officer, the *Tyger* mounted twelve carriage and swivel guns and carried ninety men, most all Frenchmen or other "foreigners" who were not Americans. Vice Admiral Clark Gayton to Comte D'Argout, Oct. 10, 1777, in Crawford et al., eds., *Naval Documents*, 10:113. See also *Cornwall Chronicle* (Montego Bay, Jamaica), May 3, 1777 (no Americans on board). However, another Caribbean source indicated the *Tyger* was commanded by a Captain Fell, likely an American, and had received a Continental Congress commission at Martinique. *Cornwall Chronicle* (Montego Bay, Jamaica), May 3, 1777. Some London newspapers reported that an American privateer captured the *Amelia* and it was taken to French-controlled Saint Domingue (later Haiti). *London Chronicle*, April 26, 1777, in Crawford et al., eds., *Naval Documents*, 8:794; *Gazetteer and New Daily Advertiser* (London), April 16, 1777; *Lloyd's List*, April 29, 1777; *General Evening Post* (London), April 28, 1777; *Daily Advertiser* (London), April 28, 1777. One source stated the African captives were sold at Guadeloupe and St. Eustatius, which sounds credible. *Cornwall Chronicle* (Montego Bay, Jamaica), May 3, 1777. Another source said the *Amelia* carried just sixty-eight captives. Deposition of the Crew of the British Sloop *Amelia*, Sept. 30, 1777, in Crawford et al., eds., *Naval Documents*, 9:986. TSTD, www.slavevoyages.org/voyage/search (voyage no. 24799), covers the *Amelia*'s capture. The *Amelia*, with Captain McNeill in command, had completed an African voyage in 1776, embarking some 149 enslaved people at St.-Louis and disembarking about 126 survivors at St. Kitts. TSTD, www.slavevoyages.org/voyage/search (voyage no. 24780).

The captured slaver was owned by the prominent London slave trading firm of Oswald, Grant & Company, which had owned Bance Island off the coast of West Africa since 1748 and had operated a major slave trading post there. This accounted for the "BI" branding—for Bance Island. Richard Oswald, the name partner, would later be appointed to negotiate the peace treaty that ended the war between Great Britain and America. For more on Oswald's slave trading activities, see Hancock, *Citizens of the World*, 186-213.

2. The sloop *Mary,* commanded by Captain William Harrison, with ninety African captives, six tons of camwood, and four tons of ivory on board, and while sailing near St. Vincent's, was taken by the *Puissance,* a privateer carrying ten carriage guns, eight swivels, and seventy men that was owned by Pierre Begozzat, a merchant at Martinique. The *Mary* was sailed to St. Lucia, where the enslaved people and the sloop were sold. The *Mary* was owned by the Liverpool firm of Tarleton & Backhouse. Henry Haffey, St. Vincent's, to Gill Slater, London, dated St. Lucia, March 10, 1777, Secretaries of State, State Papers Foreign, France, Lord Stormont, SP78/302, f. 334, British National Archives (owned by John Tarleton), British National Archives; Ashburner, Hind & Co., Grenada, to Tarleton & Backhouse, Liverpool, March 17, 1777, in ibid., f.336; Capt. William Harrison to Tarleton & Backhouse, April 2, 1777, Grenada, in ibid., f.337. Other sources, not accurate, stated that the slaver was seized by an American privateer. "The *Mary,* Capt. Harrison, from Africa to the West Indies, with a number of slaves on board, is taken by the Provincials, and sent to some port in America." *London Chronicle,* May 24, 1777; *London Evening Post,* May 24, 1777. "The *Mary,* Harrison, from Africa to Grenada, was taken in sight of that island by a Rebel privateer." *Lloyd's List,* May 27, 1777. This vessel and its captain were reported as making the voyage from Liverpool and, in about January 1777, arriving at Africa. See *Public Advertiser* (London), March 4, 1777; *Morning Chronicle* (London), March 5, 1777. The *Mary*'s capture is reported in TSTD, www.slavevoyages.org/voyage/ search (voyage no. 92437). The listing indicates the *Mary* was just thirty-five tons and owned by T. Tarleton of Liverpool. John and Thomas Tarleton, the brothers of famous British army officer Banastre Tarleton, were third-generation slave merchants. The Tarleton family as a whole undertook some two hundred slaving voyages and disembarked more than fifty thousand captives from Africa. TSTD, www.slavevoyages.org/ voyage/search (search in "vessel owner" the name Tarleton).

3. Deposition of the Crew of the British Sloop *Amelia,* Sept. 30, 1777, in Crawford et al., eds., *Naval Documents,* 9:986.

4. Lord Macartney to G. Germain, Oct. 24, 1777, in ibid., 10:277-78, to which was attached Deposition of Charles Meyers, Oct. 24, 1777, in ibid., 278-79. Two Caribbean Indians were also seized at Tobago, but they apparently were not sold. Ibid., 279.

5. Henry Haffey, St. Vincent's, to Gill Slater, London, dated St. Lucia, March 10, 1777, Secretaries of State, State Papers Foreign, France, Lord Stormont, SP78/302, f.334, British National Archives.

6. See O'Malley, *Final Passages,* ch. 5.

7. Extract of a Letter from Grenada, dated 30th March, 1777, in *General Evening Post* (London), May 29, 1777, and *London Evening Post,* May 29, 1777. See also Report of Arthur Piggot, July 3, 1777, in Crawford et al., eds., *Naval Documents,* 9:458-59 (similar report, except stating that the sloop carried "54 slaves on board"); Extract of a Letter from An English Gentleman at Martinico, dated March 21, in ibid., 8:183; Almon, ed., *Remembrancer* [1777], 5:141-42 (similar, by the Tobago purchaser of the captives).

8. See also Report of Arthur Piggot, July 3, 1777, in Crawford et al., eds., *Naval Documents,* 9:458-59; *London Chronicle,* June 3, 1777, in ibid., 8:183.

9. *North Carolina Gazette,* Sept. 26, Oct. 3, 1777, in Crawford et al., eds., *Naval Documents,* 9:971, 10:31. The second newspaper squib makes it clear that the slave ship capture in each squib refers to the same ship, *Invermay.*

10. See Oliver Pollock to Continental Congress Commerce Committee, April 2, 1778, in Crawford et al., eds., *Naval Documents,* 12:20; Petition of David Ross & Company to Don Bernardo de Gálvez, April 11, 1778, in ibid., 93-94; editor's notes, in ibid., 110n14. The author thanks Michael Thomin for bringing this capture to his attention.

11. For the *Sally's* capture, see main text in chapter 6 accompanying notes 49-50. For its fate, see main text in chapter 7 accompanying note 44. For the *Fort Rose's* capture, see main text in chapter 6 accompanying notes 56-58. For its fate, see main text in chapter 8 accompanying notes 43-45. For captures of various shallops and other small boats with enslaved people on board, see chapters 6 and 7.

12. *Daily Advertiser* (London), June 7, 1777; *Morning Post* (London), June 7, 1777. The June 7, 1777, edition of the *Public Advertiser* indicated that the attacking American privateersmen suffered a calamity:

> The *Brooks*, Noble, from Africa, is arrived at St. Vincent's, after an Engagement with a Privateer of ten guns to the windward of that place, in which the privateer lost her mainmast, and was so much damaged that the people quitted her, and got on board a schooner that was in Company, which blew up soon after they were on board, and fifty-five people perished. Ten were saved (among whom was the Captain of the Privateer) and lodged in gaol [prison] at St. Vincent's.

The *Brooks*, commanded by Captain Clement Noble, was a two-hundred-ton ship that mounted ten guns. TSTD, www.slavevoyages.org/voyage/search (voyage no. 92521). See also Williams, *Liverpool Privateers*, 560 (Captain Noble "had fifty of our strongest slaves armed, who fought with exceeding great spirit"). This *Brooks* was not the same ship in the famous drawing of the exposed hull showing the captives crammed together.

13. *Gazetteer and New Daily Advertiser* (London), May 23, 1777; *London Evening Post*, May 24, 1777. This Fisher was Ralph Fisher and was not Joseph Fisher of the *Kitty* that was captured by the *Marlborough*. See TSTD, www.slavevoyages.org/voyage/search (voyage no. 78277).

14. From the supplement to the *Jamaica Gazette* of January 10, in *London Packet*, March 2, 1778, in Crawford et al., eds., *Naval Documents*, 11:93. See also Letter from St. Vincent, dated December 27, 1777, *Adams's Weekly Current* (Chester, England), Feb. 24, 1778, and *Morning Chronicle* (London), Feb. 24, 1778 (a Liverpool "Guineaman," the *Jane*, commanded by Captain Robert Syers, gave a "rebel privateer" a severe drubbing near Barbados, reportedly resulting (with likely exaggeration) in thirty-three of the privateer's crew being killed and some forty-seven wounded); Deposition of Josiah Durham, Dec. 13, 1777, St. Vincent, in Crawford et al., eds., *Naval Documents*, 10:732 (while he was at Martinique, "a Captain Mansfield in a very fine sloop of 14 guns came in very much shattered by an engagement she had with two Liverpool Guineyman [*sic*], that Captain Mansfield lost his arm, or hand in the engagement, and nine men on his own deck, besides [illegible] very much wounded & besides considerable numbers [were] killed on board the Guiney vessels in attempting to board them"); Extract of a Letter from Liverpool, Feb. 13, 1778, in *Morning Chronicle* (London) ("A Guineaman of this place beat off an American privateer of 14 guns," presumably referring to the *Jane*). See also Williams, *History of Liverpool Privateers*, 560-61 (a Black "boy" was killed helping the *Jane* repulse an attack by an American privateer off Barbados). The *Jane* was a 140-ton ship that mounted sixteen guns. TSTD, www.slavevoyages.org/voyage/search (voyage no. 92014).

15. Extract of a letter from an Officer on board the snow *Adventure*, Capt. Muir, at Tobago, dated Feb. 27, 1778, in *Daily Advertiser* (London), May 14, 1778. The *Adventure*, commanded by Captain John Muir, was a 140-ton ship that mounted twelve guns. TSTD, www.slavevoyages.org/voyage/search (voyage no. 75016).

Bibliography

PRIMARY SOURCES, UNPUBLISHED

Admiralty Papers. Rhode Island State Archives, Providence.

Articles of Agreement for the Armed Sloop Called the *Revenge*. Mystic Seaport, Mystic, CT.

Bingham, William. Papers. Library of Congress, Manuscript Reading Room, Washington, DC.

Births, Marriages, Deaths. Exeter Town Clerk's Office, Exeter, RI.

Boss, John Linscom. Journal of an Intended Cruise in the Good Ship General Mifflin George Wt. Babcock Commander (By God's Permission against the Enemies of the United States of America), Kept by John Linscom Boss, April 8–July 9, 1779, microfilm and PDF. Morristown National Historical Park, Morristown, NJ, and Naval History and Heritage Command, Washington, DC.

———. Journal of an Intended Cruise in the Good Ship Marlborough George Wt. Babcock Commander (By God's Permission) Against the Enemies of the United States of America Kept by John Linscom Boss from the Port of Boston, Sept. 13–Dec. 20, 1778, microfilm and PDF. Morristown National Historical Park, Morristown, NJ, and Naval History and Heritage Command, Washington, DC.

———. Journal of a Voyage in the Good Ship Marlborough George Wt. Babcock Commander Bound on a Five Month Cruise Against the Enemies of the United States of America from Rhode Island, Dec. 23, 1777–June 12, 1778, microfilm and PDF. By John Linscom Boss, Morristown National Historical Park, Morristown, NJ, and Naval History and Heritage Command, Washington, DC.

British Admiralty Records, Captain's Logs, ADM 51. British National Archives, Kew Gardens, England.

Brown, Beriah. Papers. Rhode Island Historical Society, Providence.

Brown Family Business Records. John Carter Brown Library, Brown University, Providence, RI.

Brown, John. Papers. Rhode Island Historical Society. Providence.

Continental Congress Papers. National Archives, Washington, DC.

Cross, Paul. Papers. South Caroliniana Library, University of South Carolina, Columbia.

Council of War Records. Rhode Island. Rhode Island State Archives, Providence.

Cutting, Nathaniel. Journal and Letterbooks, 1786–98. Massachusetts Historical Society, Boston.

Dalzell, Archibald. Papers. Centre for Research Collections, Edinburgh University Library, Edinburgh, Scotland.

Donald Grady Shomette Collection, CMM MS 074. Revolutionary War Information on Privateers, Box 1. Calvert Marine Museum, Solomons, MD.

Exchequer, King's Remembrancer, Exhibits, E140/2/5. British National Archives, Kew Gardens, England.

French, Christopher. Journal of Lieutenant-Colonel Christopher French, 1756–1778. Library of Congress, Manuscript Reading Room, Washington, DC.

Gail and Stephen Rudin Slavery Collection. Division of Rare and Manuscript Collections, Cornell University Library, Ithaca, NY.

General Assembly Papers, Revolutionary War Suspected Persons Record Book. Rhode Island State Archives, Providence.

Howe, Admiral. Correspondence, ADM 1/488. Transcripts. Library of Congress, Manuscript Reading Room, Washington, DC.

Inferior Court of Common Pleas, Newport, Record Book 1 1/2. Rhode Island Judicial Archives, Supreme Court Judicial Records Center, Pawtucket.

Journal of the Regiment von Huyn, Lidgerwood Collection. Microfilm. Morristown National Historical Park, Morristown, NJ.

Land Evidence Records. North Kingstown Town Clerk's Office, Wickford, RI.

Land Records. East Greenwich Town Clerk's Office, East Greenwich, RI.

Letters of Marque: Declarations Against America, 1777–1783, HCA26/60-70, ADM7. Microfilm. Archives and Special Collections, Harriet Irving Library, University of New Brunswick, Fredericton, New Brunswick, Canada.

Letters to the Governor. Rhode Island State Archives, Providence.

Maritime Papers, Bonds, Masters of Vessels. Rhode Island State Archives, Providence.

Maritime Papers, Letters of Marque, Petitions and Instructions. Rhode Island State Archives, Providence.

Maritime Papers, Outward and Inward Entries. Rhode Island State Archives, Providence.

Military Papers of the Revolutionary War. Microfilm. Rhode Island State Archives, Providence.

Percy, Hugh. Diary. Hugh Percy Papers. British Manuscript Project. Microform Reading Room, Library of Congress. Washington, DC.

Petitions to the General Assembly. Rhode Island. Rhode Island State Archives, Providence.

Ralph Carpenter Collection. Redwood Library and Athenaeum, Newport, RI.

Records of the African Companies. Detached Papers, T70/1538. British National Archives, Kew Gardens, England.

Records of the African Companies. Inward Letter Books, T70/32. British National Archives, Kew Gardens, England.

Records of the African Companies. Letters to and from Richard Miles, T70/1479/2. British National Archives, Kew Gardens, England.

Records of the African Companies. Richard Miles Letter Book, 1776–1777, T70/1534. British National Archives, Kew Gardens, England.

Records of the African Companies. Richard Miles Letter Book, 1778, T70/1483. British National Archives, Kew Gardens, England.

Register of Vessels. Rhode Island. Rhode Island State Archives, Providence.

Registry of Shipping and Seamen: Agreements and Crew Lists, Series I, Port of Registry, Liverpool, BT98/37, British National Archives, Kew Gardens, England.

Revolutionary War Loyalist Claim, British Public Records Office. Microfilm. American Philosophical Society. David Library Collections, Philadelphia.

Revolutionary War Pension Applications. National Archives, Washington, DC.

Revolutionary War Prize Cases: Records of the Court of Appeal in Case of Capture, 1776–1787. National Archives, Washington, DC.

Schofield Archive. Wilberforce Institute. University of Hull, Hull, UK.

Secretaries of State, State Papers Foreign, France, Lord Stormont, SP78/302. British National Archives, Kew Gardens, England.

Ship's log of the *Dolphin*, *Rising Sun*, *Fame*, and *William*. Rhode Island Historical Society, Providence.

Smeathman, Henry. Journal. University of Uppsala Library, Uppsala, Sweden.

South Carolina Pre-Federal Admiralty Records. National Archives, Atlanta.

Town Council and Probate Records. Exeter Town Clerk's Office, Exeter, RI.

PRIMARY SOURCES, PUBLISHED

The African Pilot, Being a Collection of New and Accurate Charts, on a Large Scale, of the Coasts, Islands, and Harbors of Africa (London: Robert Laurie and James Whittle, 1804), G2446, .P5L37, 1804. Library of Congress, Geography and Map Room, Washington, DC.

Allen, Gardner Weld. *Massachusetts Privateers of the Revolution*. Boston: Massachusetts Historical Society, 1927.

Almon, J., ed. *The Remembrancer, or Impartial Repository of Public Events*. London: 1775–1784.

American Vessels Captured by the British during the Revolution and War of 1812. Records of the Vice-Admiralty Court at Halifax, Nova Scotia. Salem, MA: Essex Institute, 1911.

The Annual Register, or a View of the History, Politics, and Literature, For the Year 1775. 4th ed. London: J. Dodsley, 1783.

Arnold, James N. "Selections from the Sheriff Brown Papers." *Narragansett Historical Society Register.* Vol. 2, 1883–84, 193-99.

———, ed. *Vital Records of Rhode Island, 1636–1850.* 21 vols. Providence, RI: Narragansett Historical Publishing, 1891–1912.

Bailey's List of Bankruptcies, Dividends, and Certificates from the Year 1772 to 1793, with the Names and Residence of the Different Solicitors Under Each. Vols. 1–2. London: T. Wilkins, 1794.

Bartlett, John R., ed. *Census of the Inhabitants of the Colony of Rhode Island and Providence Plantations Taken by the Order of the General Assembly, in the Year 1774.* Providence, RI: Knowles, Anthony, 1858.

———, ed. *Records of the Colony of Rhode Island and Providence Plantations in New England.* 10 vols. Providence, RI: A. C. Greene & Bros., 1856–1865.

Blake, William Phipps. *A brief account of the life and patriotic services of Jonathan Mix of New Haven* [. . .] . New Haven, CT: Tuttle, Morehouse and Taylor, 1886.

Boardman, Timothy. *Log-Book of Timothy Boardman; Kept on Board the Privateer Oliver Cromwell, During a Cruise from New London CT., to Charleston, S.C., and Return in 1778; also a Biographical Sketch of the Author by the Rev. Samuel W. Boardman, D.D.* Albany, NY: Joel Munsell's Sons, 1885.

A British Merchant [Malachy Postlethwayt]. *The African Trade, The Great Pillar and Support of the British Plantation Trade in America.* London: privately printed, 1745.

Chamberlain, Mildred M., ed. *The Rhode Island 1777 Military Census.* Baltimore: Genealogical Publishing, 1985.

Chesnutt, David R., C. James Taylor, Peggy J. Clark, Philip M Hamer, and George C. Rogers, eds. *The Papers of Henry Laurens.* 16 vols. Columbia: University of South Carolina Press, 1968–2002.

Commerce of Rhode Island, 1726–1774. Collections of the Massachusetts Historical Society, 7th ser., vols. 9–10, 1914.

Crawford, Michael J., ed. *The Autobiography of a Yankee Mariner: Christopher Prince and the American Revolution.* Washington, DC: Brassey's, 2002.

Crawford, Michael J., William B. Clark, William J. Morgan, et al., eds. *Naval Documents of the American Revolution.* 13 vols. Washington, DC: Government Printing Office, 1964–2019.

Desmarais, Norman. *The Guide to the American Revolutionary War at Sea, 1775–1783.* 7 vols. PDF format. Lincoln, RI: Revolutionary Imprints, 2016.

Dexter, Franklin B., ed. *Literary Diary of Ezra Stiles, D.D., L.L.D.* 2 vols. New York: Charles Slocum, 1901.

Donnan, Elizabeth, ed. *Documents Illustrative of the History of the Slave Trade to America.* 4 vols. Washington, DC: Carnegie Institution, 1930–35.

Douglass, William. *A Summary, Historical and Political, of the . . . British Settlements in North-America.* Vol. 2. Boston: Daniel Fowle, 1751.

Eltis, David, and David Richardson. *Atlas of the Transatlantic Slave Trade.* New Haven and London: Yale University Press, 2010.

Equiano, Olaudah. *The Interesting Narrative of the Life of Olaudah Equiano, Written by Himself.* Robert J. Allison, ed. Boston: Bedford/St. Martin's, 1995. Originally published in London in 1789.

Les États de L'Enterprise Barber, undated (probably around 1784). In annex to Yvan Debbasch, "L'Espace du Sierra Leone et La Politique Francaise de Traite a La Fin de L'Ancien Regime." In *De la Traite à L'Esclavage: du V au XVIII Siècles. Actes du Colloque International sur la traite des Noirs. Nantes 1985*, edited by Serge Daget. Vol. 1, 205-12. Nantes, France: Centre de Recherche sur L'Histoire du Monde Atlantique, 1988.

Falconbridge, Alexander. *An Account of the Slave Trade on the Coast of Africa.* 2nd ed. London: James Phillips, 1788.

Firth, C. H., ed. *Naval Songs and Ballads.* London: Navy Records Society, 1908.

Force, Peter, ed. *American Archives.* 4th ser., vol. 1, 5th ser., vol. 2. Washington, DC: M. St. Clair Clarke and Peter Force, 1837, 1851.

Ford, Worthington C., ed. *The Journals of the Continental Congress.* 34 vols. Washington, DC: Library of Congress, 1905–37.

Golberry, Silvester Meinrad Xavier. *Travels in Africa* [. . .]. 2 vols., 2nd ed. London: Jones and Bumford, 1808. Originally published in French in 1794.

Hawkins, Joseph. *A History of a Voyage to the Coast of Africa and travels into the interior of that country: containing particular descriptions of the climate and inhabitants, and interesting particulars concerning the slave trade.* 2nd ed. Troy, NY: Luther Pratt, 1797.

Holbrook, Jay Mack. *Rhode Island 1782 Census.* Oxford, MA: Holbrook Research Institute, 1979.

Hopkins, Stephen. "Remonstrance of the Colony of Rhode Island to the Lords Commissioners of Trade and Plantations, Jan. 1764." In *Records of the Colony of Rhode Island and Providence Plantations in New England*, edited by John R. Bartlett. Vol. 6, 378–83. Providence, RI: A. C. Greene & Bros., 1861.

Ledward, K. H., ed. *Journals of the Board of Trade and Plantations.* Vols. 13 and 14. London: His Majesty's Stationary Office, 1937 and 1938.

Lincoln, Charles H., ed. *Naval Records of the American Revolution, 1775–1788. Prepared from the Originals in the Library of Congress.* Washington, DC: Government Printing Office, 1906.

Lloyd's Register of Shipping 1777-1778. London: Lloyd's Register Foundation, Heritage & Education Centre, 1778. Reprinted by Gregg Press Limited, London.

Mackenzie, Frederick. *Diary of Frederick Mackenzie, Giving a Daily Narrative of his Military Service as an Officer of the Regiment of Royal Welch Fusiliers During the*

Years 1775–1781 in Massachusetts, Rhode Island and New York. 2 vols. Cambridge, MA: Harvard University Press, 1930. Reprint, New York, New York Times, 1969.

Massachusetts Soldiers and Sailors in the War of the American Revolution. 17 vols. Boston: Commonwealth of Massachusetts, 1896–1908.

Otis, James. "The Rights of the British Colonies Asserted and Proved." In *The American Revolution, Writings from the Pamphlet Debate 1764–1776*, edited by Gordon Wood. Vol. 1, 43-119. New York: Library of America, 2015.

Report of the Lords of the Committee of Council appointed for the Consideration of all Matters relating to Trade and Foreign Plantations; submitting to His Majesty's consideration the evidence and information they have collected in consequence of his Majesty's order in Council, dated the 11th of February 1788, concerning the present state of the trade to Africa, and particularly the trade in slaves; and concerning the effects and consequences of this trade, as well as in Africa and the West Indies, as to the general commerce of this kingdom. London, 1789.

Rhode Island Historical Society, ed. *Papers of William Vernon and the Navy Board, 1776–1794.* Providence, RI: Snow & Farnham, 1901.

Smith, Joseph J., ed. *Civil and Military List of Rhode Island.* 2 vols. Providence, RI: Preston and Rounds, 1900.

Smith, Paul H., ed. *Letters of Delegates to Congress, 1774–1789.* 26 vols. Washington, DC: Library of Congress, 1976–2000.

Smith, Venture. *A Narrative of the Life and Adventures of Venture, a Native of Africa: But Resident above Sixty Years in the United States of America, Related by Himself.* New London, CT: privately printed, 1835. Originally published in New London in 1798.

Twohig, Dorothy, Philander D. Chase, Theodore J. Crackel, W. W. Abbot, and Edward G. Lengel, eds. *The Papers of George Washington.* Revolutionary War Series. 24 vols. Charlottesville: University of Virginia Press, 1985–2016.

Willcox, William B., Barbara B. Oberg, and Claude A. Lopez, eds. *The Papers of Benjamin Franklin.* Vols. 26-30. New Haven, CT: Yale University Press, 1987–93.

PUBLISHED SECONDARY SOURCES: BOOKS

Alberts, Robert C. *The Golden Voyage. The Life and Times of William Bingham, 1752–1804.* Boston: Houghton Mifflin, 1969.

Allen, Gardner Weld. *A Naval History of the American Revolution.* Boston: Houghton Mifflin, 1913.

Ammerman, David. *In the Common Cause: American Response to the Coercive Acts of 1774.* Charlottesville: University Press of Virginia, 1974.

Anstey, Roger. *The Atlantic Slave Trade and Abolition.* London: Humanities Press, 1975.

Armstrong, Benjamin. *Small Boats and Daring Men: Maritime Raiding, Irregular Warfare, and the Early American Navy.* Norman: University of Oklahoma Press, 2019.

Babcock, Stephen. *Babcock Genealogy.* New York: Eaton & Mains, 1903.

Baker, David Sherman, Jr. *Historical Sketch of North Kingstown.* Providence, RI: F. A. Johnson, 1876.

Banks, Charles Edward. *The History of Martha's Vineyard, Duke's County, Massachusetts.* Vol. 1. Boston: G. H. Dean, 1911.

Berry, Stephen R. *A Path in the Mighty Waters: Shipboard Life & Atlantic Crossings to the New World.* New Haven, CT: Yale University Press, 2015.

Boatner, Mark M. *Encyclopedia of the American Revolution.* New York: D. McKay, 1974.

Bolster, W. Jeffrey. *Black Jacks: African American Seamen in the Age of Sail.* Cambridge, MA: Harvard University Press, 1997.

Boss, William G. *Inquiry Concerning the Boss Family and the Name Boss.* Chicago: Ben Franklin Co., 1902.

Brooke, Richard. *Liverpool as It was During the Last Quarter of the Eighteenth Century, 1775–1800.* Liverpool: J. Mawdsley and Son, 1853.

Burnard, Trevor. *Jamaica in the Age of Revolution.* Philadelphia: University of Pennsylvania Press, 2020.

Carrington, Selwyn H. H. *The British West Indies during the American Revolution.* Dordrecht, Holland: Foris, 1988.

———. *The Sugar Industry and the Abolition of the Slave Trade, 1775–1810.* Gainesville: University Press of Florida, 2002.

Chitwood, Oliver Perry. *Richard Henry Lee: Statesman of the Revolution.* Morgantown, WV: West Virginia Library, 1967.

Clarkson, Thomas. *An Essay on the Impolicy of the African Slave Trade. In Two Parts.* 2nd ed. London: J. Phillips, 1788.

———. *The History of the Rise, Progress and Accomplishment of the Abolition of the African Slave Trade, by the British Parliament.* 2 vols. London: John W. Parker, 1839. Originally published in London by Longman, Hurst, Reese and Orme in 1808.

Cole, J. R. *History of Washington and Kent Counties, Rhode Island.* New York: Preston, 1889.

Corbett, Julian S. *England in the Seven Years War.* 2 vols. 2nd ed. London: Longmans, Green, 1918.

Coughtry, Jay. *The Notorious Triangle: Rhode Island and the African Slave Trade, 1700–1807.* Philadelphia: Temple University Press, 1981.

Crane, Elaine Forman. *A Dependent People: Newport, Rhode Island in the Revolutionary Era.* New York: Fordham University Press, 1985.

Curtin, Philip D. *The Atlantic Slave Trade: A Census.* Madison: University of Wisconsin Press, 1969.

Du Bois, W. E. B. *The Suppression of the African Slave Trade to the United States of America, 1638–1870.* New York: Longmans, Green, 1896.

Dull, Jonathan R. *The French Navy and the Seven Years' War.* Lincoln: University of Nebraska Press, 2005.

Earle, Peter. *The World of Defoe.* London: Atheneum, 1977.

Elder, Melinda. *The Slave Trade and the Economic Development of 18th-Century Lancaster.* Edinburgh: Edinburgh University Press, 1992.

Fenn, Elizabeth A. *Pox Americana: The Great Smallpox Epidemic of 1775–1782.* New York: Hill and Wang, 2001.

Flavell, Julie. *When London Was Capital of America.* New Haven, CT: Yale University Press, 2010.

Fowler, William M., Jr. *Rebels Under Sail: The American Navy during the Revolution.* New York: Charles Scribner's Sons, 1976.

Fried, Stephen. *Rush: Revolution, Madness and the Visionary Doctor Who Became a Founding Father.* New York: Crown, 2018.

Hancock, David. *Citizens of the World: London Merchants and the Integration of the British Atlantic Community, 1735–1785.* Cambridge: Cambridge University Press, 1995.

Hawes, Alexander Boyd. *Off Soundings: Aspects of Maritime History of Rhode Island.* Chevy Chase, MD: Posterity Press, 1999.

Hedges, James B. *The Browns of Providence Plantations: The Colonial Years.* Providence, RI: Brown University Press, 1952.

———. *The Browns of Providence Plantations: The Nineteenth Century.* Providence, RI: Brown University Press, 1968.

Herreshoff, L. Francis. *Capt. Nat Herreshoff: The Wizard of Bristol; The Life and Achievements of Nathanael Greene Herreshoff.* Dobbs Ferry, NY: Sheridan House, 1953.

Hochschild, Adam. *Bury the Chains: Prophets and Rebels in the Fight to Free an Empire's Slaves.* Boston: Houghton Mifflin, 2005.

Hulbert, Kylie A. *The Untold War at Sea: America's Revolutionary Privateers.* Athens: University of Georgia Press, 2022.

Kelley, Sean M. *The Voyage of the Slave Ship* Hare: *A Journey into Captivity from Sierra Leone to South Carolina.* Chapel Hill: University of North Carolina Press, 2016.

Latimer, John. *The Annals of Bristol in the Eighteenth Century.* Bristol, UK: privately printed, 1893.

Machat, Jules. *Documents sur les éstablissements Français de L'Afrique Occidentale au xviii siècle.* Paris: privately printed, 1906.

Macpherson, David. *Annals of Commerce. Manufactures, Fisheries and Navigation, etc.* Vol. 4. London: Nichols and Son, 1805.

Marques, Leonardo. *The United States and the Transatlantic Slave Trade to the Americas, 1776–1867.* New Haven, CT: Yale University Press, 2012.

McBurney, Christian. *Abductions in the American Revolution: Attempts to Kidnap George Washington, Benedict Arnold and Other Military and Civilian Leaders.* Jefferson, NC: McFarland, 2016.

———. *A History of Kingston, R.I., 1700–1900: Heart of Rural South County.* Kingston, RI: Pettaquamscutt Historical Society, 2004.

————. *Kidnapping the Enemy: The Special Operations to Capture Major Generals Charles Lee & Richard Prescott.* Yardley, PA: Westholme, 2014.

————. *The Rhode Island Campaign: The First French and American Operation in the Revolutionary War.* Yardley, PA: Westholme, 2011.

————. *Spies in Revolutionary Rhode Island.* Charleston, SC: History Press, 2014.

McGrath, Patrick. *Bristol in the Eighteenth Century.* Newton Abbot, UK: David and Charles, 1972.

McManemin, John A. *Captains of the Privateers during the Revolutionary War.* Spring Lake, NJ: Ho-Ho-Kus Publishing, 1985.

Millar, John F. *Early American Ships.* Williamsburg, VA: Thirteen Colonies Press, 1986.

New Cambridge Modern History. 14 vols. Cambridge: Cambridge University Press, 1957–1979.

Niles, John. *The Life of Oliver Hazard Perry.* Hartford, CT: R. Storrs, 1820.

O'Malley, Gregory E. *Final Passages: The Intercolonial Slave Trade of British North America, 1619–1807.* Chapel Hill: University of North Carolina Press, 2014.

O'Shaughnessy, Andrew Jackson. *An Empire Divided: The American Revolution and the British Caribbean.* Philadelphia: University of Pennsylvania Press, 2000.

————. *The Men Who Lost America. British Leadership, the American Revolution, and the Fate of the Empire.* New Haven, CT: Yale University Press, 2013.

Pares, Richard. *Yankees and Creoles: The Trade between North America and the West Indies before the American Revolution.* London: Longman, 1956.

Park, Stephen. *The Burning of His Majesty's Schooner Gaspee.* Yardley, PA: Westholme, 2016.

Patton, Robert H. *Patriot Pirates: The Privateer War for Freedom and Fortune in the American Revolution.* New York: Pantheon Books, 2008.

Porter, Ray. *English Society in the 18th Century.* London and New York: Penguin, 1982.

Ragatz, Lowell Joseph. *The Fall of the British Planter Class in the British Caribbean, 1763–1833.* New York and London: Century, 1928.

Rappleye, Charles. *Robert Morris, Financier of the American Revolution.* New York: Simon & Schuster, 2010.

————. *Sons of Providence: The Brown Brothers, the Slave Trade, and the American Revolution.* New York: Simon & Schuster, 2006.

Rawley, James A. *London, Metropolis of the Slave Trade.* Columbia: University of Missouri Press, 2003.

————, with Stephen D. Behrendt. *The Transatlantic Slave Trade: A History.* Rev. ed. Lincoln: University of Nebraska Press, 2005.

Rediker, Marcus. *Between the Devil and the Deep Blue Sea: Merchant Seamen, Pirates and the Anglo-American Maritime World.* Cambridge: Cambridge University Press, 1987.

Rediker, Marcus. *The Slave Ship: A Human History.* New York: Viking, 2007.

Richardson, David, ed. *Bristol, Africa and the Eighteenth-Century Slave Trade to America. The Final Years, 1770–1807.* Vol. 4. Bristol Record Society's Publications, vol. 47. Bristol, UK: Bristol Record Society, 1996.

Robertson, E. Arnot. *The Spanish Town Papers, Some Sidelights on the American War of Independence.* New York: Macmillan, 1959.

Searing, James. *West African Slavery and Atlantic Commerce.* Cambridge: Cambridge University Press, 1993.

Sheffield, William P. *An Address Delivered by William P. Sheffield, Before the Rhode Island Historical Society, in Providence, February 7, A. D. 1882. With Notes.* Newport, RI: Sanborn, 1883.

Shomette, Donald G. *Privateers of the Revolution: War on the New Jersey Coast, 1775–1783.* Atglen, PA: Schiffer, 2016.

Smith, Adam. *An Inquiry into the Nature and Causes of the Wealth of Nations.* London: 1776.

Smith, Billy G. *Ship of Death: A Voyage that Changed the Atlantic World.* New Haven, CT: Yale University Press, 2013.

Sparks, Randy J. *Where the Negroes Are Masters: An African Port in the Era of the Slave Trade.* Cambridge, MA: Harvard University Press, 2014.

Staples, William R. *Annals of Providence: From Its First Settlement to the Organization of the City.* Providence, RI: privately printed, 1843.

St. Clair, William. *The Door of No Return: The History of Cape Coast Castle and the Atlantic Slave Trade.* New York: BlueBridge, 2007.

Stone, Edwin M. *Life and Recollections of John Howland, Late President of the Rhode Island Historical Society.* Providence, RI: G. H. Whitney, 1857.

Syrett, David. *The Royal Navy in European Waters during the American Revolutionary War.* Columbia: University of South Carolina Press, 1998.

———. *Shipping and the American War, 1775–1783: A Study of British Transport Organization.* London: Anthlone Press, 1970.

Thomas, Evan. *John Paul Jones: Sailor, Hero, Father of the American Navy.* New York: Simon & Schuster, 2003.

Thomas, Hugh. *The Slave Trade: The Story of the Atlantic Slave Trade: 1440–1870.* New York: Touchstone, 1997.

Thompson, Mack. *Moses Brown: Reluctant Reformer.* Chapel Hill: University of North Carolina Press, 1962.

Tillman, Stephen F. *Christopher Reynolds and His Descendants.* Chevy Chase, MD: privately printed, 1959.

Truxes, Thomas M. *Irish-American Trade, 1660–1783.* Cambridge: Cambridge University Press, 1988.

Updike, Wilkins. *History of the Episcopal Church in Narragansett.* New York: Henry M. Onderdonk, 1847.

Ward, John R., and Jessica Bird Ward. *British West Indian Slavery, 1750–1834: The Process of Amelioration.* Oxford: Clarendon Press, 1988.

Wheeler, Richard Anson. *History of the Town of Stonington, County of New London, Connecticut, from Its First Settlement in 1649 to 1900.* New London, CT: Press of the Day, 1900.

Williams, Gomer. *History of the Liverpool Privateers and Letters of Marque with an Account of the Liverpool Slave Trade.* London: W. Heinemann, 1897.

Withey, Lynne. *Urban Growth in Colonial Rhode Island: Newport and Providence in the Eighteenth Century.* Albany: State University Press of New York, 1984.

Zilversmith, Arthur. *The First Emancipation. The Abolition of Slavery in the North.* Chicago: University of Chicago Press, 1967.

PUBLISHED SECONDARY SOURCES: ARTICLES

Baugh, David. "Elements of Naval Power in the Eighteenth Century." In *Maritime History: The Eighteenth Century and the Classic Age of Sail,* edited by John B. Hattendorf. Vol. 2, 119-35. Malabar, FL: Krieger, 1997.

Behrendt, Stephen D. "The Transatlantic Slave Trade." In *The Oxford Handbook of Slavery in the Americas,* edited by Robert L. Paquette and Mark M. Smith, 251-74. Oxford: Oxford University Press, 2010.

Behrendt, Stephen D., David Eltis, and David Richardson. "The Costs of Coercion: African Agency in the Pre-Modern Atlantic World." *Economic History Review* 54, no. 3 (Aug. 2001): 454-76.

Coleman, Deirdre. "Henry Smeathman and the Natural Economy of Slavery." In *Slavery and the Cultures of Abolition: Essays Marking the Bicentennial of the British Abolition Act of 1807,* edited by Brycchan Carey and Peter J. Kitson, 130–49. Cambridge: D. S. Brewer, 2007.

Crawford, Michael J. "The Privateering Debate in Revolutionary America." *Northern Mariner le marin du nord* 21, no. 3 (July 2011): 219-234.

Der, Benedict. "Edmund Burke and Africa, 1772–1792." *Transactions of the Historical Society of Ghana* 11 (1970): 9-26.

Deutsch, Sarah. "The Elusive Guineamen: Newport Slavers, 1735–1774." *New England Quarterly* 55, no. 2 (June 1982): 229-53.

Dull, Jonathan R. "Was the Continental Navy a Mistake?" *American Neptune* 45 (1985): 167-70.

Eltis, David, Frank D. Lewis, and David Richardson. "Slave Prices, the African Slave Trade, and Productivity in the Caribbean, 1674-1807." *Economic History Review,* New Series, 58, no. 4 (Nov. 2005): 673-700.

Eltis, David, Paul E. Lovejoy, and David Richardson. "Slave-Trading Ports: Towards an Atlantic-Wide Perspective." In *Ports of the Slave Trade (Bights of Benin and Biafra),* edited by Robin Law and Silke Strickrodt, 12-34. Stirling, UK: Centre of Commonwealth Studies, University of Stirling, 1999.

Eltis, David, and David Richardson. "Prices of African Slaves Newly Arrived in the Americas, 1673–1865: New Evidence on Long-Run Trends and Regional Differentials." In *Slavery in the Development of the Americas*, edited by David Eltis, Frank Lewis, and Kenneth Sokoloff, 181-218. Cambridge: Cambridge University Press, 2004.

Farnham, Charles W. "Crew List of the Privateer *Independence*, 1776." *Rhode Island History* 26, no. 4 (Oct. 1967): 125-28.

Foy, Charles R. "Eighteenth Century 'Prize Negroes': From Britain to America." *Slavery & Abolition* 31, no. 3 (Sept. 2010): 379-83.

Herzog, Keith P. "Naval Operations in West Africa and the Disruption of the Slave Trade during the American Revolution." *American Neptune* 55, no. 1 (1995): 42-48.

Inikori, Joseph E. "Market Structure and the Profits of the British African Slave Trade in the Late Eighteenth Century." *Journal of Economic History* 41 (Dec. 1981): 745-76.

Jamieson, Alan. G. "American Privateers in the Leeward Islands, 1776–1778." *American Neptune* 43, no. 1 (1983): 20-30.

Jones, Peter E. "Grant Us Commission to Make Reprisals upon Any Enemies Shiping." *Rhode Island History* 34, no. 4 (Nov. 1975): 105-119.

Kelley, Sean. "The Dirty Business of Panyarring and Palaver: Slave Trading on the Upper Guinea Coast in the Eighteenth Century." In *Slavery, Abolition and the Transition to Colonialism in Sierra Leone*, edited by Paul E. Lovejoy and Suzanne Schwarz, 90-107. Trenton, NJ: Africa World Press, 2014.

Klein, Herbert S. "Economic Aspects of the Eighteenth-Century Atlantic Slave Trade." In *The Rise of Merchant Empires: Long-Distance Trade in the Early Modern World, 1350–1750*, edited by James D. Tracy, 287-310. Cambridge: Cambridge University Press, 1990.

Lamb, D. H. "Volume and Tonnage of the Liverpool Slave Trade 1772–1807." In *Liverpool, the African Slave Trade, and the Abolition: Essays to Illustrate Current Knowledge and Research*, edited by Roger Anstey and Paul Hair, 91-112. Liverpool: Historic Society of Lancashire and Cheshire, 1976.

Lin, Rachel Chernos. "The Rhode Island Slave-Traders: Butchers, Bakers and Candlestick-Makers." *Slavery & Abolition* 23, no. 3 (2002): 21-38.

Lovejoy, Paul E. "Forgotten Colony in Africa: The British Province of Senegambia (1765–83)." In *Slavery, Abolition and the Transition to Colonialism in Sierra Leone*, edited by Paul E. Lovejoy and Suzanne Schwarz, 109-141. Trenton, NJ: Africa World Press, 2014.

Marsh, A. J. "The Taking of Gorée, 1758." *Mariner's Mirror* 51 (May 1965): 117-30.

McBurney, Christian. "The American Revolution Sees the First Efforts to Limit the African Slave Trade." In *Journal of the American Revolution, Annual Volume 2021*, edited by Don N. Hagist, 153-87. Yardley, PA: Westholme, 2021.

————. "British Treatment of Prisoners during the Occupation of Newport, 1776–1779: Disease, Starvation and Death Stalk the Prison Ships." *Newport History* 79, no. 263 (Fall 2010): 1-41.

Minchinton, Walter E. "The Voyage of the Snow *Africa*." *Mariner's Mirror* 37 (1951): 187-96.

Morgan, Kenneth. "Liverpool Ascendant: British Merchants and the Slave Trade on the Upper Guinea Coast, 1701–1808." In *Slavery, Abolition and the Transition to Colonialism in Sierra Leone*, edited by Paul E. Lovejoy and Suzanne Schwarz, 29-50. Trenton, NJ: Africa World Press, 2014.

Morse, Sydney G. "State or Continental Privateers?" *American Historical Review* 52, no. 1 (Oct. 1946): 68-73.

Mouser, Bruce L. "Illes de Los as Bulking Center in the Slave Trade, 1750–1800." *Revue Française d'Histoire d'Outre-mer, tome 83, n313, 4e trimester* (1996): 77-90.

Parmentier, Jan. "The Sweets of Commerce: The Hennesys of Ostend and Their Network in the Eighteenth Century," 67-92. In *Irish and Scottish Mercantile Networks in Europe and Overseas in the Seventeenth and Eighteenth Centuries*, edited by David Dickson, Jan Parmentier, and Jane Ohlmeyer. Gent, Belgium: Academia Press, 2007.

Platt, Virginia Beaver. "'And Don't Forget the Guinea Voyage': The Slave Trade of Aaron Lopez of Newport." *William and Mary Quarterly*, 3rd ser. vol. 32 (1975): 601-18.

Radburn, Nicholas. "'Keeping 'the Wheel in Motion': Trans-Atlantic Credit Terms, Slave Prices, and the Geography of Slavery in the British Americas, 1755–1807." *Journal of Economic History* 75, no. 3 (Sept. 2015): 660-89.

————. "'[M]anaged at First as if They Were Beasts': The Seasoning of Enslaved Africans in Eighteenth-Century Jamaica." *Journal of Global Slavery* 6 (2021): 11-30.

Richardson, David. "Profits in the Liverpool Slave Trade: The Accounts of William Davenport, 1757–1784." In *Liverpool, the African Slave Trade, and Abolition: Essays to Illustrate Current Knowledge and Research*, edited by Roger Anstey and Paul Hair, 60-90. Liverpool: Historic Society of Lancashire and Cheshire, 1976.

Wax, Darold D. "The Browns of Providence and the Slaving Voyage of the Brig *Sally*, 1764–1765." *American Neptune* 32 (1972): 171-79.

CONTEMPORARY NEWSPAPERS

Adams Weekly Current (Chester, England)
American Journal and General Advertiser (Providence)
Boston Gazette
Connecticut Courant (Hartford)
Connecticut Gazette (New London)

Connecticut Journal (New Haven)
Constitutional Gazette (New York)
Continental Journal (Boston)
Cornwall Chronicle (Montego Bay, Jamaica)
Daily Advertiser (London)
Evening Post (London)
Gazetteer and New Daily Advertiser (London)
General Evening Post (London)
Independent Chronicle (Boston)
Independent Ledger (Boston)
Liverpool Advertiser and Mercantile Chronicle (England)
Lloyd's Evening Post (London)
Lloyd's List (London)
London Chronicle
London Courant and Westminster Chronicle
London Evening Post.
Manchester Mercury and Harrop's General Advertiser (England)
Maryland Gazette (Baltimore)
Maryland Journal (Baltimore)
Massachusetts Spy (Worcester)
Morning Chronicle and London Advertiser
Morning Post (London)
New England Chronicle (Boston)
New Hampshire Gazette (Portsmouth)
Newport Gazette (Rhode Island)
Newport Mercury (Rhode Island)
New York Gazette
Norfolk Chronicle, or the Norwich Gazette (England)
Northampton Mercury (England)
Pennsylvania Evening Post (Philadelphia)
Pennsylvania Gazette (Philadelphia)
Pennsylvania Journal (Philadelphia)
Pennsylvania Packet (Philadelphia)
Providence Gazette (Rhode Island)
Public Advertiser (London)
Reading Mercury and Oxford Gazette (England)
Rhode Island Republican (Providence)
South Carolina Gazette (Charleston)
Stamford Mercury (England)
St. James's Chronicle or the British Evening Post (London)
United States Chronicle (Providence)

INTERNET SOURCES, THESES, AND UNPUBLISHED SECONDARY SOURCES

American War of Independence—At Sea. www.awiatsea.com.

Bell-Romero, Nicholas. "A Series of Unfortunate Events: Chichester Cheyne's Revolutionary War, 1778–1783." *Journal of the American Revolution*, Jan. 19, 2016. https://allthingsliberty.com/2016/01/a-series-of-unfortunate-events-chichester-cheynes-revolutionary-war-1778-1783/.

"Boss, John Linscom, Jr." Biographical Directory of the United States Congress. http://bioguide.congress.gov/scripts/biodisplay.pl?index=B000650.

Casey, Michael Scott. "Rebel Privateers—The Winners of American Independence." Master's thesis, US Army Command and General Staff College, 1990.

Center for Digital Scholarship, Brown University Library. "Voyage of the Slave Ship Sally, 1764–1765." http://cds.library.brown.edu/projects/sally/.

Conrad, Dennis. "A Sea Change." Naval History and Heritage Command. https://www.history.navy.mil/content/history/nhhc/research/library/online-reading-room/title-list-alphabetically/s/conrad.html.

Coughtry, Jay. Guide to the Microfilm Edition. In Papers of the American Slave Trade. Series A: Selections from the Rhode Island Historical Society, Part 1: Brown Family Collections. Microfilm project. Edited by Jay Coughtry. University Publications of America, 1998.

Eltis, David, and Martin Halbert. "History of the Project." Voyages: The Trans-Atlantic Slave Trade Database, 2009. https://www.slavevoyages.org/about/about#history/1/en/.

Flynn, Peter Erik. "H.M.S. *Pallas*: Historical Reconstruction of an 18th-Century Royal Navy Frigate." Master's thesis, Texas A&M University, 2006.

Huddleston, Jonathan. *And the Children's Teeth Are Set on Edge: Adam Hodgson & the Razing of Canton Chapel.* Self-published PDF, 2nd. ed., 2011. PDF in the author's possession.

Inhabitants and Estates of the Town of Boston, 1630–1800 and The Crooked and Narrow Streets of Boston, 1630–1822. New England Historic Genealogical Society, 2014. https://www.americanancestors.org/DB530/i/14226/2007/260079292, reference code 3694.

"Local Rally Expresses Opposition to Racism." *Newport Daily News*, Aug. 13, 2017. https://www.newportri.com/lifestyle/2017/08/13/local-rally-express-opposition-to/1275815.

MacGunnigle, Bruce. "Strolling in Historic East Greenwich: The Silas Jones House, 1515 South Rd." *East Greenwich Pendulum*, Aug. 25, 2018. https://www.ricentral.com/east_greenwich_pendulum/news/local_news/strolling-in-historic-east-greenwich-the-silas-jones-house-1515-south-rd/article_6e5d35fe-a6dd-11e8-a6c8-fbde4b1a7799.html.

Papers of William Davenport & Co., 1745–1797. *British Records on the Atlantic World, 1700–1900.* Wakefield: Microform Academic Publishers, 1998. British Online Archives, http://www.britishonlinearchives.co.uk/9781851171767.php.

Radburn, Nicholas. "The Long Middle Passage: The Enslavement of Africans and the Trans-Atlantic Slave Trade, 1640–1808." PhD diss., Johns Hopkins University, 2016.

——. "William Davenport, the Slave Trade, and Merchant Enterprise in Eighteenth-Century Liverpool." Master's thesis, Victoria University of Wellington, 2009.

"Raleigh I (Frigate), 1776–1778," Naval History and Heritage Command. https://www.history.navy.mil/research/histories/ship-histories/danfs/r/raleigh-i.html.

Rhode Island Historical Cemetery Commission. Cemetery Database. https://rihistoriccemeteries.org/searchgravesnameonly.aspx.

"Slavery, the Slave Trade, and Brown University." In *Slavery and Justice: Report of the Brown University Steering Committee on Slavery and Justice*, 2006. http://www.brown.edu/Research/Slavery_Justice/documents/SlaveryAndJustice.pdf.

Sterner, Eric. "Captain John Peck Rathbun: As Audacious as John Paul Jones." *Journal of the American Revolution*, Sept. 6, 2016. https://allthingsliberty.com/2016/09/captain-john-peck-rathbun-audacious-john-paul-jones/.

Thomin, Michael. "The 'P' Is for Profit: Revolutionary War Privateers and the Slave Trade." *Journal of the American Revolution*, Dec. 2, 2016. https://allthingsliberty.com/2016/12/p-profit-revolutionary-war-privateers-slave-trade/.www.allthingsliberty.com.

Voyages: The Trans-Atlantic Slave Trade Database. www.slavevoyages.org.

"A Wedge Grows." In Slavery in the Revolution, https://amrevnc.com/slavery-american-revolution/.

Acknowledgments

*T*he key document upon which this book is based is *The Journal of the Good Ship* Marlborough. I first heard about it on March 25, 2017, at a talk given by Dennis Conrad, then senior historian at the Naval History and Heritage Command of the US Navy (NHHC), at the sixth Annual Conference on the American Revolution in Williamsburg, Virginia. Dennis spoke about the highlights of the most recently released volume (number 12) of the *Naval Documents of the American Revolution* (*NDAR*), a massive project publishing original documents relating to the US Navy and the Revolutionary War. I was already friendly with Dennis, as he had assisted me in reviewing manuscripts for a few of my Revolutionary War books, and we got along well. As Dennis continued his talk at the Williamsburg conference, he mentioned *The Journal of the Good Ship* Marlborough and the ship's voyage to Africa, and I immediately perked up. The fact that the *Marlborough* had sailed from Rhode Island, the topic of many of my books and articles, made my heart rate increase significantly. I had also previously studied slavery in Rhode Island. I was further intrigued about Dennis's idea that the Royal Navy, due to its many commitments after the outbreak of the Revolutionary War, had trouble making available warships to patrol waters in the distant parts of the British Empire, including to protect British slave trading posts and forts in Africa. Later in the day, after speaking with Dennis more about the subject, my excitement grew—I knew what the topic would be for my next Revolutionary War book.

The NHHC made this book possible. In addition to Dennis Conrad providing the spark for the idea, the NHHC, in volume 12 of the *NDAR*, published for the first time, in an appendix, lengthy extracts of *The Journal of the Good Ship* Marlborough. Furthermore, its staff provided me with a PDF of the full original text of the journal, much of which has never been published. I also benefitted mightily from the NHHC's outstanding work in uncovering original sources relating to captures by American privateers of British slaving vessels during the early part of the Revolutionary War and including them in volumes 7 through 12 of the *NDAR*. The NHHC has made a substantial contribution toward our understanding of the impact of the Revolutionary War on Britain's African slave trade by making available these original sources. On an individual basis, in addition to Dennis, I thank Peter Luebke and Christine Hughes of the NHHC. Peter also provided me with a PDF of a 1779 log book of the privateer *General Mifflin* that is used here for the first time in a publication.

I also thank Dennis Conrad, now retired from the NHHC, for reviewing a draft of this book. Terrence Cuff, a careful student of the American Revolution, gave me excellent advice on an early draft of the book. Eric Jay Dolin, one of our country's top popular historians, read a draft and gave me helpful advice, particularly on writing. Others who reviewed parts or all of my draft manuscript, and whom I thank, are Nicholas Radburn, Peter Luebke, Joanne Pope Melish, Tim Phelps, John Millar, and Kenneth Cozens.

I want to give special thanks to Nicholas Radburn, a lecturer at Lancaster University in the United Kingdom and a leading scholar of the British transatlantic slave trade. Nicholas was very generous in sharing what information he had on Britain's role in the Atlantic slave trade during the American Revolutionary War. He is probably the leading scholar on that topic. Nicholas is also a co-manager of the Voyages: Transatlantic Slave Voyages Database at www.slavevoyages.org. This amazing website is a vital resource to those studying the African slave trade. Nicholas intends to revise the descriptions of a number of slave voyages on the database and add more slave ship voyages to it to reflect the results of my research on American privateers capturing British slave ships from August 1776 to August 1778. (See appendix B and appendix C, which I encourage readers to review.)

Unfortunately, the original of *The Journal of the Good Ship* Marlborough could not be located where it was reportedly deposited, at the Morristown National Historical Park, in Morristown, New Jersey. According to an archivist there, the original logs may not have been touched by a researcher since the 1950s or 1960s. After an extensive search, the original logs were not found. They were likely misfiled or stolen. I was disappointed not to have been able to feel and smell the eighteenth-century paper and see the original handwriting, and one drawing in particular. Morristown National Historical Park does have the journal (and the journal for the *General Mifflin*'s voyage) in its microfilm collections.

I thank Tim Tezer at Bonham's in New York City for assisting me in locating the owner of another key document for this book, the written orders George W. Babcock gave, when off the coast of West Africa, to Francis Bradfield, commander of the *Fancy*, dated March 7, 1778.

I also thank the staffs of the Rhode Island State Archives (especially Ken Carlson), Redwood Library and Athenaeum (especially Michelle Farias), Rhode Island Judicial Archives (especially Andrew Smith), Newport Historical Society (especially Bert Lippincott), Rhode Island Historical Society (especially Rebecca Valentine), Cornell University Library, Harriet Irving Library at the University of New Brunswick, John Carter Brown Library (especially Kimberly Nusco), South Caroliniana Library at the University of South Carolina, South Carolina Historical Society, South Carolina Department of Archives and History (especially Wade H. Dorsey), Calvert Marine Museum (especially Robert J. Hurry), Society of the Cincinnati Library, Library Company of Philadelphia, Daughters of the American Revolution Library, and Library of Congress. I also thank Tim Cranston of North Kingstown and Bruce MacGunnigle of East Greenwich for their contributions to the local history of those towns, Bert Caudron for French translation services, Michael Thomin for providing me with information on a few intercolonial slave voyages he had discovered, and eminent slave-trade historians, David Richardson, for reviewing the Schofield Archives at the University of Hull for information on a few slave trading voyages, and Steven Behrendt, for providing me with the muster roll for the *Pearl* and other muster rolls. For converting the value of historic pounds sterling to current (2022) dollars, I used Eric Nye's website at www.uwyo.edu.numimage/currency/htm.

I further deeply appreciate Ron Silverman for his diligent and careful copyediting and Bruce H. Franklin, publisher of Westholme Publishing, for believing in this project from the beginning to the end. Any errors that remain in this book are my own.

For any reader interested in learning more about the transatlantic African slave trade in the eighteenth century, I recommend two readable books: Sean M. Kelley, *The Voyage of the Slave Ship* Hare*: A Journey into Captivity from Sierra Leone to South Carolina* (Chapel Hill: University of North Carolina Press, 2016) and Marcus Rediker, *The Slave Ship: A Human History* (New York: Viking, 2007).

Two recently published books that were released after I turned in my manuscript to my editor are the best of the lot on American privateering: Eric Jay Dolin, *Rebels at Sea: Privateering in the American Revolution* (New York: Liveright, 2022) and Kylie A. Hulbert, *The Untold War at Sea* (Athens: University of Georgia Press, 2022).

Index